From Colony to Nationhood in Mexico

Laying the Foundations, 1560–1840

In an age of revolution, Mexico's creole leaders held aloft the Virgin of Guadalupe and brandished an Aztec eagle perched upon a European tricolor. Their new constitution proclaimed "the Mexican Nation is forever free and independent." Yet the genealogy of this new nation is not easy to trace. Colonial Mexico was a patchwork state whose new-world vassals served the crown, extended the empire's frontiers, and lived out their civic lives in parallel Spanish and Indian republics. Theirs was a world of complex intercultural alliances, interlocking corporate structures, and shared spiritual and temporal ambitions. Sean F. McEnroe describes this history at the greatest and smallest geographical scales, reconsidering what it meant to be an Indian vassal, nobleman, soldier, or citizen over the course of three centuries in northeastern Mexico. He argues that the Mexican municipality, state, and citizen were not so much the sudden creations of a revolutionary age as the progeny of a mature multiethnic empire.

Sean F. McEnroe is a historian of Spanish America and the broader colonial world. His previous publications address frontier diplomacy in colonial Mexico; the encounters between Spaniards, North Americans, and indigenous peoples in the Philippines; and the place of Mexico in the Atlantic world. His work has appeared in *Ethnohistory*, the *Oregon Historical Quarterly*, and *Oxford Bibliographies Online*. He earned his Ph.D from the University of California, Berkeley, and holds a graduate degree in education from Lewis and Clark College. He is an assistant professor of Latin American and Atlantic history at Southern Oregon University and a contributing editor for the Library of Congress's *Handbook of Latin American Studies*.

From Colony to Nationhood in Mexico

Laying the Foundations, 1560–1840

SEAN F. McENROE

CAMBRIDGE
UNIVERSITY PRESS

CAMBRIDGE
UNIVERSITY PRESS

32 Avenue of the Americas, New York NY 10013-2473, USA

Cambridge University Press is part of the University of Cambridge.

It furthers the University's mission by disseminating knowledge in the pursuit of
education, learning and research at the highest international levels of excellence.

www.cambridge.org
Information on this title: www.cambridge.org/9781107690714

© Sean F. McEnroe 2012

First published 2012
First paperback edition 2014

A catalogue record for this publication is available from the British Library

Library of Congress Cataloguing in Publication data
McEnroe, Sean F. (Sean Francis)
From colony to nationhood in Mexico : laying the foundations, 1560–1840 / Sean F. McEnroe.
  p.   cm.
ISBN 978-1-107-00630-0 (hardback)
1. Nuevo León (Mexico : State) – History.   2. Nuevo León (Mexico : State) –
Ethnic relations – History.   3. Tlaxcalan Indians – Colonization – Mexico, North.
4. Mexico – History – Spanish colony, 1540–1810.   5. Mexico – History – Wars of
Independence, 1810–1821.   6. Mexico – History – 1821–1861.   I. Title.
F1316.M44   2012
972´.13–dc23   2012003511

ISBN 978-1-107-00630-0 Hardback
ISBN 978-1-107-69071-4 Paperback

In memory of John F. McEnroe (1945–2010)
My father and first history teacher

Contents

Maps and Illustrations

Acknowledgments

The labors for this book began during my time as a graduate student at U.C. Berkeley and continued through my years on the faculties of Reed College, Oakland University, and Southern Oregon University. For financial support, I wish to thank all of these institutions, as well as the Fulbright-Hays Foundation, the Doris Quinn Foundation, and the Muriel McKevitt Sonne Chair.

William B. Taylor advised me at every step of this project and has shown me a model of mentorship to which I will always aspire (but likely never match). Margaret Chowning provided extraordinary guidance on research, writing, and publishing. In this long period of composition and reflection, Sylvia Sellers-García was an indispensible peer. Again and again, she helped me to close the gap between what I wished to explain and what was printed on the page. At home and abroad, in the archives and taverns, our colleague Paul Ramirez fueled my thinking and lifted my spirits. A broader circle of fellow Bay Area student-historians read and commented on much of my early work: Brianna Leavitt-Alcantara, Julia Sarreal, Heather Flynn-Roller, Melisa Galván, Brian Madigan, Eloina Villegas, and Bea Gurwitz. Several members of the Berkeley faculty read and commented on my writing during the same period: Mark Healey, Thomas Dandalet, Peter Sahlins, and José Rabasa. At Reed College, David Garrett, Mary Ashburn, and Margot Minardi all helped me with later stages of the project.

The research for this book was conducted at a number of archives in the United States, Mexico, and Spain. The whole project would have been impossible without the assistance of skilled librarians at the Archivo General de la Nación de México, Archivo General del Estado de Nuevo León, Archivo Municipal de Monterrey, Archivo del Arzobispado de Monterrey, Instituto Nacional de Antropología e Historia de México, Archivo General de Indias, Archivo General de Simancas, Archivo Histórico Nacional de España, Biblioteca Nacional de España, Bancroft Library, Benson Latin America Collection, and the De Golyer Library. For access to restricted collections, my thanks to Theresa Salazar of the Bancroft Library and to the Archbishop of Monterrey, Mons. Francisco Robles Ortega. Several librarians provided me with assistance above and beyond the call of duty, most notably Walter Brem and Margarita Domínguez.

It has been a pleasure to work with Cambridge University Press. Lewis Bateman and Anne Lovering Rounds offered precisely the right kind of help to shepherd this inexperienced author through his first academic monograph. My thanks to David Cox for producing the maps in this volume and to Elisabeth Butzer for offering the use of her map of Tlaxcalan colonization routes. For their assistance locating images, I wish to thank Barbara Mundy, Mary Ashburn Miller, Gerlinda Riojas of the Corpus Christi Public Library, and Gabriel Swift of Princeton Special Collections. For assistance with reproduction and permissions, my thanks to Martin Mintz of the British Library, Susan Snyder of the Bancroft, Thomas Lisanti and Tal Nadan of the New York Public Library, Niki Russell of the University of Glasgow Library, Liz Kurtulik of Scala Archives, and Kajette Bloomfield of Bridgeman Art Library.

The following scholars, friends, and acquaintances gave valuable academic and practical advice during my research travel abroad: Charles Walker, David J. Weber, Miguel Ángel Quiroga, María Gabriela Márquez Rodríguez, Raul García Flores, Kristin Huffine, Jessica Delgado, Karen Melvin, Richard Chun, and Rita Lorenzo Quiros. The Escuela de Estudios Hispano-Americanos and its director Salvador Bernabéu greatly facilitated my work at the Archivo de las Indias by providing housing and after-hours library access. Paul Kasper provided inspiration and advice during a decade of travels in the Spanish-speaking world.

For a long time, this book has claimed too great a share of my waking hours. All the while my wife, Moneeka Settles, has helped me to inhabit the real world even while living and breathing the colonial past. To her and to our son Casey, I owe my thanks for providing a sense of urgency to all matters professional, and a sense of levity to all matters personal.

Introduction

FIGURE I. The Library of Philip II at El Escorial Palace projects a global vision of Habsburg Christendom joining many lands and peoples under a common faith and sovereign. (Scala Archive, Florence/Art Resources, New York, 2006)

THE WHIPPING OF ANTONIO GONZALES

In November 1782, Vicente González de Santianes the governor of Nuevo León, received a sheaf of documents from a protracted legal dispute in the Indian town of San Miguel de Aguayo.[1] At first glance, the case seems so utterly commonplace as to be beneath the notice of the region's chief magistrate. One of San Miguel's Tlaxcalan stoneworkers had been accused of an adulterous liaison with a townswoman. The local *alcalde*, believing him guilty of the offense, ordered him jailed and whipped. This would have been an open-and-shut case, were it not for one crucial detail: the mason claimed to be a Tlaxcalan nobleman. The legal privileges of Tlaxcalan elites rested on two centuries of colonial law and custom, and they could not be taken lightly even by the Spanish governor.[2]

The initial complaint came from the stonemason, Antonio Gonzales. According to his testimony, the unreasonable *alcalde* of San Miguel, Marcos Suarez, subjected him to a humiliating whipping "without any cause or motive." Suarez maintained that he simply meted out the appropriate punishment for adultery. When Gonzales made an appeal to the governor, the *cabildo* began gathering testimony to resolve the dispute. Initially, Gonzales vigorously denied the story of his midday dalliance with a neighbor woman. Later, he conceded that he was, indeed, laboring at the woman's home on the day in question, but he still insisted that, despite the suspicions of her jealous husband, he was only moving rocks and committed no sin or crime of any kind. Gonzales claimed the whole scandal was provoked by malicious rumors. The preponderance of evidence was stacked against Gonzales, and even today, his story seems less than convincing. In truth, though, he was not so interested in refuting the specific charge of adultery as he was in proving his status as a Tlaxcalan nobleman and his consequent categorical immunity from the *alcalde*'s corporal punishment.

Gonzales described himself as "a Tlaxcalan son of the pueblo of San Miguel de Aguayo" and "sergeant of the militia." He offered these facts not merely for the purposes of identification, but also to establish his legal standing. Colonial magistrates needed these facts to determine the jurisdiction of the tribunal and the legal privileges of the petitioner. The individual's place of birth and residence, ethnicity, language, ancestry, and profession were all relevant to the case. Gonzales's status as a *vecino* (local resident and citizen) was vital to his appeal, and his military post might have conferred additional

---

[1] Several histories treat San Miguel de Aguayo's (Bustamante's) distinctive history as a Tlaxcalan colony: David B. Adams, "At the Lion's Mouth: San Miguel de Aguayo in the Defense of Nuevo León, 1686–1841," *Colonial Latin American Historical Review* 9, no. 3 (2000), 324–46; Elisabeth Butzer, *Historia social de una comunidad tlaxcalteca: San Miguel Aguayo (Bustamante, N.L., 1686–1820)* (Saltillo, Mexico: Archivo Municipal de Saltillo, 2001); Héctor Jaime Treviño Villarreal, *El Señor de Tlaxcala* (Monterrey, Mexico: Archivo General del Estado, 1986).

[2] The following story of Antonio González is reconstructed from documents contained in AMM Correspondencia vol. 121, exp. 4.

legal immunities. In this case, however, it was upon his ancestry that Gonzales staked his most important claim. Gonzales proclaimed himself a Tlaxcalan nobleman and maintained that he was thus legally protected from the sort of abuse he had suffered:

> I am a Tlaxcalan. I am from the nobles and the elites like you … that never have been accustomed to be punished thus in this village, nor with exile, when they are not remanded to Royal Justice or to the judgment of the Republic, leaving the penalty of whipping for the commoners who have not had and do not have an office in the Republic, nor did their ancestors.

Gonzales was claiming that he possessed an elite form of Tlaxcalan citizenship transmitted by heredity.[3]

The *cabildo*, which promised to conduct a full investigation of the matter, took the issue of ancestry quite seriously, collecting the information needed to verify or disprove Gonzales's noble genealogy. To substantiate his claims, Gonzales cited a history of family service to the state: "My grandfather served the king and republic in the employ of the governor and ministers of justice; in the same post, my father don Ignacio Gonzales has and still serves." Gonzales hastened to add that he himself had served in the elite frontier forces and was now the sergeant of the town's militia. Marcos Suarez, the very man who had whipped Gonzales, was the head of the *cabildo* that prepared the report. Yet the *alcalde* was in no position to dismiss Gonzales's complaint out of hand. The legal principle involved was too weighty.

In the final report to the governor of Nuevo León, San Miguel's *cabildo* challenged Gonzales's claim of immunity on several grounds: first, it cast doubt on his ancestry; second, it asserted that, though Gonzales may have been a noble, even nobles were subject to whipping for certain offenses. The one thing never disputed by any party was the underlying principle of Tlaxcalan privilege and Tlaxcalan nobility. These were universally recognized elements of colonial law in the north. Neither Suarez (who himself claimed Tlaxcalan *hidalguía*), nor Gonzales, nor Santianez had anything to gain from tampering with the time-honored Tlaxcalan-Spanish compact.[4]

---

[3] On Indian law in the region and viceroyalty, see Charles R. Cutter, *The Legal Culture of Northern New Spain, 1700–1810* (Albuquerque: University of New Mexico, 1995); Brian P. Owensby, *Empire of Law and Indian Justice in Colonial Mexico* (Stanford, CA: Stanford University Press, 2008); Jovita Baber, "Native Litigiousness, Cultural Change and the Spanish Legal System in Tlaxcala, New Spain (1580–1640)," *Political and Legal Anthropology Review* 24, no. 2 (2001), 94–106. On Spanish notions of *vecindad* and citizenship, see Tamar Herzog, *Defining Nations: Immigrants and Citizens in Early Modern Spain and Spanish America* (New Haven, CT: Yale, 2003).

[4] The *cabildo* was informed by elements of the 1591 Tlaxcalan charter, which transfered privileges held by Tlaxcala to its daughter colonies in the north. 14 Mar. 1591 mercedes, *San Esteban de la Nueva Tlaxcala: documentos para conocer su historia* (Saltillo, Mexico: Consejo Editorial del Estado, 1991), 53; Andrea Martínez Baracs, *Un Gobierno de Indios: Tlaxcala, 1519–1750* (Mexico City: CIESAS, 2008), chap. 6 notes that while the principle of nobility long remained important in Gran Tlaxcala, the phenomenon of false titles of nobility was widespread.

The population of Tlaxcala, like that of other Nahua societies, was divided between two orders: the *pilli* and the *macehualli*. The *pipiltin* enjoyed both political and economic privileges denied the *macehualtin*. They were exempt from labor levies, dominated the *cabildo* system, and marked their status with luxury goods forbidden their inferiors.[5] Though this division between orders softened gradually in Tlaxcala, and dramatically in the Tlaxcalan colonies, it remained legally relevant throughout the eighteenth century. Spaniards recognized this distinction between the orders as being similar to contemporary European distinctions between nobles and commoners and to the ancient Roman distinction between plebs and patricians. It was common, in fact, for Spaniards to refer to the *macehualtin* as *plebeyos* and to the *pipiltin* as *principales* or *hidalgos*. Like the native nobility among Rome's allies, Tlaxcalan nobles were the first to taste the fruits of colonial citizenship. In the northern colonies, both the founding families and all of their descendants were guaranteed by charter the status of *hidalgos*. Some among them, like Antonio Gonzales, claimed an even higher order of birth. The people of northern New Spain viewed Spanish and indigenous hierarchies as paralleling each other – each with its own distinctions between noble and common, governors and governed. This case from the town of San Miguel de Aguayo suggests that all parties shared an assumption that Tlaxcalans were legally distinct from non-Tlaxcalans, and that a nobility among Tlaxcalans could claim further privileges in contradistinction to the commoners around them.[6]

New Spain's vision of empire and citizenship was reflected in colonial charters and in the historical discourse of early chroniclers. However, the most common invocation of the principles of citizenship was in the application of normal criminal and civil law. Spanish law recognized a variety of legal standings based on nobility, caste, and membership in the military or clergy. In the New World, the *república de indios* and *república de españoles* were two separate legal spheres that converged only when cases were appealed above the local level. Tlaxcalans enjoyed an intermediary form of citizenship between that of other Indians and that of the Spanish – a condition that was most clearly articulated in practice.[7] To understand this hybrid political system, one must consider Spanish expectations about multiple modes of citizenship and the long history of the relationship between Nahuas and the Spanish crown.[8]

---

[5] Charles Gibson, *Tlaxcala in the Sixteenth Century* (New Haven, CT: Yale, 1952), chap. 6; on Nahua social and political hierarchies, see James Lockhart, *The Nahuas after the Conquest* (Stanford, CA: Stanford University Press, 1992), chaps. 8–9.

[6] In Tlaxcala, the hereditary group of *principales* was well defined, institutionalized, and long lasting, Lockhart, *The Nahuas after Spanish Conquest*, 125–39; Martínez Baracs, *Un gobierno de indios*, chap. 4.

[7] On law and political culture, Susan Kellog, *Law and the Transformation of Aztec Culture, 1500– 1700* (Norman: University of Oklahoma, 1995), and Owensby, *Empire of Law*.

[8] The tradition of examining central Mexico as a distinctive civilization with persistent elements of Nahua civilization was begun in earnest by Charles Gibson in *The Aztecs Under Spanish Rule: A*

TLAXCALANS AND THE ORIGINS OF THE MEXICAN NATION

The modern nation of Mexico that emerged in the nineteenth century incorporated a multitude of ethnically distinct peoples. It did so, in part, by building upon a process of political integration inherited from a long history of hybrid colonial rule.[9] Early New Spain was a colony whose political structures were grafted together from Iberian and indigenous ones. The early success of this colonial state owed a great deal to the alliance between Spain and Tlaxcala. Spaniards and Tlaxcalans cooperated first to conquer Tenochtitlan and later to colonize dangerous frontier areas. From the sixteenth to the eighteenth century, Tlaxcalan settlers created webs of self-replicating colonies that drew nomadic frontier peoples into the emerging colonial society. Tlaxcalans were both cultural intermediaries between Europeans and other Indians and the authors of their own local political systems.[10]

The long history of Tlaxcala's frontier colonies reveals the ongoing success of the Spanish-Nahua political system in binding together distinct ethnic groups as corporate elements of a larger empire. This colonial system created both new towns and a new type of citizen. Tlaxcalans introduced northern Chichimecs to

History of the Indians of the Valley of Mexico, 1519–1810 (Stanford, CA: Stanford University Press, 1964) and continued through the use of Nahuatl language sources by James Lockhart in *The Nahuas after Spanish Conquest* and Martínez Baracs, *Un Gobierno de Indios*. Similar inquires into other regions of New Spain may be found in Nancy M. Farriss, *Maya Society Under Colonial Rule: The Collective Enterprise of Survival* (Princeton, NJ: Princeton University, 1985); Kevin Terraciano, *The Mixtecs of Colonial Oaxaca: Ñudzahi History, Sixteenth through Eighteenth Centuries* (Stanford, CA: Stanford University Press, 1996); Rebecca Horn, *Postconquest Coyoacan. Nahua-Spanish Relatioins in Central Mexico, 1519–1650* (Stanford, CA: Stanford University Press, 1997).

[9] In using the term *hybrid*, I borrow loosely from a tradition begun by Homi K. Bhabha. While the term is most commonly applied to post-Colonial societies, I use it throughout this book to describe the mingling of political structures and cultures in colonial New Spain. Homi K. Bhabha, *The Location of Culture* (New York: Routledge, 1994). On Nahua-Spanish hybridity, see Arij Ouweneel, "From Tlahtocayotl to Gobernadoryotl: A Critical Examination of Indigenous Rule in 18th-Century Central Mexico," *American Ethnologist* 22, no. 4 (Nov. 1995), 765–85; as viewed through other media, Jaime Cuadriello, ed., *El origen del Reino de La Nueva España, 1680–1750* (Mexico City: Instituto de Investigaciones Estéticas, 1999) and *Las Glorias de la república de Tlaxcala: o la conciencia como imagen sublime* (Mexico City: UNAM, 2004); with respect to syncretism, Viviana Díaz Balsera, "A Judeo-Christian Tlaloc or a Nahua Yahweh? Domination, Hybridity and Continuity in the Nahua Evangelization Theater," *Colonial Latin American Review* 10 (2001), 209–28; with respect to language, Laura E. Matthew, "El náhuatl y la identidad mexicana en la Guatemala colonial," *Mesoamerica* 40 (2000), 41–68; and political geography, Barbara Mundy, *The Mapping of New Spain: Indigenous Cartography and the Maps of the Relaciones Geográficas* (Chicago: University of Chicago. 1996).

[10] On the structure of Spanish Empire, see Henry Kamen, *Empire: How Spain Became a World Power, 1493–1763* (New York: Penguin, 2002); John Elliott, *Imperial Spain, 1469–1716* (New York: Pelican, 1970); Elliott, *Spain and Its World: Selected Essays* (New Haven, CT: Yale, 1989); John Chávez, *Beyond Nations: Evolving Homelands in the North Atlantic World, 1400–2000* (New York: Cambridge, 2009). The conquest of Mexico is a well-trodden subject, and the role of Tlaxcalans has been noted repeatedly in widely read works such as Hugh Thomas, *Conquest: Montezuma, Cortés and the Fall of Old Mexico* (London: Hutchinson, 1993) and Matthew Restall, *Seven Myths of the Spanish Conquest* (New York: Oxford University Press, 2003).

the political culture of the *república de indios* and integrated them into local militias. The incorporation of these local military and political systems into the regional militias and governments of the Bourbon period created a land of Indian and Spanish citizen-soldiers, who at first inhabited separate civic spheres, but whose shared interests would eventually yield a surprising level of interethnic solidarity. These interethnic relationships determined the region's alignment during the Hidalgo Rebellion and Independence periods and the application of new political systems under the Constitution of Cádiz and the Mexican Constitution of 1824. Ultimately, the political culture transmitted through the Tlaxcalan colonies helped to produce the modern citizens and modern municipalities of the nineteenth century.[11]

Mexico's 1824 Constitution speaks of the nation as a body of formally equivalent individuals, each of whom is termed a "citizen of the state" and "citizen of the Republic." It is a notion of citizenship that takes no account of ethnicity or language – one in which all citizens are theoretically interchangeable. This is a familiar notion for modern readers, but it is a very different model than that which prevailed at the time of Spanish conquest. Spain's early North American empire was a patchwork of European and indigenous communities, whose separate ethnic "republics" were united by a shared allegiance to the crown. In local political life, Spaniards and Indians spoke of themselves as *vecinos*; and in relation to the broader empire, they spoke of themselves as the king's *vasallos*. The former term described the lateral political ties between legitimate members of a town, and the latter expressed the hierarchical relationship between the subject and sovereign. *Vecindad* described the possession of both active and passive elements of citizenship: protection for property and contract rights, and the ability to vote and stand for local offices. *Vasallaje* conferred both obligations and privileges. The vassal was protected by the king's law and, at the same time, obligated to render him service. In New

---

[11] On the application of the Bourbon reforms to northern New Spain, see Peter Gerhard, *Colonial New Spain, 1519–1786: Historical Notes on the Evolution of Minor Political Jurisdictions* (Washington, DC: Library of Congress, 1967); Gerhard, *The North Frontier of New Spain*, rev. ed. (Norman: University of Oklahoma, 1993); and Gerhard, *A Guide to the Historical Geography of New Spain*, rev. ed. (Norman: University of Oklahoma, 1993). On local systems, see José Cuello, "The Economic Impact of the Bourbon Reforms and the Late Colonial Crisis of Empire at the Local Level: The Case of Saltillo, 1777–1817," *The Americas* 44, no. 3 (1988), 301–24. The changes to military systems and jurisdictions are treated in Christon I. Archer, *The Army in Bourbon Mexico, 1760–1810* (Albuquerque: University of New Mexico, 1977); María del Carmen Velásquez, *Tres estudios sobre las Provincias Internas de Nueva España* (Mexico City: Colegio de México, 1979); Luis Navarro García, *Las Provincias Internas en el siglo xix* (Seville: Escuela de Estudios Hispano-Americanos, 1965) and *La política americana de José de Gálvez según su "Discurso y reflexiones de un vasallo* (Málaga, Spain: Algazara, 1998); Isidro Vizcaya Canales, *En los albores de la independencia: las Provincias Internas de Oriente durante la insurgencia de Don Miguel Hidalgo* (Monterrey, Mexico: ITESM, 1976). For a general overview of the Hapsburg and Bourbon periods, see John Lynch, *Spain under the Hapsburgs* (Oxford: Basil Blackwell, 1981) and *Bourbon Spain, 1700–1808* (Oxford: Basil Blackwell, 1989), as well as Anthony H. Hull, *Charles III and the Revival of Spain* (Washington, DC: University Press, 1980).

Spain, citizenship (among both Indians and Spaniards) was defined by the individual's exercise of the obligations and privileges entailed by *vecindad* and *vasallaje*.[12]

Spaniards' ideas about Indians were complex and changed over time.[13] When Europeans first arrived in the Americas, Tlaxcala was an independent polity that lay just to the east of the Valley of Mexico. The Tlaxcalans and the Mexica (the so-called Aztecs) were both Nahua peoples and, as such, shared a common language as well as many commonalities in economic life, political structure, and religious practice. In the era of Spanish rule, Nahuas would remain central to the economy and governance of New Spain. Tlaxcalans, among Nahuas, proved especially adept at defending their interests within this colonial society. The Tlaxcalans of the sixteenth century built themselves into the emerging Hispano-American empire by making first their armies, and later their civil society, indispensable to the Iberian invaders.[14]

---

[12] In a statutory sense, many of the elements of citizenship for both Europeans and Indians within the American empire were articulated under the Laws of the Indies, see Alberto Sarmiento Donate, ed., *De las leyes de indias: antología de la recopilación de 1681* (Mexico City: Consejo Nacional de Fomento Educativo, 1985). Tamar Herzog, *Defining Nations*, has added to our understanding of citizenship among Spaniards by investigating the daily exercise of legal prerogatives and standards of naturalization among Europeans in the empire. My work considers some of the same questions, but begins its analysis in the Indian political sphere, rather than the Spanish one. On notions of local citizenship among frontier colonists, see Okah L. Jones, *Los Paisanos: Spanish Settlers on the Northern Frontier of New Spain* (Norman: University of Oklahoma, 1979). Also helpful in understanding the legal culture of the north and its multiple modes of citizenship are Charles R. Cutter, *The Protector de Indios in Colonial New Mexico, 1659–1821* (Albuquerque: University of New Mexico, 1986) and *The Legal Culture of Northern New Spain*.

[13] Anthony Pagden, *The Fall of Natural Man: The American Indian and the Origins of Comparative Ethnology* (New York: Cambridge University Press, 1982); Serge Gruzinski, *Painting the Conquest: The Mexican Indians and the European Renaissance* (Paris: UNESCO, 1992); Gruzinski, *The Conquest of Mexico: The Incorporation of Indian Societies into the Western World, 16th–18th Centuries* (Cambridge, U.K.: Cambridge, 1993); Ilona Katzew, *Casta Paintings: Images of Race in Eighteenth-Century Mexico* (New Haven, CT: Yale, 2004); Patricia Seed, *American Pentimento: The Invention of Indians and the Pursuit of Riches* (Minneapolis: University of Minnesota, 2001); Jorge Cañizares-Esguerra, *How to Write the History of the New World: Histories, Epistemologies, and Identities in the Eighteenth-Century Atlantic World* (Stanford, CA: Stanford University Press, 2001).

[14] Analysis of Nahua representations of alliance and conquest may be found in Stephanie Wood, *Transcending Conquest: Nahua Views of Spanish Colonial Mexico* (Norman: University of Oklahoma, 2003); Susan Schroeder, "Looking Back at the Conquest: Nahua Perceptions of Early Encounters from the Annals of Chimalpahin," in Eloise Quiñones Keber, Susan Schroeder, and Frederic Hicks, eds., *Chipping Away on Earth: Studies in Prehispanic and Colonial Mexico in Honor of Arthur J. O. Anderson and Charles E. Dibble* (Lancaster, CA: Labyrinthos, 1994); Florine Alsselbergs, *Conquered Conquistadors: The Lienzo of Quauhquechollan: A Nahua Vision of the Conquest of Mexico* (Seville: Escuela de Estudios Hispano-Americanos, 1997). On the privileged status of Tlaxcalans under Habsburg rule, Baracs, *Un gobiernor de indios*, 76–102; and in the north, Offutt, "Defending Corporate Identity on Spain's Northeastern Frontier: San Esteban de Nueva Tlaxcala, 1780–1810," *The Americas* 64, no. 3 (2007), 351–75; Patricia Martinez, "'Noble Tlaxcalans': Race and Ethnicity in Northeastern New Spain, 1770–1810," (Ph.D Dissertation, U.T. Austin, 2004).

After helping to conquer the Valley of Mexico, Tlaxcala made a place for itself in the Hapsburg Empire. It became an early center of institutional Christianity, an important part of the Euro-American economy, and a major contributor of soldiers to the frontier wars that continued throughout the sixteenth century. Tlaxcalans soon functioned not just as soldiers, but also as colonists who helped to export Nahua and Spanish institutions to the fringes of the empire. Beginning in the 1590s, the Tlaxcalan nation and the Spanish colonial state set out to remake the northern frontier in the image of the Tlaxcalan heartland. To this end, the Spanish viceroy and the Tlaxcalan council negotiated an elaborate partnership. The Tlaxcalans agreed to colonize the north and suppress the northern Chichimecs in return for generous royal concessions: titles of nobility, land grants, and the authority to form self-governing towns. Spaniards considered the Tlaxcalans ideal emissaries for transmitting the emerging Hispano-Indian civilization to the north: they were expert agriculturalists, skilled craftsmen, reliable soldiers, and enthusiastic converts to Christianity. Spaniards viewed Chichimecs, in contrast, as the very antithesis of civilization: they lacked cities, complex political hierarchies, sedentary agriculture, and Christian faith.[15]

The application of European empire to local governance in the Americas was shaped by the colonizers' distinct approaches to sedentary versus mobile Indian populations. The northern frontier of New Spain was a point of interaction, both between Europeans and non-Europeans and among Indians with radically different patterns of subsistence and social organization.[16] The relationships

---

[15] On Tlaxcalan colonization, José de Jesus Dávila Aguirre, *La colonización tlaxcalteca y su influencia en el noreste de la Nueva España* (Coahuila, Mexico: Colegio Coahuilense de Investigaciones Históricas, 1977); David B. Adams, *Las colonias tlaxcaltecas de Coahuila y Nuevo León en la Nueva España: un aspecto de la colonización del norte de México* (Saltillo: Archivo Municipal de Saltillo, 1991); Adams, "At the Lion's Mouth"; Eugene B. Sego, *Aliados y adversarios: los colonos tlaxcaltecas en la frontera septentrional de Nueva España* (San Luis Potosí: Colegio del Estado de Tlaxcala, 1998); Butzer, *Historia social*; Cecilia Sheridan Prieto, "'Indios madrineros': colonizadores tlaxcaltecas en el noreste novohispano." *Estudios de Historia Novohispana* 24 (Jan.–Feb. 2001); Phillip Wayne Powell, *Mexico's Miguel Caldera: The Taming of America's First Frontier, 1548–1597* (Tucson: University of Arizona, 1977); Vito Alessio Robles, *Francisco Urdiñola y el norte de la Nueva España* (Mexico City: Imprenta Mundial, 1931); Pedro de Antonio Escalante Arce, *Los Tlaxcaltecas en Centro América* (San Salvador: Biblioteca de Historia Salvadoreña, 2001).

[16] David J. Weber, *Bárbaros: Spaniards and Their Savages in the Age of Enlightenment* (New Haven, CT: Yale, 2005); Cynthia Radding, *Wandering Peoples: Colonialism Ethnic Spaces and Ecological Frontiers in Northwestern Mexico, 1700–1850* (Durham, NC: Duke, 1997); Marie-Areti Hers et al., eds., *Nómadas y sedentarios en el noreste de México: Homenaje a Beatriz Braniff* (Mexico City: UNAM, 2000); Donna J. Guy and Thomas E. Sheridan, eds., *Contested Ground: Comparative Frontiers on the Northern and Southern Edges of the Spanish Empire* (Tucson: University of Arizona, 1998); Susan Deeds, *Defiance and Deference in Colonial Mexico: Indians under Spanish Rule in Nueva Vizcaya* (Austin: University of Texas Press, 2003); William B. Griffen, *Utmost Good Faith: Patterns of Apache-Mexican Hostilities in Northern Chihuahua Border Warfare, 1821–1848* (Albuquerque: University of New Mexico Press, 1988); Griffen,

between Spaniards, Tlaxcalans, and Chichimecs produced the central elements of a new political culture. On the northern frontier, Tlaxcalans built towns, farms, and irrigation systems. They established their own Indian governments, frontier militias, and local religious organizations. They also used a combination of force and persuasion to bring Chichimec bands into their settlements. This strategy produced Indian towns composed of multiple ethnic *barrios*. Over time, the Chichimec residents acquired the attributes of colonial citizenship by entering into Tlaxcalan systems of landholding, military service, and corporate governance. For more than two centuries, these Tlaxcalan-Chichimec towns provided the civic mechanisms for the growth of a functional, multiethnic state.[17]

The Spaniards' attitude toward Indian subjects was informed by classical notions of imperial citizenship. They recognized different types of citizenship based both on European notions of cultural hierarchies, and on the relative position of subordinate states within the military systems of the empire. Generally speaking, Hapsburg New Spain interpreted Spanish and Tlaxcalan subjects as the modern analogs of Roman citizens and their Latin allies respectively. Like the Latin allies of antiquity, Tlaxcalan communities were internally self-governing and their members possessed specific legal privileges within the empire.[18] Chichimecs were initially categorized as noncitizens. Yet, in time, they

Apaches at War and Peace: The Janos Presidio, 1750–1858 (Albuquerque: University of New Mexico, 1988); Martha Rodríguez García, *Historias de resistencia y exterminio: los indios de Coahuila durante el siglo xix* (Mexico City: CIESAS, 1995); Griffen, *Indian Assimilation in the Franciscan Areas of Nueva Vizcaya* (Tucson: University of Arizona, 1979); Martha Rodríguez García, *La guerra entre bárbaros y civilizados: el exterminio del nómada en Coahuila, 1840–1880* (Saltillo, Mexico, 1998); Edward Holland Spicer, *Cycles of Conquest: The Impact of Spain, Mexico, and the United States on the Indians of the Southwest, 1553–1960* (Tucson: University of Arizona Press, 1962); Susan Deeds, "First Generation Rebellions in Seventeenth-Century Nueva Vizcaya," in *Native Resistance and the Pax Colonial in New Spain*, ed. Susan Schroeder (Lincoln: University of Nebraska, 1998).

[17] Tlaxcalans are on one of several gropus that served as intermediaries between Europeans and other indigenous groups. On this social phenomenon, see Alida Metcalf, *Go-Betweens and the Colonization of Brazil, 1500–1600* (Austin: University of Texas, 2005); Camilla Townsend, *Malintzin's Choices: An Indian Woman in the Conquest of Mexico* (Albuquerque: University of New Mexico Press, 2006), Yanna Yannakakis, *The Art of Being In-Between: Native Intermediaries, Indian Identity, and Local Rule in Colonial Oaxaca* (Durham, NC: Duke, 2009); Juliana Barr, *Peace Came in the Form of a Woman: Indians and Spaniards in the Texas Borderlands* (Chapel Hill: University of North Carolina Press, 2007); Daniel H. Usner, *Indians, Settlers, and Slaves in a Frontier Exchange Economy: The Lower Mississippi Valley before 1783* (Chapel Hill: University of North Carolina, 1992).

[18] The links between Roman political models and those applied to New Spain are of several types: cases in which Hapsburg administration preserved premodern vestiges of Roman political organization, legal precedents transmitted through canon and secular law, and modeling based on classical education. On the political integration of early modern Italy and Iberia, see Thomas Dandalet, *Spanish Rome, 1500–1700* (New Haven, CT: Yale, 2001). On the transfer of ideas and economic practices from the Mediterranean to the Americas, see William D. Phillips, *Slavery from Roman Times to the Early Transatlantic Trade* (Minneapolis: University of Minnesota, 1985) and *The Worlds of Christopher Columbus* (Cambridge: Cambridge University, 1992). Two recent works have treated Roman models in the Andes: David Lupher,

entered the Spanish realm, either as defeated captives or as co-opted allies, and they advanced their fortunes in the colonial system by emulating the Tlaxcalans. Subsequent waves of Chichimec allies ascended the imperial hierarchy by assuming the functional role of their predecessors. In many ways, Chichimecs became Tlaxcalans, proclaiming their virtues as Christians, subjects, and frontier soldiers in distinctly Tlaxcalan terms.

In the long run, the north's pluralistic society, so much in keeping with the corporate structures of the Hapsburg Empire, gave way to a more uniform political culture. Spanish towns grew up beside the Tlaxcalan-Chichimec colonies, creating local economic and political systems that bound the three populations more closely together. In the late Bourbon period, the Tlaxcalan-Chichimec towns continued to attract Indian outsiders, but the place of these towns in the larger imperial system was changing as Tlaxcalan practices were universalized in the region. The distinctive political status of Tlaxcalans had always been linked to their service as militiamen.[19] Now, faced with the military and fiscal crises of the Seven Years' War, Bourbon administrators sought to apply the Tlaxcalan soldier-settler model to the larger society. Soon, garrison towns and militia rolls included northerners of all castes. Just as the previous pattern of colonization had eroded the boundary between Tlaxcalan and Chichimec, so too did this new military and administrative system erode the boundary between Spaniard and Indian. The economic, political, and military relationships among neighboring ethnic enclaves laid the groundwork for the interethnic alliances that prevailed during the Hidalgo Rebellion and shaped a new society that emerged in the wake of national independence. Under the national and state constitutions of the 1820s, all legal distinctions between Indians and Spaniards were formally abolished. At the same time, the Indian and Spanish towns, once clearly geographically delineated, were merged into larger municipalities.

In many respects, the Tlaxcalan colonies succeeded in their original mission of transforming dangerous Chichimecs into civilized Indian citizens. Ultimately,

Romans in the New World: Classical Models in Sixteenth Century Spanish America (Ann Arbor: University of Michigan, 2003) and Sabine MacCormack, *On the Wings of Time: Rome, the Incas, Spain and Peru* (Princeton, NJ: Princeton University, 2007). Daniel Reff has noted underlying similarities in the material and cultural conditions of Christianity's expansion in late antiquity and in colonial Spanish America in *Plagues, Priests, and Demons: Sacred Narratives and the Rise of Christianity in the Old World and the New* (New York: Cambridge, 2005). The classic explanation of multiple layers of Roman citizenship has its origins in Adrian Nicholas Sherwin-White, *The Roman Citizenship* (Oxford, U.K.: Oxford University, 1939).

[19] On the role of non-European soldiers in Spanish North America, see Laura Matthew and Michel R. Oudijk, *Indian Conquistadors: Indigenous Allies in the Conquest of Mesoamerica* (Norman: University of Oklahoma, 2007); Matthew Restall, *Maya Conquistador* (Boston: Beacon Press, 1998); Rebecca B. Bateman, "Africans and Indians: A Comparative Study of the Black Carib and Black Seminole," *Ethnohistory* 37, no. 1 (Winter, 1990), 1–24; Roberto Mario Salmon, *Indian Revolts in Northern New Spain (1680–1786)* (Lanham, MD: University Press of America, 1991); Ben Vinson, *Bearing Arms for His Majesty: The Free-Colored Militia in Colonial Mexico* (Stanford, CA: Stanford University Press, 2001); Herbert S. Klein, "The Colored Militia of Cuba 1568–1868," in *Caribbean Studies* 6, no. 2 (1966), 17–27.

the political machinery of the Tlaxcalan-Chichimec towns exerted an even broader influence on the formation of the state. The same civic mechanisms that had transformed Chichimecs into Tlaxcalans converged with forces in the larger polity to replace a corporate society with a unitary state. The political apparatus that had created Tlaxcalan citizens was now producing Mexican citizens.

Studying state formation in northern Mexico calls for a careful assessment of multiple cultural intersections in a region that has long been the center of border-lands and frontier studies.[20] Frontiers are often studied because they help us to understand one cultural system in contrast to another, or because they permit us to see how individuals navigate areas of ambiguous or conflicting authority. The northeastern frontier of New Spain was a point of contact between Tlaxcalans, Spaniards, a variety of northern Indian cultures, and, later, growing numbers of mestizos, mulattos, and Anglo-Americans. Tlaxcalan colonies were portals of communication between Spanish and Chichimec worlds. They channeled trade goods, brokered peace agreements, hosted and supported missionary efforts, and served as a point of entry for mobile Indians groups as they entered the more sedentary colonial world.[21]

Sixteenth-century New Spain belonged to a complex and heterogeneous empire. Structurally, the Hapsburg Empire comprehended estates and towns, monasteries and missions, free cities and subordinate kingdoms. The construction

[20] A number of works have explored the fluidity of national identities in frontier areas and the notion that cultures are defined on the periphery. Many such discussions have been influenced by Peter Sahlins, *Boundaries: The Making of France and Spain in the Pyrenees* (Berkeley: U.C. Berkeley, 1989) and *Unnaturally French: Foreign Citizens in the Old Regime and After* (Ithaca, NY: Cornell, 2004). The following collections include a wide variety of relevant studies: Donna J. Guy and Thomas E. Sheridan, eds., *Contested Ground*, and Christine Daniels and Michael Kennedy, eds., *Negotiated Empires: Centers and Peripheries in the Americas, 1500–1820* (New York: Routledge, 2002).

[21] The U.S.-Mexican borderlands have given rise to an enormous amount of scholarship on frontiers, boundaries, and national identity: Elizabeth John, *Storms Brewed in Other Men's Worlds: The Confrontation of Indians, Spanish, and French in the Southwest, 1540–1795* (College Station: Texas A&M, 1975); Stuart Voss, *On the Periphery of Nineteenth-Century Mexico: Sonora and Sinaloa, 1810–1877* (Tucson: University of Arizona, 1982); Andrés Reséndez, *Changing National Identities at the Frontier: Texas and New Mexico, 1800–1850* (New York: Cambridge 2005). Readers interested in debates over the cultural and political qualities of this borderland may wish to consult the following historiographic pieces: Jeremy Adelman, "From Borderlands to Borders: Empires, Nation-States, and the Peoples in between in North American History," *American Historical Review*, June 1999, 814–41; Albert L. Hurtado, "Parkmanizing the Spanish Borderlands: Bolton, Turner, and the Historians' World," *Western Historical Quarterly* 26, no. 2 (Summer 1995), 149–67; David J. Weber, "The Spanish Borderlands, Historiography Redux," *The History Teacher* 39, no. 1 (Nov. 2005), 43–56. Useful reference works on the region include David J. Weber, *The Spanish Frontier in North America* (New Haven, CT: Yale, 1992); and Gerhard, *The North Frontier of New Spain*. Several recent works have enriched our understanding of black populations in this region: Jane Landers, "Black Community and Culture in the Southeastern Borderlands," *Journal of the Early Republic* 18, no. 1 (Spring 1998), 117–34; Landers, "Gracia Real de Santa Teresa de Mose: A Free Black Town in Spanish Colonial Florida," *American Historical Review* 95, no. 1 (Feb. 1990), 9–30.

of colonial military forces required the successful translation of shared notions about alliance and vassalage, but the nascent colonial state would also demand the translation of European and Mesoamerican ideas about local production, exchange, and leadership. In peacetime, the emerging Hispanic state employed theories of local governance that were as mutually intelligible to Iberians and Mesoamericans as the notions of alliance and vassalage. The Nahua notion of the *altepetl* as the basic political unit was functionally compatible with Spanish notions about towns as basic constituents of the state. Both were local political entities with internal hierarchies and elements of sovereignty that could function either autonomously or as elements of a larger empire. New Spain was intentionally built from both. It was a political system whose smallest units were *repúblicas de indios* and *repúblicas de españoles*, whose leaders were bound together as fellow vassals of a global monarch. Any comprehensive description of colonial citizenship must take stock of Spaniards' and Indians' notions of themselves as *vecinos* of local communities and vassals of the distant king.

Tlaxcala's northern colonies were created in partnership with the church, and were an important vehicle for Franciscan missionary work, but they were not "missions" in the sense that that the word is commonly used in the United States.[22] It was not the missionaries who built the environment in which Tlaxcalans lived; on the contrary, it was the Tlaxcalans who built towns and hosted missionaries within them. A close look at these mission-towns reveals an environment in which Indians served as the most important agents of colonization and acculturation. Missionary activity was part and parcel of a broader cultural and political project in which Tlaxcalans transmitted the economic, cultural, and political practices of the hybrid *altepetl-pueblo* to the north.

A close examination of late colonial civic life tells us much about the origins of modern notions of nation, ethnicity, and nationality.[23] In the past several

---

[22] On missions to the northern frontiers, Thomas E. Sheridan, Charles Polzer, Thomas E. Naylor, and Diana W. Hadley, eds., *The Franciscan Missions of Northern Mexico* (New York: Garland, 1991); David J. Weber, *How Did Spaniards Convert Indians?* (Waco, TX: Baylor University Press, 2004); Steven W. Hackel, *Children of Coyote, Missionaries of Saint Francis: Indian-Spanish Relations in Colonial California, 1769–1850* (Chapel Hill: University of North Carolina Press, 2005); Kent Lightfoot, *Indians, Missionaries, and Merchants: The Legacy of Colonial Encounters on the California Frontier* (Berkeley: U.C. Berkeley, 2004). Dated in some respects, but still quite valuable, are Robert Ricard's *The Spiritual Conquest of Mexico: An Essay on the Apostolate and Evangelizing Methods of the Mendicant Orders, 1523–1572*, trans. Lesley Byrd Simpson (Berkeley: University of California, 1966) and John Leddy Phelan, *The Millennial Kingdom of the Franciscans in the New World*, 2d ed. (Berkeley: U.C. Berkeley, 1970). On religious life in the emerging urban environment, see William B. Taylor, *Magistrates of the Sacred: Priests and Parishioners in Eighteenth-Century Mexico* (Stanford, CA: Stanford University Press, 1996); Karen Melvin, "Urban Religions: Mendicant Orders in New Spain's Cities, 1570–1800," (Ph.D Dissertation, U.C. Berkeley, 2005); and Matthew O'Hara, *A Flock Divided: Race, Religion, and Politics, 1749–1857* (Durham, NC: Duke, 2009).

[23] On state formation, Fernando López-Alves, *State Formation and Democracy in Latin America, 1810–1900* (Durham, NC: Duke, 2000); Gil Joseph and David Nugent, eds., *Everyday Forms of State Formation* (Durham, NC: Duke, 1994); Brian Connaughton, "Conjuring the Body Politic from the

decades, historians have introduced appealing new theories on the evolution of ethnic and national identities. In borderlands studies, several recent works have explored the fluid relationships between Spaniards and "barbaric" Indians, raising questions about ethnic redefinition and ethnogenesis in frontier spaces. Our growing understanding of the plasticity of ethnic and national identities among marginal groups and in frontier spaces should also inform our understanding of the origins of mainstream Mexican citizenship. Scholarship on Indian governance, frontiers, identity formation, citizenship, and state formation can help us to arrive at a fuller description of how "civilized" and "barbaric" Indians integrated themselves into the imperial and later republican state.[24] This undertaking requires a crossing of common

Corpus Mysticum: The Post-Independence Pursuit of Public Opinion in Mexico, 1821–1854," *The Americas* 55, no. 3 (1999), 459–80; Connaughton, *Clerical Ideology in a Revolutionary Age* (Calgary: University of Calgary, 2003); David Frye, *Indians into Mexicans: History and Identity in a Mexican Town* (Austin: University of Texas, 1996); Michael T. Ducey, *A Nation of Villages: Riot and Rebellion in the Mexican Huasteca, 1750–1850* (Tucson: University of Arizona, 2004); Peter Guardino, *Peasants, Politics, and the Formation of Mexico's Modern State: Guerrero, 1800–1857* (Stanford, CA: Stanford University Press, 1996); Guardino, *In the Time of Liberty: Popular Political Culture in Oaxaca, 1750–1850* (Durham, NC: Duke, 2005); John Tutino, *From Insurrection to Revolution in Mexico: Social Bases of Agrarian Violence, 1750–1940* (Princeton, NJ: Princeton University, 1998); Alan Knight, "Peasants into Patriots: Thoughts on the Making of the Mexican Nation," *Mexican Studies/Estudios Mexicanos* 10, no. 1 (1994), 135–61; Annick Lempériere, "¿Nación moderna o república barroca? Mexico, 1823–1857," in *Inventando la nación: Iberoamerica, siglo xix*, ed. Francois-Xavier Guerra and Monica Quijada (Mexico City: Fondo de Cultura Económica, 2003); Eric Van Young, *The Other Rebellion: Popular Violence, Ideology, and the Mexican Struggle for Independence, 1810–1821* (Stanford, CA: Stanford University Press, 2001s); Mario Rodríguez, *The Cádiz Experiment in Central America, 1808–1826* (Berkeley: U.C. Berkeley, 1978); Jaime Rodríguez O., *The Independence of Spanish America* (New York: Cambridge, 1998); Stanley C. Green, *The Mexican Republic: The First Decade, 1823–1832* (Pittsburgh: University of Pittsburgh, 1987); Luís Jáuregui, "El Plan de Casa Mata y el federalismo en Nuevo León, 1823," *Secuencia* 50 (2001), 140–67; Benedict Anderson, *Imagined Communities: Reflections on the Origin and Spread of Nationalism*, rev. ed. (London: Verso, 1991); Sarah Castro-Klarén and John Charles Chase, eds., *Beyond Imagined Communities: Reading and Writing the Nation* (Baltimore: Johns Hopkins, 2003); Jacques Lafaye, *Quetzalcóatl and Guadalupe: The Formation of Mexican National Consciousness, 1531–1813* (Chicago: University of Chicago, 1976).

[24] The literature on identity formation with respect to race and nationality is extensive: *Imperial Subjects: Race and Identity in Colonial Latin America*, eds. Andrew B. Fisher and Matthew D. O'Hara (Durham, NC: Duke, 2009), Anthony Pagden, "Identity Formation in Spanish America," in *Colonial Identity in the Atlantic World, 1500–1800*, eds. Nicholas Canny and Anthony Pagden (Princeton, NJ: Princeton University, 1987); David Brading, *The First America: The Spanish Monarchy, Creole Patriots, and the Liberal State-1492–1867* (Cambridge, U.K.: Cambridge, 1991); Patricia Seed, "Social Dimensions of Race: Mexico City, 1753," *Hispanic American Historical Review* 62 (1982), 559–606; Magnus Mörner, *La Corona española y los foráneos en los pueblos de indios de América* (Madrid: Ediciones de Cultura Hispanica, 1999); Harold Dana Sims, *The Expulsion of Mexico's Spaniards* (Pittsburgh: University of Pittsburgh, 1990); Frye, *Indians into Mexicans*; Raul García Flores, *Formación de la sociedad mestiza y la estructura de castas en el noreste: el caso de Linares* (Monterrey, México: Archivo General del Estado de Nuevo León, 1996); Ann Wightman, *Indigenous Migration and Social Change: The Forasteros of Cuzco* (Durham, NC: Duke University Press, 1990); Karen Viera Powers, *Andean Journeys: Migration, Ethnogenesis and the State in Colonial Quito* (Albuquerque: University of New Mexico Press, 1995). Works treating identity formation in Anglo-America and the borderlands:

boundaries between fields and specialties. Historians have too often treated Mexican and European history as discrete topics. Even among Mexicanists, there is a long tradition of separating the study of colonial and modern history. It has become increasingly clear, however, that a complete description of the origins of the modern Mexican state must address the long history of colonial governance and the complex relationship between European and Mesoamerican political cultures.

THE "CHICHIMECS" OF THE NORTH

New Spain was a state built outward from the Hispano-Nahau heartland of central Mexico, and its colonial culture defined itself in contrast to peripheral societies. Nahuas and Spaniards called northern cultural outsiders "Chichimecs" – an exonym that paid no heed to distinctions of language or heredity. In the Mixtón and Chichimec wars of the sixteenth century, Spaniards and their indigenous allies fought to bring ever larger areas of the Gran Chichimeca under colonial control. In colonial parlance, "Chichimec" signified all things alien to New Spain: barbarism, rootlessness, paganism, and ignorance.[25] Yet the long-term strategy of the vice-royalty was more often to conquer, co-opt, and integrate than to displace and exclude. For this reason the colonial north soon included Chichimecs who considered themselves loyal subjects of the crown; and "Chichimec" – once a word without much underlying ethnographic substance – came to describe a real social category.

Several common characteristics of so-called Chichimec nations shaped their interactions with the expanding colonial empire. In contrast to Mesoamericans and Europeans, the members of these northern societies were more mobile, employed simpler technologies, and belonged to much smaller political entities. Spaniards used the words *nación* and *ranchería* to describe northern political organizations. A *nación* at times described a broad ethno-linguistic group under no single authority; at other times it described any individual band under recognizable leaders. *Ranchería* had a more precise definition. It described a community that resided or traveled together. Usually comprising less than a hundred people, a *ranchería* might describe a mountain village or a similar-sized

Gary B. Nash, "The Hidden History of Mestizo America," *Journal of American History* 82, no. 3 (1995), 941–64; Noel Ignatiev, *How the Irish Became White* (New York: Routledge, 1995); Neil Foley, *The White Scourge: Mexicans, Blacks, and Poor Whites in Texas Cotton Culture* (Berkeley: U.C. Berkeley, 1997). On translations between ethnicity, class, and political alignment in later Mexican history, see Christopher R. Boyer, *Becoming Campesinos: Politics, Identity, and Agrarian Struggle in Postrevolutionary Michoacán, 1920–1935* (Stanford, CA: Stanford University Press, 2003) and Jennie Purnell, *Popular Movements and State Formation in Revolutionary Mexico: The Agraristas and Cristeros of Michoacán* (Durham, NC: Duke, 1999).
[25] Charlotte M. Gradie, "Discovering the Chichimecas," *The Americas* 51, no. 1 (1994), 67–88; Gradie, "Chichimec," *Oxford Encyclopedia of Mesoamerican Culture*, ed. Davíd Carrasco (New York: Oxford, 2001).

group of Chichimecs on the move.[26] The small scale of the Chichimecs' political organization was a source of both vulnerability and adaptability, as they struggled to survive and thrive both outside and inside the Spanish colonial system.[27]

The cases presented in this book come largely from the northeastern frontier of Mexico, a region with a highly diverse Indian population.[28] Spaniards identified northern nations by language, appearance, subsistence patterns, or trade goods.[29] In most cases, we do not know what these groups called themselves. Spaniards named some groups for their piercings, face paint, or tattoos (for instance, the Borrados and Rayados). Others were identified by a food staple or eating practice (Caracoles, Cometunas, Comecrudas). Geographical terms, such as *serranos*, also became ethnic labels. Terms like Tobosos described large ethnic groups with great geographical dispersion, while other names of *naciones* were applied only to a single *ranchería*. Recent scholarship on the phenomenon of ethnogenesis (the process of creative integration among disparate mobile groups) shows that we should never assume a northern Indian nation named in the records was eternal, monolithic, or permanently bound to a specific

[26] Eugenio del Hoyo describes a pattern in which Spanish opportunists first identified recently "discovered" *rancherias* of Chichimecs to magistrates, who then recognized them as *naciones* under encomienda, *Historia del Nuevo Reino de León (1577–1723)* (Monterrey, Mexico: ITESM, 1972), 316–18. On the basis of the writings of Martín de Zavala, Israel Cavazos Garza describes seventeenth-century Nuevo León as including more than 200 *rancherías* or *naciones*, see *Breve historia de Nuevo León* (Mexico City: Colegio de México, 1994), 15–16.

[27] David Frye notes that Spaniards generally assumed all northern peoples were organized into *rancherías* of a consistent size under the military command of individual Indian captains, "The Native Peoples of Northeastern Mexico," *Cambridge History of Native Peoples of the Americas*, vol. II, eds. Richard E. Adams and Murdo J. Macleod (New York: Cambridge, 2000), 98–99.

[28] García Flores, *Formacion de la sociedad mestiza*, identifies the following groups in sacramental registers from the area: Borrados, Gualaguises, Pelones, Pintos, Serranos, and Pames, as well as Tlaxalans and Otomis. In the early eighteenth century, Pedro Gómes Danés has arrived at the following demographic estimate from church records: 5.75% Spanish, 5.75% mestizo, 47.75% Indian outsiders, 23.45% Indians from the region, and 17% blacks and mulattos, *San Cristóbal de Gualaguises: haciendas, ranchos y encomiendas, siglo xviii* (Monterrey, Mexico: Archivo General del Estado de Nuevo León, 1990). Napoleón Nevarez Pequeño finds the early site at Hualahuises to have contained Gualaguises, Tlaxcalans, Borrados, and Cadimas. For two *pueblos de indios* on the site of today's Monetemorelos, Pedro Gómez Danés has identified the following groups in missionary records: Nazcas, Cacabras, Cacalotes, Pelones, Aguatinejos, Tortugas, Otomis, Narices, Domisaguas, Guarames, Lumbres, "paysanos," Guasames, Mexitillos, and Cadimas, as well as the standard mixed-caste designations, *Las misiones de Purificación y Concepción* (Monterrey, Mexico: UANL, 1995). The work of José Jesús Martínez Perales finds Pelones, Pames, Cadimas, Borrados, and Rayados, along with Tlaxcalans, Otomis, and mixed castes, José de Jesus Martínez Perales, *Montemorelos, Nuevo Leon* (Monterrey, Mexico: Congresso del Estado, Comite de Archivo Biblioteca, 2003).

[29] On Spanish naming and classification of Chichimecs, see Chantal Cramaussel, "De cómo los españoles clasificaban a los indios. Naciones y encomiendas en la Nueva Vizcaya central," in *Nómadas y sedentarios*. Gary Clayton Anderson notes that the Spanish distinguished between groups like the Jumanos (among them Tobosos), which shared some "civilized" traits with Pueblo Indians, and Coahuiltecans whom the Spanish described as hunter-gatherers, *Indian Southwest, 1580–1830: Ethnogenesis and Reinvention* (Norman: University of Oklahoma, 1999), 4–28.

area.[30] The northeastern Indians produced no written records prior to colonial contact; and with the notable exception of Pame, their languages have not survived.[31] Despite the many uncertainties about the identity and culture of the northeastern Chichimec nations, a number of shared traits determined similar experiences among these groups in the face of colonial settlement.

The Indians of the northeastern frontier mixed horticulture with hunting, fishing, and forage. They cultivated Mesoamerican crops such as maize and beans, but they also collected wild foods such as nopal fruits, and they hunted for deer and other game. Most did not live in year-round settlements, but they did construct fixed structures and revisit the same sites in the course of their seasonal rounds. The Indians of the coastal northeast were connected by language to the Maya world, and by commerce to the peoples of the Nahua center and the Chichimec periphery. Northern nations had never lived isolation, but the colonial era was a time of accelerated contact, exchange, violence, and displacement. With the arrival of Spanish and Nahua colonists, raiding and trading with colonial settlements become a central part of the Chichimec economy. Both forced and voluntary settlement in colonial agricultural communities would further transform the subsistence and culture of these Chichimec nations.[32]

---

[30] On ethnogenesis, ethnic redefinition, and community membership, see Anderson, *The Indian Southwest, and Pekka Hämäläinen, The Comanche Empire* (New Haven, CT: Yale, 2008). On the permeable boundaries between European and Indian communities, see James F. Brooks, *Captives and Cousins: Slavery, Kinship, and Community in the Southwest Borderlands* (Chapel Hill: University of North Carolina, 2002). Charlott M. Gradie, *The Tepehuán Revolt of 1616: Militarism, Evangelism, and Colonialism in Seventeenth-Century Nueva Vizcaya* (Salt Lake City: University of Utah, 2000) notes the flexible organization of communities led by shamans and war chiefs, and organized on the scale of *rancherías*.

[31] David Frye, "Pame," *The Oxford Encyclopedia of Mesoamerican Cultures.* The Chichimec-Jonaz language survived to the modern period, though in a different region, Harold E. Driver and Wilhelmine Driver, *Ethnography and Acculturation of the Chichimeca-Jonaz of Northeast Mexico* (Bloomington: Indiana University, 1963). According to García Flores, Pames were at the center of the Chichimec wars and they continued to appear at new settlements in Nuevo León and Nuevo Santander throughout the eighteenth century,"También aca hubo Pames: Nuevo León, 1770–1830," *Actas* 2, no. 3 (2003). Frye notes the lone survival of the Pame language in "The Native Peoples of Northern Mexico."

[32] Luis Gonzalez Rodríguez, "Los tobosos, bandoleros y nómadas: experiencias y testimonios históricos," in *Nómadas y sedentarios; Isidro Vizcaya Canales, Invasión de los indios bárbaros en el norte (1840–1841)* (Monterrey, Mexico: ITESM, 1968); David B. Adams, "Embattled Borderland: Northern Nuevo León and the Indios Bárbaros, 1686–1870," *Southwestern Historical Quarterly* 95, no. 2 (1991), 205–20; Frye, "The Native Peoples of Northeastern Mexico," 98–99. The coastal Huasteca had pre-Conquest trade relationships to the Nahua center through the Río Panuco zone, Lorenzo Ochoa, "Huastec," *Oxford Encyclopedia of Mesoamerican Cultures.* A wide range of labor arrangements existed in the eighteenth century in areas where Indian towns, Spanish towns, and Spanish estates neighbored each other. In the first decades of the eighteenth century, this variety is apparent in Gómez Danés, *San Cristóbal de Gualaguises.* Radding, *Wandering Peoples,* describes a similar northern environment in which Otomí and Tarascan settlers entered a region of more mobile northern Indian communities. She describes groups engaged in sporadic planting and harvest and occupying small rancherías. On Indians laboring within the colonial sphere, see Susan M. Deeds, "Land Tenure Patterns in Northern New Spain," *The Americas* 41, no. 4 (1985), 446–61.

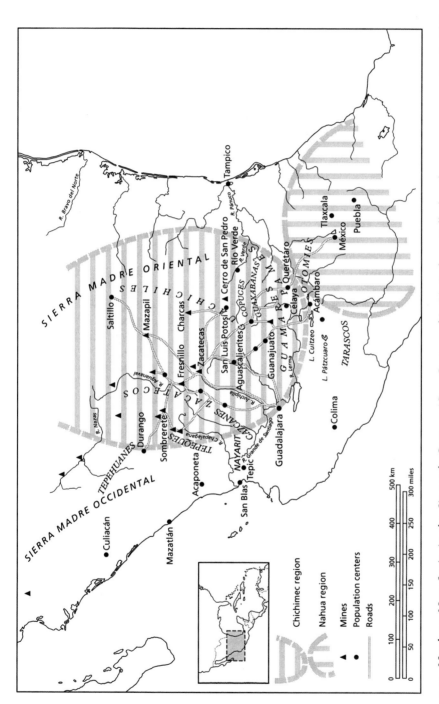

MAP 1. Northern New Spain in the Sixteenth Century (Cox Cartographic Limited, partially based on a map appearing in Philip Wayne Powell, *Capitán mestizo: Miguel Caldera y la frontera norteña* [Mexico: Fondo de Cultura Económica, 1980], 33–34)

OVERVIEW

This book opens by reconstructing how Spaniards and Tlaxcalans understood their standing as vassals of the empire and *vecinos* of their local communities. Spaniards derived their notions of empire from Roman precedent and transmitted them to the Tlaxcalans, who established a position for themselves as subordinate self-governing allies. This created two spheres of citizenship: one that existed within the semiautonomous Tlaxcalan client states and one with broader currency in the larger empire. Like Rome's Latin allies, the Tlaxcalans possessed a clearly defined form of citizenship within the empire that was predicated on their military service. Tlaxcalans helped to conquer the north of New Spain, shaping the categories of colonial citizenship in that region. The Tlaxcalan towns retained their own governments and their own military hierarchies, but they also recruited and incorporated other northern Indian populations to settle beside them. Chapter 1 describes the early history of the Tlaxcalan-Chichimec colonies in Nuevo León. It explores the relationship of the Neoleonés daughter colonies to their immediate mother colonies, and to the original nation of Tlaxcala. It also considers the relationship of these Indian towns to nearby Spanish estates, and to the mobile Indians who continued to live outside the political systems of colonial New Spain.

In the seventeenth century, two political economies existed side-by-side in northern New Spain: one based on Indian republics, the other on Spanish estates. Chapter 2 describes the construction of stable local administration in areas that combined Spanish, Tlaxcalan, and Chichimec communities. Chichimecs often lived and worked in both environments. The Indian republics, which were established by Tlaxcalan settlers, followed the rules of land tenure and political authority for *repúblicas de indios* as defined under imperial law. Spanish estates, which were first formed under early grants of land and labor (*encomienda*), operated differently. Spanish estates did not create a civic sphere for Indian political institutions, nor did they grant land titles to their Indian workers. Under the original terms of *encomienda*, and under the modified principle of *congregación*, Spanish farmers, ranchers, and miners were able to exact labor from Chichimec nations. Conflicts involving mobilie Indian bands, *pueblos de indios*, and Spanish estates provoked a series of early-eighteenth-century administrative reforms, which curtailed Spanish control of Indian labor and expanded the Tlaxcalan civic model, opening the path for new waves of Chichimecs to enter the *pueblos de indios*. This period, associated with the administration of royal visitor Francisco Barbadillo, codified and strengthened existing Tlaxcalan practices.

The labor regime on early Spanish estates too often left Chichimec workers with no choice other than to submit themselves to cruel conditions or flee. The Tlaxcalan-Chichimec *pueblos de indios* were a far more desirable environment. There a path of opportunity lay open for those who were willing to operate within colonial norms. Chapter 3 describes how non-Tlaxcalan Indians acquired the cultural traits and legal prerogatives of Tlaxcalans. Strong groups of Chichimec nomads were able to negotiate settlement in Tlaxcalan communities on favorable terms, retaining their weapons and their internal social hierarchies within the Indian towns. Those that took up permanent residence soon learned the rules of colonial society by emulating the Tlaxcalans. Over time, settled Chichimecs gained most of the civic and legal privileges originally reserved for Tlaxcalans. This chapter traces the incorporation of Chichimec populations as barrios within Indian towns. It also examines the language used by long-settled Chichimecs to explain and justify their acquisition of Tlaxcalan privileges.

Multiethnic colonies served, not just the interests of their inhabitants, but also those of the empire. Spanish leaders of the eighteenth century considered the Tlaxcalan-Chichimec *repúblicas de indios* in Nueva Vizcaya and Nuevo León the best available model for numerous new settlements in Texas, Tamaulipas, and the upper reaches of the Río Grande. Chapter 4 recounts how the system of colonization, land tenure, and governance established by Tlaxcalans and codified by Francisco Barbadillo now became the template for further settlements among previously uncolonized peoples in the north. Tlaxcalan towns also made important practical contributions to the colonies by furnishing supplies, transport, soldiers, and settlers. In many cases, though, it was the Tlaxcalan precedent, rather than the Tlaxcalans themselves, that was most decisive in shaping the frontier. The founders of eighteenth-century colonies borrowed from both the codified and customary elements of the Tlaxcalan colonial system that already existed in Coahuila and Nuevo León. As in the older colonies, new multiethnic frontier towns were based on the accretion of distinct Indian barrios. Newer residents learned from previously "civilized" groups, eventually becoming members of local defense forces and local governments. In these later ventures, a variety of populations was employed as "civilized" founders and tutors to the local Indians. In some communities, Tlaxcalans served this function; in others, previously acculturated Chichimecs, mestizos, or mulattos provided the nuclei for growing multiethnic towns. *Cabildos* with mixed representation and multiethnic militias emerged in this environment, paving the way for the casteless civic institutions of republican Mexico.

While the growth of pueblo governance created a new civic environment (and with it new local citizens of many stripes), it was the long history of military service that bound together the inhabitants of separate communities as subjects of an empire and later as citizens of a modern state. Chapter 5 describes the conditions of violence and the modes of military cooperation that cultivated a shared imagination of citizenship within a larger polity. In the eighteenth century, the confluence of two historical forces expanded and redefined citizenship: the continued growth of Tlaxcalan-Chichimec garrison towns and a new system of imperial militias. In the 1760s, Bourbon military reformers integrated local militia units into vast new regional militias. They believed that a region of small landholders, armed for militia service, was most likely to create population growth, economic growth, and security. Strategists often invoked the history of the Tlaxcalan-Spanish alliance as the model for frontier diplomacy, and the Tlaxcalan mission-towns as the model for further settlement.

With the outbreak of the Hidalgo Rebellion, the latent democratizing forces of a fully armed citizenry had sweeping effects throughout the region. As Hidalgo's armies moved northward from central Mexico, viceregal authorities mobilized the largest armies ever assembled in the region. The militia armies were mobilized to resist the invaders, but the militiamen soon voted with their feet and joined the insurgency. The confrontation (and collaboration) between the two citizen armies was a powerful demonstration of the link between military service and political participation that joined members of distinct communities in a broader consciousness of regional (even proto-national) citizenship. The Constitution of Cádiz further legitimized the association between local, regional, and imperial forms of citizenship by creating hierarchies of representation that linked provincial government to the mother country, and by abolishing caste distinctions between European and New World populations. The crown repudiated the constitution between 1815 and 1820, but the political changes already underway in the north of New Spain took on a life of their own.

Chapter 6 is a study of citizenship and state formation at the municipal level. It describes the evolution of local political economies from the 1790s to 1830s, focusing on the relationship between Spanish, Tlaxcalan, and Chichimec populations during the years in which *repúblicas de indios* and *repúblicas de españoles* merged into larger municipalities. The notion of uniform, casteless citizenship, which arose with the Constitution of Cádiz and the 1824 Mexican Constitution, was a legal theory that could only be operationalized through local systems of government. On Mexico's northern frontier, local systems composed of Tlaxcalan-Chichimec pueblos and neighboring Spanish communities had already adopted administrative practices that connected the economic and political lives of Spaniards, Tlaxcalans, and Chichimecs. During the half-century considered in this chapter, northern communities made a gradual transition from colonial corporate systems to casteless republican ones. The Indian republics, composed of aggregated Tlaxcalan-Chichimec barrios, now merged with the Spanish political community. Old barrio-based organizations continued to define local political geography and to shape the fight for land and water rights. During this transitional period, Indians continued to invoke legal privileges and property rights using the lexicon of colonial law. Meanwhile, they selectively employed language and tactics from the new constitutional order. The same habit of pragmatic emulation that had allowed Tlaxcalans to master Spanish law, and Chichimecs to attain Tlaxcalan status, now allowed both groups to rearticulate their political demands in the language of modern republican citizenship.

I

Tlaxcalan Vassals of the North

Rome came to be the ruler of the whole world, and the policy of its foundation was none other than the admission of all those trouble-makers who didn't fit in their own kingdoms, assigning them lands and granting them proportional honors, according to the circumstances, populating well the colonies that they were acquiring through conquests; and if this worked in those remote times, why should we not apply it to our fine part of the Spanish Empire?[1]

–1805 Report on the Northern Frontier

Xochipilla.

FIGURE 2. This battle scene from the Lienzo de Tlaxcala records Tlaxcalan service beside Spaniards in the Mixtón War. (Nineteenth-century copy from the lost sixteenth-century original in Alfredo Chavero, *Antigüedades Mexicanos*, 1892, Bridgeman Art Library)

A SPANISH VIEW OF EMPIRE: VISIONS OF ROME IN AMERICA

New Spain was a colony forged by two kinds of conquerors, one European, the other indigenous – and this is the key to understanding the institutions and

[1] Biblioteca Nacional de España, Madrid (hereafter BNE) MSS 19709, no. 37, fols. 3–5.

customs of the imperial frontier. Though Mexicas, Tarascans, and Otomís all served as soldiers and colonizers at different times, no indigenous group so thoroughly shaped the practices of colonization as the Tlaxcalans. The relationship between Castile and Tlaxcala was formalized in the sixteenth century and rearticulated over the next three centuries. The Spanish Empire was multiethnic, multilinguistic, and composed of many semiautonomous principalities. However, the member states, both European and American, shared common understandings about law, religion, warfare, and royal authority. Like the many kingdoms and communes of Iberia, unified under a common sovereign, Tlaxcala retained its own political institutions and local liberties within the empire.[2]

The Spanish Empire was consciously modeled on Rome, and we must reconstruct Spain's memory of Rome to understand the principles of citizenship and statecraft that ordered life in New Spain. Like Roman Europe, much of Spanish America was built from constituent substates. Consequently, Spanish law recognized several types of citizenship, as well as the principle of plural citizenship. Looking deep into their own past, the *vecinos* of Spanish cities often knew that their towns were once Roman colonies with special charters describing their internal governance and their relationship to the empire. To this day, several of these charters, inscribed in bronze, may be seen in Spanish museums.[3] New Spain's Tlaxcalan charters were recorded on parchment or paper rather than bronze or stone, but their authority was enduring. The kings of Spain issued colonial charters to Tlaxcalan leaders, who then guarded, studied, and recopied them with diligence. These documents are less specific than their Roman antecedents with respect to the details of internal law and governance, but they are meticulous in their account of each community's heritable privileges. The charters, along with the legal and administrative records of Spanish and Indian magistrates, produce a clear picture of the Spanish-Tlaxcalan colonial order.

Discussing the similarities between the Roman and Spanish empires would be no more than an amusing glass-bead game, were it not for one important fact: the colonizing Spaniards were as fascinated by these parallels as we

---

[2] Herbert Bolton and Thomas Marshall, *The Colonization of North America, 1492–1787* (New York: Macmillan, 1920), 39; Phillip Wayne Powell, *Soldiers, Indians, and Silver: The Northward Advance of New Spain, 1550–1600* (Berkeley: University of California, 1952), 67–72; Andrea Martínez Baracs, "Colonizaciones Tlaxcaltecas," *Historia Mexicana*, vol. 43, no. 2, pp. 201–3; Pedro de Antonio Escalante Arce, *Los Tlaxcaltecas en Centro America*; Matthew and Oudijk, *Indian Conquistadors*. On other colonizing groups, such as the Otomí, see Martínez Baracs, *Un Gobierno de Indios*, 273–4. John Chávez, *Beyond Nations: Evolving Homelands in the North Atlantic World, 1400–2000* (Cambridge, 2009), explores the functions of subordinate alliances and federalism in the history of colonial and modern state formation.

[3] The first century *Lex Irnitana*, inscribed on still-legible bronze plates, is currently displayed at the Museo Arqueológico de Sevilla. Both the text and its monumental presentation suggest the importance and specificity of Roman municipal charters for Ibero-Roman communities.

are.[4] Spanish administrators saw the world though the veil of their own classical education and imposed on New Spain notions of empire and citizenship patterned on Rome.[5] In this vision of the world, Tlaxcalans assumed the role of Rome's early Latin allies: a separate nation in a dependent alliance, whose elites (and later entire population) enjoyed many of the privileges of imperial citizenship. These allies were distinguished from subject peoples by their civil status, their corporate autonomy, and their exemption from tribute. The Latin allies of antiquity retained their own internal governance and military command structure, but lacked independent diplomatic functions. Their populations enjoyed the civil protections of imperial law but did not participate in the political life of the imperial capital.[6] Ancient Iberia was itself a frontier for Rome, wooed in alliances, punished by invasion, and drawn slowly into the political and linguistic culture of the empire. In the sixteenth-century Americas, Spain reenacted its own classical past, but now played the role of the conqueror rather than the conquered.

Educated Spaniards often reflected on the parallels between the Roman conquest of Iberia and the Iberian conquest of the Americas. Rome absorbed Spain through strategic alliances with Celtiberian tribes, pitting one against the other until the empire prevailed. In the midst of a Mediterranean-wide contest against Carthage, Rome sought control of Iberia for silver and slaves. It proved a great source of wealth for Rome, but also of endless rebellions. The Romans put down insurrections with a combination of carrot and stick, frequently enslaving defeated enemies and sometimes meting out exemplary mass-executions, but at other moments co-opting their enemies with grants of military posts and Roman

---

[4] It was once common for Anglophone historians to describe all empires by analogy to Rome. The protracted fall described by Edward Gibbon became the model for the decadence of any crumbling empire. Early twentieth-century historians like Arnold Toynbee and Oswald Spengler saw in the story of Rome a set of eternal truths about the life cycle of all civilizations. Edward Gibbon, *The Decline and Fall of the Roman Empire* (New York: Random House, n.d. [1787]); Oswald Spengler, *The Decline of the West*, trans. Charles Francis Atkinson (New York, Knopf, 1957 [1926]); Arnold Toynbee, *A Study of History* (Oxford: Oxford University, 1972 [1934]).

[5] In the past two decades, several works have traced the intellectual history of classical imagery in Latin America. Sabine MacCormac's *On the Wings of Time: Rome, the Incas, Spain and Peru* (Princeton, NJ: Princeton University, 2007) is a thorough exploration of the analogies drawn between Rome and the Incan empire by both Spanish and Andean writers. Lupher demonstrates the patterning of Spanish imperial thinking and historical composition on Roman precedents in *Romans in the New World*; Pagden has argued that the French, English, and Spanish empires were built on a psychology of fulfilling ideals inherited from Rome in *Lords of All the World*. Brading notes many examples of conscious links between Spanish and Roman institutions in *The First America*, 184–9; Jorge Cañizares-Esguerra describes the classical analogies applied by Europeans to the Americas in *How to Write the History of the New World: Histories, Epistemologies, and Identities in the Eighteenth-Century Atlantic World* (Stanford, CA: Stanford University Press, 2001), 11–59; on the dynamic relationship between classical learning and new colonial experience, see Anthony Grafton, *New Worlds, Ancient Texts: The Power of Tradition and the Shock of Discovery* (Cambridge, MA: Harvard University, 1995).

[6] Sherwin-White, *The Roman Citizenship*, chapter 4.

citizenship. Roman emperors settled veteran soldiers on Spanish lands, planting gridiron towns on the Iberian landscape. These towns became the nuclei of Ibero-Roman cities, and the loci of a cultural exchange that would eventually yield a large population of Latin-speaking Christians.[7]

Many centuries later, with heads full of classical memories and grand ambitions, the Spanish in North America moved outward from the Valley of Mexico seeking silver. They and their Tlaxcalan allies approached the Chichimecs of the north with the same Roman tactics of carrot and stick, and with the same flexible diplomacy of war and peace, cooptation, and conquest. Some Chichimec enemies were taken as mining slaves; others were drawn into the sedentary regime of the mission-towns. At the core of the early colonial population were Tlaxcalan soldier-settlers who built around themselves communities of northern Indians.

Sixteenth-century Spaniards gazing at America sometimes saw their former selves and felt the sting of conscience. They imagined Spain in the role of Rome, and New World peoples as conquered Spaniards. Bartolomé de las Casas used this analogy to good effect in his critique of Indian slavery and his attack on its apologist, Juan Ginés de Sepúlveda. Las Casas pointed out that Spaniards were once themselves barbarians on the fringe of a civilized empire. In the following passage, he notes the savage state of early Celtiberians, quoting the Roman historian Trogus Pompey:

> Let Sepúlveda hear Trogus Pompey: "Nor could the Spaniards submit to the yoke of a conquered province until Caesar Augustus, after he had conquered the world, turned his victorious armies against them and organized that barbaric and wild people as a province, once he had led them by law to a more civilized way of life." Now see how he called the Spanish people barbaric and wild.[8]

Here las Casas's analogy is put to the purpose of defending the rights of Indians. Though not all Spaniards shared his moral cause, many saw the

---

[7] On the intellectual history of Spansh notions of empire, see John Eliot, *Spanish Imperialism and the Political Imagination: Studies in European and Spanish-American Social and Political Theory, 1513–1830* (New Haven, CT: Yale, 1990); Eliot, *Empires of the Atlantic World: Britain and Spain in America, 1492–1830* (New Haven, CT: Yale University Press, 2006); Elliott, *The Old World and the New, 1492–1650* (Cambridge, U.K.: Cambridge, 1970); Pagden, *Lords of All the World*; Pagden, *The Idea of Europe: From Antiquity to the European Union* (Cambridge, U.K.: Cambridge University, 2002); On theories of conquest, see Patricia Seed, *Ceremonies of Possession in Europe's Conquest of the New World, 1492–1640* (Cambridge, U.K.: Cambridge University, 1995); Silvio Zavala, "*La filosofia politica en la conquista de América*" (Mexico City: Fondo de Cultura Economica, 1972); Zavala, *Ensayos sobre la colonización español en America* (Mexico: Editorial Porrua, 1978); Zavala, *La defensa de los derechos del hombre en América Latina (siglos xvi-xviii)* (Mexico: UNAM/UNESCO, 1982).

[8] Bartolomé de las Casas, *In Defense of the Indians . . .*, trans. Stafford Poole (DeKalb, Ill.: Northern Illinois University Press, 1992) [1552], 43. Trogus Pompey, a historian writing in the time of Augustus, was himself a Gaul from Vocontium, a community first bound to Rome as ally and then granted Latin status.

same similarity between the two periods of history, and many believed that Spain would civilize the New World in the same way Rome civilized the old.

At other times, Spaniards imagined themselves to be like the early Christians who conquered the souls of pagan Rome.[9] Sixteenth-century Jesuit missionary José de Acosta described the conversion of Rome and the conversion of the Americas as part of the same prophetic story: "The Almighty decreed that the stone mentioned in the Book of Daniel which broke the kingdoms and monarchies of the world, should also break those of this other New World; and just as the law of Christ came at a time when the monarchy of Rome had reached its height, thus it was also in the Indies."[10] Acosta believed that the Andean and Mesoamerican civilizations, like pre-Christian Rome, attained a high level of material and political refinement while suffering profound spiritual ills. Running though Acosta's work is the conviction that evangelization inevitably wins the hearts of pagans, and that empire can bring civilization to the uncivilized; savages can become subjects, and pagans Christians.

Acosta divided the world's non-Christian cultures into three categories for the purposes of evangelization: first, civilized and literate societies; second, civilized nonliterate societies; and finally, savage peoples. At the time of first contact, missionaries to North America placed Tlaxcalans in the second category and Chichimecs in the third. Acosta believed that nations like China, which were urban, literate, and well governed, should be brought to the faith by persuasion and reason. Peoples of the second rank, like the Mexican and Andean civilizations, who possessed sophisticated economies and governance but lacked literature and philosophy, should be governed by Europeans – but governed with a light hand. In matters unrelated to the Christian faith, their own customs were to be respected. The savage peoples of the earth possessed souls and natural reason, and thus could, and must, be converted to Christianity. However, their want of true government and civilized customs would necessitate direct imperial rule. The Hapsburg Empire's hierarchy of citizenship followed Acosta's taxonomy and remained rooted in Roman precedent. The application of the Acosta taxonomy to the northern frontier is predictable. Tlaxcalans, who were already "civilized" peoples before the time of Cortés, were placed under loose imperial oversight, retaining their customs and internal hierarchies. Having acquired the traits of literacy and Christianity, Tlaxcalans passed into the ranks of civilized Christian peoples. The Chichimecs, who were considered savages, would have a longer path to membership in the empire. To save the

---

[9] Reff, *Plagues, Priests, and Demons*, argues that early New World missionaries likened their position in the ruins of the Aztec Empire to that of Christian evangelizers who spread the faith amid the epidemics and invasions of the late Roman Empire.

[10] José de Acosta, *Natural and Moral History of the Indies*, ed. Jane E. Mangan, trans. Frances López-Morillas (Durham, NC: Duke, 2002), bk. 7, chap. 28.

souls of Chichimec *bárbaros*, the empire first had to govern their bodies and their communities.[11]

The Roman Empire had at its core a body of hereditary citizens bound together by common language, culture, and history. However, as Rome expanded its military reach, it gathered power through a network of alliances with neighboring states, referred to as Latin allies (or *socii*). Over time, these Latin allies were granted a form of Roman citizenship even while they retained citizenship in their own polities. They became passive citizens with limited rights in the former, but remained active citizens with full privileges in the latter. This pact between Romans and Latins expanded over time to include new states and peoples in a larger confederation. Slowly, the Latin allies became full Roman citizens, while new arrivals rose to the status of Latin allies. On the fringes of the empire, recently conquered enemies were often subjected to Roman administration without any form of citizenship. However, opportunistic leaders of enemy peoples were sometimes drawn under the patronage of the empire by status grants of Roman citizenship. All of these practices were part of Spain's strategy for the expansion of New Spain.[12] To extend the Roman analogy, Tlaxcalans were like Spain's Latin allies, and the barbaric Chichimecs were like Gauls or Goths who, once co-opted by the empire, sought to climb the ranks toward Latin status.

Spaniards first entered Nuevo León in the 1580s under the command of the first governor and *encomendero* Luis de Carvajal. Carvajal's brief and unsuccessful conquests, motivated by the profits of slave raiding and mining, provoked fierce resistance from local populations. The hostility stirred up by Carvajal's activities, and the power vacuum created by his subsequent arrest, led Spain to temporarily abandon the area.[13] His successors also sought profit, but through more stable, long-term investments in mining, farming, and ranching.

The seventeenth century brought a remarkable confluence of different ethnic groups into Nuevo León. The indigenous inhabitants were seminomadic peoples who spoke a wide variety of languages and possessed a simple material culture, but were formidable warriors.[14] Over the course of the seventeenth

---

[11] Though this schema is not set out by Acosta in one place, it is clear in his treatment of North America, South America, and China in *Natural and Moral History of the Indies*. A similar taxonomy of civilization and barbarism is articulated by las Casas, *In Defense of the Indians*, chaps. 1–5. See also Zavala, *La defensa de los derechos del hombre*, 36–42; Pagden, *The Fall of Natural Man*, chap. 3; and Brading, *The First America*, 184–9.

[12] The classic description of these forms of alliance and dual imperial citizenship may be found in Sherwin-White, *The Roman Citizenship*.

[13] The earliest Spanish settlement on the site of Monterrey was established a few years before when Alberto Canto, after creating a settlement Saltillo in 1577, began prospecting for slaves and minerals in Nuevo León. The area was abandoned from 1588–1596. On the early *entradas* in Nuevo León, see Israel Cavazos Garza, *Breve historia de Nuevo León*, 20–32; Silvio Zavala, *Entradas, congregas y encomienda en el Nuevo Reino de León* (Seville, Spain: Universidad de Sevilla, 1992).

[14] On the region's indigenous peoples see Frye, "The Native Peoples of Northeastern Mexico."

century, great numbers of the region's Indians were rounded up by *encomenderos* to be used as agricultural workers or be sold to mine operators. During these same years, the Franciscan order sent out missions and established *doctrinas* throughout Nuevo León.[15] The cumulative effect was a colony that, though technically under the control of a Spanish governor and integrated into the legal and political structures of New Spain, was, in practice, a loosely governed zone subject to continuous conflict among its indigenous and Spanish inhabitants. Spanish soldiers took Indian captives from ungovernable frontier areas and sometimes even from mission lands. Meanwhile, semi-Hispanicized Indians moved in and out of the mission system, sometimes themselves attacked by unassimilated tribes and sometimes joining in attacks against Spanish authority. In addition to Spanish and indigenous peoples, colonial Nuevo León's population included some people of African origin. Carvajal included forty African slaves in his expedition to found Nuevo León, and African slaves remained a small part of the regional economy thereafter.[16] The Spanish crown's New Orders of 1575 had forbidden the enslavement of Indians (though many elaborate legal devices permitted Indian slavery to continue in a variety of guises), but African slavery remained legal.[17] Free Africans and mulattos sometimes filtered into Nuevo León from the cities of the Gulf Coast and a few Africans continued to enter as slaves. In the mid eighteenth century, Nuevo León had a substantial free mulatto population.[18]

The final decades of the seventeenth century was a period of conflict and instability in Nuevo León. Alonso de León and his contemporaries anticipated the rapid colonization of northern New Spain, including the newly explored territories of Texas, but their ambitions were soon frustrated. The flight of Indians from Spanish estates and mission communities was common, and rates

[15] I use the current state name, "Nuevo León," as well as "New Kingdom of Léon," throughout this chapter. However, the latter is more historically accurate. Contemporary documents used "Nuevo Reino de León."

[16] Cavazos Garza, *Breve historia de Nuevo León*, 47.

[17] Weber, *The Spanish Frontier in North America*, 125-7; on Indian slavery and *encomienda* in Nuevo León, see Zavala, *Entradas, congregas, y encomiendas en el Nuevo Reino de León*; Frye, "The Native Peoples of Northeastern Mexico," 90-107; on Nueva Vizcaya and Nuevo León, Gerhard, *The North Frontier of New Spain*, 220-1.

[18] The free mulatto population of this region remains understudied. Once manumitted from formal chattel slavery, people of African ancestry mixed into urban populations, making them difficult to trace in the documentary record. On the documentary traces of African and mulatto populations in Pilón, see José de Jesús Martínez Perales, *Montemorelos, Nuevo León* (Monterrey, Mexico: Congresso del Estado, Comité del Archivo Biblioteca, 2003), 14. Some parish records indicate the presence of at least a few black slaves in Nuevo León as late as the 1750s; see "Libros de defunciones de la Purísima Concepción," in Pedro Gómez Danés, *Las Misiones de Purificación y Concepción* (Monterrey, Mexico: UANL, 1995), 88. For a general estimate of the ethnic composition of Linares in the eighteenth century, see Raúl García Flores, *Formación de la sociedad mestiza y la estructura de castas en el noreste: el caso de Linares*, serie Orgullosamente Barajaros . . ., no. 12 (Monterrey, Mexico: Archivo General del Estado de Nuevo León, 1996); on Hualahuises, see Gómez Danés, *San Cristóbal de Gualaguises*, 97.

of death by disease astronomical. Many Indian communities were largely depopulated and, in several cases, completely abandoned in the 1690s.

The Spanish leaders of the northern frontier viewed their own era as one of great historical import. They sought to describe their actions in the context of world history and to harmonize the story of New Spain with the story of Europe. To the learned men of the day, the backdrop of Roman antiquity loomed over all subsequent events; it guided their statecraft and served as the measure of their accomplishments.[19] For literate Spaniards, history had two foci: Rome and the Bible. The Bible was the source of authority invoked in discussions of conversion, just war, and kingship; the history of Rome in discussions of statecraft, citizenship, and military strategy. Drawing from both sources, Spanish leaders incorporated the colonization of the north into a global narrative of human history.

Three seventeenth-century sources are of particular interest for reconstructing Spanish visions of empire on the northeastern frontier: the report of Alonso de la Mota y Escobar who, as the bishop of Guadalajara, toured the region and described its peoples; and the chronicles of Alonso de León and Juan Bautista Chapa who recorded the first histories of Nuevo León. All three men described a northern empire rooted in the Roman model, and a system of settlement and conversion shaped by Acosta's taxonomy of civilizations. Alonso de León and Juan Bautista Chapa make direct reference to José de Acosta, and de la Mota seems also to have been informed by him.[20] All three describe a tripartite social organization of Spaniards, Tlaxcalans, and Chichimecs that corresponds to both the Acosta taxonomy and Roman notions about citizens, allies, and barbarians.

Between 1602 and 1605, Bishop Alonso de la Mota y Escobar recorded his visits to the colonies of the northeastern frontier. He traveled through Nueva Galicia, Nueva Vizcaya, and Nuevo León, preparing a report on their lands and inhabitants for the church and crown. De la Mota had a classical education

---

[19] Discussions of history *qua* history were always dominated by the Roman analogy. However, we should also consider the unarticulated transfers of colonial psychology and practice from the Castilian administration of Andalucía to the New World. On the roots of Mexican racial categories in the *Reconquista*, see Claudio Lomnitz, *Deep Mexico, Silent Mexico: An Anthropology of Nationalism* (Minneapolis: University of Minnesota, 2001), 42–45; on *vecindad* as originating in the *reconquista*, Tamar Herzog, *Defining Nations*, 6–7; on crusade and *reconquista* imagery in the politics of war, Zavala, *Ensayos sobre la colonization español*, 61; on the transposition of Islamic images onto Indians, Serge Gruzinski, *Images at War: Mexico from Columbus to Blade Runner (1492–2019)*, trans. Heather MacLean (Durham, NC: Duke University, 2001), 31, 97–98; on the transfer of *encomienda* practices, Peter Bakewell, *A History of Latin America: 1450 to the Present* (Oxford: Blackwell, 1997), 46, 82–89; on *reconquista* psychology in the north of New Spain, Weber, 20–23, and Phillip Wayne Powell, *Capitán Mestizo: Miguel Caldera y la frontera norteña: la pacificación de los chichimecas (1548–1597)*, trans. Juan José Utrilla (Mexico: Fondo de Cultura Economica, 1980), 46.

[20] Alonso de León, Juan Bautista Chapa, Gral Fernando Sánchez de Zamora, *Historia de Nuevo León, notas de Israel Cavazos Garza* (Monterrey, Mexico: Ayuntamiento de Monterrey, 1980) [17th century], De León, introduction; Bautista Chapa, 161–73.

and viewed the world in classical terms. He compared his tour of the north to Rome's provincial inspections; he likened his enormous dispatch to Livy's history of Rome; and he described his cartography as following the tradition of Pomponius Mela's *Geography*. He ornamented the report with many classical flourishes and even quoted Cicero in the original Latin.[21] One is not surprised to find that de la Mota's strategy for the north was a Roman one.

In the eyes of de la Mota, all the inhabitants of North America were Spanish vassals (*vasallos*), but vassals of several different types. He wrote the report to inform the king of his "distant kingdoms and vassals," carefully elucidating the differences among them. His broadest classification of the northern population designated inhabitants as Spaniards, Tlaxcalans, or Chichimecs.[22] He considered Tlaxcala a true civilization with a long history of complex political and religious institutions. De la Mota acknowledged that the Tlaxcalans were once pagan idolaters, but explained that they had since become Christians and proper subjects of the crown. In contrast, he described the unassimilated Chichimecs as savages without government or civilization:

> one will not find any town in [New] Galicia or [New] Vizcaya, that obeys a coat of arms or flag from their [the Chichimecs'] land like those that the Mexica and Tlaxcalans possessed in their paganism, the people being so barbarous and violent, nor did they even have any type of writing or hieroglyphics to serve in any way for history or as a record of their ancestors."

He presented the Nahuas of central Mexico (the Mexica and Tlaxcalans) as true civilizations, whose military prowess and state-level organization made them the equals of Old World peoples. According to de la Mota, the Chichimecs' only saving grace was that they were too primitive to construct temples and become idolaters.[23] However, he did not place them forever beyond the reach of civilization. Much of his text is concerned with the process of their Christianization and acculturation. De la Mota shared las Casas's optimistic belief that even the most primitive peoples could be brought to the faith. To him, Spain had succeeded in transforming Nahuas from civilized pagans into civilized Christians. Among the Chichimecs, the project was just beginning; they were a people without civilization, religion, or government, who must now be given all three.

---

[21] Mela seems to have been chosen by the author to remind us of the historical parallels between Roman Spain and Spanish Mexico. The first-century geographer was himself an Iberian from Baetica.

[22] He also speaks of Mexica individuals when making historical comparisons between north and center. In the latter case, the same traits are generally ascribed to Tlaxcalans and Mexica.

[23] Alonso de la Mota y Escobar, *Descripción geográfica de los Reinos de Nueva Galicia, Nueva Vizcaya y Nuevo León, Colección histórica de obras facsimilares* (Gobierno del Estado de Jalisco, 1993) [1602–1605], 17–22, 91–92.

Spaniards embraced the notion of civilization in the original Roman sense of *civitas* – the embodiment of the society in the city.[24] The *pueblos de indios*, which structured local life in central Mexico, had the essential characteristics of Iberian towns and thus matched de la Mota's expectations for civilized life. He, like the architects of the 1590 Spanish-Tlaxcalan pact, hoped to see the Tlaxcalan town spread civilization northward. De la Mota was pleased to see that the Tlaxcalan-Chichimec colonies had implemented the system of governance and record keeping of Nahua *pueblos de indios*. The new towns, he noted, have "a house that they call a community where they appropriately convene their Republic, and in this house they have a box with keys into which they put the money that they call the goods of the community (*bienes de la comunidad*) ... these keys are customarily guarded, one by the *alcalde* and the other by the *mayordomo* and *escribano*."[25] The Tlaxcalan colonies, as described by de la Mota, would have been immediately recognizable to any Spaniard as ordinary towns within the empire.

De la Mota was one of the first Spanish writers to comment on the success of the Tlaxcalan colonies in settling and civilizing the region's Chichimecs. He gave a glowing report on the colony of Venado, which had been established by Tlaxcalans near the silver mines of Charcas. The pueblo contained "*vecinos* of Chichimec birth, peaceful ones among whom have settled a certain number of Tlaxcalan Indians." They, along with the Spanish captain and a few of his soldiers, had reportedly created an environment in which the Chichimecs became good Christian subjects. De la Mota observed that stationing soldiers among the community's Chichimecs was no longer necessary because "as the old [Chichimecs] that were warlike people are dying off, those that are now born and raised in the *doctrina* ... [are] gentle and Christian."[26] Here he described the success of what was, in fact, a widespread social system in the north – one in which interdependent settlements of Spaniards and Tlaxcalans became the sites of acculturation for nearby Chichimecs.

Alonso de León provides us with the first attempt at a general history of the New Kingdom of León. De León established the first Spanish settlement in the Valley of Pilón and cooperated with Tlaxcalan colonists to found San Juan de Tlaxcala. In the 1640s, he wrote a regional chronicle that contextualized local events in a grand narrative of world history. His timeline began with the Book of Genesis and the story of how the fall of Babel fractured the world's primeval linguistic unity. For de León, the fall of Rome was a second blow to the dream of human unity. Both ruptures were now to be healed by the Spanish crown acting on behalf of the universal church. De León understood his efforts on behalf of Spain as part of a theological project

---

[24] Pagden describes the history of the association between "city" and "civilized" in *Lords of All the World*, chap. 1.

[25] De la Mota y Escobar, 72, 22.

[26] De la Mota y Escobar, 72.

to reconstitute the divided peoples of the earth as a single Christian community.[27]

The question of how to forge a common society from the varied peoples of the north was one of de León's main preoccupations. Like Acosta, de León saw the peoples of the world through a hierarchical taxonomy. Following the Aristotelian-scholastic tradition, he judged human societies by their progress toward a true knowledge of God. De León believed that all peoples had at least some notion of the Divine, but that the fall of Babel and consequent scattering of peoples had left many nations with only a faint memory of theological truth. De León believed that only in the area between New Spain and Florida could one find a population with no notion of kingship and no notion of God. He thought the Nahuas' gods were a distorted memory of the Apostles, but that the Chichimecs lacked even that. The Chichimecs were both more innocent and more terrible than the other peoples of the earth, and thus were in urgent need of conversion. Viewed through either lens, they were true primitives.

De León emphasized the shared frailties of all human beings, drawing parallels between the Old World's pre-Christian past and the northern frontier's present. His representations of the Chichimecs alternated between images of noble savage and ruthless barbarian. At some points, he described them as cannibals and sodomites possessed by Satan; at others points, as simple people who in their nakedness exemplified "the perfect poverty that Our Lord Christ said his disciples must have."[28] De León's grand-scheme history admits a certain cultural relativism. He condemned the Chichimecs for sodomy, but reminded readers that it was a vice shared by the Greeks; he described their cruelty in war, but compared it to that of pre-Christian Europe; and he bemoaned their polygamy while conceding that it was common among the Patriarchs of the Old Testament. History provided inspiration and cautionary tales for all concerned. To de León, the barbarians, in their moral depravity, could be seen as Canaanites who turned their backs to God. Many of his stories were warnings meant for Spanish ears. He believed that Spaniards, in their time of victory, should watch their step lest they fall prey to the prideful sins of the House of David. However, if all went well, Spain could become a Christian Rome for the people of the north. Alonso de León, who was granted the very Roman title of "*Procurador General*," certainly embraced that end.[29]

Juan Bautista Chapa, a younger comrade in arms of Alonso de León, continued his mentor's chronicle from the 1660s to the 1690s. Bautista Chapa, the *procurador* of Monterrey and the proud owner of a large classical library, also walked self-consciously in Roman footsteps. His references to governance show how commonplace the language of Roman statecraft was in his time. As

---

[27] De León, Bautista Chapa, Sánchez de Zamora, *Historia de Nuevo León* [17th century], 7–17.
[28] Alonso de León, 17–22.
[29] Alonso de León, chaps. 10–11.

procurador, he ruled in conjunction with the "the *cabildo* sitting as *naturales* of the land who care for the republic." As a magistrate, he placed great stock in the authority of historic texts. Bautista Chapa, like de León, used discussions of Christian ethics and Roman history to analyze local events. His descriptions of military actions were accompanied by exacting just-war arguments; and those arguments were, in turn, supported by reference to decrees of the Roman Catholic Church, papal donations, and historical precedents. He believed that governance should be rooted in law (positive and divine), and he sought out such law in authoritative texts. When his personal library was insufficient to the task, Bautista Chapa consulted the collections of Cerralvo; that failing, he wrote to the Franciscans at the College of Zacatecas that they might glean from their library a final answer.[30] For Bautista Chapa, to be a good leader was to be a good student of scripture, law, and classical history.

Bautista Chapa judged contemporary leaders against the yardstick of Roman ones, heaping special praise on his predecessor Alonso de León. The latter appears in the chronicle as a brilliant student of Roman military tactics and diplomacy who prevailed against his Chichimec adversaries and even staged something akin to a Roman triumph. Bautista Chapa admired de León for his shrewd diplomacy and his ability to play one nation against another. De León's strategy triggered frequent retribution against his men and their Indian allies, fueling a pattern of warfare and slave taking, but Bautista Chapa made of him a great hero.

Bautista Chapa's view of the Chichimecs was inconsistent. In some passages they are described as unclothed barbarians without law, religion, or governance; in others as conspirators, cagey negotiators, and formidable warriors. In a moment of grudging admiration, he likened their skill and resolve in warfare to that of the Flemish rebels. While his impressions of the Chichimecs varied, his view of the colonizers was constant: he saw Spaniards as the successors of the Romans, and the Tlaxcalans who came north through Saltillo as their faithful and civilized allies. Not a word of criticism does Bautista Chapa have for the Tlaxcalans, whom he describes as supplying armies of up to a hundred skilled soldiers and playing a vital role in the foundation of several Neoleonés communities.[31]

It is hard to ignore how much of the record of Spanish colonial expansion in the Americas is overwritten with and shaped by older narratives. Sixteenth- and seventeenth-century Spaniards arrived at an understanding of new frontiers and new peoples that could be accommodated within their mental map of the world and their stories about the Spaniard's place in world history. Their larger narrative was a Roman one – Roman in a sense that comprehended Habsburgs as Romans, Rome as the heart of Christendom, and classical Rome

[30] Juan Bautista Chapa, "Historia de Nuevo León de 1650 a 1690," in De León, Bautista Chapa, Sánchez de Zamora, *Historia de Nuevo León*, chaps. 10, 22.

[31] Bautista Chapa, chaps. 18–19 on Caesar and de León; on his conflicting notions about Chichimecs, chap. 20; Tlaxcalans as admirable military allies, chap. 8.

as the great author of European multiethnic empire. Some of the peoples of the Americas would place themselves within this Spanish vision; others would not.

A TLAXCALAN VIEW OF EMPIRE: THE CHARTERS AND COUNCILS OF SPAIN'S "LATIN ALLY"

From the sixteenth to eighteenth century, Tlaxcalans were widely recognized as a distinct cultural group with a special political status under the empire.[32] References to this elite Tlaxcalan status appear regularly in Tlaxcalan petitions and in the descriptions of Tlaxcalan mission-towns recorded by their clergy. Tlaxcalans described themselves as vassals (*vasallos*), conquerors (*conquistadores*), and nobles (*nobles* or *principales*). To understand what Tlaxcalans meant by these words, we must explore their early relationship with Castile and the circumstances under which they colonized the frontiers of New Spain.[33]

The Spanish-Tlaxcalan alliance began in the wars of conquest of 1519–1521, but by the mid sixteenth century, it had evolved into a stable, institutionalized pact, and Tlaxcala became a state within the empire. Agreements between Tlaxcala and Spain guaranteed the former's system of internal governance and affirmed its inhabitants' status as knights and vassals under the Castilian crown. Spanish magistrates took very seriously the authority of agreements between the Spanish crown and Indian communities. Perhaps no such agreements were as elaborate or as often invoked as those of the Tlaxcalans.[34] Charles Gibson was

---

[32] Frye's *Indians into Mexicans* examines the history of the Tlaxcalans of Mexquitic and finds that they retained Tlaxcalan privileges and a distinct identity until the mid eighteenth century, but that, from the mid eighteenth to mid nineteenth centuries, their historic, corporate identity and its recognition under the law melted away, leaving almost no collective memory of the Tlaxcalan past. I do not see signs of this collective amnesia in eighteenth-century Nuevo León.

[33] On elite indigenous subjects in Spanish America, Chance, "The Caciques of Tecali: Class and Ethnic Identity in Late Colonial Mexico," *The Hispanic American Historical Review* 76, no. 3 (Aug. 1996), 475–502; Robert Haskett, *Visions of Paradise: Primordial Titles and Mesoamerican History in Cuernavaca* (Norman: University of Oklahoma, 2005); Kevin Gosner, "Caciques and Conversion: Juan Atonal and the Struggle for Legitimacy in Post-Conquest Chiapas," *The Americas* 49, no. 2 (Oct. 1992), 115–29; Delfina Esmeralda López Sarrelangue, *La Nobleza Indígena de Pátzcuaro en la Época Virreinal* (Mexico City: UNAM, 1965); Scarlett O'Phelan Godoy, *Kuracas sin sucesiones: del cacique al alcalde de indios, Perú y Bolivia, 1750–1835* (Cuzco: Centro de Estudios Regionales Andinos Bartolomé de las Casas, 1997); David T. Garrett, *Shadows of Empire: The Indian Nobility of Cusco, 1750–1825* (New York: Cambridge, 2005); Sinclair Thompson, *We Alone Rule: Native Andean Politics in the Age of Insurgency* (Madison: University of Wisconsin, 2002); Ward Stavig, *The World of Túpac Amaru: Conflict, Community, and Identity in Colonial Peru* (Lincoln: University of Nebraska Press, 1999).

[34] English translations of the Nahuatl *cabildo* records of sixteenth-century Tlaxcala have been published in Lockhart, *The Tlaxcalan Actas*. The charters, unlike the early *cabildo* records, were issued in Spanish, not just Nahuatl, and many are available in published form. See *San Esteban de la Nueva Tlaxcala: documentos para conocer su historia: investigación y paleografía*, comp. Carlos Manuel Valdes Dávila and Ildefonso Dávila del Bosque (Saltillo, 1991); *Los*

first to systematically explore the Spanish-Tlaxcalan relationship in *Tlaxcala in the Sixteenth Century*.[35] Gibson demonstrated Tlaxcala's success in utilizing its early status as an indispensable military ally of Spain to justify its high level of political autonomy during a century of ever-increasing Spanish influence. He showed that Spanish political traditions favored subjects who could present all petitions as rooted in past service to the crown. The Tlaxcalans represented themselves as the first Christians of New Spain and as the faithful allies who had persevered with Cortés though the *noche triste* and the conquest of Mexico. Among the indigenous populations of New Spain, they were uniquely positioned to curry viceregal favor.[36] Throughout the sixteenth century, Tlaxcalan leaders sought special recognition through the petitioning process, even sending delegations to the royal court in Spain in 1534 and 1535. These efforts, along with their continuing military service, secured for the Tlaxcalans near-complete self-governance, symbolic honors, and exemption from many taxes.[37]

Culturally, and linguistically, Tlaxcalans, like the Mexica, were Nahuas, central Mexican agriculturalists with a complex material and political culture.[38] James Lockhart's *The Nahuas after Spanish Conquest* focuses on cultural continuity in the Nahua zone of Mexico from before European contact to the late colonial period. Just as Gibson sees a natural compatibility between Nahua and Spanish military systems and patronage practices, Lockhart sees a natural compatibility between Nahua and Spanish social organizations. The mutually beneficial relationship that evolved between the two was rooted in a shared perception of analogous social hierarchies. Both Spaniards and Nahuas belonged to societies ordered in one way by the distinction between noble and commoner, and in another by hierarchies of patronage and military service.[39] Both cultures understood a polity to be comprised of corporate elements with higher functionaries defending both their own caste prerogatives and the broader interests of the communities that they represented. Because of these similarities in Spanish and Tlaxcalan political culture, the two systems could be functionally integrated without fundamentally disrupting either. Lockhart perceives this to be so seamless an integration that the municipalities and parishes of the late colonial period were merely new descriptions for the earlier political structures called *altepeme*. Under the colonial

Tlaxcaltecas en Coahuila, fuentes documentales, 2d ed., comp. *Carlos Manuel Valdés Dávila and Ildefonso Dávila del Bosque* (San Luis Potosí: Colegio San Luis, 1999); J. de Jesus Dávila Aguirre, *La colonizacion tlaxcalteca;* also the the appendices of Gibson, *Tlaxcala in the Sixteenth Century.*

[35] Gibson, *Tlaxcala in the Sixteenth Century.*

[36] Tlaxcalan efforts to create authoritative pictorial representations of their faithful Christianity and past service to the crown is treated at length in Cuadriello, *Las Glorias de la República de Tlaxcala.* The production of the narrative artwork in question seems to appear in the *cabildo* records for 17 June 1552, *The Tlaxcalan Actas,* 51.

[37] Gibson, *Tlaxcala in the Sixteenth Century,* 160–79.

[38] Gibson sometimes follows traditional U.S. usage in referring to Nahuas as "Aztecs"; Lockhart and more recent writers prefer "Nahuas."

[39] Lockhart, *The Nahuas after Spanish Conquest,* 100–139.

regime, Tlaxcala was composed of four *altepeme* governed by a *cabildo* of elected elites – much the same social organization that existed in the preconquest period.[40]

In Gibson's view, the Tlaxcalan *cabildo* was a public body that served to negotiate the relationship between the autonomous internal sphere of the four Tlaxcalan *altepeme* and the Spanish viceroyalty.[41] This is a perspective corroborated by the more recently translated Nahuatl *cabildo* records.[42] The extant records of the sixteenth-century Tlaxcalan *cabildo* provide us with an opportunity to observe the Tlaxcalan *cabildo*'s internal functions, its place in the fiscal and military systems of New Spain, and the relationship between the Tlaxcalan community and the Franciscan order.[43]

The *cabildo* records of the sixteenth century show that Tlaxcalan leaders considered their central charge to be the protection of their community's corporate privileges and of their peers' noble privileges. Tlaxcala was assigned a viceregal *corregidor* but his power was far from absolute. In the *cabildo* deliberations of 1555, Tlaxcalan leaders entered into negotiations with their *corregidor*, exacting concessions in the process of arriving at a mutually acceptable contract for his own salary and benefits.[44] Even viceregal decrees seem, in practice, to have been subject to a sort of regional nullification by the Tlaxcalan council. In 1560, the *cabildo* succeeded in reversing the application of a viceregal mandate for the congregation of Indian populations within Tlaxcalan lands. The matter is treated in the records of two sessions of the *cabildo* that conclude with the confident report that "Juan Jiménez, *alcalde*, and Buenaventura Oñate, *regidor*, went to Mexico City to request of the lord viceroy that the congregation not be permitted to be carried out yet; let a little more time [pass]. The lord viceroy accepted very gladly that the congregation not be carried out and things stay as they are."[45] On one hand, the Tlaxcalan *cabildo* addressed the viceroy and sovereign in terms of deepest reverence and phrased its demands as humble requests; on the other hand, the frequent success of its petitions suggests that Tlaxcala held considerable power in this political relationship.[46]

Tlaxcalans expended a great deal of time and money defending their local prerogatives before the Spanish government by sending frequent embassies to Mexico City, maintaining lawyers on retainer at the viceregal court, and even

---

[40] The pre-Columbian Tlaxcalan state was composed of four *altepeme* which, in turn, were composed of smaller social units called *calpulli*. Lockhart emphasizes the compatibility of the Nahua state's *altepetl-capulli* structure with the Spanish kingdom's *cabecera-sujeto* structure. For a more detailed structural analysis, see Martínez Baracs, *Un Gobierno de Indios*, 91–97.

[41] Gibson, *Tlaxcala in the Sixteenth Century*, 193.

[42] *The Tlaxcalan Actas*. All passages quoted from this source are the editors' translations from the Nahuatl into English.

[43] On the Franciscan-Tlaxcalan relationship, see Martínez Baracs, *Un gobierno de indios*, chap. 3.

[44] 10 Oct. 1555, *The Tlaxcalan Actas*, 95–97.

[45] 12 Jan. 1560, 15 June 1560, *The Tlaxcalan Actas*, 103–6.

[46] On the system of goverance in Tlaxcala under the viceroyalty, see Martínez Baracs, *Un gobierno de indios*, 135–95.

sending delegations directly to Spain in 1527, 1534, and 1562.[47] Nearly all their
petitions were prefaced with a recitation of the community's past service to the
crown. In 1562, the *cabildo* appended to a normal administrative report a
lengthy explanation of Tlaxcalan service over the previous half-century:

> it was necessary that it [this story] begin back when Hernando Cortés first came
> leading the Spaniards as captain and how the Tlaxcalan rulers, our fathers and
> grandfathers, just met and received him in friendship; they did not meet him
> with warfare, but gave him everything needed. And then began the war in
> Mexico City and everywhere here in New Spain. Very many were the rulers,
> legitimate nobles, and commoners who died in that war, and much of their
> property was destroyed by it.[48]

Both in these sixteenth-century records and in those of the Tlaxcalan colonies in
the two centuries that followed, the same themes were constantly repeated in
justifying Tlaxcalans' status: their history as unconquered allies, loyal vassals,
and generous subordinates who contributed more to the colonial state than they
demanded in return.

Plural citizenship and multiple forms of authority were at the heart of
Tlaxcalan political culture and of Spain's imperial system. Tlaxcalan colonists
in the north were both citizens of a greater Tlaxcala and vassals of the kings of
Castile. The Tlaxcalan communities throughout New Spain maintained communications and perpetuated a culture of collective citizenship. To become a
vecino of a new colony did not mean renouncing one's membership in the old
community. An eighteenth-century petition from the northern colony of San
Miguel de Aguayo illustrates this principle. In 1723, Estevan González, one of
leaders of San Miguel de Aguayo, presented himself in a petition as follows:
"Don Estevan González, cacique and principal of the City of Gran Tlaxcala,
vecino, settler, and conqueror of the town of San Miguel de Boca de Leones and
its frontiers, and discoverer of the Royal Mines of Our Lady of San Juan del
Nuevo León." Before proceeding to the contents of his petition, González
summarized the military contributions of his Tlaxcalan compatriots and promised to be ready "for the invasion of any enemy, providing arms and vassals at
my own cost, not only I but all the Tlaxcalans that find ourselves settled on the
frontier."[49] González presented himself as belonging to all of the following
categories: Indian, Tlaxcalan, nobleman, vassal of the king of Castile, citizen
of greater Tlaxcala, and citizen of Boca de Leones.

Tlaxcalan petitioners were well acquainted with European history and sought
to present themselves in ways that matched Spanish notions of modern and
classical empire. In 1812, the *cabildo* of the City of Tlaxcala prepared a petition
to the viceroy asking that its current assessor be appointed *alcalde de cortes* to

[47] Gibson, *Tlaxcala in the Sixteenth Century*, 164–5; 1 May 1562 *The Tlaxcalan Actas*, 118–19.
[48] 1 May 1562, *The Tlaxcalan Actas*, 119–120.
[49] Petition of Estevan González, 23 Aug. 1723, Archivo General de Indias (herafter AGI), Audiencia
    de Guadalajara, 173.

the royal *audiencia* of Mexico. The petition recites the military feats of the assessor's ancestors and praises his education, Christian orthodoxy, and past service to the crown. In typical Tlaxcalan form, the document seeks to enhance the community's status at court, both through the record of community merits and through the craftsmanship of the petition itself. It notes Tlaxcala's service in the age of Spanish conquest and its recent steadfast loyalty to the crown during the Hidalgo Uprising. The elegant document is written in the most elevated prose, attends to every point of etiquette, and in a flourish of classical sophistication, references the writings of Pliny and the reign of Emperor Trajan. Such nods to the Roman imperial tradition, on the part of the Tlaxcalans, show a precise understanding of Spain's self-image as the successor of Rome. Trajan was a Spaniard, raised on the imperial frontier, but he was also a Roman emperor famed for his suppression of colonial rebellions. Like las Casas, the Tlaxcalans sought to remind their readers that Spain, too, was once the frontier of the great empire. Tlaxcalans knew their history and they knew their patrons well.[50]

TLAXCALAN VASSALS AND THE SPREAD OF THE NAHAU PUEBLO

In the first century of Spanish colonization, Tlaxcalans were vital allies in the subjugation of lands outside the core of Nahua civilization. Their settlements, which combined the functions of garrison, mission, and town, were soon widely distributed across North America. Tlaxcalan soldiers fought under the direction of Pedro de Alvarado, establishing communities in Guatemala and El Salvador in the 1520s, and in the long series of conflicts that secured Spanish access to the mining regions of northern New Spain.[51] Spaniards first confronted the problem of the Chichimec frontier as they attempted to extend colonial control into the northern highlands in mid sixteenth century. In the resulting Chichimec wars, Tlaxcalan allies fought on behalf of the Spanish. It represented no radical departure from established policy when in 1590, the viceroy reached an agreement with the *cabildo* of Tlaxcala to found mission-towns in the north. In 1591, four hundred Tlaxcalan families established the first settlements. Perhaps the most successful of these was San Esteban de Nueva Tlaxcala, a strategic village near Saltillo, which lay on the route to the newly explored valleys of Nuevo León. San Esteban was a vital element of New Spain's plans for future security against nomadic attackers, but its function was also economic and cultural.[52]

---

[50] "Serenisimo Señor. La Ciudad de Tlaxcala ..."AGI, Audiencia de Guadalajara, 297.

[51] Escalante Arce's *Los Tlaxcaltecas en Centro America* shows that Tlaxclans fulfilled the same military and settlement functions in Central America that have been noted by Dávila Aguirre's *La colonización Tlaxcalteca* in northern New Spain.

[52] On San Esteban and the initial northern Tlaxcalan colonies, see Davila Aguirre, *La colonización Tlaxcalteca*; David B. Adams, *Las colonias Tlaxcaltecas*; the best secondary treatment of San Esteban may be found in Sego, *Aliados y adversarios*, 67–92. See also Martínez, "'Noble Tlaxcalans.'"

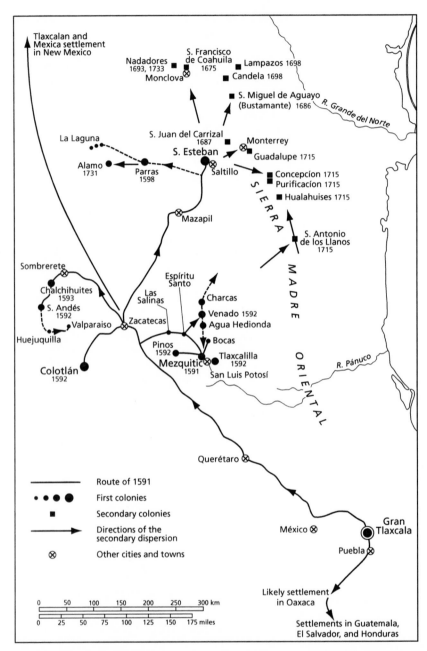

MAP 2. Tlaxcalan Colonization from the Sixteenth to Eighteenth Centuries (Map redrawn and modified by Cox Cartographic Limited from an original in Elisabeth Butzer, *Historia social de una comunidad tlaxcalteca* [Saltillo, Mexico: Archivo Municipal de Saltillo, 2001])

It is clear from the *cabildo* records and royal charters that the Tlaxcalans colonized the north, not merely at the order of the king, but by means of a mutually beneficial agreement. In 1560, the viceroy had proposed an earlier plan for northern colonization, but the Tlaxcalans declined the offer. The *cabildo*'s response to the viceroy noted Tlaxcala's ongoing cooperation with the crown in shorter military campaigns, but claimed that maintaining permanent colonies would be an undue hardship.[53] Thirty years later, when the agreement was finally struck, the official documents made clear Tlaxcala's position with respect to the crown. The royal charter of 1591 referred to the Tlaxcalan families as "my faithful vassals" who undertook the project, "not by compulsion, but voluntarily."[54] It stipulated many of the specific conditions of settlement, but its most important provision was one that transferred to the colonies all of the legal prerogatives of Tlaxcala itself, proclaiming "that the Tlaxcalan Indians and their successors and descendants as well as being *hidalgos* and free from all tribute shall enjoy all the liberties, immunities and privileges which the city of Tlaxcala enjoys and will in the future enjoy."[55]

The Tlaxcalan settlements in the north were created to serve a variety of purposes. They were military outposts, sites for agricultural and infrastructural development, and centers for civilizing and Christianizing northern Indians. The *cabildo* records explain that the colonization was undertaken in order that

> the leading Indians of the city of Tlaxcala might help with four hundred of their married Indians to settle with the aforementioned Chichimecs to instruct them and aid them that they may live in political order ... forming a harmonious and lasting republic following the order and form of villages of fortunate, Christian people that the clerics that are in charge of them may teach them and administer the sacraments for the salvation of their souls.[56]

This civilizing mission was celebrated by eighteenth-century Tlaxcalans of San Esteban who bolstered their petitions with notarized copies of the town's founding documents. A 1768 copy of a letter from the governor of Nueva Vizcaya proclaims that the Tlaxcalans' purpose in coming to Saltillo was "to settle in the lands of the Guachichil Indians ... so that the Guachichil Indians may be industrious and live in order and Christianity in the way of life of the Tlaxcalans."[57]

The later Tlaxcalan colonies of the northeast were settled in the seventeenth and eighteenth centuries by colonists from San Esteban de Saltillo. The original founders of Saltillo-San Esteban understood the Spanish, Tlaxcalan, and acculturated Chichimec populations of the area to be culturally and institutionally separate, yet interdependent and joined by a common purpose; this set of understandings set the pattern of settlement for Nuevo León. Spanish

[53] 15 June 1560, *The Tlaxcalan Actas*, 106–8.
[54] 14 Mar. 1591, *San Esteban de la Nueva Tlaxcala: documentos*, 52.
[55] 14 Mar. 1591, *San Esteban de la Nueva Tlaxcala: documentos*, 53.
[56] 14 Mar. 1591 mercedes, *San Esteban de la Nueva Tlaxcala: documentos*, 52.
[57] *San Esteban de la Nueva Tlaxcala: documentos*, 18.

Saltillo and Tlaxcalan San Esteban were planted back-to-back and took their water from a common canal (*acequia*), which defined the boundary between them. Both communities received religious guidance from the same church and convent of Franciscans, but each was internally self-governing.[58] These structures of segregation and autonomy were prized by the Tlaxcalans. Their charter included the guarantee that "said populations settle themselves and make their own homes in separate barrio plots with neither the Chichimecs nor the Spanish settling among them."[59] In the beginning, Tlaxcalan settlers were happy to fight, to lead, or to teach the northerners, but not to integrate with them.

When Tlaxcalans from San Esteban established new communities in Nuevo León, they took pains to document the transfer of legal privileges, just as the founders of Saltillo had done before them.[60] Written nearly two centuries later, a 1760 document from Saltillo suggests that the chain of mother-daughter settlements continued to cooperate in military expeditions and new foundations in the mid eighteenth century. It refers to the failed settlement of San Sabá and the defeat of the colonizers by the Comanches:

> The settlers have come from the town of Parras, San Francisco de Coahuila, Our Lady of Candela, San Miguel de Aguayo in Boca de Leones, Guadalupe, Purificación and Concepción, and from the foundation of the aforementioned towns to the present have been and are giving aid with armed men to subdue the hostilities of the barbarous Indians: and finally that in the month of May of the last year of 1759, the troop having come from Charcas for the undertaking of San Sabá from the day they arrived at said town to that which followed their defeat, maintained themselves as a cavalry.[61]

The document, prepared by a Franciscan friar at the behest of the Tlaxcalan *cabildo*, has several purposes: it recites the military services of the Tlaxcalans, celebrates their service to the church as faithful Christians, and connects all of their communities in a clear genealogy back to San Esteban, and thus to Tlaxcala itself. It also attests to the Tlaxcalans' ongoing activities as allies and colonizers as far north as Texas.

The genealogy connecting Tlaxcalan settlements is visible in their charters, in their leaders' individual chronicles of merit, and even in colonial maps. In northern New Spain, one encounters communities with names like Asunción Tlaxcalilla (beside San Luis Potosí), San Esteban de Nueva Tlaxcala, San Miguel de Tlaxcala (San Miguel de Aguayo), and San Antonio de la Nueva Tlaxcala. These daughter colonies bear the name of the mother, but naming patterns for the constituent barrios also suggest kinship ties from mother community to

---

[58] Sheridan Prieto, "'Indios madrineros,'" 32–34.

[59] 14 Mar. 1591, *San Esteban de la Nueva Tlaxcala: documentos*, 52.

[60] A 1711 document records the transfer of the 1591 privileges via Saltillo to the settlement of Salinas. Archivo Municipal de Monterrey (hereafter AMM), Civil, vol. 36.

[61] Letter of Fray Joseph Antonio Lazo of the Church of San Francisco in *San Esteban de la Nueva Tlaxcala: documentos*, 159.

colony. Tlaxcala itself was a polity comprised of four interdependent states (*altepeme*): Quiahuiztlan, Tizatlán, Ocotelulco, and Tepetíptac.[62] All the initial Tlaxcalan settlers in San Esteban were described in its founding documents as "vecinos de Tizatlán."[63] Thus, San Esteban takes its name from the patron saint of Tizatlán. San Esteban was composed of five barrios: Concepción, Purificación, San Buenaventura, Santa Ana, and San Esteban. The later mission-towns of Concepción and Purificación, established in the Valley of Pilón by Tlaxcalans from San Esteban, appear to be named for the San Esteban barrios from which their founders came. These naming patterns hint at the genealogical relationships between specific *altepeme* and *calpultin* in Tlaxcala and chain of successor communities in the north.[64] Thus the web of colonies linking the northern frontier to San Esteban and linking San Esteban back to Tlaxcala amounted to a network of settlements paralleling that of the European communities. At times the population of the Tlaxcalan diaspora, linked through these genealogies of colonization, functioned as a state within a state.

Many of the later missions of Nuevo León were designed in imitation of San Esteban, and drew upon its Tlaxcalan population as settlers. The missions of Purificación, Concepción, San Cristóbal de los Hualahuises, and Guadalupe all mixed newly settled Chichimecs with Tlaxcalans. A 1749 document attests to the fact that fourteen family groups of Tlaxcalans, originating in San Esteban, set out in 1686 to establish the settlement of San Juan de Carrizal. When San Juan proved a poor site, they then relocated to Purificación in 1715. The families described themselves as vassals of the king, with ongoing military responsibilities, who moved to Nuevo León of their own free will. The provenance of their charters stretched from Tlaxcala to San Esteban to San Juan to Purificacíon.[65]

---

[62] In Nahua civilization, a *calpulli* was a subunit of an *altepetl*. Both words are sometimes used to describe the four divisions of Tlaxcala that, because of their size, entailed an additional layer of four-part territorial divisions. On the structure of Tlaxcala, see Lockhart, *The Nahuas After Conquest*, 15–24; on the *barrio* structure of San Esteban *vis* Tlaxcala, Vito Alessio Robles, *Bibliografía de Coahuila, histórica y geográfica* (Mexico: Secretaría de relaciones exteriores, 1927), 362–7; on *barrio* genealogies, Martínez Baracs, *Un Gobierno de indios*, 224–37.

[63] "Relación de los tlaxcaltecas que vinieron a poblar la colonia de San Esteban de la Nueva Tlaxcala junto al Saltillo en 1591," J. de Jesus Dávila Aguirre, *La colonización tlaxcalteca*.

[64] Lockhart has raised the possibility that Nahua polities followed the same practices as their noble clans, periodically subdividing and colonizing in a process that he calls "hiving off." *The Nahuas after Conquest*, 20–21, 436–8; Frye shares the same perspective on *barrio*-based colonization.

[65] "Certificación de dos fundaciones hechas por los Tlaxcaltecas (1749)," *San Esteban de Nueva Tlaxcala*. Gómez Danés (*Las misiones de Purificación y Concepción*, 145–8) has argued that the Tlaxcalans of Nuevo León did not retain the special status of those in San Esteban, but the above document (and those that follow) demonstrates otherwise. David Frye ("The Native Peoples of Northeastern Mexico," 90) contends that the settlement of the north forced the Spaniards of New Spain to develop a broader notion of "indio" that could encompass both civilized Mesoamericans and northern nomads. It appears to me, however, that in Nuevo León, Spaniards saw Tlaxcalans and *indios bárbaros* as very different from each other. José de Dávila Aguirre goes so far as to suggest that in San Esteban, the Tlaxcalans amounted to a third legal and social category (a third *república*), *La Colonización tlaxcalteca*, 14–15. "Mercedes otorgadas a los frailes franciscanos y los tlaxcaltecas y guachichiles en 1591 (copia del siglo XVIII)," *San Esteban de Nueva Tlaxcala:*

This sense of legal and historical continuity was characteristic of Tlaxcalan colonization in the north.

One of the earliest, most prosperous, and most strategically important colonies of Nuevo León was San Miguel de Aguayo. The community was founded in the 1680s by explorers and miners from the Tlaxcalan town of San Esteban and the neighboring Spanish settlement of Saltillo.[66] Tlaxcalan prospectors discovered the first of many mining sites in the area and soon established a community of miners, frontier soldiers, and farmers. Following the typical Tlaxcalan settlement pattern, San Miguel grew up in partnership with a Spanish community (Boca de Leones) and a Chichimec *pueblo de indios* (San Antonio). The strategic importance of the town was threefold: it protected the nearby mines, protected Monterrey from northern invasions, and protected the route from Monterrey to Monclova.

Records from the seventeenth century provide striking examples of elite Tlaxcalan citizenship in San Miguel. Most of San Miguel's founding families were Tlaxcalans who retained their status as *vecinos* of Saltillo, and thus, by extension, of Gran Tlaxcala. All Tlaxcalan settlers were soldiers and *hidalgos*, but some held higher honors than others. The elite founding families, identified as *principales* in late seventeenth-century sources, wielded considerable political and economic power. The town's five original Tlaxcalan founders prepared documents in 1685 and 1686, both in Spanish and in Nahuatl, to confirm their land and mining claims before Spanish and Tlaxcalan authorities.[67]

One of the founding Tlaxcalan couples, Bernabé González and his wife Ana María, could almost be termed Tlaxcalan aristocrats. Bernabé, who was one of San Miguel's five leading founders, held the military rank of captain and also served as governor of San Miguel. His power in the mining economy was formidable. Records of mining transactions identify him as "Bernabé González, *indio tlaxcalteca principal* miner [and] discoverer of the mines." González bought and sold mining rights and prospered from mining receipts. His transactions were sometimes in excess of 1,000 pesos.[68] Several wealthy noblewomen among the Tlaxcalans also played important roles in the community after the deaths of their husbands. María Magdalena continued to wield influence as the widow of Agustín de la Cruz, one of the founding *principales* and

---

documentos; the best secondary treatment of San Esteban's regional role may be found in Sego, *Aliados y adversarios,* 67–92.

[66] The town owed its name to the patronage of the Marqueses of San Miguel de Aguayo, the region's largest landowners. Butzer points out that the family was intermarried with that of Francisco Urdiñola, the first protector of San Esteban de Saltillo, *Historia social,* 34.

[67] Butzer notes the 1685 Nahuatl petition and the 1686 Spanish one, Butzer, 32–33.

[68] 23 June 1698, AMM Protocolos, vol. 6, exp. 1, fol. 126; 20 Jan. 1701, AMM Civil, vol. 22, exp. 9, fol. 6. The transaction cited here was for 1,500 pesos. For comparison, consider that twenty years later, the standard daily wage for Indian workers was two *reales* per day ("Instrucciones y ordenanzas … Barbadillo," Zavala, *Entradas, Congregas, y Encomiendas,* 119–20). At 8 *reales* per peso, this transaction represented the equivalent of more than 15 years of day labor wages.

"first discoverer of the mines of Our Lady of San Juan Hill." She retained ownership of the mine of San Francisco de Assisi at Boca de Leones after her husband's death. María Magdalena along with Ana María, the widow of Bernabé González, were among the wealthiest people in the area. These elite Tlaxcalan women bought and sold mining rights and retained their titles and social stations after the death of their husbands.[69] Ana María was the owner of a miraculous image of Christ that became the center of a cult in San Miguel which survives to this day. She received special recognition as the patroness of the image from the bishop of Guadalajara. Toward the end of her life, she entrusted the image to the town's church and established an endowment and *cofradía* for its care.[70]

San Miguel de Aguayo came very close to achieving the ideal for a Tlaxcalan colony. Its mining and agriculture prospered and its founders retained their status as Tlaxcalan citizens and frontier soldiers. San Miguel also fulfilled its intended function as a place of settlement and acculturation for Chichimecs. Some of the same Tlaxcalan families who had helped to settle Guachichil Indians in their colony of San Esteban became the founders of San Miguel. Now they helped to settle the Alasapa Indians that inhabited the area near San Miguel de Aguayo. From 1786 to 1791, Alasapas and Tlaxcalans lived in adjacent barrios usually referred to as San Miguel and San Antonio. From 1691 to 1709, the Alasapas reverted to a seminomadic life, only to return later to San Antonio and become a permanent part of the local economy, military, and political culture thereafter.[71]

In the 1690s, San Miguel had an established local political system. The pueblo registered its elections in Monterrey, its governor and *cabildo* played an important role in regional defense, and its mining magnates (usually the same men who sat on the *cabildo*) concluded business agreements with Nuevo León and Coahuila's Spanish merchants and magistrates. They undertook mining ventures through shareholding partnerships in which individual miners put up the necessary capital, worked the mines, and reaped proportional profits. Most of San Miguel's Tlaxcalans were transplanted from San Esteban de Saltillo, and they maintained political and economic ties to their place of origin. Those born in San Esteban de Saltillo (and perhaps also their progeny) continued to regard themselves as *vecinos* of both San Esteban and San Miguel. Tlaxcalans continued to come to San Miguel; and, on at least one occasion, a group of families from San Miguel returned to Saltillo. San Miguel was the northernmost satellite of San Esteban, which was, in turn, a spoke that tied its colonists back to Gran Tlaxcala.

---

[69] 16 July 1698, AMM Protocolos, vol. 6, exp. 1, fol. 122; 16 Aug. 1699, AMM Civil, vol. 24, exp. 6, fol. 8; 16 Sept. 1698, AMM Protocolos, vol. 6, exp. 1, fol. 130.

[70] Treviño Villarreal, *El Señor de Tlaxcala*, 24–30.

[71] This history of the relationship between the Alasapas and Tlaxcalans is treated at length in Chapter 3.

SPANISH VASSALS AND CHICHIMEC LABORERS
IN A NORTHERN VALLEY

At the site of today's Montemorelos, the river Pilón moves in a twisted course
through a broad valley. In an arid and mountainous region, the valley's flat,
abundantly watered lands have long permitted it to sustain a large population
and have made it a natural route of transit. In the late sixteenth and early
seventeenth centuries, Spaniards, Tlaxcalans, and the northern tribes all
moved through this area and made use of its resources. Though permanent
agricultural settlements did not take root in the area until the 1640s, half a
century of previous contact established a set of practical expectations for the
interactions of Spaniards, Tlaxcalans, and local Chichimecs. From the first
Spanish forays of the 1570s, the Valley of Pilón was in the midst of the
mineral prospecting and slaving expeditions carried out first from Saltillo
and later from Monterrey and Cerralvo. Northern tribes gained experience
both as allies and enemies of Spanish expeditions. They traded with the
Spanish, fought against them, and fought beside them. They were often seized
as slaves, but also took Spanish captives of their own. In the records of the 1630s
and 1640s one encounters Chichimecs who speak Spanish or Nahuatl and
whose experience with the language and customs of the colonizers informs
their interactions with them.

Spanish governance and agriculture arrived in the Valley of Pilón in the person
of Alonso de León. De León was, by his own account, and in point of fact, a
conqueror. Born into a Mexico City family and its martial tradition, de León
described his northern conquests in the same terms a previous generation used to
describe the conquest of Mexico. De León considered himself a vassal of the
king and a conqueror and missionary among northern nations. Yet, in other
respects, he belonged to a new generation of military adventurers whose diverse
business interests distinguished them from their sixteenth-century predecessors: he
was a cattle rancher, a mining speculator, and a slave raider. Like the rest of
the leading Spanish colonizers, de León's personal authority in the region
was military, economic, and legal in character. From his headquarters at the
presidio of Cadereyta, de León's sphere of operations encompassed the entire
northeastern frontier. He commanded a small group of full-time soldiers and a
larger number of Spanish volunteers, and worked in cooperation with Tlaxcalan
and Chichimec allies. The crown granted him vast tracts of land, tribute from its
Indian inhabitants (*encomienda*), a military command with corresponding
fueros (*capitán a guerra*), and judicial authority in his domains (as *justicia
mayor*). To call him a feudal lord would not overstate the breadth of his authority.
However, in one crucial respect, the situation of northern conquistadors like
Alonso de León differed from that of the European feudal ideal; their rule did
not yet rest on the surplus wealth of a large and stable agricultural population.
Alonso de León, like many of his successors, would strive to transform the seminomadic population of the northeast into productive peasant-subjects, and himself into a proper feudal lord.

De León entered the New Kingdom of León in 1637 from Saltillo. In the same year, Governor Martín de Zavala (himself a military commander and *encomendero*) made five land grants in the valley; Alonso de León received a plot corresponding to the modern city of Montemorelos. De León distinguished himself in military expeditions against northern Indian tribes, and we may surmise that his hacienda, San Mateo de Pilón, was populated with his war captives.[72] Saltillo provided not only many of the men and goods needed for the new communities, but also the model of settlement. Like Saltillo and San Esteban, de León's new headquarters of Cadereyta was a Spanish town paired with a Tlaxcalan one. Yet the terms under which Tlaxcalans first settled in the Valley of Pilón are not entirely clear. Whether or not they were yet permanent residents of the valley, Tlaxcalan soldiers frequently cooperated with de León's military operations in the area. Certainly the bulk of the population of the valley was made up of its pre-Colonial inhabitants. On paper, de León held an *encomienda* over the Indians in the area. In practice, though, enforcing his privileges as *encomendero* was no easy matter.

Though neither the enslavement of Indians nor the grant of new *encomiendas* was legal, Alonso de León and many of his contemporaries were adept at exploiting the penal system to retain a supply of forced labor. De León carried out military expeditions, ostensibly to suppress rebellion and punish Indians for banditry, both inside and outside the sphere of existing Spanish settlements. He brought the captives before Governor Martín de Zavala, who summarily convicted them of the charges and assessed monetary fines, which were to be remitted in the form of labor. A portion of these captives was sold, and the proceeds surrendered to the crown to satisfy the *quinto real* (the royal tax). The records from Zavala's governorship show that adult captives were typically sentenced to ten years of labor; children remained the wards of the contract-holder until the age of twenty-five.[73] Given the number of captives deeded to Alonso de León and the scarcity of labor in Nuevo León, there can be little doubt that his lands were often worked by Chichimecs who were slaves in all but name.

In the Valley of Pilón, Alonso de León established the Hacienda San Mateo around 1637 on one of the many plots deeded to him in that year, and the colonial community of Pilón grew up around it.[74] De León maintained several residences, at first living principally in Cadereyta and running the Hacienda San Mateo through his *mayordomo*. De León, along with other land-grant beneficiaries and their collective dependents, comprised the small, initial Spanish population of the Valley of Pilón – a population of Spanish elites whose haciendas relied on Indian labor. What little official governance there was in the valley came from the *alcalde mayor* at Cadereyta whose jurisdiction extended to a

---

[72] Ciro R. Cantú, *Origen de la ciudad de Montemorelos: Síntesis de una investigación histórica* (Nuevo León: Universidad Autonoma de Nuevo León, 2002), 137–40; Martínez Perales, 10–11.

[73] Silvio Zavala, *Entradas, congregas y encomiendas, en el Nuevo Reino de León*, 13–17.

[74] Martínez Perales, 17–19.

number of communities in the region. Pilón was originally possessed by a small, closed group of Spanish landholders; but over time it evolved into a community of both small and large estates. The early landlords of Pilón did not secure entailed land titles, and in the generations that followed, the five great estates were divided both through inheritance and through land sales. By the end of the century, the Valley of Pilón was a patchwork of properties of varying sizes.[75]

Beginning in 1651, de León and the other *encomenderos* were faced with widespread flight and frequent attacks from the Indian nations they claimed to rule. A charismatic Indian war leader called "Cabrito" rallied a number of Indian *rancherías* into a unified war band, luring Indians away from the haciendas, and seizing Spanish wealth (primarily cattle) wherever they found it. In 1653 Cabrito's followers attacked and sacked much of San Mateo, in the process killing its *mayordomo*, Miguel Angel. In 1658 de León took up residence at his Pilón estate, but even then his control of the valley was far from absolute.[76] In the seventeenth century, the Valley of Pilón lacked a permanent parish or mission, and there was no resident cleric with responsibility for the daily welfare and instruction of the Indians.[77] Alonso de León was legally obliged to provide his Indian workers spiritual instruction, and by 1658 he had constructed a chapel on the lands of San Mateo de Pilón. It soon operated as a *visita* for Cadereyta, which is to say that a priest from Cadereyta was charged with making regular visits to Pilón to administer the sacraments to the Indians and the Spanish of the valley.

Alonso de León died in 1661, dividing his lands equally among his offspring. Thus began the fragmentation of his once vast land grant.[78] In the generations that followed, the Valley of Pilón was transformed from a unitary estate to a political community dominated by the holders of the smaller successor estates. From the late seventeenth to the early nineteenth century, this group of landed elites, generally numbering between ten and twenty, and describing themselves as the *vecinos del valle de Pilón*, constituted the enfranchised Spanish citizenry of the valley. As a group, and as individuals, these *vecinos* sought to defend their inherited and purchased land and water rights, and to exact labor from the area's Indian population.

[75] Ciro R. Cantú provides a detailed explanation of the division of the great estates, *Origen de la ciudad de Montemorelos*, 137–44.

[76] Juan Bautista Chapa, "Historia de Nuevo León de 1650 a 1690," in *Historia de Nuevo León*, 126–30.

[77] In contemporary usuage, *misión* could mean either the act or the site of religious instruction. Institutionally, the places of missionary activity were described as *conversiones* when inhabited by new converts and as *doctrinas* when they held Indians being instructed in Christianity by friars (these terms were not mutually exclusive). A *parrochia* (parish) was the basic geographical unit for populations under the administration of bishops. A parish was considered a secular jurisdictioin rather than a regular one (meaning that it was theoretically under an ordinary *cura*, not under a missionary friar). In many cases, however, doctrinas were "secularized" only in the sense that their friars were placed under the administration of bishops.

[78] This process of fragmentation has been investigated in Cantú, *Origen de la ciudad de Montemorelos*, 134–44.

In the final decades of the seventeenth century Captain Cipriano García de Pruneda, a Spaniard and newcomer to the Valley, sought and attained a political status and economic position much like that of Alonso de León. From 1680 to 1687, he held the position of *alcalde mayor* of Cadereyta, which still included the Valley of Pilón in its jurisdiction. Like de León, his personal estate was in the Valley of Pilón, and his military activities allowed him to either attract or compel Indian bands to labor on his lands. In 1699, García de Pruneda received official, legal recognition of his status as an *encomendero*. Both the petition and the grant that followed explain a great deal about the legal relationship between the region's Spanish landowners and Indian workers. The Indians in question were two groups called Alopuycapanes (meaning "arrow shafts") and Quitamoquapanamas (pork-eaters). In his petition, García de Pruneda claimed that their former *encomendero*, Baltasar de Treviño, died without issue, leaving the *encomienda* vacant. García de Pruneda pointed out that, since most of his Indian workers had been killed in a recent epidemic, and since the two groups were in need of Christian instruction, it would benefit all parties for him to take over the grant. Before the petition could be approved, the governor of Nuevo León had to determine whether the estate met several key legal requirements: first, that the Indians on his lands were the same ones treated by Treviño's grant; second, that the Indians submitted to the *encomienda* of their own free will; and finally, that they were not already being served by a *doctrina*. To this end, the governor visited García de Pruneda's hacienda (Nuestra Señora de la Soledad) and interviewed the Indians using two interpreters. Capitán Cristóbal de Villarreal translated between Castilian and Nahuatl, and an Indian named Bartolo translated between Nahuatl and the languages spoken by the two Chichimec groups. The following year, García de Pruneda received the royal grant of *encomienda*. The 1699 document asserts that "the formation of the *congrega* on that hacienda is by their [the Indians'] will" and is carried out in order that they "may be reduced to political life and that they may be industrious in the matters of Our Holy Catholic Faith and that their souls may be saved." To these ends, it orders that "Captain Don Cipriano García de Pruneda be sent the title of *protector* of said Indians."[79]

These documents shed some light on the terms used to describe Spanish-Indian relations in the late seventeenth century. The term *hacienda* describes Pruneda's land, *congregación* a community of Indians living and working on that land, and *encomienda* the right to demand an amount of annual labor from a specific group of Indians who might reside on or off of Pruneda's land. The crown instructed Pruneda to notify the *padre ministro* of the "new doctrina" on his lands. Presumably, like Alonso de León, Pruneda received regular visits from

---

[79] 1698 Solicitud de *Congregación de Indios*, AMM Civil, vol. 26, leg. 3, exp. 2; 1699 Visita a *Congregación de Indios*, AMM Civil, vol. 26, leg. 3, exp. 2; 1699 Título de *congregación de indios*, AMM Civil, vol. 26, leg. 3, exp. 2. All three are transcribed in Eugenio del Hoyo, *Esclavitud y encomienda de los Indios en el Nuevo Reino de León (siglos xvi y xvii)* (Monterrey, Mexico, 1985).

the parish priest of Cadereyta, who ministered to the Indians on his lands. In the 1699 document, Pruneda was awarded the title of *"protector"* over the two bands of Indians. Here the term is used as an equivalent for *encomendero* – a Spaniard who collects labor tribute and in return provides religious instruction and protection from other groups. In the following century, the protectorate remained central to Spanish and Indian understandings of the legal relationship between the two groups, though the role of the *protector* would evolve and change.

In 1709, Juan García de Pruneda, a landowner in the Valley of Pilón, found himself in a fortunate position. His father, Luis García de Pruneda (governor of the New Kingdom of León), and his mother Juana de León (descendant of Alonso de León) along with his uncle, Cipriano García de Pruneda, opened a path for his ambitions. When Juan García de Pruneda petitioned for the recognition of his privileges in the Valley of Pilón, he used much the same language and logic that was routinely employed in the previous century. Though the term *encomienda* was by then under a cloud of suspicion, Juan García invoked all other forms of authority commonly recognized in the valley.[80] He called himself a *vecino* and cattle rancher of the Valley of Pilón, a descendant of *conquistadores* (including Alonso de León), and a faithful vassal of the king. He noted that his family had always ruled over the descendants of two Chichimec leaders and their followers: Aseama, captain of the Piehuanes and Zuñigas, and Ariscapanes, captain of the Borrados and Pelones. García made his claim to the protectorate based on a family *encomienda*, but he did so without requesting the now legally suspect title *encomendero*. Juan García asked to be confirmed as *protector y amparador* of these populations and promised, in return, to pay the Indians for their labor and to ensure their religious instruction through the *doctrina* of Cadereyta.

At the beginning of the eighteenth century, we begin to discern the emergence of a set of Spanish institutions binding together the Pilón landowners as a political community. In 1700, Pilón was a valley under the political jurisdiction of Cadereyta and received its sacraments from Cadereyta's parish priests. In 1702, on the lands of the Hacienda of Nuestra Señora de Soledad, a dozen *vecinos* of the valley met to form a compact for local governance and to request the recognition of the community as a *villa* and parish.[81] The *vecinos* argued that the ultimate purpose of the community was the reduction and Christianization of the area's dangerous Chichimecs. Much like Nuevo León's Tlaxcalan communities, this Spanish town justified its political claims based on

---

[80] First in the *Leyes Nuevas* of 1542 and subsequently in the *Recopilación de leyes de los reinos de las Indias* of 1681, the crown condemned the abuses of early encomenderos. These bodies of law limited intergenerational transmission of encomienda, forbid new grants of encomienda, and forbid direct servitude, or *servicio personal*. See *De las Leyes de Indias: Antología de la recopilación de 1681*, títutlos 8–12.

[81] Achivo General de la Nación de México (hereafter AGN) Reales Cédulas, vol. 38, exp. 105, fols. 134–7.

its military and missionary service to the crown. The compact between *vecinos* defined the valley's first legally constituted public spaces, recognizing the existence of a town commons and providing land for the construction of the parish church.

The early history of the Valley of Pilón illustrates one path by which Neoleonés towns were populated. Politically favored Spanish settlers received large land grants and explicit, or virtual, rights of *encomienda* over neighboring Indian populations. It was on these estates that many Chichimecs first entered the colonial sphere. One of Nuevo León's basic political units was the *valle*. Cultivated valleys so designated comprised the nameable Spanish populations grouped together as *alcaldías maiores*. Initially, these were not so much towns as they were political communities coordinating the interests of Spanish estates. In the early eighteenth century, however, Tlaxcalans and Franciscans would establish two *pueblos de indios* in the Valley of Pilón, initiating a long period of political coexistence between Spanish and Indian governments much like that which prevailed between Linares and San Cristóbal.

CONFLICT AND COOPERATION BETWEEN SPANIARDS, TLAXCALANS, AND CHICHIMECS

In the seventeenth century, San Antonio de los Llanos (today's Hidalgo, Tamaulipas) was the easternmost beachhead of Tlaxcalan settlement and the final outpost between colonial society and the long-impenetrable region separating Nuevo León from the Gulf Coast. The area surrounding Río Blanco and the upper Río Purificación, and encompassing the mines of Matehuala and the plains of San Antonio, was rich in the resources most dear to settlers: water, arable lands, and mineral deposits.[82] Despite these advantages, colonization of the area was dogged by one persistent problem: almost continuous attacks from the Indians of the Sierra Tamaulipas. The region's mountainous terrain offered only three reasonable routes for commerce and communication with the world

---

[82] Though today's city of Hidalgo belongs to the modern state of Tamaulipas, its colonial predecessor, San Antonio de los Llanos, was under the jurisdiction of the New Kingdom of León. The inconsistent use of geographical names makes local descriptions of this area difficult. Early maps represent Río Blanco and San Antonio as lying between two tributaries of the same river, sometimes labeled San Antonio and Purificación, which flowed in turn into the Conchas. A 1739 document indicates that the Río Blanco and San Antonio missions were 18 leagues apart, though most visual representations make them appear closer. Don Antonio Ladrón de Guevara, *Noticias de los poblados del Nuevo Reino de León (1738)* (Monterrey, Mexico: ITESM, 1969), 20; Joseph Antonio Fernández de Jáuregui Urrutia, "Copia final del mapa enviado por Hauregui en el año 1736," in Pedro Gómez Danés, *Las misiones de Purificación y Concepción*; "Plano corografico de los dos Reynos de Nueva Extremadura ó Coahuila y el nuevo de León ... 1729," Bancroft 18(n) 1729b; Gerhard notes further confusion caused by the interchangeable use of San Fernando and Conchas to refer to the same river, *The North Frontier*, 358. Frequent changes in geographical names have made made tracing its history difficult. For the sake of convenience, I will use "San Antonio de los Llanos" to describe this area of interrelated missions, mines, and haciendas.

outside the New Kingdom of León: one route led to through Monterrey to
Saltillo, another southwest to San Luis Potosí, and a third down the watershed
to the Río Pánuco and the Gulf Coast. Until the late eighteenth century, only
the first of these was a reliable path, since the second was rough and largely
without water, and the third passed through the lands of hostile Indians. For all
of these reasons, the area's colonial population fluctuated, and individual settlements came and went.

In the early seventeenth century, the southern parts of the New Kingdom of
León were not truly colonized. Opportunists from the mining economies of San
Luis Potosí and Charcas found in the region a source of Indian labor and of
pasturage for the ever-expanding sheep flocks and cattle herds. They entered the
area seasonally with their livestock, or intermittently on slaving expeditions, but
left little in the way of permanent settlements. The first settlements in the area of
San Antonio de los Llanos were established by soldier and mine operator
Fernando Sánchez de Zamora and two missionaries, Juan Caballero and Juan
García. Sánchez de Zamora was, at times, the *alcalde mayor* of San Luis Potosí,
and always a soldier and mineral prospector. His military expeditions
included Tlaxcalan allies, and his mines and haciendas employed northern
Indians attracted or forced into service. His expeditions established a pattern
of joint Spanish-Tlaxcalan settlements and Chichimec labor recruitment in the
south of the New Kingdom of León modeled on the practices of San Luis
Potosí and Tlaxcalilla. For twenty-two years, Sánchez de Zamora operated a
mine and hacienda in Río Blanco. Unlike most of his contemporaries, he left
behind a narrative account of his activities.

The New Kingdom's governor, Martín de Zavala, granted Sánchez military
authority in the area and instructed him to defend the missionaries and facilitate
their efforts. Beginning in 1648, Franciscans established a number of *doctrinas*
in the Río Blanco area and attempted to instruct the local Indians in agriculture,
but their efforts were generally unsuccessful.[83] Chichimecs wandered in and out
of the communities, rarely accepting settlement on the terms desired by the
missionaries. According to Sánchez's own account, Caballero and García
begged him to mount an expedition to return errant Indians to the mission
system. Perhaps discerning some shared interests, Sánchez helped the missionaries establish the mission of Santa María de los Angeles de Río Blanco beside the
estates that included his mine, foundry, and home.[84] In 1660, Sánchez supported
Fr. Salvador Barranga's efforts to establish Mission San Antonio de los Llanos
on the nearby plains. Barranga and Sánchez sought out wandering bands of
Janambres and Rayados. Though the Rayados were still "bárbaros" unschooled
in colonial culture, the Spanish found other Indians accustomed to the
colonial system and able to serve as cultural intermediaries. The most important
of these were several Indians who had worked under the *encomienda* of one
Jacinto García and were "*indios ladinos* in the Mexican language and already

[83] San Joseph (also called San Cristóbal) was located on the current site of Aramberri, Nuevo León.
[84] Current site of General Zaragosa.

baptized." With their help, Barranga and Sánchez gathered a population of Janambres and Borrados, constructed a primitive chapel, distributed tools and supplies, and set the agricultural economy in motion. Under the leadership of Fr. Antonio Belasco, Indians streamed in at an impressive rate: "in the year and a half that he was there he advanced the *conversión* so much, that it already appeared an old pueblo; putting each family in its barrio, and in the same manner the *milpas*, making them build *"jacales de adobe."* Thus San Antonio developed into a *pueblo de indios* with the residential pattern that would be typical in the Nuevo Reino de León. Both the adobe homes at the core of the settlement and the *milpas* surrounding them were clustered in groups determined by kinship and by the order of settlement.[85]

San Antonio came into existence just as the cattle boom in the New Kingdom León began. While the mission swelled in size, so too did the surrounding colonial population of Spanish and *ladino* cattle herders arriving from zones of earlier settlement. In its first decade, San Antonio flourished, but in 1673 it fell victim to its own rapid growth. Preexisting enmities between the pueblo's constituent nations, as well as conflicts over land use, labor, and expanding sheep ranches, led to rebellion, war, and flight.[86]

The story of the 1673 rebellion comes to us from two contemporary sources: the chronicle of Juan Bautista Chapa and that of Fernando Sánchez de Zamora. Bautista Chapa's shorter account attributes the uprising largely to the personal leadership of the Indian rebel, Cuatliteguache. We are told that Cuatliteguache was a *ladino* raised in a Spanish home. He settled in the pueblo of San Antonio and soon inspired a conspiracy against the neighboring haciendas. He and his men struck by surprise, killing the valley's *teniente* and thirty-eight local shepherds and terrorizing the mission. The colonial population of San Antonio evacuated to Río Blanco and Pilón; Cuatliteguache and his men withdrew to the hills. His followers, numbering more than 600, continued to menace the other settlements in the region.[87]

The Sánchez de Zamora account is far more detailed – often to the point of confusion – but it is also far more attentive to the complex relationships and grievances between different Indian groups in the area. In his narrative, the institutions and the local economy are designed by the Spanish, but the most important local conflicts are between Indian leaders. Sánchez describes a complex population whose alliances and conflicts revolved around a vast new sheep hacienda belonging to Martín Pérez Romo. The hacienda is best understood as a rival community beside the mission-town of San Antonio. Though some laborers moved between the two environments, these communities had separate hierarchies, and were peopled by separate and antagonistic Indian nations. Pérez Romo came to San Antonio with enormous herds of sheep, a group of Indian

[85] Fernando Sánchez Zamora, 231–4.

[86] Descriptions of the rapid growth of sheep and cattle ranching and consequent conflicts appear in AMM Protocolos, vol. 16, fol. 64, no. 27.

[87] Juan Bautista Chapa, *Historia de Nuevo León, 1650–1690*, chap. XXIV.

allies under the *cacique* Mariman, and an Indian *mayordomo* from Querétaro, the "cacique Juan Díaz." Mariman's people were inveterate enemies of the Janambres who were now settled at the San Antonio mission. Janambres from the mission worked on Pérez Romo's lands. Mistreated by the *ladino mayordomo*, the Janambres soon conspired against him. The leader of this conspiracy was the mission's *fiscal*, an Indian *cacique* who goes unnamed in the text, but who may be identified by his actions as Cuatliteguache from Bautista Chapa's account. The *fiscal* rallied the Janambres and Guaripas to attack the surrounding missions, killing a great number of shepherds and wranglers. The Indian soldiers under Mariman arrived at the scene to find thirty-seven dead. Mariman's men then vented their wrath upon the mission, killing some Janambres, putting the rest to flight, and burning down the settlement. When the dust settled, the mission was destroyed, all of the local Indian groups had fled, and sheep and cattle from the local haciendas were loose in the hills. A few miles away, the author experienced the uprising firsthand when rebel Indians besieged his home. The regional crisis was so acute that the governor ordered the abandonment of San Antonio and Río Blanco, and the former residents sought refuge in what became an emergency garrison at Matehuala. According to Bautista Chapa, it was only through the skillful negotiation of Padre Caballero, accompanied by twelve armed men, that the rebels' *ladino* commander was dissuaded from killing all the residents of Río Blanco.[88]

Some have claimed that San Antonio was abandoned from the time of the 1673 uprising until its reestablishment by Francisco Barbadillo in 1715.[89] Yet there is much evidence to the contrary. Land grants and administrative correspondence from the period indicate the ongoing presence of Spanish landholders. In the first decade of the eighteenth century, Tlaxcalans of San Antonio de los Llanos attested to their continuous occupation of the land, and several early documents add credibility to this claim. The bulk of the evidence suggests that the rebellion of 1673, though larger than most, conformed to the usual pattern of mission-town disruptions. A set of specific grievances in the community led to an attack on the haciendas followed by Indian flight. The disruption of the local hacienda economy had lingering effects, but the Spaniards returned to the area shortly after the violence subsided. Many mission Chichimecs, both combatants and bystanders, eventually returned; and it appears that the Tlaxcalans never left. The Monterrey government, perhaps convinced that Río Blanco and San Antonio were more trouble than they were worth, sought to limit Spanish activities that might trigger a renewal of hostilities.

---

[88] Sánchez Zamora, 234–41. On the scale and impact of European cattle and sheep in New Spain, see Elinor G. K. Melville, *A Plague of Sheep: Environmental Consequences of the Conquest of Mexico* (Cambridge, UK: Cambridge University, 1997).

[89] The notion that the site was abandoned is put forward in Cavazos Garza, *Breve historia de Nuevo León*, 33.

The regulations issued by Governor Pedro Fernández de la Ventoza reveal his understanding of the sources of conflict: large-scale sheep ranching invited Indian poaching; and unregulated conscription of Indian labor undermined the missions, provoked rebellions, and created conflicts over preexisting claims of *encomienda*. His 1688 regulations ordered

> that the *mayordomos* of the haciendas of ewes and sheep that enter the New Kingdom of León neither pasture their cattle nor establish their ranches, except from the river San Cristóbal to the Valley of Pilón, not passing under any pretext to the other bank of the river or into the area of the Sierra Tamaulipas ... the *mayordomos* may not lodge in said haciendas any Indian from the pueblos and missions of this Kingdom nor any which might belong to an *encomienda*; nor shall they seize any young Indians or *naturales* of this kingdom ... I order this because of the risk from the rebel Indians of the Sierra Tamaulipas and llanos de San Antonio that have killed many soldiers and obliged many military campaigns.[90]

The 1673 rebellion demonstrated the limits of colonial authority in the south of the New Kingdom of León and limited Spanish economic activity. It did not, however, lead to a general abandonment of the area. A set of 1683 correspondence shows that Francisco Salvador Jiménez received a land and water grant that bordered San Antonio de los Llanos, indicating ongoing Spanish agricultural development during the same period of more modest settlement.[91] In the 1690s, Fernando Sánchez de Zamora still appears in public records as the *alcalde mayor* of Río Blanco and los Llanos de San Antonio. Not only did the Spanish colonial presence persist through the late seventeenth century, but there was also some continuity in leadership though the entire period.[92] Tlaxcalan elites retained their foothold throughout the period. In 1686 Antonio Jiménez sought and received formal confirmation of his title to lands on the river Purificación. The documents identify him as a Tlaxcalan *principal* and the son of a *vecino* San Antonio de los Llanos.[93]

In 1706, several parties sought to strengthen their claims to land and water rights in the area of San Antonio de los Llanos and the Río Blanco mining district. The area's Tlaxcalan and Negrito populations brought a suit against neighboring Spaniards in order to defend the holdings of their *pueblo de indios*. The old hacienda of Matehuala, linked to the nearby mines, was expanding its agricultural production with lands and waters claimed by the *pueblos de indios*. The legal complaint was signed by twenty-two Tlaxcalan and eighty Negrito *vecinos*. The leaders of this body are identified in the document as Negrito *caciques* and as descendants of Gran Tlaxcala. Most of the arguments in this case relied on a simple set of principles for determining property rights:

---

[90] AMM Protocolos, vol. 16, exp. 64, no. 27.
[91] AMM Civil, vol. 32, exp. 137.
[92] AMM Civil, vol 23ª, exp. 3b, fol. 27.
[93] 2 Sept. 1686, AMM Civil, vol. 15, exp. 4.

prior discovery and continuous occupation. No one contested the claim by the Tlaxcalans that they were descended from original frontier settlers and in continuous occupation of the site. Similarly, the early history of Negrito participation in the pueblos' foundations went unchallenged. The case hinged on the question of continuous occupation. The Negritos had apparently fled the settlements in times of crisis, and may have only occupied the lands seasonally even in times of peace. The Spaniards of Matehuala believed that the Negritos had thus forfeited their title to the land.

The questions of precedence and jurisdiction were complex. Miners and missionaries had sometimes established conflicting claims independent of each other. All matters were complicated by the fact that, though the area fell within the official boundaries of the New Kingdom of León, its communities had been established by Tlaxcalan and Spanish explorers coming sometimes from Monterrey, the capital of Nuevo León, and at other times from Charcas and Venado, which were under the jurisdiction of Nueva Galicia. The most important disputes treated the boundaries and usufructory rights of San Antonio de los Llanos versus those of Matehuala.[94]

Both the mission-town and the mining town had their origins in the expeditions of Martín de Zavala in the 1620s and Don Juan de Zúñiga Almaraz in the 1630s. The narrative of Zúñiga's expedition shows that, from the outset, San Antonio de los Llanos was rooted in a typical pattern of partnership between Spaniards and their Chichimec and Tlaxcalan allies. His account of the 1638 journey notes the important role of a Chichimec interpreter and military officer "Captain Juan Domínguez, a Chichimec of the Negrita nation who understands well said languages [those of the area] and is *muy ladino* in the Mexican language." A mestizo translator, Juan de la Cruz, who was "*ladino* in the Mexican language and Castilian," could complete the chain of translation between the local peoples and the Spanish commander. Later land disputes demonstrate that this original mixture of populations persisted in the area. Spaniards, Tlaxcalans, and Negritos would continue to claim privileges as founders for the century that followed.[95]

The Tlaxcalans and Negritos vindicated their legal claims by describing the history of their community. This material reveals a good deal about the relationship between the two groups. The Tlaxcalans often called their pueblo the "the frontier of San Antonio" and spoke of their "frontier privileges." This language carried legal weight, since frontier communities of the north, whether Spanish or Indian, were entitled to exemptions from certain types of taxation and accorded a high measure of military autonomy. Their account of the creation of the pueblo mentions that Tlaxcalans directed all the necessary construction projects and held policing powers in the community. The Tlaxcalans were, in these respects, the senior partners in this civic union. Still, though the

---

[94] AGN Tierras, vol. 3044, exp. 4, fols. 1–15.
[95] AGN Tierras, vol. 3044, exp. 4.

Negritos may have been the clients of the Tlaxcalans, they were in no sense their slaves or serfs. Both parties recognized – and, in fact, jealously defended – the Negritos' property rights, and both parties gave full recognition to their internal governance under the group of leaders alternately referred to as *capitanes* and *caciques*.

Material contained in a 1712 episcopal visit indicates that the Río Blanco area now comprised three political communities: the Spanish town of San José and the Indian pueblos of San Antonio de los Llanos and Santa María de Río Blanco. The three communities were all served by the same missionary. We may surmise (though it goes unremarked in the *visita*) that the three communities continued to be linked economically to each other and to the Matehuala mines. However, it appears that from the 1640s to 1715, the demographic and legal structure of the area was such that Tlaxcalan, Chichimec, and Spanish populations, each with defined land rights, constituted internally governed subpopulations joined together by economic exchange and military cooperation.[96]

The early north frontier of New Spain was a region shaped by the political imagination of Spaniards and Tlaxcalans and by the political reality of many ethnic groups inhabiting a rugged landscape in a time of violence. Spanish soldier-settlers cast themselves in the mold of Roman frontier statesmen; missionaries imagined themselves to be living in a new apostolic age; and Tlaxcalan colonists went forth to plant Nahua towns for their new European lords. These visions were constantly checked by the instability of military and political relationships in the north. Northern Indians moved in and out of the emergent colonial sphere, and Spanish settlers repeatedly disrupted fragile interethnic pacts through their appetite for silver and Indian labor. One constant in the development of the region was the operation of Tlaxcalan mission-towns. Tlaxcalans maintained long-term relationships with the missionary orders and the viceroyalty, and maintained a consistent strategy of pueblo-based settlement. While the Spanish regime fluctuated in its use of slave labor, *encomienda*, and wage labor, and experimented with a variety

---

[96] The bishop of Guadalajara, who did not personally inspect the Río Blanco area, relied on the report of Monterey leader, Capt. Juan Esteban Ballesteros. Ballesteros' categorization of populations is a bit confusing. He describes San José as "Spanish," Santa María as entirely populated by "gentiles," and San Antonio as having no more than five Indians. It is not clear whether the Tlaxcalans are absent from his count of the Indian population because Ballesteros considered them non-Indians, or if Tlaxcalans had disappeared from the community. The former seems more likely, since Tlaxcalans reappear in the records two years later. Likewise, one cannot tell whether the "gentiles" that make up the population of Santa María are the Negrito population, or a new group that has replaced them. 1712 Episcopal visit "Autos de visita" in Eugenio del Hoyo, *Indios, frailes y encomenderos en el Nuevo Reino de Leon* (Monterrey, Mexico: Archivos del Estado, 1985) [original in Benson, W.B. Stephens collection, no. 1411]. Note that the term *gentiles* among missionaries is used to descibe non-Christians in contrast to Christians, rather than to describe Christians in contrast to Jews.

of political and military configurations, the Tlaxcalan system operated largely by design. Tlaxcalans established their place within the empire by writing themselves into the narrative of conquest and conversion, consolidating their legal position as vassals and nobles, and rendering themselves indispensible to the extension of colonial authority in the north. In geographical, diplomatic, and legal terms, they made themselves vital intermediaries between northern Indians and the crown.

Multiethnic Indian Republics

FIGURE 3. The foundational myths of the Nahuas include stories of origins, migration, and colonization connecting the peoples of Mesoamerica and the Chichimec North. This painting from the sixteenth-century Historia Tolteca-Chichimeca describes the birth of seven nations from the cave-wombs of Chicomoztoc. (Bibliothèque Nationale de France, Mexicain 46–58, Manuscrits orientaux, Historia Tolteca-Chichimeca/Annales de Cuauhtinchan, p. 29)

PETITIONERS WITH PAINTED FACES

In 1725 an Indian from New Spain's distant northern frontier traveled to Mexico City in order to bring legal accusations against the governor of Nuevo León. The Indian's name was Joseph Antonio, and the court scribe described him as being "from the Chichimec nation, with stripes on his face." He was "a *vecino* and *natural* of the pueblo of Nuestra Señora de Guadalupe" and he had journeyed to the capital with three other members of his nation to bring accusations of war crimes and slave trafficking against Governor Juan de Arriaga y Brambila and several of Nuevo León's leading landowners and military commanders.[1] These four Chichimecs were only a few of the many interested parties in the case. They, along with Guadalupe's special legate Francisco Díaz Serrano, accused some of the region's most powerful Spaniards of gross transgression of the laws that governed warfare, captivity, and labor.[2]

The story told by the four Chichimec witnesses was as follows. In 1714, Spanish soldiers from Monterrey attacked and captured a group of Indians, then took them to the Hacienda García where they forced them to labor as slaves. The community of slaves, recognizing that their captivity was illegal, sent these four men to seek help from the Tlaxcalan-Chichimec pueblo of Guadalupe. Their plan was to negotiate an agreement by which the entire group of captives might resettle in Guadalupe. However, the plan was interrupted when armed Spaniards arrived in pursuit of the messengers. Fearing for their lives, the four men sought sanctuary in the mission church. When its friar refused to surrender them to the Spanish soldiers, a standoff ensued. A rumor soon spread among the Indians of Guadalupe that the soldiers intended to hang both the fugitives and the missionary. This provoked an Indian uprising against Nuevo León's Spanish authorities, and a harsh counterattack against the Indians by Spanish landowners. According to the Indian witnesses, the Spanish reprisals that followed were so severe that the town was nearly destroyed.[3]

The four Indians who appeared before the *audiencia* were knowledgeable about the law and assertive in pressing their case. If the *oidores* of the *audiencia* were surprised by the appearance of Indian plaintiffs with tattooed faces, their shock does not show in the records. Despite the Chichimecs' exotic appearance, they were quite familiar with Spanish culture and governance. They were

---

[1] 12 Mar. 1725 Testimony of Indio Joseph Antonio, Audiencia de Guadalajara 173, fol. 7.

[2] 28 July 1725 Memorial de parte de los indios presos, AGI Audiencia de Guadalajara 173. This case took years to resolve because it involved so many parties and such complex determinations of fact. Governor Arriaga was removed from office for his crimes, leaving a variety of unresolved civil claims. Barbadillo, while still in office as governor of Nuevo León, dispensed with the separate post of provincial *protector de indios*, taking on the functions of the office himself. When Arriaga entered office, he did the same thing. The man who lost his post as protector, Nicolás Villalobos, sought reinstatement and compensation. He sought to prove to the *audiencia* that the absence of a protector was partly to blame for the transgressions of the Arriaga administration.

[3] 7 Aug. 1725 Memorial por indios de Nuestra Señora de Guadalupe, AGI 173, fols. 5–6; Don Juan de Arellano, 10 May 1724, AGI Audiencia de Guadalajara 173, fol. 6.

Christians, Spanish speakers, and citizens of the realm; and as such, they were treated seriously by the magistrates. The court scribe remarked with interest that Joseph Antonio, "despite the fact that he speaks the Castilian language perfectly clearly," demanded a translator as matter of legal privilege. Antonio entered the *audiencia* well informed about court procedures and about his own prerogatives.[4]

The Indian witnesses were detained as prisoners pending the resolution of the case, but they were far from defenseless. Joseph Antonio was aided by Guadalupe's attorney, Francisco Díaz Serrano, who held power of attorney for "the community and *naturales* of the New Settlements of the New Kingdom of León." Díaz Serrano began by demanding the release of the prisoners, but this was only the beginning his demands. He and his clients argued that the court should first free them, and then issue official letters vindicating their reputations. The Indians insisted, not only that they were innocent of any wrongdoing, but also that four highly ranked Spaniards were guilty of slave trafficking, and that these four men should be jailed in their stead.[5] They asserted that if the court did not meet their demands, they would appeal directly to the Council of the Indies in Spain.[6]

This courtroom scene was only a small chapter in a much larger struggle between two factions and two political systems in Nuevo León. The surrounding litigation would eventually involve the dismissal of Governor Arriaga, his demands for reinstatement, and a fight over the status of Nuevo León's one-time *protector de indios* Nicolás de Villalobos. In this legal saga, there were no clear personal victors. Governor Arriaga, who had already been deposed from the governorship, was not reinstated, and Nicolás de Villalobos, his supposed *protector de indios*, was not restored to office either. In fact, the *audiencia* took no action on the disputes over the governorship and protectorate. It noted that questions of political appointment were not within the purview of the *audiencia*. Nor did the Indian plaintiffs win a conviction against the alleged slave traders. The Indian witnesses were eventually permitted to return to their homes, though one of their number had already died before the order was given.[7]

In a long-term institutional sense, however, there *were* winners and losers in this struggle. The Audiencia's refusal to reinstate Arriaga confirmed in practice a set of policies and agreements that had been carefully orchestrated between Indian and Spanish communities in the previous decade. In Nuevo León, the period between 1710 and 1725 had witnessed a struggle between two competing models of settlement, labor, and exchange: one based on parallel Indian and Spanish town governments, and the other based on Spanish estates with

---

[4] 12 Mar. 1725 Testimony of Indian Joseph Antonio, AGI Audiencia de Guadalajara 173, fol. 7.

[5] Juan de Arriaga y Brambila, Juan García de Quintanilla, Mateo Leal, and Joseph Pheliz de Almandos.

[6] 28 July 1728 Memorial por parte de de los indios de Nuestra Señora de Guadalupe, AGI Audiencia de Guadalajara 173.

[7] 16 July 1726 Respuesta fiscal, AGI Audiencia de Guadalajara 173.

subordinate Indian laborers. The political phase of this struggle began in 1714 when Francisco Barbadillo was sent to Nuevo León as the viceroy's special envoy in order to suppress slave raiding and replace Spanish *congregas* with Tlaxcalan-led *pueblos de indios*. As royal visitor and acting governor, Barbadillo codified this system of Indian pueblos. Governor Báez Treviño and the Governor Arriaga, whose political networks centered on Nuevo León's landed estates, made every attempt to dismantle the Barbadillo system. Ultimately, however, local Franciscans, Tlaxcalans, and Chichimecs were able to protect the emergent system by enlisting the aid of viceregal authorities. Warfare did not come to an end, and slave raiding did not entirely disappear, but the mission-towns advocated by Barbadillo weathered the assaults of the Treviño and Arriaga administrations. Through a series of legal and political battles, the proponents of the mission-towns successfully defended the Barbadillo system.

THE STRUGGLE BETWEEN *PUEBLOS DE INDIOS* AND SPANISH *CONGREGAS*

In the seventeenth century, the New Kingdom of León became a semicolonized patchwork of Spanish and Indian communities. Tlaxcalans colonized the region by drawing northern Indians into the *pueblos de indios* system while the Spaniards colonized by exacting labor though the mechanism of *congregación*. Both systems had their roots in the history of central Mexico during the early years of Spanish colonization. The *pueblo de indios* was a self-governing Indian community with clearly delineated lands, whose residents sustained themselves through individual and collective agriculture. The area's Spanish estates, in contrast, were owned by Spaniards, but worked largely by Indians. They operated on the legal theory of *congregación*, a procedure by which Spanish landholders exacted tributary labor from Indian groups on a seasonal basis. By the mid seventeenth century, the New Kingdom of León became an accidental laboratory for competing systems of governance, land tenure, and labor. Within its borders, one could find all of the following social organizations: Spanish *alcaldías*, which governed collections of Spanish estates and their dependent laborers; *pueblos de indios*, led temporally by Indian *cabildos* and spiritually as Franciscan *doctrinas*; nomadic Indian bands, which were loosely allied to Spanish and Indian communities; and fully independent Indian bands that did not acknowledge Spanish sovereignty.[8]

During the sixteenth century, the Spaniards who conquered the Nahua heartland of central Mexico won grants of *encomienda* over specified groups of

---

[8] Readers more familiar with the history of central Mexico than of the north may be surprised by regional usage of the term *congrega*. In the center of Mexico, *congregación* aimed to produce denser permanent settlements. In the north, the term often described seasonal labor by Indians with no fixed year-round habitation. This evolved from the northern variant of *encomienda*, which exacted tributary labor from mobile populations.

Indians. These grants entitled the holder to tribute rendered in goods. Through this legal relationship, Indians became subjects of the crown and tributaries of the *encomendero*. Grants of *encomienda* were rarely tied to land grants. Thus, it was common for Indian communities with their own land rights and their own governments to be subject to tribute demands or labor drafts from the Spanish *encomenderos*. Early Spanish conquerors generally drew their wealth from their Indian tributaries, not from Spanish sites of production. The tributary Indians continued to live in their own communities, whose land titles and governments were recognized as *pueblos de indios* under the protection of royal law. Consequently, the power of central Mexican Indian pueblos was more clearly rooted in fixed land rights than was that of the Spaniards.[9] In the north of New Spain very different conditions prevailed. The precontact indigenous economy was fundamentally different from that of Nahua lands, and the institution of *encomienda* was adapted accordingly. When Spaniards first entered Nuevo León, they found no sedentary Indian towns to conquer. Early governors issued vast land grants to Spanish settlers creating a class of conquistadors that was land-rich, but labor-poor. Northern Indians were frequently on the move; thus grants of *encomienda* were based on tributary Indian nations or bands, rather than on towns or kingdoms. The early Spanish elites exacted their tribute in the form of labor, frequently extorting work from nonresident Indians during the seasons of planting and harvest.

Nuevo León's Tlaxcalan-Chichimec colonies were distinct from the Spanish estates and from the precontact economies of the north. These colonies were intended to re-create the type of territorial *pueblos de indios* that existed in central Mexico. When successful, the resulting towns had a sedentary Indian population with fixed land rights and an autonomous government. The residents were landholding farmers – no distinction existed between a laboring and landowning class. Thus, in the seventeenth century, Nuevo León evolved two separate agricultural regimes: a Spanish sphere in which land was trans-actable and labor alienable, and an Indian sphere of nontransactable lands under the *pueblos de indios*. Missionaries moved in both environments: they operated *doctrinas* in the *pueblos de indios*, but also administered the sacraments to Indians laboring on Spanish estates. The Tlaxcalan and Spanish agricultural systems were, in some respects, rival entities competing for the allegiance of the local Chichimec population. In other respects, the two systems were symbiotic, growing closer together through the colonial period. This chapter explores the early history of the Tlaxcalan-Chichimec colonies, their internal cultural inter-actions, and their relationship to Spanish society.

The final decades of the seventeenth century were a period of conflict and instability in Nuevo León. Although Alonso de León and his contemporaries had

---

[9] On the manifestations of *encomienda* throughout New Spain, see Silvio Zavala, *La encomienda indiana* (Mexico City: Editorial Porrúa, 1992); on the regional form of *encomienda* known as a *congrega*, see Andrés de Montemayor Hernández, *La Congrega: Nuevo Reino de León, siglos XVI-XVIII* (Monterrey, Mexico: Cuaderno del Archivo, 1990).

anticipated the rapid colonization of the northeastern frontier, their successors proved unequal to the task. The flight of Indian workers from haciendas and missions was common, and the rate of death by disease astronomical. In the 1690s several missions were largely depopulated, and others abandoned altogether. Spanish settlers' aspirations of a stable and prosperous north were soon frustrated. Nor were the goals of the Spanish crown quickly realized. The *encomiendas*, which were originally a short-term expedient, became a tradition difficult to suppress. A royal cédula of 1672 forbade *encomiendas* and mandated in their stead the creation of *congregas* or *pueblos-misiones* in the hope of both protecting the Indians from exploitation and averting their flight into the wilderness. The *encomenderos* of the past were now to become *capitanes-protectores*, men who directed the employment of Indians, but did not own their labor. By most accounts, however, the system of forced labor continued with little modification in the four decades following the royal proclamation. Both the Indian-led pueblos and the Spanish-run *congregas* fared badly in these years.[10]

The Tlaxcalan-Chichimec mission-towns were fundamentally different from the Indian communities linked to Spanish estates. They were structured around the system of *repúblicas de indios* that prevailed in the center of New Spain.[11] A Tlaxcalan pueblo possessed clearly defined land rights and a legally constituted *cabildo*, which governed most internal relations between *vecinos*. Chichimec pueblos, settled beside the Tlaxcalans ones, also received land titles. The government of these barrios assumed a variety of forms. Some barrios were ruled internally by traditional headmen (generally referred to by Spaniards and Tlaxcalans as *capitanes*), while other barrios were apportioned a fixed number of representatives in a joint Tlaxcalan-Chichimec *cabildo*; still others possessed separate *cabildos* making them effectively pueblos within pueblos. All of these

---

[10] Cavazos Garza, *Breve historia de Nuevo León*, 48–57; on the development of the office of *protector de indios*, see Cutter, *The Protector de Indios*, 5–20. On the evolution of coerced labor, see Silvio Zavala Udo Oberem, Jan Bazant, and Hermes Tovar, *Peones, conciertos, y arrendamientos en América Latina* (Bogotá: Universidad Nacional de Colombia, 1987) and José Cuello, "The Persistence of Indian Slavery and Encomienda in the Northeast of Colonial Mexico, 1577–1723," *Journal of Social History* 21, no. 4 (Summer 1988), 683–700. The statutory size of both Spanish and Indian towns was set at twenty leagues according to Losada, p. 134, and AGI Audiencia de Guadalajara 166, exp. 7, fols. 130–46. The 1672 order was transmitted to Nuevo León through the Audienca of Nueva Galicia; it forbade the enslavement of Indians, ordering that they be "congregated in pueblos distributing to them land and exempting them from tribute for ten years, "Instrucciones y ordenanzas que se han de practicar para el régime y conservación de los pueblos nuevamente fundados en este Reino de León," reproduced from W.B. Stephens Collection no. 1.410, U.T. Austin Library in Zavala, *Entradas, congregas, y encomiendas*, 112–13. The theory of the appointment of impartial protectors paid by the crown is described in a letter from Barbadillo to Viceroy Valero, 16 Sept. 1716, AGI Audiencia de Guadalajara 166, exp. 7, fols. 145–6.

[11] Note that in practice the Indians of Nuevo León were rarely year-round residents of the lands. Barbadillo acknowledged that departures for hunting and gathering, such as the collection of cactus fruits, was necessary for the survival of many of the new communities, and that these trips did not constitute an act of rebellion against the colonial state, Zavala, *Entradas, congregas, y encomiendas*, 117; AGI Audiencia de Guadalajara 166, fol. 110.

communities recognized new Chichimec converts as legitimate landholders and civic actors. Tlaxcalan towns, like the Chichimec *congregas*, had Spanish *protectors*, but *protectors* of a very different sort. The *protector* of a Tlaxcalan pueblo was typically the highest-ranking Spanish functionary in the area. He served as a point of contact between the Spanish and Indian realms when organizing joint military operations, negotiating contracts, or adjudicating legal disputes between Indians and non-Indians.

In the second decade of the eighteenth century, the legal relationship between the Spaniards and the Indians of Nuevo León was transformed by New Spain's viceregal authorities who, alarmed by incessant warfare and frequent allegations of slavery, intervened in regional affairs. In the preceding decade, the cycle of Indian flight and captivity threatened the survival of the northern colonies. Indian attacks carried off Spanish property, sapped military resources, and made the region more vulnerable to future attacks by nomadic nations beyond the current frontier. The theft of cattle and the disappearance of much of the Indian labor force placed the regional food supply in jeopardy. In 1714 the viceroy convened a *junta de guerra* to consider the crisis in Spanish-Indian relations. To confront what they understood to be a moral, economic, and military crisis, the viceroy and *junta* appointed Mexico City barrister Francisco Barbadillo as a visitor to the New Kingdom of León, granting him the authority to restructure systems of land tenure, labor, and defense.[12]

The proposed reforms were so sweeping that by 1715, the prominent Spaniards of Nuevo León were locked in a dispute against Barbadillo over the place of Chichimecs in northern colonial society: the former urged the perpetuation of *congregas*; the latter demanded the incorporation of Chichimecs into *pueblos de indios*. The Tlaxcalans were in the enviable position of being indispensable to the execution of either plan. The loose military system of the region had long relied upon them as mounted soldiers to defend against external attack, suppress rebellion, and recover escaped Indian laborers; for the time being, the Spanish *vecinos* could not survive without them. The *pueblos de indios* envisioned by Barbadillo, following the Saltillo-San Esteban model, relied on Tlaxcalans as soldiers, farmers, and tutors to their Chichimec neighbors. Spanish appeals for military and material aid referred repeatedly to the cooperation of Tlaxcalans in recent engagements. In his design for every one of the new

---

[12] The intentions of the Junta de Guerra are spelled out in AGI Audiencia de Guadalajara 166, fols. 85–96; Barbadillo's belief that warfare was perpetuated by slavery is explained in his 24 April 1716 to the Audiencia of Mexico, AGI Audiencia de Guadalajara 166, fols. 119–29. Elsewhere Barbadillo described the typical practices of slave taking as follows: first an interested party would purchase a license for the formation of a *congrega*, "then ten or twelve war comrades gathered to go into the lands where the Indians live in barbarism, and at the head *rancherías* ... with arms pointed at them if the Indians resisted or defended themselves; and already beaten they chain them and put them in collars ... in order that these Indians may then belong to the *congrega*," Barbadillo to the Audiencia of Mexico, 24 Apr. 1716, AGI Audiencia de Guadalajara 166. See also Cavazos Garza, *El lic. Francisco Barbadillo: fundador de Guadalupe, Nuevo León* (Monterrey, Mexico: Ayuntamiento de Ciudad Guadalupe, Nuevo León, 1980), 14–17.

Chichimec towns, Barbadillo planned the deployment of groups of Tlaxcalan families.[13]

CODIFYING THE MISSION-TOWNS

Francisco Barbadillo sought to codify the Tlaxcalan-Chichimec system of governance where it already existed and to impose it on those communities formerly organized as *congregas*. Barbadillo returned the existing missions of San Miguel and San Cristóbal to Franciscan administration, and he founded the new mission-towns of Purificación, Concepción, and Guadalupe. He invited Tlaxcalans to settle in all *pueblos-misiones* in order to bolster their populations and to provide an example of civilization to the newly settled and converted Chichimecs.[14]

To Barbadillo, the conversion and settlement of nomads, the proper administration of the *pueblos de indios*, and the imposition of new regulations for Spanish estates were all parts of a broad strategy for regional defense and economic development. His diagnosis of the woes of Nuevo León was straightforward. Spanish landowners' practice of using captive laborers fueled two types of military crises: Spanish aggression in the hunt for captives, and Indian rebellion and retribution. His solution was to end the current system of *congregación* in which estate owners captured and coerced Indian labor under the guise of Christianization. In its place, he proposed a uniform system of *pueblos de indios* like that of central New Spain. The Indians' relationship with local landowners was to be both voluntary and purely economic, with the landowners no longer empowered to govern the Indians or obliged to provide their religious education. As in the world described by the *Leyes de Indias*, Barbadillo imagined internally autonomous Indian and Spanish spheres. They were to be autonomous in some respects, but interdependent in others. Though the property of the two would not be mingled, both labor and goods would cross the boundary, and defense would be cooperative.

The Barbadillo code also defined important aspects of Indian citizenship in the pueblos. Tlaxcalans retained all the privileges and exemptions that were a part of their previous colonial charters. Chichimecs were granted some of these privileges and denied others. For the first time, all settled Indians in Nuevo León were to be formally enrolled as members of pueblos. Membership had several advantages: it placed the Indian *vecinos* under their own communities' *cabildos* and guaranteed them both land and water rights and the spiritual services of the mission. Most importantly, it protected them from capture and servitude. An enrolled member of a pueblo could not be considered a barbarian and subjected to capture and forced labor by Spanish landowners. An Indian might choose to

---

[13] On Tlaxcalans in the Barbadillo plan, 20 Feb. 1715 AGI Audiencia de Guadalajara 166, fols. 45, 90. On Tlaxcalan functions and their basis in the Saltillo model, AGI Audiencia de Guadalajara 166, fols. 85–96.

[14] Israel Cavazos Garza, *El lic. Francisco Barbadillo Vitoria*.

work on a hacienda, but he remained a legal resident of his own pueblo and retained its legal protections.[15]

This new form of Indian *vecindad* conferred both obligations and immunities. Northern Indians were required to obtain permission from their governor and missionary when they traveled off of pueblo lands, and to carry letters of passage with them. This was both a form of social control to suppress Chichimec flight and a mechanism by which to protect legitimate Indian travelers from capture. It was not, however, intended to bar the free mobility of Indians, a right that was acknowledged in the same period by Fray Juan de Losada, the head of the Franciscan missions to Nuevo León.[16] Barbadillo recognized that Chichimecs needed to leave the pueblos for a substantial part of each year for seasonal hunting and gathering, and he expected that these activities would continue to be an important source of village food supplies. The new policies would permit Chichimecs to forage in the wilderness and to take payments from Spanish ranchers for rounding up lost cattle. Barbadillo maintained that these activities were economically vital, and that the free mobility of Indians would reduce the likelihood of rebellion.

The regulations surrounding travel, along with the new system of pueblo enrollment, were part of a general attempt to more clearly differentiate enemy Indians from those within the colonial community. Progress toward this end would be a military advantage; it would also be a tremendous advantage in Barbadillo's efforts to suppress slave raiding, a practice which had in the past been so widespread that it frequently resulted in the illegal capture of Christianized Indians. The limited restrictions on Indian travel provoked little resistance, but other proposals drew stiff opposition. In 1717, colonial authorities proposed mandating special haircuts (*balcarrotas*) of different lengths to distinguish Tlaxcalans from Chichimecs and both types of Indians from Spaniards. After conferring with Tlaxcalan leaders, however, Barbadillo rejected the plan. He explained to his superiors that the Tlaxcalans took great pride in their appearance. Requiring the haircuts would so offend the Tlaxcalans that they would likely leave Nuevo León in protest and return to their homes in Saltillo and Venado.[17] Barbadillo knew that maintaining good relations with both the Tlaxcalans and Chichimecs was vital to northern security and economic development. He constantly reasserted the Tlaxcalans' traditional military role and also recommended that reliable Chichimec archers be put on the payroll as armed night watchmen in the pueblos and as soldiers on northern campaigns. He dismissed as anachronistic the old regulations against Indians riding horseback (a rule that had never applied to the Tlaxcalans) and sought to arm, rather than disarm, pueblo Indians. In this he saw eye-to-eye with Juan de Losada who expressed his concern that depriving Indian allies of their military privileges or

---

[15] Zavala, *Entradas*, 119–22.
[16] "Carta del lic. Francisco de Barbadillo Vitoria . . . 6 agosto," 1717, AGI Audiencia de Guadalajara 166, exp. 8, fol. 165.
[17] 6 Aug. 1717, AGI Audiencia de Guadalajara 166, exp. 8, fols. 141–54.

insulting them by mandating distinctive haircuts would turn them against the kingdom. Those Chichimec soldiers, like the Tlaxcalan ones, were vital to regional defense.[18] In the end, Tlaxcalans would retain their customs and privileges, and Chichimecs would begin to gain them.

The new mission-towns of Nuevo León were modeled on the Tlaxcalan-Chichimec pueblo of San Esteban de Saltillo. Newly settled Chichimec groups were to pass through a sort of apprenticeship to the Tlaxcalans before assuming their permanent economic and political role in the community. In order to be farmers, the Chichimecs first had to learn the basics of agriculture (or so it seemed to Spaniards unfamiliar with indigenous horticulture in the north). Barbadillo ordered that new Chichimec populations initially farm all of their lands in common under the supervision of groups of eight to ten Tlaxcalans. This period of instruction was eased by temporary grain subsidies distributed by the Franciscan missionaries. Once the Chichimecs acquired the skills needed to raise crops, the community lands would be partitioned into individual family lots, leaving an appropriate share for common fields and public spaces.[19]

The Barbadillo ordinances described the approximate political geography for all the Tlaxcalan-Chichimec mission-towns. An *acequia* was to be the axis of each town, dividing Tlaxcalan from Chichimec barrios. At the center of the grid, a town plaza was to be surrounded by the church, *casas reales*, and hospital. Each Tlaxcalan family would be granted thirty *varas* of land, and each Chichimec family twenty. Additionally, each community would possess substantial common lands for crops and grazing to support public expenses such as hospital operations and church furnishings. Barbadillo's instructions might lead a reader to believe that he was creating all such communities from whole cloth. In practice, however, he was giving a rough description of the arrangements that already existed in several Tlaxcalan-Chichimec pueblos. In other places, such as Guadalupe and the Valley of Pilón, his guidelines would dictate the form of new *pueblos de indios*.[20]

Barbadillo's guidelines for the internal structures of the pueblos were nothing new, but his regulations on labor and exchange between Spaniards and Indians were. Foremost on Barbadillo's agenda was the suppression of slavery. Though both Indian slavery and *encomienda* had long been illegal, northern landowners had successfully veiled several forms of slavery or near-slavery behind the definitions of just war, penal servitude, and *congregación*. To avoid another generation of legal obfuscation, Barbadillo forbade, in very concrete terms, the specific practices that in his eyes constituted slavery: forced labor, labor without compensation, the confinement of Indians in chains and collars, and interference

---

[18] Barbadillo to Audiencia of Mexico, 6 Aug. 1717, Audiencia de Guadalajara 166, fols. 149–54.
[19] Zavala, *Entradas*, 118–19.
[20] On the ordinances, see Cavazos Garza, *Ciudad Guadalupe*, 81–3; Fr. Juan de Losada explains the same elements in the design of the *pueblos de indios* in a letter of 20 July 1717, AGI Audiencia de Guadalajara 166, exp. 7, fols. 130–40. On conditions antedating Barbadillo's visit, see "Carta al Rey, 1690," in del Hoyo, *Indios, frailes y encomenderos*.

in their right to marry freely and maintain households. His ordinances guaranteed Indians membership in *pueblos de indios* and mandated a minimum wage for employment on Spanish estates. Barbadillo's measures sought to eliminate the most common causes of slavery: capture and debt. His system of pueblo enrollment and his new military measures aimed to end slave raiding. New restrictions on Spanish lending to Indians, and a prohibition on the exaction of debt from the children of Indian debtors, aimed to end debt peonage. To prevent similar forms of labor exploitation from developing within the pueblos, the clergy, like Spanish landowners, were forbidden from exacting unpaid labor from their Indian communicants.

Prior to Francisco Barbadillo's arrival, there was no uniform set of written rules governing the relationships between the missions, towns, and haciendas of Nuevo León. Franciscan missionaries followed the institutes of their order, Tlaxcalans brandished their charters, other Indians could seek protection under the *Leyes de Indias*, and Spanish landowners clung to their early land grants and the legal vestiges of *encomienda*.[21] However, this body of law generally treated these distinct ethnic spheres as separate entities, and failed to codify the customs governing their interaction. Interaction between them took place for many reasons: because Tlaxcalans and Chichimecs formed joint pueblos, because Indians labored on Spanish lands, and because both Tlaxcalans and Chichimec allies traded with Spaniards and cooperated with them in joint military operations. Barbadillo transformed many customary community interactions into legally definable ones.[22]

Barbadillo expected the central Mexican system of parallel Indian and Spanish republics to be the backbone of the improved northern system. To this end, he made the most important institutional distinctions between the Spanish and Indian legal spheres: "all the Tlaxcalan Indians, Chichimecs and those of any other nation in the kingdom remain insulated from the jurisdiction of the governors and the *alcaldes mayores* of the *partidos* [and] *alcaldes ordinarios* of *villas* and pueblos."[23] Interactions between pueblo Indians and Spaniards were to be mediated through the *protectores de indios* (both local and provincial) and the missionaries. The pueblos were internally self-governing and the Indian magistrates were granted jurisdiction over many criminal matters and over all internal civil disputes regarding land and water. Many of the most important *pueblos de indios* were joint Tlaxcalan-Chichimec communities. Though the

[21] Lockhart (*Nahuas After Conquest*, 413–18) has explored the widespread production of "false titles" by enterprising Nahua scribes. His findings should lead us to read corporate land titles with caution. However, given how often the basic historical narratives of Tlaxcalan documents from the north can be corroborated from other sources, it is my view that there is much to be gained from a cautious reading of Tlaxcalan records. It goes without saying that the falsification of documents by interested parties was also common among Spaniards in the production of records of merit, titles, and records of *limpieza de sangre*.

[22] Zavala, *Entradas, congregas y encomiendas*, 117–22; Cavazos Garza, *El lic. Francisco Barbadillo*, 19–23; Cavazos Garza, *Ciudad Guadalupe*, 81–4.

[23] "Ordenanzas de Barbadillo," in Silvio Zavala, *Entradas*, 117.

homes and fields of the two populations were to be segregated, the *cabildo* that ruled over them was to include officers from both. Barbadillo's code specified that the governor and *escribano* were to be Tlaxcalans, but that the other councilmen should be a mix of Chichimecs and Tlaxcalans. It is not surprising that the governor, who held military responsibilities, and the *escribano*, who must be literate and familiar with colonial law, should be Tlaxcalans. The governor, working with the *escribano* and missionary, was also responsible for community accounts, tracking and auditing the revenues from community holdings and the debts incurred from community expenses. Elections for all offices were to be held annually for one-year renewable terms.[24]

The Indian governors, missionaries, and *escribanos* in partnership with the *protectores de indios* were to account for all economic transactions between Indians and Spaniards and ensure that those transactions followed the regulations on wages, labor, and exchange. Pueblo accounts would record transactions between the individual and the commons, and transactions between the commons and outside economic agents. For instance, the cost of tools supplied by Spaniards to the Indian community was repaid with revenue derived from sales of grain produced on pueblo lands. Barbadillo and Fray Juan de Losada defined the minimum daily wage for Indian laborers on Spanish lands and for Indian archers serving with Spanish troops.[25]

Before Barbadillo's time, the defense of the Neoleonés frontier was in the hands of several types of military forces: Tlaxcalan soldiers, Spanish landowner militias, a small number of presidial troops, and an unpredictable assortment of Indian allies. Barbadillo endeavored to create command structures that would more effectively link these disparate forces.[26] He envisioned provincial defense as a well-orchestrated effort by the five Tlaxcalan garrisons, the twenty-six major haciendas (which were to maintain a total of 104 horsemen), the fixed presidio forces, and the seventy horsemen of the *compañías volantes* that would move between the presidios.[27] Major landowners had always been obligated, as a provision of their property grants, to defend the frontier. In practice, virtually all men of the landowning class were already *de facto* members of armed militias. Likewise, the charters of all Tlaxcalan communities outlined the settlers' military privileges and responsibilities. Barbadillo went a step further in explaining the place of the Tlaxcalans in the military system. Tlaxcalan men were to be armed

[24] Ordenanzas de Barbadillo, arts. 13–52, in Zavala, *Entradas*, 118–19.

[25] Cash was dispensed from the *cajas reales* of San Luis Potosí to the *padre comisario* and *protector* in Nuevo León, 23 Mar. 1716, Consulta de Francisco Barbadillo, AGI Audiencia de Guadalajara 166, fols. 107–10. Juan de Losada argued that these expenditures were far cheaper than the price of war, Carta de Fr. Juan de Losada, 20 July 1717, AGI Audiencia de Guadalajara 166, fols. 134–8.

[26] Barbadillo to Viceroy Valero, 16 Sept. 1716, AGI Audiencia de Guadalajara 166, fols. 145–6; Barbadillo to Audiencia de México, 6 Aug. 1717, AGI Audiencia de Guadalajara 166, fol. 176.

[27] AGN Historia 30, exp. 15, fols. 218–19; AGI Audiencia de Guadalajara 166, fols. 51–4; AGI Audiencia de Guadalajara 166, exp. 15, fols. 218–19; AGI Audiencia de Guadalajara 166, fol. 166.

and at the ready. It was the responsibility of their governor, and ultimately the *protector de indios*, to make sure that they complied with this obligation. Barbadillo's code stated that "Tlaxcalan Indians use horses and arms, and the *protector* shall insure that each one has a musket."[28] Yet, it appears that the primary function of these forces was local and defensive, and that Tlaxcalan participation in other military ventures was largely at their own discretion. Barbadillo explained that much of the time the Tlaxcalans did not engage in war, and that "if those in the frontier pueblos are needed, they may go of their own volition, not by compulsion, and only in an urgent case and by order of the *protector*."[29]

Chichimecs were usually disarmed when they first entered the mission system, but Barbadillo's writing often refers to settled Chichimec archers. Once incorporated into the towns, it was not so much that the Chichimecs were disarmed, but that they were permitted to carry arms only when the circumstances justified it. His regulations recognize that Indians periodically left the pueblos to hunt. Chichimec villagers armed themselves for hunts, and Indians on guard duty patrolled the perimeter of the pueblo with bows and arrows.[30]

When Barbadillo arrived in Nuevo León, he came in part to investigate the accusation, put before the Council of the Indies, that the governor of Nuevo León was granting licenses to carry out slave raids for a fee of 100 to 200 pesos.[31] Eugenio del Hoyo, in his documentary collection on Indians in the colonial north, has described the workings of what he terms "pseudo-*encomienda*," along with a persistent form of chattel slavery. He argues that the *encomenderos*, when forced to renounce their official rights over tribute labor, used their military commands and land rights to justify the seizure of Indian laborers. The *congrega*, which he considers a pseudo-*encomienda*, was legally excused as a sort of privately held mission in which the landowners exacted labor from the Indians in return for care, protection, and religious instruction. Indians who refused to live on the *congregas*, or who fled from them, could be declared rebels and then captured, sentenced to hard labor, and sold in the slave markets of Mazapil, Sombrerete, and Charcas, or the *obrajes* of Puebla, San Miguel, or Querétaro.[32]

When Barbadillo entered Nuevo León, he was walking into a war zone (or, in the parlance of the day, a *guerra viva*). The costs of war had provoked petitions from the *vecinos* of Monterrey for royal grants of arms and supplies,

---

[28] "Ordenanzas," Zavala, *Entradas*, 118. The same requirements for the maintenance of arms and mounts for the Tlaxcalans of San Cristóbal appear in a copy of the pueblo charter of 15 Jan. 1725, AGI Audiencia de Guadalajara 173.

[29] "Ordenanzas," Zavala, *Entradas*, 117.

[30] On the function of Indian soldiers, 15 Feb. 1715 document, AGI Audiencia de Guadalajara 166, fols. 51–4. These obligations were shared with Spanish settlers, who were also required to maintain arms and mounts, 12 May 1719, AGI Audiencia de Guadalajara 166, fols. 185–7.

[31] Orders of the Consejo de Indias, 11 Feb. 1716, in Zavala, *Entradas*, 114–16.

[32] Eugenio del Hoyo, *Indios, frailes y encomenderos*, 10–13.

inadvertently attracting attention to their military and labor practices.[33] Rather than merely providing the muskets and shot requested by the *vecinos*, Barbadillo took over the military operation, transforming it from a series of slave raids to a series of diplomatic encounters orchestrated by Juan de Losada and backed by a mixed force of Spanish and Indian soldiers. Among the first groups approached by Losada were the Indians who had fled San Cristóbal de los Hualahuises. Losada and Barbadillo employed a force of twenty-five Spaniards and twenty-five Indian archers. Through the indirect exchange of tokens such as gift goods and the peace sign of an arrow without a point, the colonial and rebel communities were soon brought into face-to-face negotiations. Ultimately, twenty-two of the San Cristóbal Indians returned to the settlement. In the year that followed, Losada claimed credit for peace agreements with 1,500 Indians whom he soon settled in pueblos.[34]

When Barbadillo summarized his accomplishments and the objectives of the new communities, he made clear that the system of Indian pueblos was to be the foundation of regional peace. He explained to the viceroy, the Duke of Linares, that the recent epidemics of violence had its roots in a flawed pattern of settlement: Spanish settlers had been given far too much land, leaving no viable sites for Indian farming towns. This enabled labor exploitation by the landowners but also encouraged Chichimecs to revert to nomadic practices. In this changing environment, Indians flocked to the mission-towns as a place of refuge. Barbadillo ascribed the hostility he received from Spanish landowners to their reasoned fear that Indian workers would flee their exploitive *congregas* for his new *pueblos de indios*.[35]

NEW *PUEBLOS DE INDIOS* AND SPANISH RESISTANCE

In 1715 Francisco Barbadillo, invoking his authority to establish missions on unoccupied land, founded the mission-towns of Concepción and Purificación in the Valley of Pilón by seizing property previously deeded to Spanish settlers. The viceroy had sent Barbadillo to Nuevo León in response to two related problems: first, the persistence of slavelike conditions under the *congrega* system; and second, the failure of existing policies to secure the concentration and settlement of Indians who had fled the missions or had never been "reduced" in the first place. Whereas at Hualahuises, Barbadillo's task was to reconstitute a failed mission, in the Valley of Pilón, he was starting from scratch.

Following the model of San Esteban, and paralleling his work in Hualahuises, Barbadillo designed each mission-town to be populated by both Chichimecs and resettled Tlaxcalans.[36] The new pueblos were to face each other on the banks of

---

[33] AGI Audiencia de Guadalajara 166, fols. 24–80.
[34] AGI Audiencia de Guadalajara 166, fols. 39–42.
[35] AGI Audiencia de Guadalajara 166, fols. 20–29.
[36] Cavazos Garza, *El lic. Francisco Barbadillo*, 15–20.

the river Pilón, each possessing "a league of land in each direction."[37] The Chichimecs who settled there came from a number of different tribes or bands, and it is difficult to determine their exact origin. Pelones are the most common group appearing in the early mission records, but whether they were captured, persuaded to settle in the missions, or drawn from existing *congregas* remains unclear. Following the intervention of Francisco Barbadillo, the same basic cultural geography would describe the Valley of Pilón for nearly a century. The valley was home to haciendas of varying sizes, a number of smaller ranches, the two missions populated with Tlaxcalans and Chichimecs, and a village (usually called Pilón) surrounding the parish church of San Mateo, which ministered to the needs of the valley's Spanish inhabitants.

In those days, Pelones, Borrados, and Pamoranes were raiding the valley's estates, capturing or destroying supplies, and carrying off livestock. The Spanish *vecino* militias responded with equal ferocity, raiding Indian camps, killing the men, and enslaving women and children. Barbadillo's solution to this chaos in the valley was to seize lands held by Nicolás Ochoa, Juan de León, and Alonso Garrido, and from them to create the two new mixed Tlaxcalan-Chichimec *pueblos de indios*. These three families, and their supporters in the valley, raised a hue and cry against the expropriations. Pilón's Spanish *vecinos* sought to defend their lands in precisely the same way that Tlaxcalans usually defended theirs: by petitioning the crown for redress of grievance and by citing their history of faithful military service. The leading families of Pilón pointed out that they were "descendants of conquistadors" and still under arms in the defense of the northern frontier. They asked, not for more missions, but for more arms and material support. Barbadillo was in no way convinced by their arguments. When he looked at Pilón, he saw a fertile valley that was producing little food, and he saw a flashpoint for further war. He pressed ahead with his plans with the ongoing support of the viceroy.[38]

When Barbadillo announced the expropriation of private land for the construction of Purificación, he earned the antipathy of much of the local Spanish population. The major landowners of the valley surmised that the creation of a mission-town in their midst would lead to a labor shortage when Indian workers departed their lands for those of Purificación. The resulting fight was both personal and institutional. Manuel Angel de Robles, leader of the outraged *vecinos*, so openly flouted the orders of Barbadillo that the latter exiled him to Coahuila, placing him in the custody of the presidio of Monclova until local affairs were put in order.[39] Robles's testimony makes clear that he and Barbadillo were advocating two different social orders. In justifying the previous operations of local estates, Robles provided a concise description of the ideal form of the

---

[37] Francisco Barbadillo, "Auto. En la Villa de S. Felipe de Linares en treinta y un día del mes de agosto de mil setecientos quince anos," reproduced in Beatriz Bazan de León de Vaquero, *Crónica de Montemorelos* (Santa Catarina, Mexico: Editorial Nogales, 2003).

[38] 1715 Testimony of Robles, AGI Audiencia de Guadalajara 166, fols. 72–5.

[39] AGI Audiencia de Guadalajara 166, fols. 68–71.

congrega system in which naked coercion would yield slowly to a wage-labor system: "Indians, that are taken in war are distributed to the owners of haciendas and fields with the title of *protectores* in order that they may be fed and may work in our Holy Faith, be baptized, and serve the haciendas.... [T]he Indians that remain on the haciendas with the title of *gañanes* being paid a salary after the fashion of New Spain." Under current practices, the *hacendados* housed both Spanish and Indian laborers on their lands, and organized a workforce of both free wage-laborers and captive ones. It was a system that the *vecinos* insisted served the common interests of the region's Indians and Spaniards. Robles cautioned that Barbadillo's program of settling nomads and rebels was tantamount to forgiving them their crimes of robbery and murder and transferring land from faithful Spanish subjects to enemies of the state. Ultimately, he feared that the system would leave the Spanish estates without *gañanes* and cause a collapse of agriculture in the region. Robles described the new foundation of Guadalupe in equally alarming terms, complaining that 1,200 Indians, arriving under peace agreements brokered by Losada and Barbadillo, poured into the area, driving out Spanish families and Christianized Indians. Robles insisted that all four of the new mission-towns (Guadalupe, Purificación, Concepción, and San Cristóbal) had produced disastrous consequences for local productivity and safety.[40]

The new mission-towns all included Tlaxcalan colonists whose position in the north was so clearly equivalent to that of neighboring Spaniards as to create both mutual respect and rivalry. The leaders of Tlaxcalan communities generally presented themselves as "*principales conquistadores*" in their petitions to the crown. In the dispute over the formation of Purificación, the four major Spanish landowners of Pilón described themselves with the same words. Robles and his copetitioners, Nicolás de Ochoa, Juan de León, and Alonso Garrido, viewed the Tlaxcalans who were arriving in the valley to found the mission-towns as rival conquistadors who were taking unfair advantage of the new legal climate. The four Pilón notables complained that Tlaxcalans, who already held viable land grants in the region, were now encroaching upon theirs: "for thirty years there has been a town called Nuestra Señora de San Juan de Carrizal, known by the name of the Tlaxcalans, administered spiritually by a priest from the city of Monterrey. They are frontiersmen who have left their former pueblo in order to pass on to the Valley of Pilón." Robles and his peers were outraged that the Tlaxcalans had left behind perfectly good agricultural land only to establish in their midst a new town that was luring away their *gañanes*.[41]

As in the other colonies, the first decade did not go smoothly for these pueblos. Attacks from outside Indians and from neighboring Spaniards led to widespread flight from the pueblos and to spotty agricultural productivity. Yet,

[40] Robles Testimony, AGI Audiencia de Guadalajara 166, fols. 72–3.
[41] Robles Testimony, AGI Audiencia de Guadalajara 166, fols. 73–5. In saying that the town is "known by the name of the Tlaxcalans," the speakers refer to the fact that the town was sometimes called Nueva Tlaxcala.

the Tlaxcalan leadership of Purificación and Concepción held firm. What looked like an uncertain start for the communities would yield a lasting and prosperous settlement by the late 1720s. Given local memory of warfare and slavery, it was not easy to earn the trust of new Chichimec populations. By 1716, after a year of Barbadillo and Losada's efforts, Purificación had a population of 867 and Concepción of 549. However a sudden panic – whether based on rumor or fact – brought an overnight depopulation of the Chichimec barrios. The Indians, who regularly attended church services, came to believe that Spaniards were planning to massacre them during mass. On the strength of this rumor, almost the entire population fled into the hills. According to the missionary, Fray Torres, only eleven new converts remained on the lands that had days before been home to more than a thousand Chichimecs.[42]

Much of the population eventually returned, but the panics of newly settled Chichimecs were rooted in realistic anxieties. In 1722, a group of Chichimecs from Purificación and Concepción traveled to las Tablas to work on the land of Joseph Benavides. There they were suddenly attacked by a group of armed Spaniards who killed most of the men and took the women and children as slaves. Several of the survivors eventually reached Mexico City and accused Governor Arriaga of complicity in the attack. An Indian named Pedro Fermín was among those who traveled to Mexico City to testify against Governor Arriaga. Fermín averred that the hangings and sales of captives were undertaken without any judicial process and that Governor Arriaga was not just negligent, but complicit in these events. Fermín claimed that the governor and his wife received a share of the slaves.[43]

Of the all the communities established or reformed by Barbadillo, the mission-town of Nuestra Señora de Guadalupe was the most ambitious in scale and the most politically contentious. Unlike San Cristóbal or San Miguel, there was no preexisting mission or Indian pueblo on the site that would become Guadalupe. The area was inhabited by Spaniards and Indians – the former as landowners, and the latter as laborers under the terms of *congregación*. In 1714, the lands that would soon become Guadalupe were still private estates owned by Pedro Guajardo, Joseph Treviño, Nicolás Escamilla, and the Ochoa family. For many years, the landowners had rounded up neighboring tribes on a seasonal basis and forced them to work their fields. When Barbadillo arrived in the valley, these tribes were in open rebellion, the Janambres and Pelones having fled the *congregaciones* and joined with Borrados to carry out raids on Spanish property. The estate owners, who considered themselves faithful "Spaniards and vassals," petitioned the viceregal government for military support in the form of arms shipments, supplies, and funding, arguing that they could bring an end to Indian rebellion and train the Indians to be peaceful workers. What they got, instead,

[42] Testimonio de la consulta que al su ex. hizo el sn. lic. Francisco Barbadillo y Victoria ... 1716, AGI Audiencia de Guadalajara 166, fols. 99–116.

[43] Memorial que presentó Fermín Indio Meco en el Juzgado gral. de los naturales. AGI Audiencia de Guadalajara 173, fols. 3–4.

was a visit from Francisco Barbadillo. Barbadillo, who viewed the landowners' petition as a pretext for endless slave wars, took the drastic step of seizing significant portions of the four large estates to form the mission-town of Guadalupe. Like the landowners, Barbadillo claimed he would create a population of peaceful Indian farmers, but his methods were very different from theirs.[44]

Barbadillo and Losada's diplomatic missions to the Janambres, Pelones, and other Chichimecs were almost too successful for their own good. Not only did wandering bands come to the new Guadalupe site, but other Indians also began leaving the *congregas* to join them. Soon more than a thousand Chichimecs were camped at the site of Guadalupe. This was a larger population than could at first be reliably provisioned, and the settlement remained unstable and plagued by continuous violence. Barbadillo blamed the conditions of war on the previous conduct of the landowners. They, in turn, accused Barbadillo of inciting rebellion by encouraging Indian workers to flee Spanish estates.

Guadalupe evolved from a camp to a village under the direction of a small but indispensable core of Tlaxcalan colonists. By 1716, Guadalupe had lost some Indians and gained others. The Pamoranes, negotiating through their war leader, joined the community on the same terms as the first Chichimec recruits. Guadalupe now had reliable corn crops, but its population stood at 244 families and comprising a total of 1,000 individuals. The sustenance of this remarkably large population still required significant amounts of hunting and gathering. In the first years of the mission-town, the Chichimec population was reportedly absent for five months out of every year. It would appear that, rather than abandoning their accustomed seasonal migrations, the members of the pueblo Guadalupe modified their calendar to incorporate seasons of cultivation and harvest into their hunting and gathering activities.[45]

The plotting of the town of Guadalupe followed the pattern prescribed by Barbadillo's ordinances. It was divided into Tlaxcalan and Chichimec barrios and surveyed into thirty-*vara* plots for the former and twenty-*vara* plots for the latter. Much of this land was already under cultivation as a part of Spanish estates, so it is possible that some of the irrigation systems predated Barbadillo's intervention. The community first constructed simple homes, and then the church and civic buildings that surrounded the plaza.[46] Guadalupe soon became one of the most important colonial communities in Nuevo León.

---

[44] Acta de 30 diciembre 1715 AMM, transcribed copy provided by Juana Margarita Domínguez Martínez, director of the archive; 16 May 1715 testimony of Monterrey *vecinos*, AGI 166, fols. 69–70.

[45] Barbadillo, AGI Audiencia de Guadalajara 166, fols. 99–116.

[46] Ordenanzas, Cavazos Garza, *Cd. Guadalupe*, 81.

CONSOLIDATING THE PUEBLOS FROM WITHIN

Of all the Tlaxcalan colonies of Nuevo León, San Miguel de Aguayo had the strongest early success in staking out its property rights and legal privileges. San Miguel was one of the first Tlaxcalan-Chichimec towns, and its strategic position was indispensable for protecting the Royal Mines of Boca de Leones and the associated refining haciendas of the Valley of Sabinas.[47] By the time Francisco Barbadillo's arrived in Nuevo León, the Tlaxcalan-Chichimec pueblo of San Miguel had already existed for thirty years or more. He did not create the pueblo, nor did he fundamentally alter it, but he did give further legal recognition to existing practices, and he altered some of the military and administrative relationships between the pueblo and the organs of colonial government in the region. Many of San Miguel's elected leaders were Tlaxcalan nobles who held military commands and owned shares in area mines. They were an important part of the region's economic and military elite; still, they and their communities were not completely immune from the Spanish backlash against the Barbadillo reforms. San Miguel was a party in the legal disputes surrounding the misdeeds of Governor Arriaga. Despite this period of antagonistic relations with the governor, the community emerged from the period with its assets and privileges intact.

In the long run, both Tlaxcalans and Chichimecs would benefit from this period of reform in which the essentials of the Barbadillo system were confirmed in practice. Though the Tlaxcalans had always been protected from forced labor, Chichimecs had not been. The Barbadillo reforms eliminated the legal basis for forced labor that had existed under the guise of *congregación*. Barbadillo's ordinances and the subsequent rulings of the *audiencia* confirmed the Tlaxcalans' arrangement with local Chichimecs (most notably the Alasapas) for joint settlement and defense. In the years that followed, San Miguel would retain a secure position in the regional political system and create the conditions for a growing population.[48]

The Tlaxcalans had themselves surveyed the lands of San Miguel long before the Barbadillo period. The arrangements of 1715 merely rubber-stamped a set of land-tenure patterns established by the Tlaxcalans in the 1680s. The town's land grants were twice the size of those in other Tlaxcalan mission-towns. Each Tlaxcalan family held an urban lot of 60 *varas* and a field of 200 *varas*. Chichimec families held 40-*vara* home sites and farmed their pueblo land in common.[49] A Chichimec barrio was delineated from the Tlaxcalan one by an *acequia*. The residents of San Miguel were governed by an Indian *cabildo* that in most years included both Tlaxcalan and Chichimec officers.

---

[47] On the special military functions of San Miguel, see Adams, "At the Lion's Mouth," 324–46.
[48] The relationship between the Alasapas and Tlaxcalans will be treated at greater length in Chapter 5.
[49] Butzer, *Historia social*, 87.

In the 1720s, San Miguel was tested by difficult circumstances originating both inside and outside the colonial community. From outside came relentless attacks by northern tribes; from within came destabilizing Spanish military reprisals and a series of fraudulent economic exactions associated with Governor Arriaga's administration of Nuevo León. Indian attacks against the colonial communities of the Boca de León area were very common and very hard to counter. Local Spaniards, uncertain as to the attackers' identities, were often unsure whether they faced an invasion or a local uprising. Barbadillo recounted that in 1719 three squadrons of enemy Indians attacked the Hacienda Mamulique, property of Don Antonio López de Villegas, killing and kidnapping several of its inhabitants. As in other times of turbulence, new mission Indians sometimes joined with the invaders, creating well-informed and dangerous groups of bandits. Barbadillo noted with concern that the owners of Mamulique were attacking Indians almost at random. The owners punished the resident Piruamas despite the fact that, according to Barbadillo, "It was not the Piruamas of said hacienda that carried out the murders, but the Tobosos, Gavilanes, and Tripas blancas." He maintained that the governor, who supplied troops to defend the interest of the *hacendados*, was taking forced confessions and executing the wrong Indians.[50]

During these years, the Tlaxcalans of San Miguel and the area's Spanish landowners had some convergent interests and some divergent ones. Both groups benefited from the continuous operation of the mines and foundries, from the safe passage of mule trains between communities, and from the growth of the farming population.[51] The Tlaxcalans and the Spanish landowners had in the past provided most of the military muscle in the area. The growth of presidios, staffed by regular soldiers, benefited regional security and the local economy, but it also diminished the political capital possessed by old Spanish and Tlaxcalan elites whose power rested on their indispensable military contributions. Francisco Barbadillo hoped to guard the frontier with a bigger force of presidials and a new group of "flying companies" that would patrol between them and respond quickly to unexpected threats. Between 1715 and 1723 the number or regulars stationed at the Boca de Leones presidio increased from four to eight, and then to fourteen.[52] The presidio became increasingly important as a point of supply and as a communications hub, but its force of regular soldiers remained small. The vast majority of those who defended the pass were militiamen from the Tlaxcalan-Alasapa colony and the Spanish haciendas.

---

[50] 12 May 1719, AGI Audiencia de Guadalajara 166, fol. 185.

[51] Monterrey helped to fund the defenses at Boca de Leones because the two populations shared vulnerability to attack through the same path, 3 Aug. 1721, AGI Audiencia de Guadalajara 166, fols. 223–37.

[52] The total force at the presidios at any given moment was far greater than the number of official presidial soldiers. Allied *indios amigos* were often present in much greater numbers. July 1721, AGI Audiencia of Guadalajara 166, fols. 217–19; 3 Aug. 1721 Representación de vecinos y mineros, Audiencia de Guadalajara 166.

By numbers, the military system of the area remained largely unchanged in the 1720s, but the administration of those forces became more regular. In the seventeenth century, Tlaxcalans and Spaniards made *ad hoc* alliances with *indios amigos* to carry out military campaigns in the area. By the 1720s, many of these *indios amigos* had become permanent members of the San Miguel community. Militia enrollment was formalized and the coordination between Spanish, Tlaxcalan, and Chichimec fighters was better orchestrated through the presidio and the *alcaldía mayor.*[53] Tlaxcalans and Spaniards both continued to benefit, in some ways, from the sale of war captives. Not only mines, but also the growing *obrajes* of Mexico City purchased northern Indians as workers.[54] Whereas area Spaniards sometimes sought to maintain a level of warfare that would guarantee a stream of captives, the Tlaxcalans of San Miguel were more reticent. Tlaxcalans took a narrower view of what constituted just war or reasonable grounds for penal servitude. The growth and prosperity of San Miguel required a steady rate of voluntary settlement by outside Indians. High levels of conflict hurt the town by undermining the recruitment of new populations and, worse still, provoking the flight of recently settled groups. For this reason, and others, the Tlaxcalans lobbied for the restoration of a strong province-wide *protector de indios.*[55]

In 1723, the Tlaxcalans of San Miguel de Aguayo put their full weight behind the movement to oust the allies of Governor Arriaga and restore both the protectorate and the safeguards of the Barbadillo system. Arriaga was at the center of a network of landowning military commanders and merchants who colluded to control the flow of goods and captives in and out of Nuevo León. One such merchant, Roque Perez, had been given control of the commerce connecting La Descubridora mine and the nearby hacienda of Manuel Zisneros to the rest of the regional economy. When Perez abruptly departed for Coahuila without paying his outstanding accounts to San Miguel, he provoked the wrath of the community. Don Esteben Gonzales spoke for the community in demanding both proper restitution and the arrest of the rogue merchant. Gonzales began his petition to the *audiencia* by demonstrating his own place in the colonial order. He described his status in San Miguel, in the Tlaxcalan nation, and in the larger Spanish Empire. He called himself "Dn Esteban Gonzalez, *casique* and *principal* of Gran Tlaxcala, *vecino*, settler, and

[53] On the formal combination of forces, 12 May 1719, AGI Audiencia de Guadalajara 166, fols. 190–1. The records of the period show the frequent deployment of these mixed forces. For example, a 1 May 1720 document records that Barbadillo and De la Garza led a campaign that included Spanish regulars and armed Spanish *vecinos* along with a group Tlaxcalan arcabusiers and Chichimec archers. The following month, a similar force included eight regular soldiers, fifteen *vecino* militiamen, and fifteen *indios amigos*, 1 May 1720, AGI Audiencia de Guadalajara 166, fol. 192; 28 June 1721, fols. 202–11; 3 Aug. 1721, fols. 221–39.

[54] In 1720 a band of Indians accused of attacking mule convoys was captured and sold to the *obrajes* of Mexico City, 15 May 1720 Consulta, Barbadillo to viceroy, AGI Audiencia de Guadalajara 166, fol. 196.

[55] 17 Aug. 1723, Pedimento del Indio Don Esteven de Gonzales, AGI Audiencia de Guadalajara 173.

conqueror of the pueblo of San Miguel de Boca de Leones and its frontiers and discoverer of the Royal mines of Our Lord San Juan of the new Kingdom of León."[56] He placed himself in a feudal hierarchy that extended from his humblest subordinates in one direction to the king of Spain in the other. Gonzalez claimed that his people conquered the land they now inhabited ("not only I did this, but all of the Tlaxcalans that we have settled on the frontier"). With the merits of the community firmly established, Gonzalez laid down his demands: not only must the debts be repaid and the perpetrator imprisoned, but the whole current administration of the kingdom needed to be cleaned up. He complained of a cycle of Indian raids and Spanish counteroffensives that was leaving the Tlaxcalans squeezed between conflicting threats. Nomadic Indians were attacking their property, but so were the Spanish clients of the governor. Spanish commanders were indiscriminately seizing settled Chichimecs as captives and illegally requisitioning (or just plain stealing) draft animals and supplies from the Tlaxcalans. He warned that without a strong *protector de indios* to regulate Spanish-Indian relations, the frontier could collapse. Arriaga had his own version of recent events, but it is clear that the *audiencia* found the Tlaxcalan perspective more credible. Governor Arriaga was removed from office and replaced by Pedro de Sarabio, a leader who would adhere more closely to rules of governance as laid out in the Barbadillo ordinances.

One of the first local systems to attract Barbadillo's attention was that of San Felipe de Linares and San Cristóbal de los Hualahuises. San Cristóbal was one of Nuevo León's first missions, but one that had experienced great vicissitudes of fortune. It had already existed for half a century when in 1711 the holder of a neighboring land grant established beside it the town of San Felipe. The landowner, Sebastián Villegas Cumplido, held the office of *alcalde mayor* and soon received a charter for the parish and town that he and a handful of Spanish residents asked to establish.[57] However, this foundation soon occasioned a dispute with the Indians of San Cristóbal who claimed the new charter was an attempt to appropriate a portion of their lands for the new Spanish town. Francisco Barbadillo, who investigated the matter, sided with the Indians, and the viceroy ordered that the young Spanish town be moved.[58]

Just upstream from Linares and on the banks of the river Hualahuises, today's city of Hualahuises occupies the site of a colonial mission-town of the same

[56] All the material from Gonzales treated here appears in his testimony of 23 Aug. 1723, Audiencia de Guadalajara 173.

[57] Villegas Cumplido's family tree tells the story of many of the early alliances binding together the powerbrokers of Nuevo León. He was born in Santa María Nativitas in Tlaxcala and may well have been a Tlaxcalan. His wife was a member of Nuevo León's powerful Cantú family. The possibility of his Tlaxcalan ancestry is raised by Gómez Danés *San Cristóbal de Gualaguises*, 91–2. Villegas Cumplido's 1713 testament claims that he is the legitimate son of a native of Mexico City and a native of castile, 21 Aug. 1713, Linares, AMM Protocolos 10, exp. 1, fol. 57.

[58] 8 June 1711, AMM Civil 38, exp. 1; on the regional dispute over grazing and boundaries, 1 Jan. 1713, AMM 99, exp. 11; the resolution of the case appears in documents of 15 and 20 Feb. 1715, AGI Audience de Guadalajara 166, fols. 39–42, 49.

name.[59] The Hualahuises Indians were its first inhabitants, along with a group of Tlaxcalan settlers sent there to structure and guide the town in its early years.[60] It is likely that the mission was built to contain members of the same tribe of Hualahuises against whom Zavala fought a taxing war in 1655.[61] Later records from the eighteenth century recall that the original settlers of San Cristóbal were fifty Tlaxcalan families who came from the Tlaxcalan pueblo of San Miguel Mexquitic near San Luis Potosí in the seventeenth century.[62] In the 1690s, visitors to the area reported the mission abandoned by its former inhabitants. Still, the settlement survived in some form. The earliest extant mission records for San Cristóbal de los Hualahuises date from 1700, and from that point forward, a variety of documentary sources connect the early mission to the municipality that emerged in the nineteenth century.

The lands surrounding San Cristóbal, like so many of the valuable bottom lands in Nuevo León, were the focus of early legal battles. The first and most significant of these struggles was between the *pueblo de indios* and a neighboring estate belonging to Sebastián de Villegas Cumplido, a Spanish settler who sought to control the area and its Chichimec inhabitants under the rules of *congregación*. In 1700, Villegas Cumplido, who identified himself as the owner of a hacienda near the Franciscan mission of San Cristóbal, petitioned for and received authority to capture "barbarous" Indians from the surrounding area in order to Christianize them and put their labor to use.[63] The document named Villegas Cumplido *"protector"* over these Indians. Villegas then helped to found the Spanish village of Linares in 1711 on lands that fell within the original jurisdiction of San Cristóbal de los Hualahuises. The founding Spanish *vecinos* immediately claimed title to the lands of the existing *pueblo de indios*. This provoked a legal dispute between the *pueblo de indios* and the emergent Spanish town that was resolved only when viceregal visitor Francisco Barbadillo reconfirmed the mission-town's title.[64] In the short term, his defense of San Cristóbal de los Hualahuises threatened the interests of Villegas Cumplido and

---

[59] Today, the name of the municipality is written "Hualahuises," though historical sources use "Gualaguises" almost as often. I have chosen to use the modern spelling throughout.

[60] Documentation for the early years of the town's history is scarce, but the rough outlines are discernable. Several regional historians have maintained that the Mission San Cristóbal was founded by Governor Martín de Zavala in the 1640s and that it was attacked and then abandoned for a time in the late seventeenth century. Relying on contemporary references, Pedro Gómez Danés has concluded that the mission was founded between 1674 and 1678. Napoleón Nevárez Pequeño, *Villa San Cristóbal de Hualahuises*, 17–24; Gómez Danés, *San Cristóbal de Gualaguises*, 13–19. Note that Nevárez Pequeño and Carrera accept the story of the mission being founded by Zavala; Gómez Danés argues, convincingly, that it was founded later in 1674–1678.

[61] Cavazos Garza, *Breve historia de Nuevo León*, 33.

[62] Archivo General de Simancas (hereafter AGS) 6966, exp. 69, chaps. 256–8.

[63] "Petición de Sebastián de Villegas Cumplido (1700) Archivo Municipal de Monterrey," in Zavala, *Entradas, congregas, y encomiendas en el Nuevo Reino de León*, 73–4.

[64] Nevárez Pequeño has suggested that the mission, after being burned by hostile Indians in 1793, was completely depopulated and was not reestablished until 1715. However, the sacramental

the area's other major landholder, Francisco de la Marcha.[65] In the long run, however, the more stable mission-town became a boon to regional security, and created local conditions conducive to the growth of Linares.[66]

In the legal dispute over the boundaries of San Cristóbal and San Felipe and in a will left by Sebastián Villegas Cumplido, we are able to glimpse the set of relationships between the area's Indian and Spanish populations in the period before the Barbadillo reforms. Villegas Cumplido described his lands as a *hacienda* that held Indians as a *congrega*. He believed his hacienda was an important defense against "the enemy of Tamaulipas" and that his oversight of the Indians on his lands facilitated their Christianization and education. In donating part of his lands for the creation of San Felipe, Villegas Cumplido expected the creation of a colonial town and parish. Villegas was connected to the other powerful families of the kingdom: he married into the Cantú family, deeded one of the first plots of San Felipe to the Jáuregui family, and coordinated his military efforts with the region's other major landowners. Villegas was born in Tlaxcala and he seems to have maintained close relations with the Tlaxcalan pueblos of Nuevo Léon. Among the assets in his will was an outstanding debt owed to him by the Tlaxcalans of Carrizal who had borrowed a substantial sum to finance the construction of a church. Sebastián Villegas Cumplido's lifeworks and the provisions made in his testament permit us to understand the social systems of Nuevo León in his time. The human community of Nuevo León was structured by Spanish haciendas and Tlaxcalan pueblos, but Villegas Cumplido was working toward a vision of the province in which Spanish *villas* and urban parishes would be the region's cultural and political centers. Francisco Barbadillo and Sebastián Villegas Cumplido differed only in their notions about the place of the Chichimecs in this northern society. Villegas expected them to remain the charges of Spanish landowners who would structure their economic and religious lives; Barbadillo sought the acculturation of new Chichimec populations in Tlaxcalan-style *pueblos de indios*.

The Chichimecs on Villegas Cumplido's estate were not slaves, nor were they entirely free. Through the logic of the *congrega* system, he was entitled to their labor, but the Indians retained their own leadership and were free to leave his estate periodically on their seasonal rounds. The haciendas of Nuevo León did not rely on African slave labor for agricultural work, and Villegas Cumplido's testament lists only one slave. The appearance of small numbers of African slaves among the assets of the biggest estates suggests that they were prized either for scarce skills or for the status that they conferred upon their owners. Barbadillo's new system would leave no place for the *congregas* or for slavery. To him, the

records published by Gómez Danés show a small Indian population present from 1700–1715, Nevárez Pequeño, 17–21; Gómez Danés, *San Cristóbal Gualaguises*, 43–4.

[65] Charts of data from parish documents provided by Gómez Danés show that Villegas Cumplido and de la Marcha possessed *encomiendas*; Villegas Cumplido appears to have been the area's wealthiest *encomendero*, Gómez Danés, *San Cristóbal Gualaguises*, 28–42.

[66] On the ongoing Indian raids of the 1720s and the military function of Tlaxcalans, see the Barbadillo documents in Zavala, *Entradas, congregas y encomienda*, 125–7.

seventeenth-century charter for the mission and pueblo of San Cristóbal was both legally valid and politically desirable. It could be the basis of a full-fledged Tlaxcalan-Chichimec *pueblo de indios* that would be connected to but not unduly dependent upon neighboring landowners like Villegas Cumplido.[67]

The *junta de guerra* and viceroy, both of which reviewed and approved Barbadillo's plans for San Cristóbal and San Felipe, were increasingly distrustful of Nuevo León's major landowners. At the same time, they took a fairly dim view of the cultural state of the region's Chichimecs. Among dishonest Spaniards and "barbarous" Chichimecs, the Tlaxcalans were often relied upon as honest brokers. A 1715 resolution of the *junta de guerra* explained that the newly restructured *pueblo de indios* at San Cristóbal was to insure that the Chichimecs would no longer live as "lazy vagabonds, from which vices and sins may originate due to their lack of political life and good instruction and Doctrine." The viceroyalty was worried on one hand about the excessive exploitation of Indian labor, and on the other hand that, in the absence of an ordered sedentary life of work, the Chichimecs would be an ongoing threat to the realm. In place of the old hacienda *congregas*, it argued for a more orderly form of wage labor in which "the governors and justices of that kingdom distribute them [the Indians] that they may go to the haciendas and pastures of cattle and sheep for a stipend and daily wage that is justly paid to them ... with the oversight of the missionary and the governor, *alcaldes*, and officials of the *república* of such communities of Indians ... in order that they may learn to cultivate and sow, and care for cattle, make their shelters and houses." This is not entirely unlike the early descriptions of the functions of Spanish-run *congregas*. However, the *junta de guerra* clearly no longer trusted the frontier Spaniards, choosing instead to place the system in the hands of Tlaxcalans. The new town of San Cristóbal was to have at its organizational core "a share of the families from some of the *pueblos de indios* from the jurisdiction of San Luis Potosí, like San Esteban de Tlaxcala in Saltillo."[68]

The revitalization of San Cristóbal can be attributed as much to the planning of its Tlaxcalan residents as to the designs of Barbadillo. Unlike the Valley of Pilón, San Cristóbal had a long-established Tlaxcalan population. Its leaders helped initiate the expanded plans for the pueblo by sending emissaries back to San Esteban and Gran Tlaxcala to request additional settler families.[69] To the local Spaniards, the revitalization of San Cristóbal was an attack on their access

[67] Villegas Cumplido's *testimonio*, 21 Aug. 1713, Linares, AMM Protocolos 10, exp. 1, fol. 57. Barbadillo (and ultimately the Audiencia of Guadalajara and the viceroy) found that Villegas Cumplido's petition for the charter of San Felipe intentionally concealed the legitimate preexisting land claims of San Cristóbal, 15 Feb. 1715, AGI Audiencia de Guadalajara 166, fols. 47–8.

[68] 1714 Report from Viceroy Duke of Linares, on the accomplishments of the Junta General that commissioned Barbadillo, AGI Audiencia de Guadalajara 166, fols. 85–96.

[69] The mission records suggest that a second wave of Tlaxcalan settlement took place between 1715 and 1720 under Barbadillo's direction. Though the pueblo was founded by Tlaxcalans in the sixteenth century, they were not continuously present in its early years. Baptism and marriage records for San Cristóbal Mission between 1700 and 1715 note the ethnic identity of residents;

to land and labor; to the viceregal government, it was the extension of the normal local administration of New Spain to the frontier; to the Tlaxcalans, it was a routine form of colonial development. Tlaxcalans were old hands at the creation of mission-towns, and they were careful to lay the proper groundwork for defending San Cristóbal's legal privileges in the future. As in all previous Tlaxcalan colonies, the Tlaxcalans demanded written agreements that specified the founders' legal prerogatives, property rights, and initial access to vital supplies.

The men who negotiated such deals moved comfortably in both the Spanish and Tlaxcalan environments. Tlaxcala's agreement with Mexico for the development of Hualahuises was negotiated by the university-educated Tlaxcalan cacique Don Manuel Salazar, a man who was at once a *bachiller*, a *cacique*, and a *principal* (a college graduate, lord, and nobleman). The final terms were worked out by Dn. Juan de Molina, a representative of the *cabildo* of Tlaxcala who traveled to the site of San Cristóbal. The charter affirmed that all the privileges transferred from Tlaxcala to San Esteban de Saltillo in 1591 would again be transferred to the Tlaxcalans of San Cristóbal. The settlers would be considered "*pobladores, conquistadores, y pacificadores.*" They would be both entitled and required to bear arms in the service of the community. They would retain their own system of governance and could expect the viceroyalty to provide tools and supplies in the first years of settlement. Though largely autonomous, the Tlaxcalans would be appointed a *protector* to serve as an intermediary to the parallel Spanish *alcaldía mayor*.[70]

Francisco Barbadillo did not create San Cristóbal from scratch. Like San Miguel it was a preexisting Tlaxcalan-Chichimec settlement. Barbadillo used San Cristóbal and San Miguel de Aguayo, along with their common mother colony of San Esteban, as the prototypes for the new *pueblos de indios* of Purificación, Concepción, and Guadalupe. Still, San Cristóbal was a struggling, underpopulated settlement in 1714, and one that was having trouble retaining its Chichimec neophytes. For Barbadillo, the first order of business was to attract and retain a larger population. As part of his diplomacy to the nomadic tribes, Barbadillo sent Fray Juan de Losada to parley with area Chichimecs. Losada traveled with fifty armed men, half of whom were Indian archers, in the search for potential converts. His first attempt yielded an agreement with a group of twenty-two Indians who agreed to settle in San Cristóbal.[71]

---

among them, no Tlaxcalans appear. However, when Governor Pedro de Barrio Junco y Espriella paid an official visit to San Cristóbal in 1754, he reported the existence of four ethnic barrios: Tlaxcalans, Hualahuises, Borrados, and Cabimos (likely the same as "Cadimas") – with Tlaxcalans accounting for 32 of the 223 residents, *Visita general del Nuevo Reino de León por el Gobernador Don Pedro de Barrio Junco y Espriella en 1754* (Monterrey, Mexico: UANL, 1979). In the first century of San Cristóbal's existence, Tlaxcalans were probably a minority population, but one which was introduced, and reintroduced, with specific objectives in mind. From the Barbadillo period, Tlaxcalans remained a permanent element of the local population.

[70] Copy of the1715 agreement, 15 July 1725, AGI Audiencia de Guadalajara 173.

[71] 20 Feb. 1715, AGI Audiencia de Guadalajara 166, fols. 39–42.

Losada's diplomacy was based on well-tested methods. His fifty-man entourage was a great show of force, but he approached wandering Chichimecs with inducements more than threats. Working through translators, and employing the regional token for peaceful intentions – an arrow with its point removed – he offered gifts of tobacco and the promise of further provisions in the mission-town. To Indians who agreed to settle, Losada issued letters attesting to their status as "valiant warriors" that could be presented as letters of passage or signs of status to other Spaniards. In this case, the twenty-two Chichimecs agreed to appear in San Cristóbal in two months' time to begin their new lives as Christian farmers.[72]

Both Barbadillo and the Franciscans were pleased with the success of San Cristóbal in the years that followed. The Tlaxcalans provided a stable core for the mission-town in its first few years, with the number of families varying between twenty and twenty-five (roughly seventy-five to one hundred individuals). The Chichimec population reached around 500, though its numbers were less stable.[73] In 1716 the community requested that an additional twenty families be sent from Mexquitic (the Tlaxcalan sister colony of San Luis Potosí) to permit the recruitment of more Pinto Chichimecs. In the same year, the Tlaxcalan leader Dn. Juan Molina requested the return of thirty settlers from San Cristóbal to Tlaxcala. These communications suggest constant coordination between Gran Tlaxcala and its daughter colonies and may indicate that the deployments of Tlaxcalan garrisons in the north were still to some extent managed from Tlaxcala.[74]

DEFENDING THE PUEBLO SYSTEM

The period between 1722 and 1725 became a showdown between two political networks in Nuevo León: the defenders of the *congrega* system (Governor Arriaga and his hacendado allies) versus the defenders of the *pueblo de indios* system (Barbadillo, the Tlaxcalans, their Chichimec allies, and the frustrated ex-*protector* Nicolás de Villalobos). As long as Arriaga and his allies controlled the governorship and Ayuntamiento of Monterrey, the *pueblos de indios* had no hope for the redress of their grievances through provincial authorities. Instead, the Tlaxcalans used their relationships with Barbadillo and with the leaders of

---

[72] 20 Feb. 1715, AGI Audiencia de Guadalajara 166, fols. 39–45.

[73] Documents from the period give the following data on the population of San Cristóbal: 25 Tlaxcalan families in 1715; 590 Indians of all descriptions in 1716 (or 16–18 Tlaxcalan families according to another source); 20 Tlaxcalan families in 1717; 75 Tlaxcalan individuals in 1725 (or 20 couples, 6 single men, 29 children), 15 Feb. 1715, AGI Audiencia de Guadalajara 166, fol. 47; 15 July 1725 copy of 1715 charter documents, AGI Audiencia de Guadalajara 173, fols. 13–16; Francisco Barbadillo, 23 Mar. 1716, AGI Audiencia de Guadalajara 166; Barbadillo, 24 Apr. 1716, AGI Audiencia de Guadalajara 166.

[74] 1716 AGN Indios 40, fols. 34–7.

Gran Tlaxcala to appeal over the heads of their opponents to the Audiencia of Guadalajara and to the viceroy himself.[75]

Predictably, many Spanish *hacendados* were outraged by the threat to their control over Indian laborers. Barbadillo's reforms threatened not just their pseudo-*encomiendas*, but also Spanish control of the land itself.[76] Early colonial land grants had deeded the most desirable bottom lands to Spanish settlers and Tlaxcalan pueblos. Barbadillo invoked broad powers of eminent domain, conferred upon him by the viceroy, to seize several choice plots of land under Spanish title and award them to new *pueblos de indios*. At the same time, he attempted to transform the New Kingdom's military system by substituting *compañías volantes* – cavalry militias linked to presidio commands – for the existing military system, which had heretofore relied almost entirely on deputizing hacienda owners for specific campaigns. As a visitor in 1715, and as the governor of the New Kingdom of León in 1722 and 1723, Barbadillo's public acts threatened the military autonomy of regional Spanish elites, undermined their claims over Indian labor, and compromised some of their land titles. Meanwhile, his efforts formalized the status of Tlaxcalan-Chichimec pueblo lands and governments. Following Barbadillo's return to Mexico City, regional Spanish elites fought tooth and nail to recover their lost lands and diminished authority.

For those wishing for the return of the old slave-raiding frontier state, the arrival of Governor Juan de Arriaga y Brambila was a prayer answered; to the Indians (both Tlaxcalan and Chichimec), he was a tyrant. Arriaga's one year in office was an orgy of warfare, labor repression, and legally sanctioned slave raiding. His ruthless conduct united Chichimecs, Tlaxcalans, and even a substantial number of Spanish elites in opposition. Complaints against him from indigenous and Spanish opponents led to an official visit of inspection, the accumulation of mountains of damning testimony, and Arriaga's eventual removal from office. Both Barbadillo's visit and the later trial of Arriaga are tremendous assets for historians. These moments of conflict provoked petitions from virtually every sector of Neoleonés society as all parties sought to vindicate their demands by presenting their conflicting versions of recent history.[77] In the end, the alliance between Tlaxcalans, settled Chichimecs, and Franciscans carried the day. The Tlaxcalan-Chichimec mission-town, originating with the Tlaxcalans and Franciscans of the sixteenth century, would be preserved and strengthened by the intervention of Barbadillo. Many regional Spanish elites struggled to overturn the Barbadillo reforms. Not only did these neo-*encomenderos* fail, but the conflict they provoked served to strengthen the

---

[75] The Villalobos materials appear throughout AGI Audiencia de Guadalajara 173; Villalobos's appeal to the crown appears in a Mexico City document of 16 July 1726.

[76] Eugenio del Hoyo was first to term the *congregas* "pseudo-encomienda," *Indios, frailes y encomenderos*, 10–13.

[77] The Arriaga case, which will be treated at length, is documented in AGI Audiencia de Guadalajara 173.

relationship between Tlaxcalans and settled Chichimecs, and to demonstrate the military and legal status of both Indian groups under the system of the *repúblicas de indios*.

A series of petitions drafted by the *cabildos* of Purificación and Concepción in 1725 expressed the essential demands of the Pilón pueblos. The Indian petitions asked for the suppression of Governor Arriaga's military adventurism, for greater material support, and for more teachers and missionaries. Most importantly, they asked for the appointment of a strong *protector* to help mediate contracts and disputes between the Indian pueblos and local *hacendados*. The Tlaxcalan colonists pushed for the continuing recognition of agreements made with the viceroyalty prior to their arrival in Pilón (in 1713), and approved again shortly afterward (in 1718). The colonists had come from San Esteban de Saltillo as free conquistadors of the "military caste" (*calidad militar*) who fought and labored in the service of the king. They touted their lineage and their competence as soldiers and farmers. The *cabildo* of Concepción, and the team that represented it at court, included educated men such as the governor *licenciado* Roldan and their attorney Francisco Díaz Serrano.[78]

In launching their political and legal opposition to the Arriaga faction, the Indian *cabildos* of Pilón reached out to distant allies. They made common cause with Villalobos, who believed their support might help him regain his post as provincial *protector de indios*. By 1725 Villalobos, the pueblos of Pilón, and the *cabildo* of Gran Tlaxcala made a joint offer to the viceroyalty in an attempt to break the back of the Arriaga regime. Arguing that the current governor and leading *hacendados* were the biggest threat to peace and to Indian settlement, they offered new Tlaxcalan colonists for the Valley of Pilón in return for the restoration of a strong protectorate. To bolster their credibility, the Tlaxcalans of Pilón sent distinguished representatives to bear their petitions to the Audiencia of Guadalajara and ultimately to Viceroy Casafuerte in Mexico City. Tlaxcalan leaders Don Antonio de Basilio and Don Ygnacio Martín traveled from Pilón with their attorney from Gran Tlaxcala to appear personally before the *audiencia*. The scribe who recorded their representations described them as "Tlaxcalans of the pueblo de Concepción of the Valley of Pilón in the New Kingdom of León in the company of Bachelor Dn. Manuel de Salazar, graduate of the Royal University and native of the City of Tlaxcala." These emissaries spoke not only on the basis of their personal status but also on the basis of the authority delegated to them from the *vecinos* of Concepción. As a preamble to their testimony, the men averred that they spoke for the "Tlaxcalans and *vecinos* of the Pueblo of Nuestra Señora de la Concepción de Pilón of the new communities of the New Kingdom of León, conquerors, pacifiers and settlers of said *pueblo* and its frontiers in the name of the governor and officials of the common republic, for whom we give voice." They called for the censure of the provincial leaders in Monterrey and the reinstatement of the provincial

---

[78] 15 Aug. 1725, Valle de Pilón, AGI Audiencia de Guadalajara 173, fols. 10–12.

protectorate as a safeguard for the land, water, and civil privileges. Their voices were heard. Though Villalobos himself was not reinstated, the office of *protector* was restored and thereafter remained an important element of Neoleonés administration and law.[79]

Francisco Barbadillo encountered two competing systems of economics and governance in the north: the *encomienda-congrega* system of the Spanish settlers, and the mission-town system of the Tlaxcalans. Historically, Monterrey had been the center of power for the Spanish *encomenderos* of Nuevo León. San Esteban de Saltillo had exported a competing mission-town model through its Tlaxcalan colonists. Unlike Monterrey, Saltillo and its immediate environs had no history of *encomienda*. From the outset, Saltillo and San Esteban were structured as twin communities of Spaniards and Indians, each with the same civic structures as the towns in the Valley of Mexico or Spain.[80] Thus Saltillo and its Tlaxcalan-Chichimec colonies in Nuevo León were in compliance with the New Laws, whereas many Spanish estates in Nuevo León were not.

Barbadillo presented his project of reform in sweeping terms, describing most of his local interventions as "foundations," and trumpeting his abolition of the *congrega* system throughout the New Kingdom of León. Israel Cavazos Garza, who has treated the subject at length, tends to view Barbadillo as an idealist and a skillful administrator. He credits Barbadillo, more than anyone else, with the suppression of the remaining traces of *encomienda*, while noting some of the setbacks faced by his new communities. In this, Cavazos Garza follows the interpretation of Eugenio del Hoyo who sees in Barbadillo both humanitarian sentiment and a jurist's commitment to bringing Neoleonés practice into conformity with preexisting royal law. Silvio Zavala, most attentive to the fate of Indian laborers, describes Barbadillo in tragic terms, both lauding his program and lamenting its collapse following his departure.[81]

The truth is that Barbadillo's system was neither a visionary transformation of northern society nor a tragic failure. It was a conservative project, inasmuch as it reinforced the cultural and military functions of the Tlaxcalan-Chichimec mission-town. Though the unfortunate interlude of the Arriaga administration made the Barbadillo ordinances appear a dead letter, the years that followed proved otherwise. The Tlaxcalan mission-towns had always been central to the settlement and defense of the north, and had always been an important avenue by which outside Indians joined the colonial order. Now, however, Barbadillo regularized this system so that the relations of the towns to their clergymen and

[79] *Pedimento de los indios de el Pilón pidiendo la restituzion de su Protector*, Oct. 1725, AGI Audiencia de Guadalajara 173, fols. 9–10.

[80] "La Visita de Barbadillo" W.B. Stephens Collection no 1.410, U.T. Library published in Zavala, *Entradas*. While Barbadillo observed correctly that there were no grants of *encomienda* for Saltillo, this does not mean that the area was free of labor coercion. War captives were taken as forced labor in military forays from Saltillo. However, the towns themselves were constituted as towns rather than as *encomienda*-based estates.

[81] Del Hoyo, 17; Zavala, 122; Cavazos Garza, *El lic. Francisco Barbadillo Vitoria*.

protectores were uniform. In the previous century, the *protectores* of the Tlaxcalan colonies had generally been respectful liaisons between Indian and Spanish governments, while the *protectores* of the *congrega* Chichimecs remained unreconstructed *encomenderos*. Under the Barbadillo regime, the latter sort of protectorship lost its legal status and was replaced by a system in which Spanish landowners who employed off-pueblo laborers were obliged to report wages to true *protectores de indios*. These *protectors*, like those of the early Tlaxcalan pueblos, were magistrates of neighboring *villas* or *valles*.[82] Arriaga delayed the implementation of the Barbadillo system, but did not prevent it. In the long run, Barbadillo, Nicolás de Villalobos, and a number of Tlaxcalan-Chichimec communities were vindicated by viceregal authorities.

In the late eighteenth century, new Bourbon administrative systems would dovetail with Barbadillo's mission-town system. One of the principal architects of late Bourbon reform in the north was Matías de Gálvez, whose reports to the crown, begun in 1784, advised the administrative integration of the *pueblos de indios* into the intendancy system. Gálvez, rather than presenting his reforms as a bold innovation, was careful to explain his work as a continuation of Barbadillo's. His brief on the history of Nuevo León's Indian communities began with a review of law and custom in the seventeenth century. This review can be summarized as follows: Nuevo León's Indian labor force was originally bound to Spanish landowners through grants of *encomienda*; the royal decree of 1685 forbade *encomienda* and the captivity of Christianized Indians; the decree was widely ignored, and the mistreatment of Indian captive labor led to large-scale rebellion; both the practice of *encomienda* and the consequent rebellion were brought to an end through the work of Francisco Barbadillo and the missionary diplomacy of Juan de Losada; by 1767, this more enlightened policy resulted in the maturation of many missions into towns. For Gálvez and the royal administrators of his generation, the ultimate goal was the complete transformation of Chichimec Indians from bands of nomads and conscripted laborers into colonial citizens who owned land, worked for wages, and paid clerical fees and taxes.[83] The late Bourbon systems for administering Indian communities matched and built upon Barbadillo's system, a system that was itself based on the earlier Tlaxcalan model. As we shall see, this long history was preserved in regional memory, and often reiterated in the writings of Tlaxcalans themselves.

[82] Cavazos Garza, *El lic. Francisco Barbadillo*, 81–4.
[83] Matías de Gálvez, "Misiones del Nuevo Reyno de León, Pertenecientes a la Intendencia de San Luis Potosí," in "Copia de informe general instruido en cumplimiento de rl. Orden de 1784 sobre las misiones del Reyno de Nueva España," AGS Guerra 6966, arts. 237–46. Note that Matías was the brother of José, who is addressed elsewhere in this piece.

3

Becoming Tlaxcalan

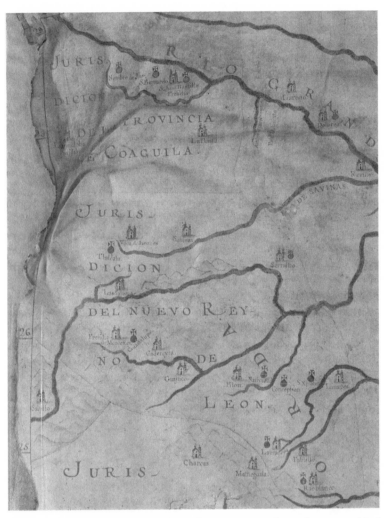

FIGURE 4. A detail from this eighteenth-century map shows the geographical relationship between many of the Tlaxcalan-Chichimec *pueblos de indios* and Spanish communities treated in this chapter. (José de Escandón, "Mapa de la Sierra Gorda y Costa del Seno Mexicano desde la Ciudad de Queretaro c. 1763," New York Public Library Archives)

In June 1782, thirty-seven Indians fled Concepción in the Valley of Pilón.[1] It seems that their leader, Joseph Montes, hoped to take them into the mountains where the rough terrain would foil pursuit. Almost immediately, the loose military system linking the towns, missions, and mines of Nuevo León was called into service, and armed men rode out in pursuit. Such events were common in eighteenth-century Nuevo León. Newly settled Indians fled mission-towns with great regularity, sometimes joining with other hostile tribes to raid settlements and carry off cattle and captives. Wandering armed bands of any kind were cause for alarm, and Montes, who had a troubled history in the colony, could not be ignored.[2]

Nuevo León's governors and *alcaldes mayores* were long accustomed to the challenges of using scarce military resources to protect colonial settlements.[3] Towns and missions were generally protected by few, if any, professional soldiers, while the capital of Monterrey and the royal mines at Boca de Leones, both considered important strategic sites, were guarded by a modest number of regulars.[4] Because most attacks and uprisings were unexpected, and because communications in Nuevo León were slow, local leaders typically responded to the first signs of danger by alerting their peers in nearby towns. Though a formal chain of command theoretically linked all towns to the governor of Nuevo León, and ultimately to the viceroy, most military actions were executed at the local level, and pulled together by cooperating *alcaldes* and mission-town governors.[5] When the Montes outbreak was discovered, the Valley of Pilón first mobilized its own forces, and then turned to officials in neighboring settlements for help. The Indian pueblos of Purificación and Concepción sent their soldiers in pursuit of the fugitives while messengers rushed to Linares and the adjacent mission of San Cristóbal Hualahuises to solicit

---

[1] 28 June 1782 letter of hacienda owner Juan Rosider to *protector* Dávila, AMM 121, exp. 5, fol. 10.

[2] Throughout the correspondence used to construct this narrative of the Concepción outbreak, we find the captive Indians referred to as "piezas," a choice of wording that opens the possibility that Indians in the region were still being taken as slaves. The first Spanish settlers in Nuevo León were slave raiders, and their commerce in captive Indians did not disappear quickly. These early *adelantados* captured Indians, whom they refered to as *piezas*, and sold them to mines and plantations, remitting a portion of the proceeds as tribute to the crown, Frye, "The Native Peoples of Northeastern Mexico," 104–12; Cavazos Garza, *Breve historia de Nuevo León*, 47–51. See also the compilation of documents on slave raids collected in Silvio Zavala, *Entradas*.

[3] The word *gobernador* was put to many uses in the eighteenth century. In this dissertation, I refer both to the "governor" of the province of Nuevo León, who resided in Monterrey and was the supreme military commander for the region, and to the Indian governors of the *pueblos de indios*. The leaders of *pueblos de españoles* are referred to as *alcaldes* or as *protectores*, when acting in their capacity as supervisors of the Indian communities. The *alcaldes* referred in this story are *alcaldes mayores*, the highest local political officers in districts that typically included several towns and missions. They should not be confused with the lesser *alcaldes* who composed local *cabildos*.

[4] Israel Cavazos Garza, *Breve historia de Nuevo León*, 79–81.

[5] On the geography of presidios and the system of commands, see Gerhard, *The North Frontier of New Spain*, 354–67; David Frye notes that, in the early eighteenth century, Monterrey was effectively on the military frontier, "The Native Peoples of Northeastern Mexico," 102.

further aid. The *alcalde* of Pilón sent out a dispatch to the governor of Nuevo León in Monterrey, apprising him of the situation and asking his counsel.[6]

Don Joseph García Antonio Dávila, the *alcalde* of Pilón, soon found himself in an embarrassing predicament. A message arrived from Monterrey ordering that Montes be arrested and deported to Nuevo Santander to stand trial for banditry, but the message arrived too late. Dávila was forced to concede to his superior not only that he had failed to arrest Montes, but also that Montes and his followers were now at large.[7] Antonio Dávila, who had less than a year before assumed his position as *alcalde* of Pilón and *protector* of its missions, was not off to a good start.[8] Like most powerful men in the region, Dávila had several public lives: he was a hacienda owner, the *alcalde* of the Valley of Pilón, and *protector* of the missions of Purificación and Concepción.[9] If all went well for such a man, he could protect the valley from nomads and bandits, resolve disputes between neighbors and neighboring communities, keep the peace in the missions, and still reap a reasonable profit in his role as arbiter of commercial and labor relations between the missions and the Spanish population. His mandate came from the governor; and when things went badly, as they did in 1782, it was to the governor that he must justify his shortcomings.

As Antonio Dávila's fortunes waned, those of his counterpart in Linares waxed. The *alcalde* of Linares, Don Ignacio del Valle, who oversaw mission San Cristóbal, was first alerted to Montes's escape by his subordinate, the *alcalde* of San Cristóbal, Juan Rodríguez.[10] Rodríguez answered the alarm by taking to the field with his soldiers. He soon overtook and captured eighteen stragglers from the fugitive group who had been unable to keep pace with Montes's swifter followers.[11] Thus, to del Valle fell the happy task of reporting his people's military success while Dávila came up empty-handed.

For Dávila the situation went from bad to worse. He had lost control of his valley and been unable to capture the Indians who fled. The troops from Linares bailed him out, but nineteen of the fugitives, including the apparently dangerous

---

[6] AMM Correspondencia vol. 121, exp. 6, fol. 7; vol. 121, exp. 7, fol. 9.

[7] The dates of the correspondence are such that one can easily imagine a second possibility: Dávila may have received the message, avoided taking action against Montes, and merely claimed ignorance. AMM Correspondencia vol. 121, exp. 2, fol. 4.

[8] AMM Correspondencia, vol. 121, exp. 7, fol. 1.

[9] Correspondence to eighteenth-century *protectores* is almost always addressed to a large estate within the same *alcaldía mayor* as the mission-town. Dávila's correspondence is addressed to, and thus indicates his ownership of, Hacienda San Juan de la Cañada.

[10] I use the word *subordinate* with caution. Hualahuises was within the area of military jurisdiction for the *alcalde* of Linares, and we see here Rodriguez acting in his military capacity as inferior officer to Dávila. In some other respects, however, the *cabildo* of Hualahuises appears to have been independent of Linares. Gerhard, *The North Frontier of New Spain*, 221–2, explains that the Tlaxcalans of San Esteban remained under the juridiction of Mexico City even while their Spanish neighbors in Saltillo fell under the juridiction of Guadalajara. The legal relationship between the Tlaxcalans of Nuevo León and the viceroyalty seems less cut and dried. I have encountered many cases appealed to Guadalajara and many others to Mexico City.

[11] AMM Correspondencia, vol. 126, exp. 6, fol. 7.

Montes, were still at large in the mountains. Worse still, the eighteen captives, held by Rodríguez in San Cristóbal, blamed Dávila for their flight and refused to return to Concepción. Ignacio del Valle's 7 July dispatch to the governor of Nuevo León explained the nature of their complaints: the fugitives insisted that they had been mistreated by the other Indians at Concepción, given insufficient provisions, and been forbidden from leaving the mission to forage for their subsistence.[12] They now asked to settle in San Cristóbal where they expected a better life.[13] In the month that followed, the governor of Nuevo León commended del Valle's service to the crown and issued further instructions for the care of missions and for diplomacy with nomadic tribes. The governor also duly noted the resignation of Dávila.[14]

It is striking how few of the particpants in this military and diplomatic drama were ethnic Spaniards. Among those involved in the fighting, we learn of only three: Joseph Antonio García Dávila, governor-*protector* of the Valley of Pilón; Ignacio del Valle, the governor-*protector* of Linares; and Vicente González de Santianes, governor of Nuevo León. Every other participant in the drama was an Indian: the thirty-seven fugitives from the nomadic Piedra and Cadima tribes, the other residents of Concepción who so mistreated them, and the governors of Purificación, Concepción, and Hualahuises. The eighteen fugitives, caught in the foothills, were run down, not by Spaniards, but by San Cristóbal's Indian governor and his four Tlaxcalan *salvaguardias* (town guards). In stories like this one, it becomes clear that the most important cultural question in eighteenth-century Nuevo León was not *whether* a person was an Indian, but rather what kind of Indian he was. The story of the Montes uprising shows the interdependence of Nuevo León's sedentary peoples (Spanish and Indian). It also illustrates the legal hierarchy that defined the relative positions of Chichimecs, Tlaxcalans, and Spaniards. Most importantly, it shows us that some newly converted Indian bands entered the mission system, acquired the traits of Tlaxcalans, and eventually gained the legal and political standing enjoyed by Tlaxcalans.

Nuevo León remained in a state of near-continuous warfare in the late eighteenth century. It was a war between those within the colonial community and those outside of it. Yet it was not, in any simple sense, a war between "the Spaniards" and "the Indians." Many of those fighting on the side of the viceroyalty were Indians; so were those fighting against it. Nor were the sides in this contest fixed. Indians and mestizos moved in and out of colonial settlements, fleeing danger and seeking material comfort. Roving Chichimec bands attacked the property of Spanish and sedentary Indian communities. Settled Chichimecs

---

[12] AMM Correspondencia, vol. 121, exp. 6, fol. 6; AMM Correspondencia 126, vol. 6, fol. 7.

[13] Since the Indians' complaints are only made known through the words of del Valle, we must, of course, reflect upon his motives. It is always possible that del Valle wanted to retain the Indians in order to increase the labor available to San Cristóbal and Linares. However, his previous refusal to permit new settlement in the mission makes this appear unlikely.

[14] AMM Correspondencia, vol. 121, exp. 3, fol. 28.

responded pragmatically, with some reverting to traditional subsistence patterns, some turning to banditry, and others coming to the defense of the colonial
order. Many of these conflicts ended in negotiated settlements that spelled out
the terms of community life for Chichimecs on pueblo lands.

Throughout the seventeenth and eighteenth centuries, Nuevo León's
Tlaxcalan-Chichimec pueblos incorporated new groups of Chichimecs into the
colonial system. Though this process was continuous, it was most clearly articulated and recorded in periods of institutional change. In the eighteenth century,
three moments of change created a clear documentary record of the inner workings of the Tlaxcalan-Chichimec communities: the Barbadillo intervention of the
1710s, the Neoleonés colonization of Nuevo Santander in the 1750s, and the
Bourbon reforms of the 1770s and 1780s.[15] The first two periods (treated in
previous chapters) show that the sixteenth-century Tlaxcalan-Spanish compact
for northern settlement persisted through the following two centuries, helping
New Spain to meet the demands of ongoing frontier warfare and colonization.
Both inside Nuevo León and in its new satellite of Nuevo Santander, Tlaxcalans
served the crown by establishing new settlements that incorporated northern
Chichimecs.

Over time, long-settled Chichimecs attained Tlaxcalan status both as groups
and as individuals, distinguishing themselves from barbarian outsiders and from
more recently settled Chichimec tribes. Now well versed in Tlaxcalan practices,
they employed standard Tlaxcalan legal tactics to defend themselves, their lands,
and their water in criminal and civil proceedings. Whereas Tlaxcalans invariably
touted their pure and separate ancestry in order to retain their sixteenth-century
privileges, settled Chichimecs were more flexible. Mission-town Chichimecs
adapted their political tactics to suit the circumstances. Chichimec communities
sometimes defended their property and status claims by remaining apart from
other indigenous groups. At other times they recruited outside tribes into their
barrios, intermingled, and intermarried.[16]

By the 1770s and 1780s, Nuevo León's colonial populations included three
distinct types of Indian members: Tlaxcalan founders, long-settled Chichimec
bands, and newly arrived or resettled Chichimec bands. The administrative,
military, and legal records of the day permit us to see the terms of settlement
for the new arrivals and the civic standing of those long-settled Chichimecs who
had emulated Tlaxcalan practices and gained Tlaxcalan status. In both cases,
groups that negotiated from a position of military strength were more likely to
gain self-governance, land rights, and civil privileges. The most successful
Chichimec groups took on the characteristics of Tlaxcalans: they became
Spanish-speaking (and sometimes Nahuatl-speaking) Christian citizens who

---

[15] Increased pressure for administrative regularization in these years forced a defensive articulation
of customary political and economic relationships. On the expansion of Bourbon tax systems in
the region, see José Cuello, "The Economic Impact of the Bourbon Reforms."

[16] Even in the pre-colonial period, Tlaxcalans had considerable experience as the dominant ethnic
group in a multiethnic polity, Martínez Baracs, *Un Gobierno de Indios*, 75.

fielded their own military forces, elected their own *cabildo* officers, and received many of the legal privileges accorded to the early Tlaxcalan conquerors.

LAW AND IMPROVISATION

In the 1780s Tlaxcalans controlled five *pueblos de indios* in Nuevo León: San Miguel de Aguayo, Guadalupe, Concepción, Purificación, and San Cristóbal. Guadalupe had emerged as the largest Tlaxcalan population in the region, but the other communities still contained a dynamic mix of Tlaxcalan and Chichimec populations. Colonial administrators recognized these five pueblos as constituting a coherent system that served the region's military needs and served to acculturate Chichimecs as colonial citizens. Tlaxcalans were exempted from most taxation and all civilian labor levies because they supplied military labor and military provisions. Though this form of Tlaxcalan frontier citizenship was established in the sixteenth century, it was reinscribed in the Bourbon military policy of the late eighteenth century. Bourbon administrators recognized and perpetuated the traditional role of the Tlaxcalans, but also extended Tlaxcalan frontier privileges to several groups of settled Chichimecs.

Spanish and Tlaxcalan troops were needed as a defense against nomadic raiders and against the frequent uprisings of new, unstable mission populations. Though the Spanish and Tlaxcalan forces cooperated in times of crisis, they were separate forces under different chains of command. In the midst of one local uprising, Governor Santianes described this parallel system while cautioning Pilón's *alcalde* about the limits of local Spanish authority over Tlaxcalan troops:

> I tell you that the *salvaguardias* are soldiers of a veteran troop and are in no sense subject to the *alcalde mayor y capitan* [illegible] whose jurisdiction is limited to the militiamen in the cases that have been anticipated; the other *salvaguardias* are sufficient in the missions for the security of the Reverend Father missionary and to obey him and be employed by him in his quarter, and [by] the *protector* [.] With respect to the benefice, they are under the governor of the missions and the Indians.[17]

Several implications are clear: the Spanish *alcalde* controlled the Spanish militia of the Valley of Pilón, but the friar of Purificación and Concepción, and the Tlaxcalan governor controlled a separate force. Santianes goes on to explain that the Indian governor should execute his military orders though a local sergeant.[18] Here we see the military cooperation between Tlaxcalans, their missionaries, and their *protectores* described in the same terms as those which governed the sixteenth-century settlements of Saltillo and San Esteban.

Tlaxcalan pueblos, as well as those Chichimec barrios now elevated to Tlaxcalan status, had special military duties and legal privileges. The status of

---

[17] 2 Feb. 1782, AMM Correspondencia, vol. 121, exp. 5, fol. 2.
[18] The same document describes the sergeant as the local functionary charged with economic administration and the review of arms and mounts.

these frontier colonies was made clear in contemporary correspondence on taxation and military service. In December of 1781, Governor Santianes submitted the tax rolls to the viceroy with an elaborate explanation of the difference between the Indian communities that paid tribute and those that were exempt.[19] Governor Santianes noted which Tlaxcalan communities defended the region against hostile Indian nations and were thus relieved of taxation. His report distinguished between three types of settled Indians: Tlaxcalans, acculturated Chichimecs, and "recently converted" Chichimecs. He had five *pueblos de indios* under his purview: Purificación, Concepción, San Cristóbal, San Miguel de Aguayo, and Guadalupe. Three of the five (Purificación, Concepción, and San Cristóbal) contained a mix of Tlaxcalans, newly settled Chichimecs, and established Chichimecs. The remaining two (San Miguel and Guadalupe) lacked *doctrinas* of new converts; they were peopled by Tlaxcalans and by long-settled Chichimecs who had already followed the path to Tlaxcalan citizenship. The obligations of these two communities were entirely military in character, rather than combining those of garrisons and missions. The governor's letter began his explanation as follows:

> Besides the *pueblos de indios* in the provinces named Purificación, Concepción, and San Cristóbal, there are two others that for many years have had no neophytes, only [illegible] Tlaxcalans, one named Guadalupe, one league distant and in the parish of this city [Monterrey], and the other named San Miguel de Aguayo in the Parish of the Royal Mines of Boca de Leones, and two leagues away – both are relieved of tribute.[20]

Having described the distinction between Tlaxcalan-status pueblos and mixed-population *doctrinas* in this report on revenues, Santianes followed up a few months later with a report on schools. Here, again, the governor distinguished between "*pueblos de viva conversión*" and the purely Tlaxcalan-status pueblos. This distinction was both legal and practical. Concepción, Purificación, and San Cristóbal were sites where the conversion of neophytes was still taking place. In the mature Tlaxcalan pueblos of San Miguel and Guadalupe, the Indians were Christian subjects already fully incorporated into the colonial system.[21]

Gonzales de Santianes sketched a general portrait of the Tlaxcalan communities, noting their economic, civic, and military characteristics. He explained that Tlaxcalan colonies were armed and organized for war. They held their land in common, setting aside fields for community revenues that funded the construction and maintenance of churches and the salaries of priests, church personnel, and schoolteachers. In compliance with a set of 1778 administrative reforms, they kept accounts of the community treasury and managed rents and common

---

[19]   All correspondence referred to in this discussion of military service and the tax status of missions is contained in AMM Correspondencia, vol. 121, exp. 1, fol. 3.

[20]   AMM Correspondencia, vol. 121, exp. 1, fol. 3.

[21]   AMM Correspondencia, vol. 121, exp. 1, fol. 7.

holdings to fund schools. They lived alongside those Indians from the region who had converted to Christianity and grown accustomed to a settled life.[22]

In his correspondence on the tax status of San Miguel de Aguayo, Santianes furnished a helpful explanation of how and why a group of Chichimecs came to be classified as Tlaxcalans. The town, he noted, though once a site for new conversions, was currently considered a frontier colony. The Borrado Indians, who settled in the community many years before, now comprised a barrio within the town and provided archers who fought beside the Tlaxcalan cavalry:

> The reason for the aforementioned tax exemption is that tribute is still not established.... [T]here still persist in the two villages and in San Miguel de Aguayo the frontier conditions of territories through which barbarous Indians still enter to carry out hostilities, to the remedy of which it [San Miguel] contributes a small company of horsemen which the aforementioned Tlaxcalans formed there and another of archers from the *antiguos borrados* that still have a separate *barrio*.[23]

In an April 1782 report on the establishment of schools, the governor explained that, of the five missions, "three are *de viva conversión* but the other two have long since ceased to be, and they are called Tlaxcalans because only they and the *antiguos borrados* are found there."[24] It seems that a "Tlaxcalan pueblo" was understood to be either a place entirely inhabited by Tlaxcalans (like Guadalupe), or a mixed community in which long-settled tribes, such as the Borrados, had become like Tlaxcalans – agriculturalists who served as a frontier militia.[25] In other words, for his purposes, the words "Tlaxcalan pueblo" described the community's rights and functions more than its strict ethnic composition.

From this correspondence emerges a general picture of the range of communities that functioned as a part of the Neoleonés mission-town system. San Miguel and Guadalupe were populated by Tlaxcalans and by northern Indian auxiliaries who had gained Tlaxcalan status. Purificación, Concepción, and Hualahuises contained the full spectrum of Indian castes. As sites of *viva conversión*, they included barrios of recently pacified and disarmed Chichimec, which mission clerics and *protectors* viewed as still barbarous and tainted with paganism; but they also included barrios of Tlaxcalans, and of established Chichimecs now armed, acculturated, and aspiring to Tlaxcalan status.

---

[22] AMM Correspondencia, vol. 121, exp. 1, fol. 3.

[23] AMM Correspondencia, vol. 121, exp. 1, fol. 3.

[24] "Tres son de viva conversión y los otros dos aunque hace algunos años que dejan de serlo, y se llaman hoy de tlascaltecos porque solo de estos y de los borrados antiguos hay en ellos." AMM Correspondencia, vol. 121, exp. 1, fol. 7.

[25] Charles Cutter asserts that all colonial frontier people were exempt from taxation regardless of caste. This administrative correspondence suggests otherwise, especially when considered in light of the Tlaxcalan charters' treatment of taxation and military services. It indicates that, at least in Nuevo León, caste was fundamental to the military system and the resulting categories for taxation. See Cutter, *The Legal Culture of New Spain*, 24–8.

The Borrado archers that Governor Santianes exempted from tribute were just the latest in a series of Chichimec groups to attain Tlaxcalan status in San Miguel de Aguayo.[26] The first were the Alasapas, who had formed a relationship with the Tlaxcalans of San Miguel a century before. Though the Alasapas began as refugees and subject laborers, they steadily ascended the colonial hierarchy, finally attaining Tlaxcalan status both as soldiers and as *vecinos* of the autonomous pueblo of San Antonio de Padua, which sat beside San Miguel. A series of eighteenth-century land and water disputes between the Tlaxcalans and Alasapas occasioned a large collection of legal briefs that permit us to reconstruct the story of how the Alasapas transformed themselves from barbarians to the peers of the Tlaxcalans in the eyes of the law. The story begins in the 1680s and culminates in the legal contests of the 1750s.[27]

The history of San Miguel and its twin colony of Alasapas at San Antonio de Padua is bound up with the military and mining history of nearby Boca de Leones. Near the mountain pass known as Boca de Leones was one of Nuevo León's most profitable, dangerous, and dynamic communities in the seventeenth and eighteenth centuries. Within a few leagues of the pass were several mines, five haciendas for the processing of ore, and a number of fertile valleys. It was also the corridor through which the hostile Indians of northern Coahuila could most easily pass in raiding the north of Nuevo León. Tlaxcalans, working as miners, soldiers, and farmers, established the community of San Miguel de Aguayo along the banks of a river they named Tlaxcala in 1686. As they had done in Saltillo, the Tlaxcalan settlers platted out two towns side-by-side: one for themselves, which they called San Miguel, and one for the local Alasapa Indians, which they named San Antonio. At first the Alasapas were subjects and laborers for the Tlaxcalan pueblo, but with the passage of time, San Antonio evolved into a twin of San Miguel. Its Alasapa residents became tax-exempt frontier warriors with land titles, their own elected officials, and Tlaxcalan standing before the courts. In the long run, they would assume the Tlaxcalans' traditional tutelary role with respect to other newly settled tribes.

During the early years of Tlaxcalan and Spanish colonization, the Alasapas lived sometimes as mobile bands in the highlands, sometimes as bonded laborers in mines and haciendas, and sometimes as residents of the *pueblo-misión* of San Antonio. Though both Tlaxcalans and Alasapas later claimed that their joint settlement had existed since 1686, it is clear that the first twenty years of contact were chaotic. The Alasapas first enter the Spanish records as enemies and as captives. Military requisitions from Monterrey in 1698 indicate the Nuevo León was conducting a war against the Alasapas and taking captives. It is likely that the first Alasapas in the colonial settlements of the Sabinas valley were war captives seized as mine laborers. Both Spaniards and Tlaxcalans held

---

[26] The lengthy political dispute that I describe in this section is drawn from AGN Tierras 3044, exp. 7.

[27] This Alasapa community of San Antonio should not be confused with San Antonio de los Llanos (on the southeastern fringe of Nuevo León) or with San Antonio Béjar (in Texas).

mining claims in the area and used local Indians as workers. It seems that the Alasapas were at first bonded laborers on Spanish estates and later released from service and brought into the Tlaxcalan-run pueblo. In 1750, the priest of Boca de Leones, in recounting this early history to the *alcalde mayor*, claimed that

> the Alasapa Indians are natives of this territory where said pueblos [San Miguel and San Antonio] and the Real de Boca de Leones are situated and where they had their origins and settlements since the time of their paganism, and in said time they were congregated by the Governors of this Kingdom with the Spaniards of the Valley of Salinas at which time they communicated with some Tlaxcalans of the Villa de Saltillo in order that by liberating them from their masters they might be brought into their service, and said Tlaxcalans might offer to teach them mining in this Real ... without any population of Spaniards in order that missionaries might come from the College of Querétaro ... placing the Alasapas in a mission.[28]

This explanation suggests that two separate political environments existed side-by-side in the area of Boca de Leones, one Spanish and the other Tlaxcalan. The Alasapas first entered the colonial sphere of the Spaniards as bonded labor on Spanish haciendas, but clearly preferred to move into the alternate colonial system of the Tlaxcalans.

San Antonio at first eked out only the barest subsistence, and its residents were subjected to frequent attacks by nomadic Indians. In the 1790s, the Alasapas abandoned the mission-town to return to their previous way of life. In these years of violence and population displacement, the Alasapas were unable to find a refuge safe from Toboso attacks. They eventually returned to San Antonio and resumed their relationship with Tlaxcalan San Miguel. Other members of the tribe, either refugees or captives, had already ended up laborers on Spanish *congregas*. In 1715, as part of Francisco Barbadillo's reorganization of Neoleonés missions, the remaining Alasapas still bound to Spanish estates were permitted to settle at San Antonio. The Alasapa community thereafter credited both the Tlaxcalans and Francisco Barbadillo with liberating them from servitude.

Initially, the Tlaxcalans controlled the distribution of goods to the Alasapas, but the latter soon attained a higher level of practical and administrative autonomy. Though the property rights granted to Tlaxcalans and Alasapas remained consistent, the political and military relationship between the two groups evolved over time. The Alasapas were gradually rearmed and incorporated into the regional militias beside the Tlaxcalan units. During the same period, the structure of their local government evolved to approximate that of San Miguel. From the beginning, the Alasapas held clearly defined land and water rights with respect to their Tlaxcalan and Spanish neighbors. The *acequia* that ran through the town, and the church at its center, divided Tlaxcalan San Miguel from Alasapa San Antonio. The Alasapas who entered the settlement in

---

[28] AGN Tierras 3044, exp. 7. Note that *real* indicates a royal mine.

the late seventeenth century were represented in negotiations by their headmen, but there are no signs of a *cabildo* that kept written records. In 1715 Francisco Barbadillo mandated that San Antonio and San Miguel each have *cabildo* representation just like the other Tlaxcalan-Chichimec mission-towns. However, later documents indicate that San Antonio's first *cabildo* was short lived, and that the Tlaxcalan governor and *cabildo* of San Miguel soon held authority over both towns.[29] Barbadillo demanded the disarmament of Chichimecs settled in mission-towns, but this proved an untenable arrangement in the invasion-prone area near the pass of Boca de Leones; it soon became clear that all hands were needed to defend the region's colonial settlements. In the 1720s and 1730s, the Alasapas were rearmed and in the process readmitted to colonial political life. San Antonio now had both a militia and a *cabildo*.

In the 1720s, the Alasapa soldiers of San Antonio appear as an important element in the defense of the region's populations and mines. A 1721 proposal for the construction of a new presidio at Boca de Leones provides a description of the area's political geography. Spanish haciendas in the valley of the Sabinas River refined ore from the mines under the jurisdiction of the Real de Boca de Leones, and the "*pueblo* of Tlaxcalans of San Miguel de Aguayo" sat beside the "Pueblo de San Antonio of the nation of Chichimec Alasapa Indians." Joseph Sotomayor protected the Sabinas settlements by commanding a mixed force of "*vecino* soldiers" and "*alasapas amigos*." These armed Alasapa *vecinos* set the pattern for a type of military citizenship among the settled Chichimecs in the area.[30]

In the 1730s, Spanish officials still described the Alasapas of San Antonio as "subject to the *pueblo* of Tlaxcala [San Miguel]," but it is clear that they also enjoyed considerable political autonomy. The Alasapas, though subject to the Tlaxcalan governor, elected an otherwise complete *cabildo* of their own. Meanwhile, the Tlaxcalans of San Miguel elected each year a full *cabildo* including a governor who served for both communities. Alasapas had assumed the Tlaxcalan role as frontier citizen-soldiers and were constituted as a *pueblo de indios* in the Tlaxcalan model. Alasapa archers served the governor of Nuevo León and sometimes came to the aid of the governor of Coahuila. They defended their own homes as well as neighboring mines and Spanish communities. Sometimes there was no clear distinction between their retaliatory expeditions and slave raiding. Mixed Alasapa and Spanish forces attacked Chichimec camps, often killing the men and taking the women and children captive. When the Alasapas were not given their accustomed share of profits for the sale of captives, they made formal complaint.

In 1733 the Alasapas launched a full-fledged legal campaign for formal recognition of their status as peers to the Tlaxcalans. Their efforts were occasioned by a dispute over the spoils of war. Alasapa archers had come to

[29] Documents dated 1733, AGN Tierras, exp. 7, fols. 1–20 and exp. 8, fols. 21–4.
[30] 28 June 1721 and 16 Mar. 1721, AGI Audiencia de Guadalajara 166, fols. 201–3, 211.

the aid of the governor of Coahuila, attacking dangerous nomads and taking many women and children captives.[31] The existing customs for the division booty on the northern frontier dictated that captives might be sold by their captors (through a veiled judicial process), earning a profit for the military expedition after a fifth of their market value was remitted to the crown. The Alasapas claimed that they were entitled to a share of recent profits proportioned on the number of archers they had supplied to the joint expeditionary forces. This was the custom in Spanish-Tlaxcalan expeditions, and the Alasapas felt entitled to the same share. In making their case, the Alasapas and their Spanish patrons (most notably the *procurador de pobres*) articulated the following functions and privileges of San Antonio: it was a self-governing pueblo whose *cabildo* elections were confirmed annually in Monterrey; it possessed a share of local lands and waters equal to that of Tlaxcalan San Miguel; its *vecinos* were frontier soldiers obligated to defend Spanish lands and to spread the faith to the unconverted; and it was a community consequently exempt from other forms of compulsory service. The governor of Nuevo León affirmed these claims, specifying that the Alasapas were obliged to supply soldiers along with arms and provisions, but that they were free from ordinary labor levies. A judge's visit of inspection in 1741 showed that this arrangement held firm. In that year, the Alasapas elected a *cabildo* that continued to manage the internal affairs of San Antonio under the authority of the Tlaxcalan governor and ultimately of the *alcalde mayor* for the Real de Boca de Leones. The signatures on the documents indicate the extent to which literacy had been transmitted from the Tlaxcalan to Alasapa population. The common practice of literate *cabildo* members signing for their nonliterate peers allows us to see that literacy was equally common among the leaders of the two communities.

In 1750, the construction of a new road through the lands of San Miguel de Aguayo provoked a disagreement between the Tlaxcalans and their Alasapa neighbors. Deprived of some land by the construction project, the Tlaxcalans tried to lay claim to a strip of real estate belonging to the Alasapas. Despite a display of typically Tlaxcalan legal maneuvering, the Alasapas held their ground. In their sixty years of contact, the Alasapas had learned the Tlaxcalan game very well. In the end, the Spanish government reaffirmed a power-sharing agreement and a land boundary based on the history of the two communities and consistent with the division of power and resources in the other Tlaxcalan-Chichimec pueblos of the region. The records from the 1750 boundary dispute include a set of legally mandated written exchanges between the Tlaxcalans and Alasapas. Each party put forward both a set of claims and a set of questions to be answered by the other. Nearby Spanish communities were consulted as impartial parties. The aim of the inquiry was to determine the exact terms of the relationship between the Tlaxcalans and the Alasapas, their systems of governance, and the boundary between them.

---

[31] On penal servitude, see documents furnished in Silvio Zavala, *Entradas*.

The recorded testimony demonstrates how thoroughly the two communities shared the same legal culture and legal tactics. The Tlaxcalan strategy was to put forward a set of questions about the characteristics of both pueblos that would emphasize Tlaxcalan priority, cultural superiority, and political authority. The Alasapas, in response, described San Antonio in the same terms that the Tlaxcalans used to describe San Miguel, besting the Tlaxcalans at their own game. The result is a matching civic blueprint. The Alasapa testimony emphasizes the following aspects of San Antonio: the literacy of its leaders, the antiquity of its land claims, the religious orthodoxy of its population, and the military service of its men. This is precisely the way that the Tlaxcalans of San Miguel represented themselves. The only salient difference in the two groups' accounts of their role in the region is to be found in the Tlaxcalans' special claim to priority in the foundation of the town. They considered themselves the founders of San Miguel–San Antonio, even while conceding that the Alasapas had lived beside them since 1686.

The Alasapas of San Antonio, themselves having been drawn into the Tlaxcalan system, in turn recruited other nomadic Indian groups into the colony. In the mid eighteenth century, the Tlaxcalan population of San Miguel continued to expand while the Alasapa population declined. This demographic shift added credibility to Tlaxcalan claims that San Antonio's land and water rights were being underutilized and should be transferred to San Miguel. Tlaxcalan orchards made heavy demands on the water supply, and the owners were anxious to increase their water rations from the shared *acequia*. Rather than conceding that their lands were underutilized, the Alasapas sought to boost their town's population. The Alasapas and their allies among the local clergy sought permission to settle other outside tribes in San Antonio, arguing that more settlement would reduce attacks on nearby mines. The settlements took place, revitalizing San Antonio and strengthening its use-based land claims. Soon the new populations of Guajolotes and Cometunas were clamoring for some of the same privileges and exemptions as the Alasapas. The Tlaxcalans sought to profit from labor drafts levied on the Guajolote and Cometuna populations. By 1755 the two groups brought suit against the Tlaxcalans claiming that the levies were an illegal form of personal service.

In the case of the Alasapa (and later the Guajolotes and Cometunas), Tlaxcalan legal culture proved to be more powerful than the Tlaxcalans themselves. Successive waves of converts settled on pueblo lands, emulating Tlaxcalan governance and imitating Tlaxcalan legal tactics. From a Tlaxcalan perspective, the project of cultural tutelage was, perhaps, too successful. The Chichimec students soon slipped from the grasp of their Tlaxcalan tutors. In 1759 warriors from San Antonio contributed to the foundation of a new colony at Carrizal where, we may surmise, this process of cultural transmission continued among new Indian populations.[32]

---

[32] AGI Audiencia de Guadalajara 327, fol. 36.

HOW CHICHIMEC BANDS NEGOTIATED SETTLEMENT AND CITIZENSHIP

The Montes incident, described at the beginning of this chapter, illustrates the common phenomenon of Chichimec flight and negotiated resettlement – a process that defined and redefined relationships between local Tlaxcalan and Chichimec communities. Spaniards described bands of Indians who withdrew from colonial settlements, in legal and political terms, as either bandits or rebels. Just as would be the case in a European context, both bandits and rebels were subject to criminal law. The penalties for banditry and rebellion (*"sublevación"*) in Nuevo León ranged from execution to penal slavery to ordinary resettlement. Stronger groups of Indian warriors could not be so easily forced under colonial authority. When powerful bands of Indians elected to enter or reenter the colonial community, they did so through negotiated settlements. This was a diplomatic, rather than judicial process, and these Indian leaders retained much of their authority within the colonial pueblos.

Montes and his Cadima followers appeared in Nuevo León in the early 1780s, first as *"indios bárbaros,"* then as *"arrimados"* of San Cristóbal (literally, those leaning against or sheltered by the pueblo), and finally as members of the Pilón communities.[33] Montes first entered the colonial sphere when he and his Cadima people moved into Nuevo León and established a relationship with San Cristóbal. Yet, they were never fully incorporated into the mission-town, and in the first weeks of 1782 they relocated to the Valley of Pilón. At Concepción mission, they settled in a new barrio where the missionary and Indian *cabildo* expected them to conform to mission life. In July, dissatisfied with their treatment at Concepción (or perhaps attracted to seasonal opportunities for forage), the Cadimas, along with a group of Piedras that had joined them, fled to the hill country to return to hunting, gathering, and poaching. Tlaxcalan soldiers from San Cristóbal captured half of the fugitives; the others eventually returned on their own. The captives requested a resumption of their earlier relationship with San Cristóbal Mission, but the governments of San Cristóbal and Linares, in consultation with the governor of Nuevo León, refused their request, returning them instead to Concepción in the Valley of Pilón. Correspondence between the mission's *protectores* and the provincial governor, both before and after the outbreak, provides us a remarkably detailed portrait of the terms of settlement and of the relationship between Tlaxcalans, *nueva conversión* Chichimecs, and *antiguos* Chichimecs.

Revisiting each step in the negotiations between Montes and the colonial authorities, it is easy to see that both parties were constrained by the limits of their power and resources. The Cadimas entered Nuevo León from Nuevo Santander, settling first in San Cristóbal, and then relocating to the Valley of Pilón where, by April of 1782, they were resettled according to Governor

---

[33] José Antonio García Dávila to Governor of Nuevo León, AMM Correspondencia 121, exp. 7, fol. 4.

Santianes's mission-town program.[34] From the perspective of García Dávila, the *protector* of Pilón, the Piedras and Cadimas warranted special concern. They were brought to Pilón under armed escort and handled with caution upon arrival. Two facts suggest that the new barrios established for these groups retained a strong identity as separate communities: first, their physical segregation from the existing population, and second, their collective negotiations over arms and provisions. García Dávila considered them an unconverted population, noting to the governor that he "assigned them a *barrio* separate from all those of the Christians."[35] Dávila exercised two kinds of power over newly arrived Indians: military threats, and material inducements, but at the moment, he did not have enough of either. Though the governor's plan called for the immediate disarmament of all newly settled Indians, García Dávila complained on 9 March that he was too sick to confiscate newly arrived Indians' arms.[36] His next letter reported that "as soon as the rations for the Piedras had been received, and the arms collected, the separate *barrios* were assigned."[37] It is not hard to read between the lines: the Indians turned in their weapons in exchange for food, and were granted thirty-by-forty-yard plots on which to build their *jacales*.[38] The two letters on the seizure of arms suggest the relative weakness of García Dávila's position. The disarmament of the Indians and the distribution of rations were not unrelated policies, but rather a clear quid pro quo: food for peace.

Despite well-laid plans, life in Nuevo León was far from pacific in the spring of 1782. On 6 April, García Dávila wrote to the viceroy describing the chronic problems of the area: the new Indians' refusal to submit to authority, their attrition from the mission-towns, and the constant robbery of livestock by Indian bandits.[39] Neither the missions nor the haciendas were closed systems. The livestock of missions and haciendas could not be secure as long as Indian populations remained outside of colonial system or subsisted on its margins. No one should have been altogether surprised in July when Montes and his Cadima and Piedra followers walked out of Concepción.

The Montes incident was a typical event in the region: a group of Indians attempted to leave the mission-town, and a body of armed men sought to return them to it. Though the Montes outbreak *was not* merely a conflict between Spaniards on one side and Indians on the other, it *was* a conflict between the

---

[34] Governor of Nuevo León to viceroy, 6 Apr. 1782, AMM Correspondencia vol. 121, exp. 1, fol. 7.

[35] "Les asign. barrio separado de todos los delos ya cristianos," García Dávila to gov. NL, 10 Mar. 1792, AMM Correspondencia 121, exp. 7, fol. 7.

[36] García Dávila to gov. NL, 9 Mar. 1782, AMM Correspondencia 121, exp. 7, fol 5.

[37] "Quanto la ración de los Piedras que la teníamos recibidos, les recolidas Armas les asign. barrio separado." Correspondencia 121, exp. 7, fol. 7.

[38] The unit of measurement was the *vara* (33 1/3 inches), which is not quite the length of an English yard; the lots were thus closer to 28-by-37. "Les medí Solares a todos los de familia dandoles a cada uno treinta V. de frente y quarenta de fondo para que baian fabricando sus jacales." AMM Correspondencia, vol. 121, exp. 7, fol. 7.

[39] García Dávila to Governor of Nuevo León, 8 Apr. 1782, AMM Correspondencia, vol. 121, exp. 7, fol. 10.

colonial order and those who transgressed its rules. The colonial forces were composed of Tlaxcalans, acculturated Chichimecs, and Spaniards; Montes's group was a marriage of convenience between Chichimecs of two distinct nations drawn together to combine their strength in the face of colonial power. It is possible that these Piedras and Cadimas who followed Montes shared no common history prior to their arrival in the Nuevo León mission-towns. From the perspective of the Spanish *protectores* of Linares and Pilón, the Cadimas and Piedras were two different tribes under different leadership.[40] The governor and *protector* considered both to be uncivilized and unconverted; beyond this, little is certain. However, once living in the new barrios of Concepción, the two tribes' shared interests bound them together and led to their joint flight. Likewise, the colonial force that opposed them was drawn from several ethnic communities who had a shared interest in the preservation of the mission-towns.

The men who pursued the Concepción fugitives were ethnically heterogeneous. However, beyond their differences in ethnicity, they had much in common as defenders of the mission-towns. It was a force made up of Spaniards, Tlaxcalans, and settled Chichimecs who had become like Tlaxcalans. It was the Indian governor of Concepción, accompanied by his Tlaxcalan *salvaguardia*, Encarnación Forres, who rode out from Pilón to solicit aid from San Cristóbal Hualahuises. Upon reaching San Cristóbal, they sought the assistance of its two Indian governors, Simón de Taso, leader of the *nueva conversión* Indians, and Juan Rodríguez, governor of the Tlaxcalans, along with militiamen of both communities. Simón de Taso had fallen ill, but a replacement was found, and the others rallied to the cause. Dávila described the group as consisting of "the soldier Encarnación, the governor of the Indians of Concepción, the governor of Hualahuises and others *de razón* from San Cristóbal with the leader Cabazos."[41] Four other Tlaxcalan soldiers are mentioned in del Valle's account.[42] This force was composed of the old Tlaxcalan militias from two mission-towns augmented by the Chichimec commander Cabazos and his followers from the established Chichimec barrios of San Cristóbal. The entire force was responsible to the governor of Nuevo León through the captain-protectors of Linares and Pilón. Their objective was to restore the fugitive tribes to a sedentary life under the spiritual supervision of the *doctrina* of Concepción. This was not so much a war as a policing action by the armed members of the mission-town establishment against unassimilated (or we might say semi-assimilated) northern tribes.

[40] Montes is frequently identified as the leader of Cadimas and sometimes of both tribes. I have not seen a separate leader of the Piedras clearly identified, though it is possible that Antonio Cortinas, who appears in later documents as an alleged instigator of the revolt, was their leader. AMM Correspondencia, vol. 121 exp. 3, fol. 17.

[41] Dávila to Governor of NL, 6 July 1782, Correspondencia, vol. 121, exp. 7, fol. 9.

[42] "El soldado Encarnación el Governador de los Yndios de Concepción el de los Gualaguses y otros de razón de San Christoval con el Cabo Cabazos." AMM Correspondencia, vol. 121, exp. 6, fol. 6.

Montes's followers separated into two bodies. The slower-moving group of fugitives was soon captured and returned to Concepción where investigations into the origins of the flight centered on a presumed instigator named Antonio Cortinas.[43] The mission-town soldiers never caught up with the swifter group, headed by Montes. Only in August did Montes and the remaining Cadimas return to Concepción of their own accord.[44] By the end of the summer, the threat of rebellion was contained and the mission-town reconstituted.

Since Barbadillo's time, advocates of the mission-town system had argued that the pacification of the region could be carried out only by combining military force with diplomatic efforts to attract Chichimecs with generous terms of peace. Neoleonés officials were acutely aware of the fact that they lacked the resources to confine groups like Montes's to the mission-towns by force alone. In these years, the conditions on the ground in Nuevo León argued for the same type of pragmatic compromises currently promoted by Bourbon military officials. Concepción's Franciscan friar, Tomás Correa, proclaimed the innocence of Antonio Cortinas and defended the returned fugitives in legal proceedings before the governor. He argued that peace would be best maintained through the same combination of vigilance and *"medios suaves"* now endorsed by the viceroy. Correa urged a mix of clemency and force both for both moral and pragmatic reasons. He conceded that soldiers were "indispensable for the stability, peace, and governance of the new converts" in order to "contain their disorders that they may not so easily execute similar flights." At the same time, he warned that the soldiers should not be used for the "punishment or terror" of the Chichimecs who were so long accustomed to life in "disordered liberty."[45] He used a different standard to judge the moral culpability of those not yet acculturated and Christianized than for those fully integrated into the pueblo system.

Though flight and resettlement continued throughout the colonial period, the methods of diplomacy and pacification endorsed by Correa seem to have gradually achieved their goals. How much the fugitives' return is attributable to military action, how much to the *"medios suaves"* of offering food and safety in the mission community, and how much to the normal seasonal rounds of the tribes is unclear. What is clear, however, is that all fully integrated communities within the colonial system rushed to its defense: the Spanish magistrates and clerics, the Tlaxcalan governors and soldiers, and the rising caste of armed and acculturated mission-town Chichimecs.

Montes's people were only one of several Indian groups from Nuevo Santander and Coahuila moving restlessly between mission-towns of Nuevo León in the early 1780s. Among these were the Chivatos, a Chichimec nation that took up temporary residence in several missions before settling ultimately in the Valley of Pilón. Like the Cadimas and Piedras, the Chivatos entered into

---

[43] AMM Correspondencia, vol. 121, exp. 7, fol. 9.
[44] Governor of Nuevo León to viceroy, 3 Aug. 1782, AMM Correspondencia, 121, exp. 1, fol. 11.
[45] Correa to Governor of Nuevo León, 12 June 1782, AMM Correspondencia, vol. 121, exp. 3, fol. 17.

repeated negotiations with mission-town leaders to shape the terms of their incorporation into Indian barrios. Governor Santianes made every effort to reconstitute these wandering bands as settled communities based on the existing Tlaxcalan model. In this he followed the design of the Tlaxcalan-Chichimec colonies of 1591 and Francisco Barbadillo's 1715 mission-towns.

The governor's correspondence with Mexico City officials outlined his methods and the practical difficulties they confronted. Even before the Montes incident, Santianes composed a series of reports on the difficulties of settling Indians from Nuevo Santander in the three *nueva conversión* communities under his supervision (Purificación, Concepción, and San Cristóbal). He assured the viceroy that he was using "gentle methods" to avert the flight of his new charges and ensure their incorporation into civil society.[46] The governor's optimism would soon be challenged by the flight of the Cadimas, the Piedras, and the Chivatos, all in the space of a few months. However, after several bouts of flight and renegotiation, the wisdom of the governor's policy was ultimately vindicated. Within a few years, this wave of Indians would be absorbed into the colonial community.

Spaniards and Tlaxcalans described Chichimec nations as composed of *rancherías* – groups of several dozen families. Spanish officialdom often described nomadic groups as *rancherías fugitivas* and considered them a major threat to regional peace. When Chichimecs entered the mission-town system, they retained their own clan structure, and the *rancherías* became geographically delimited barrios. At the beginning of 1782, many nomadic Chichimecs settled in new barrios in Purificación, Concepción, and San Cristóbal. However four *rancherías fugitivas* from the Chivato nation remained at large. These Chivatos began settling in the mission-towns when Peono Chivau (elsewhere "Capitán Chivato") agreed to bring his people to San Cristóbal. Peono Chivau soon impressed local Spaniards who spoke in praise of "the Indian Peono Chibau who was the first of those who settled themselves with the other four from his family or *ranchería* and has thus remained until the present a subject with faithful attention to the work and teachings of the community."[47]

The members of the first Chivato *ranchería* to settle seemed the sort of Indians most welcome in the mission. Colonial officials praised them for their Christian observances and their productivity. However, when more Chivatos arrived, the picture began to change. The other three *rancherías fugitivas*, encouraged by the good fortune of their settled counterparts, petitioned to the governor of Nuevo León to join San Cristóbal, but both the governor and the local *protector* had serious misgivings. They believed that San Cristóbal already had too many Indians and too little water. As the governor explained to the viceroy, more settlement of *nueva conversión* Indians would lead to predictable and dangerous consequences: with insufficient rations and crops, the missionaries would be

---

[46] "Cuidarse de la seguridad de los Indios refugiados a esta Provincia como fugitivos [illegible] de Nuevo Santander que procurarse por media suabe evitan su fuga."

[47] Note that captains as eponymous leaders of Indian nations are common in colonial records, AMM Correspondencia, vol. 121, exp. 1, vol. 5, fol. 44.

forced to permit the Indians to forage in the hills. This would put them in contact with unsettled Indians who might lure them away from the customs of colonial life. Santianes noted that Indians had routinely "joined up with vagrants from the settlements to celebrate pagan rites" and that they had then assaulted and robbed travelers.[48] Stories of Indians who, like Montes, slipped out of the mission system and returned to hunting (or poaching) and gathering were very common.[49]

Fearing that scarcity would lead to rebellion among the Chivatos, Piedras, and Cadimas, mission and military leaders undertook a general relocation of these tribes. The Spanish leaders of Nuevo León reached what they believed would be a practical, permanent solution for the settlement of the four Chivato *rancherías* that were overtaxing the resources of San Cristóbal. The Indians would be taken to the Valley of Pilón where the *medios suaves* of food distribution, and supervision by *salvaguardias*, would keep them in the communities of Purificación and Concepción until they learned to work the land. Governor Santianes's instructions to the *alcalde* of Pilón were lengthy and detailed – almost a blueprint for the construction of *nueva conversión* communities. The governor instructed the *alcalde* and mission friar to select the site for a new barrio and to immediately settle the Chivatos there. The Pilón missions were already home to a composite population of Tlaxcalans and northern Indians in accordance with Barbadillo's settlement plan from the beginning of the century. New *rancherías* of Indians had been settled in the Pilón mission-towns, one barrio at a time, since at least 1715.[50] The Santianes plan for settlement involved the following stages: mission guards were to disarm the Indians; then the *protector* and friar would issue them individual sites (*solares*) for the construction of their shelters (*jacales*); and finally, the *protector* would distribute farming tools and *metates* (mortars and pestles) for grinding corn, along with food rations to help sustain them in the first year.[51]

The Chichimec newcomers were first to be neutralized as a military threat, then instructed in Tlaxcalan subsistence practices and incorporated into the *doctrina*. Santianes devoted much thought to the recurrent problems in Neoleonés missions: scarcity, rebellion, flight, and banditry. A letter on these matters addressed to García Dávila was full of stern admonitions. He emphasized that the supply of food was an important inducement to the Indians to

---

[48] "Se ha seguido juntan se con los vagos de la colonia a celebrar mitotes gentiles, roban quanto encuentran y aun a saltar los caminantes y quando menos volven a la misión destruidos," AMM Correspondencia, vol. 121, exp. 1, fol. 5, no. 44.

[49] AMM Correspondencia, vol. 121, exp. 1, fol. 5, no. 44.

[50] Israel Cavazos Garza maintains that all Tlaxcalans in Nuevo León were resettled in Guadalupe in 1756 in accordance with a plan proposed by the bishop of Monterrey. If such resettlement took place, the former Tlaxcalan mission-towns must have been soon reconstituted by reverse migration or by additional Tlaxcalan settlement from San Esteban, since Tlaxcalans are visible in a variety of documents for the towns in question from the 1770s to the early 1900s. Cavazos Garza, *Ciudad Guadalupe*, 90–1; Cavazos Garza, *Breve historia de Nuevo León*, 37–40.

[51] AMM Correspondencia, vol. 121, exp. 5, fol. 2.

remain at the missions. Too scarce a supply of food could drive them away, but real abundance also might undermine the Indians' dependence on the colonial system. The governor counseled a middle path: "In the collection of corn, the customary theft must be avoided, and in the distribution of rations there must be an order that avoids teaching any bad habits.... [D]istribute the rations daily because he who does not eat is not able to work and is on the verge of pursuing robbery or deserting." Yet there seemed to be some question about whether the food supply would hold out during the first year. Consequently, Santianes alludes to two alternative sources to supplement the Indians' meager subsistence: hunting and loans of food and seed secured against the first harvest from farmers who rented nearby mission lands. The governor was aware that both hunting and commerce with the Spanish population, though necessary, involved risks to the tranquility and integrity of the mission. He also worried that the lure of wages from Spanish planters would prevent the Indians from developing their own lands. Hunting was even more problematic because it required weapons: "if it is necessary to give a few [Indians] permission to hunt deer, they [arms] may be given to them as long as all are collected again when they return; outside of this case, under no circumstances should they have them, especially in their dances, games, and drinking binges." Clearly, a fear of armed rebellion was ever present in the minds of Spanish leaders, but it was the Tlaxcalans and the *antiguos* Chichimecs who were to enforce this regime. Dávila was told that the weapons of the incoming neophytes should be collected by "the other Indians" of the pueblo. At the same time, the pueblo rapidly conferred systems of self-governance upon the newly settled Indians. Santianes expected an Indian fiscal, selected (or perhaps elected) from among their ranks, to serve as the primary policeman of public conduct in the community. The gravest of offenses were to be referred from the fiscal to Santianes. The first elements of colonial civic life were planted in the planned community from the outset.[52]

Yet, despite this careful planning on the part of mission-town and provincial leaders, Pedro Chivato and members of his *ranchería* fled Concepción in the summer of 1782, as did Montes's Cadimas and Piedras. The danger of Indian flight from Nuevo León's missions even became a matter of concern to Martín de Mayorga, the viceroy of New Spain. On 16 July he wrote to Governor Santianes, urging him to avoid harsh treatment of the *nueva conversión* Indians that might spark conflict. The viceroy noted that the three Chivato clans that had fled the missions did so when provoked by rough treatment at the hands of a *salvaguardia*. The viceroy hoped to avoid any repetition of this sort of provocation. He urged the governor to treat gently the four *rancherías* from Nuevo Santander that had been transferred from San Cristóbal to the Valley of Pilón.[53] Colonial officials believed these tribes could be brought back into the fold. Yet, as always,

[52] AMM Correspondencia, vol. 121, exp. 5, fol. 2.
[53] AMM Correspondencia, vol. 121, exp. 2, fol. 4. There is some ambiguity in these documents; at some points there appear to be three *rancherias*, and at other times four.

each new settlement entailed negotiations over barrio sites, land and water, and the terms of citizenship.

In the early phases of settlement, Chichimecs took little on trust. When the conditions did not meet their expectations, they left the colonial environment, returning only when faced with worse conditions elsewhere. Meanwhile, within the colonial community, the rules of diplomacy and settlement were being standardized as colonial leaders sought to minimize unnecessary warfare. Nuevo León was learning that the carrot was cheaper than the stick; for prudent administrators, second chances were the rule rather than the exception. A punitive military strategy or harsh terms of settlement would only lead to heightened regional conflict. Instead, the *pueblos de indios* offered a sort of conditional citizenship. They granted newly pacified tribes limited instruments of self-governance; and those that remained within the colony could expect property rights, political representation, and incorporation into the military system of the north.

ETHNIC STATUS AND IDENTITY WITHIN THE COLONIAL COMMUNITY

The social and political hierarchy of Indian communities was determined, in part, through warfare against the nomads and the terms of settlement that followed. Much was also determined by the evolving political relationships between the Indian barrios that constituted each mission-town. The earliest Tlaxcalan colonies were created by pacts between the Tlaxcalan and local Chichimec groups; by the eighteenth century these binary settlements had become more complex. The Chichimec pueblos grew by adding distinct barrios drawn from other tribes and even by intermingling and intermarrying with the newcomers. Tlaxcalans had a stronger motive to remain distinct from other groups, and they routinely recruited additional families from distant Tlaxcalan towns to bolster their numbers. If Tlaxcalans did, indeed, intermarry with other Indians or invite them to settle on their pueblo lands, they did so as personal acts, not as a matter of public policy. The Tlaxcalan attitude was logical. Tlaxcalan communities held centuries-old charters, and many elite Tlaxcalan families held titles of nobility granted in the sixteenth century. To maintain a community apart from other Indians was to maintain their special status.

Settled Chichimecs tribes took a variety of approaches to other groups. Generally pragmatic in their negotiations with Spaniards, Tlaxcalans, and other Chichimecs, they sought alliances apt to advance their status and protect their assets. Thriving Chichimec barrios often sided with Tlaxcalans against outsiders or against less acculturated barrios in order to advance their own standing in the colonial hierarchy. But when faced with dwindling populations, or when their resources were threatened by Spaniards or Tlaxcalans, they were quick to build alliances with other Chichimec nations. The members of new and old Chichimec barrios frequently intermarried and often cooperated to recruit new settlers into the mission-towns, or to launch legal suits in defense of common interests. Powerful Chichimec barrios invoked the purity of their bloodlines only when there was something to be gained by it. Advancing toward the political status of the Tlaxcalans was not a matter of heredity. Chichimecs became Tlaxcalan by acquiring Tlaxcalan civic traits and by rendering themselves indispensable to the local economy and military.

The neighboring communities of San Cristóbal de los Hualahuises and Linares contained the full spectrum of citizenship. One finds the same terminology used to describe these types of citizens whether consulting diocesan, military, or legal records and regardless of the identity of the speaker. The relationships between these groups formed a rough hierarchy: Spaniards and Tlaxcalans at the top, long-settled Chichimecs beneath them, and newly settled Chichimecs in the most humble position. Linares was a town of Spanish *vecinos*, but Hualahuises was a *pueblo de indios*, and only its Indian residents could possess *vecindad*. Indians defined their privileges in reference to other groups: Tlaxcalans asserted their status relative to Chichimecs; established Chichimecs barrios asserted their higher status relative to newer barrios; and new barrios differentiated themselves from the barbarians beyond the fringe of colonial life. A 1763 census notes that the colony was established by "Gualaguises' Indian founders . . . that today distinguish themselves from those of the new *conversión* as *gente de razón* though their origin is from the *nueva conversión*."[54]

The characterization of the Hualahuises' attitude toward new arrivals presented in the census is confirmed in their own petitions. In 1784 a rift developed between the old and new populations of Hualahuises. The Jasos tribe, which had recently settled in the community, occupied the lowest political stratum. The Jasos' frequent wanderings and suspected banditry and paganism provided an opportunity for more established groups to demonstrate their loyalty and status in contrast to the Jasos. Between May and November of 1784, the friar of the Hualahuises *doctrina* transmitted to the governor of Nuevo León a series of petitions for official intervention against the Jasos. Speaking as a block, the Tlaxcalans, Hualahuises, and *antiguos* Borrados all requested that more soldiers and missionaries be sent to confront the problem population of Jasos whom they described as dangerous apostates.[55]

Each external threat to the mission offered the faithful Indians an opportunity to confirm their membership in the community. Each new settlement of a nomadic *ranchería* lifted the established groups one step higher in the local hierarchy. From a Spanish perspective, the true outsiders were of two types: barbarians who remained untouched by Christianity and civilization, and *ladino* rebels who had once entered colonial society but then renounced it. Among the criminal and military cases of the 1780s, we find both types in Hualahuises. In 1787 the mission-town authorities described the local rebel Cavezón as "without reason." Cavezón and the ten families that followed him had been residents of the

[54] 10 Dec. 1783, AGN Provincias Internas, vol. 135, exp. 6, fols. 326–50.

[55] 30 May 1784, AMM Correspondencia, vol. 123, exp. 19, fol. 15; 29 Nov. 1784 AMM Correspondencia, vol. 123, exp. 19, fol. 37.

pueblos, but reportedly failed to attend *doctrina* and failed to contribute labor to the community's farms.[56] Cavezón's people were not fully integrated into the pueblo, and more established Indian groups continued to regard them as barbarians. The Borrados, who were ascending the colonial hierarchy, emphasized their own status by joining with the Tlaxcalan and Spanish colonial establishment and closing ranks against the outsiders.

The mid eighteenth century in the Valley of Pilón was a time of near equilibrium in the power wielded by Tlaxcalans, Spaniards, established Chichimec communities, and hostile outsiders. Defending the colonial community required careful negotiations between all parties, and even between the colonial establishment and menacing outsiders. The legal arrangements between sedentary peoples recognized this balance of power. In 1756 the Guajolotes of Concepción petitioned the governor of the New Kingdom of León asking that some land and water rights be transferred to them from their Tlaxcalan neighbors.[57] In justifying their request, the Indians presented the history of their military service and of their incorporation into the New Kingdom of León. The Guajolotes were once nomads of the Sierra Madre. Their leader, Santiago, allied the tribe to the Spanish, receiving the title of *capitán* from Governor Pedro de Barrio. Later, Santiago and de Barrio agreed that the Guajolotes should join with the Cometunas and settle on lands belonging to the Tlaxcalans of Concepción. They began to take up agriculture under the tutelage of the Tlaxcalans, and to learn Christian doctrine from a Franciscan missionary. Don Antonio Ladrón y Guevara was appointed their *protector*.

The Guajolotes became true citizens of the Tlaxcalan type: educated Christian, citizen-soldiers who understood their new civic standing. Yet, with the passage of time, the Guajolotes came to believe that their Tlaxcalan mentors had deprived them of their fair share of the mission-town's land and water. The Tlaxcalans denied the charge, but the Guajolotes were not easily brushed off. By this point, the Guajolote barrio had become indispensable to the larger community. It boasted a substantial population and a captain at the command of thirty-six soldiers. In case this was lost on their neighbors, the Guajolotes, like most Tlaxcalan communities, now retained paid legal counsel. In these years, the *protectors* of the valley were often arbiters between Indian communities, but this dispute rose to a higher level. In true Tlaxcalan style, the Guajolotes began to press their case before a series of Spanish magistrates. Thus it was that in 1756 the Guajolotes, employing the services of their attorney, Manuel Caro y Carillo, began to negotiate for a reapportionment of the land and water rights that had once been dictated by the Tlaxcalans.

---

[56] 1791 AGN Provincias Internas, vol. 135, exp. 6, fols. 326–50.

[57] All material on this dispute comes from the 1775 legal filings in AMM Civil, vol. 108, exp. 1. Other legal cases demonstrate the extent to which Indian communities distinguished themselves from the Spanish population in order to retain exclusive control of Indian pueblo resources. In a 1781 case, the entire mission-town of Purificación brought suit against a soldier, Gregorio Antonio Silva, for infringing on their common water rights when he began drawing water from Purificación's *acequia*, AMM Civil, vol. 118, exp. 12.

The mission-towns, composed of Tlaxcalans and successive waves of Chichimec nations, were places of cultural exchange and synthesis; yet distinct ethnic communities persisted within them. In 1775, a dispute in Purificación over a new Indian governor's eligibility for office holding reveals many of the political subcommunities within the mission-town. The plaintiffs in the case described themselves as *mecos* (Chichimecs) from the Hacienda de los Pelones within the mission of Purificación, in the Valley of Pilón. Represented by their attorney, Mariano Pérez de Tagle, this group of leading citizens complained that the normal rules for selecting their governor had been ignored – and with disastrous consequences. They asserted that their barrio was populated by an unmixed nation of Pelones who had never intermarried with Tlaxcalans or with other outsiders. A self-governing community, they had always selected their governor by lot from among the descendants of their founding *indio principal*, Eugenio de la Garza. The current governor, who goes unnamed in the documents, was reportedly an outsider and a *coyote* – that is, a person of mixed mestizo and Indian parentage – who gained office by ingratiating himself with the ruling family. They presumably permitted him, amongst the legitimate members of the family, to draw a lot for the governorship. The plaintiffs charged that the *coyote* interloper, unfamiliar with the customs of the nation, had done great harm to the community. The complaint asked that the viceroyalty intervene, both to expel the rogue governor and to affirm the principle that their community was an internally governed ethnic franchise: "in the pueblos and reductions of Indians, one should not be permitted to mix with other nations or castes ... nor is it fitting that those of other nations be governors or officials of the republics because of the distinct customs that each has." They claimed that their lands, water rights, cattle, and governance had always been separate from those of the other peoples who inhabited Purificación. The Pelones insisted that their claims were consistent with the customs of their nation, the traditions of the valley, and with the *Recopilacíon de Leyes de los Reynos de las Indias*. Ultimately, however, they resorted to the argument that had historically carried the most weight in Nuevo León: that the viceroyalty must ensure proper governance to the Indians "in order that they not desert their pueblos and *reducciones*."

Chichimec communities fought for legal recognition of their property rights and autonomy on the basis of law, merit, and utility. They borrowed their tactics from the Tlaxcalans and often insisted that their barrios were equivalent to Tlaxcalan communities. Sometimes they, like the Tlaxcalans, sought an exclusive ethnic identity to bolster their claims; at other times they did not. Whereas the Tlaxcalans and Pelones defended their hereditary privileges by insisting on endogamy, the Guajolotes advanced their interests by merging with the Cometuna tribe. Clearly, the constituent ethnic bodies of Purificación were prepared to enter into legal conflicts autonomously, in partnerships with other groups, or in common cause with all members of the mission-town, depending on where their interests lay. These barrios were claiming Tlaxcalan legal standing, but without in any sense seeking a Tlaxcalan ethnic identity.

INDIVIDUAL CITIZENSHIP IN THE *PUEBLOS DE INDIOS*:
BECOMING "MEN OF REASON"

Thus far, this chapter has discussed the path open to Chichimec communities that aspired to the status of Tlaxcalan pueblos. The colonial regime recognized a hierarchy of Indian communities and permitted an elevation of status to those groups that fulfilled its expectations about Indian civilization and provided important services to the crown. The same was true of individuals. The colonial state recognized a number of distinctions between Indians. Their civil status under the law depended on language, religion, cultural traits, place of residence, military service, and heredity. Except in regard to privileges based on birth, such as Indian nobility, Indians could move between legal categories based on their conduct and community affiliations.

The capture and trial of several Borrado Indians from San Cristóbal de los Hualahuises shows how citizenship categories based on cultural traits and military participation defined the legal status of local peoples.[58] Between 1783 and 1791, the colonial authorities of Spanish Linares and Indian San Cristóbal de los Hualahuises struggled to control periodic violence and theft committed by some of the seasonal residents who drifted in and out of the mission's new *conversión*. Indians loyal to the colonial order were victims of the thefts, participants in the manhunts, and witnesses in the resulting trials. Their involvement in these court cases helped them to secure their place in the colonial hierarchy by contrasting themselves with the rebels and bandits. The trials of the bandits also articulated the differences between Indian citizens and those Indians beyond the pale.

A series of disorders began at San Cristóbal in 1783 with a wave of sheep poaching. Some of the offenders (or supposed offenders) were quickly seized; others long eluded the grasp of local authorities. Indian and Spanish leaders cooperated to capture and punish the poachers. The Indian governor and *alcaldes* determined that the men must be whipped, and the friar and sergeant oversaw the punishment. It seems that both legal and practical requirements were met by this arrangement. The *cabildo* held proper temporal jurisdiction over the *pueblo de indios*, but the friar had special authority over the new members of the *doctrina* who were not yet assimilated into the community. Maintaining a monopoly of force to carry out the will of the colonial state was a delicate matter; and it was most prudent to carry out official acts of violence through the orderly cooperation of officials representing all local castes. The hunt for bandits, like their punishment, required the cooperation of several local communities.

Many of the bandits remained at large after the exemplary whippings, so Simón de Taso and his company of Indian soldiers were brought into service,

---

[58] This 1791 trial concerns a series of offenses reaching back to 1783. All of the material presented here is drawn from AGN Provincias Internas, vol. 135, exp. 6, fols. 326–50.

keeping watch over the town and pursuing the remaining fugitives.[59] The project of pacification appeared to be a success until three bodies were found on the road near the outlying Rancho Muñoz. Word of the deaths quickly reached de Taso who, according to his later testimony, was unable to locate the pueblo's governor, but quickly marshaled three militiamen and one "*indio amigo*" as an emergency force. Word soon reached the *protector de indios* and the chief of the *salvaguardias* who set out in search of the bandits.

Three Indians were later captured in the hills and taken first to Linares and later to Monterrey to stand trial. Because the bodies found beside the road to Rancho Muñoz were those of a Spanish landowner and his peons, several jurisdictions were crossed, and the case could no longer be handled within the *pueblo de indios*. The Indians' murder of Spanish landowner Manuel Gómez Flores and his two dependents involved all levels of Neoleonés law. The three captives were tried in 1791, but were initially charged with an improbably large collection of crimes beginning as early as 1783. Though the accusations seem broad, if not arbitrary, the investigation and judgment were even-handed and deliberate.

The prisoners denied any involvement in a general rebellion but admitted to killing Manuel Gómez Flores. According to their testimony, the three Indians were in the midst of an expedition to gather peyote when they encountered an armed man whom they described as a strange, foreign Spaniard. In the ensuing confusion, they shot and killed him. The Indians were, at some level, members of San Cristóbal de los Hualahuises and at one point admitted that they were fleeing work obligations when they departed for their peyote-gathering expedition.

The court's judgment hinged both on the facts of the case and on an important determination about the prisoners' status as citizens. The judicial records describe the prisoners as "*muy ladino*" Borrados and as Christians, which is to say that they were Chichimecs, but also baptized and fully conversant in Castilian. However, much of their acculturation had taken place between the time of the first crimes and the time of the trial. Their advocate argued that although the men were Christians at the time of the trial, they had not yet been converted at the time of the crimes. He insisted that the relevant laws regarding theft and murder had their origin in the Ten Commandments; consequently, Indians not yet instructed in the Commandments could not be held fully morally responsible for transgressing them. He also argued that the thefts were for subsistence, rather than immoderate gain, and did not fit the legal definition of the crime. The men were acquitted on several grounds: the perpetrators' ignorance of law at the time of the crimes, the categorization of their poaching as subsistence, and the insufficient testimony against them. The most revealing

[59] A further reconstruction of the relationship between de Taso and the colonial community beginning with his baptism could be made on the basis of the documents contained in AMM Correspondencia, vol. 119, and from those included in documents from the Real Academia de la Historia de Madrid recorded in David Alberto Cossío, *Historia de Nuevo León* (Monterrey, N.L.: Consejo de Educación Publica, 1924), 104–15.

aspect of the case is the decision to stay the punishments for their prebaptismal transgressions as *ex post facto* penalties. The state placed non-Castilian-speaking gentiles in one category and *ladino* Christians in another. Its ruling made clear that in the years preceding the trial, the three men had crossed from the status of barbarian noncitizens into the realm of colonial citizens.[60]

The coordinated response to the Montes outbreak of 1782 illustrated the cooperative arrangements between Spanish authorities, Tlaxcalan militias, and the acculturated Chichimec militias.[61] The Chichimec captain Simón de Taso and his subordinate, Cavazos, appear in the records of the Montes outbreak as the military commanders of a force of *nueva conversión* Indians from Mission San Cristóbal. In a similar occurrence in 1784, Simón de Taso appears again as a respected political and military leader. In this case, we see de Taso, a northern Indian, present himself as a Tlaxcalan-style leader acting in cooperation with Spanish authority against a local bandit.

Before the courts, the status of a citizen was at issue whether he appeared as a defendant, plaintiff, or witness. In the case of the three Borrado bandits, the defendants' status as Christian subjects, both at the time of the offense and at the time of the inquest, were crucial to the verdict. The story of these bandits illustrates the mobility of individuals through the lowest rungs of colonial citizenship. In contrast, contemporary documents from San Cristóbal illustrate the mobility of Chichimec Indian leaders among the highest ranks of Indian citizenry. Here one sees rivalries between elite Indians in the mission-towns expressed through the language of citizenship that prevailed in the legal system.

On the morning of 28 October 1784, Don Antonio del Valle, *alcalde mayor* of Linares, received troubling news from Hualahuises: five Indians led by one Joseph Francisco Almaras Tevando (also known as "Julián") had fled town the previous night bound for Mexico City, and in possession of mules and horses. Del Valle immediately began collecting the facts that he would use to respond to the crisis and to bring the wrongdoers to justice. In the trial, as was customary, colonial magistrates evaluated testimony based on the status of the speaker. Consequently, the records of del Valle's investigation reveal much about the civic standing of the Indians who came before him. Here, as in other legal and political records, we see that petitioners and witnesses had to accredit themselves before speaking. The first news of Julián's activities came to the *alcalde* from a trusted source, Juan Antonio Silva, the head of the confraternity of mission San Cristóbal who could be trusted as an "*indio de razón.*" José Palomo and José María Treviño, accredited as Spanish "*vecinos*" of Linares, reported seeing Julián and his followers armed with bows and arrows and in possession of the

---

[60] On other occasions, heavy penalties were inflicted on Indians classified as barbarians. This case is something of an anomaly in the mercy shown to the accused. It is, however, typical in the language that it uses to describe the range of caste stations under the law.

[61] All facts and quotations from this case are drawn from AMM Correspondencia, vol. 121, exp. 6, fol. 7.

stolen animals at the gates of the pueblo of San Juan del Río. José Palomo also spotted the band of outlaws in Santa María del Río.

Simón de Taso corroborated the stories of other witnesses, swearing that he saw Julián and his henchmen in Santa María del Río. For our purposes, however, the description of de Taso himself is more interesting than his testimony. His accreditation as a witness includes the following biographical information: "Simón de Taso Governor of the *indios de nueva conversión* of the Mission San Cristóbal, a Catholic Christian by whose conduct all the Indians of his nation have been conquered and made subjects of the mission; and furthermore, on account of his solicitude and work has calmed the other missions of Concepción and Purificación in the Valley of Pilón." Not only does de Taso represent himself as a pious man and the head of the local *cabildo*, but he also touts his credentials as "warrior and conqueror." In an interesting variation on the theme, de Taso seems to take credit for conquering his own people. Clearly a man to be reckoned with in regional diplomacy, de Taso had brokered agreements between neighboring tribes and missions. The passage quoted here suggests that he may even have been responsible for ending the period of hostilities in Pilón at the time of the Montes outbreak.

From Simón de Taso, we also learn a bit more about Julián and about the community in which, until a few days before, both de Taso and Julián had lived. De Taso explains that Julián, who was very "*ladino*" and fluent in Castilian, had previously asked the mission's priest to appoint him to the post of *alguacil*.[62] Julián received the post with the understanding that he would use his authority to reform wicked members of the community; but, according to de Taso, Julián "didn't help in any way."[63] Under his negligent watch, disorders and rebelliousness previously kept in check now reemerged.

Through this muddle of local politics, we are able to discern important norms of community membership and civic status. Both men were northern Indians, but Simón de Taso parlayed his military command and his cultural knowledge into an authoritative civic standing. One might say that they possessed Tlaxcalan status. It appears that his despised adversary, Julián, was nearly a success at the same game, acquiring the cultural knowledge as a *ladino* that permitted him to assume an important local office. However, with his flight, Julián fell into the social category of an Indian bandit and slipped out of the colonial order. Spanish *vecinos* of Linares and Indian *vecinos* of Hualahuises considered him a common threat. As in the case of the Montes incident, the members of the colonial order closed ranks to defend the mission-town system against those who sought to

---

[62] The term *ladino* rarely occurs in the official writing of this period in Nuevo León. It seems to have been a foregone conclusion that Tlaxcalans were fully conversant in Spanish language and customs. Here Julián is called "ladino" because, as an *indio de nueva conversion*, his level of acculturation is noteworthy and relevant to his earlier success in the mission-town.

[63] "Dijo que conoce es de su propia gente y que por ser indio tan ladino en la ydioma castellano pidó al Reverendo Padre ministro se lo dieran de Alguasil para que le ayudara arreglar los yndios malos pero ... no le [h]a ayudado en nada."

break free from or subvert it. In doing so, men like Simón de Taso could affirm their positions in the colonial hierarchy.

The relationship between Tlaxcalans, *antiguos* Chichimecs, and *indios de nueva conversión* was both customary and legal in character. The varying privileges of these groups were reflected in local governance, the courts, the military system, and the tax code. Informed by Tlaxcalan political practices and legal discourse, many Chichimec groups and individuals laid claim to the privileges of Tlaxcalan citizenship. In violent times, the political capital of individuals derived, to a great extent, from their contributions to common defense. Every military threat and every deployment of Indian soldiers was an opportunity for the renegotiation of the warriors' status. Banditry, flight, and rebellion could lend power and status to the instigators, but they also could lend power to those who came to the defense of the community. In either case, Indian groups that could negotiate from a position of strength had the most to gain. Some nomads and bandits were captured or surrendered in desperate circumstances. They were subject to disadvantageous settlements or even trial for rebellion or banditry, which could result in sentences of death or penal servitude. More fortunate Indian bands were able to negotiate a settlement on mission-town lands. They were typically disarmed and settled as subject peoples in new Indian barrios. The most powerful Indian bands represented a greater threat as enemies and, conversely, a greater potential asset as allies, and thus had the widest range of choices. Some such groups retained their arms and their own military commands when they entered the mission-town community. Their path to Tlaxcalan citizenship was a shorter one, and many took full advantage of the opportunity.

4

Exporting the Tlaxcalan System

FIGURE 5. This detail from a late colonial map shows the new settlements established in Nuevo Santander from bases in Nuevo León. (José de Escandón, "Mapa de la Sierra Gorda y Costa del Seno Mexicano desde la Ciudad de Queretaro c. 1763," New York Public Library Archives)

The Tlaxcalan model of colonization was applied to frontier regions of northern New Spain for more than two centuries. Though all such efforts began with the Tlaxcalan colonies of 1590, the long history of subsequent exploration and settlement extended Tlaxcalan influence far beyond the first generation of colonies. The Tlaxcalan communities of Nuevo León were the progeny of earlier colonies near Saltillo and San Luis Potosí. These daughter colonies of Tlaxcala eventually became mother colonies to other more distant settlements, spreading the web of Tlaxcalan towns farther and farther from the original Nahua heartland. In the eighteenth century, the Neoleonés settlements seeded more colonies in Coahuila, Texas, and Nuevo Santander. The geographical dispersion of the Tlaxcalans diluted their numbers, creating concentric rings of colonization with ever-smaller populations of ethnic Tlaxcalans in each community. However, though their numbers decreased, their influence did not. The Tlaxcalan-Chichimec pueblo was a versatile political organism that reproduced itself and its distinctive type of indigenous colonial citizen. In the eighteenth century, the Tlaxcalan-Chichimec pueblos of Nuevo León sent out citizen-soldiers to create new settlements in neighboring territories. At these sites local Indians were drawn into the same civic environment now shared by Chichimecs and Tlaxcalans throughout the north.

The later colonies, however, differed from their predecessors in one important respect. In colonizing Texas, Coahuila, and especially Nuevo Santander, Spanish officials studied the characteristics of the old Tlaxcalan-Chichimec towns, codified them, and applied them more systematically. They now drew not just on Tlaxcalan colonizers, but also on Spaniards, mestizos, mulattos, and "civilized" Chichimecs.[1] By the mid eighteenth century, a regional civic culture was emerging based on the Tlaxcalan precedent. Planned towns of soldier-settlers now dotted the landscape, mixing different ethnic populations and functioning as sites of conversion, colonial acculturation, and shared governance.

The colonization launched from Nuevo León was motivated, in part, by a desire for natural resources, but more urgently by the need to protect the existing province from the Indians of neighboring territories.[2] In the early eighteenth century, the administration of Nuevo León's Spanish and Indian communities was regularized, and a clearer system of military cooperation between communities created some modicum of regional stability. In the years that followed, the greatest threats to Nuevo León would come from Texas, the upper Río Grande, and the Sierra Tamaulipas. Many Indians entered Nuevo León through these paths, with some settling permanently in its mission-towns and others moving

---

[1] Tlaxcalans were the most important, but not the only, North American peoples to serve in this capacity. On plans for the use of Otomís as a civilized settler population in the north, see Philip Wayne Powell, "Franciscans of the Old Silver Frontier of Old Mexico," in *The Franciscan Missions of Northern Mexico,* ed. Thomas E. Sheridan (New York: Garland, 1991), 20–29. The use of black settlers is more unusual. Mulattos were sometimes seen as skilled laborers but also often considered a cultural threat.

[2] This mix of economic and security concerns is evident in the three colonization proposals included in AGS 6966.

between missions or disappearing into the hills. The mobility of these groups was a cause of great concern to Nuevo León's governors and to the *protectores* of the mission-towns. Spanish governors used a variety of tactics to incorporate the tribes that subsisted on the margins of the colonial community. Local magistrates and missionaries employed both the carrot and the stick to attract mobile populations to the missions and convince them to stay. In times of successful engagement, they wooed the tribes with trade goods and alliances. When these methods failed, Spanish governors reverted to military means. Close contests between colonial and noncolonial groups typically resulted in negotiated settlements; but after hard-fought colonial victories, Indian captives were sometimes subjected to judicial punishments and penal servitude. When the mobile tribes prevailed, they carried off Spanish cattle and goods and disappeared back into Texas, the mountains of Tamaulipas, or the Bolsón de Mapimí. Only by bringing neighboring regions and peoples into the colonial system could Nuevo León become more secure.

FORAYS INTO NUEVO SANTANDER

In the 1720s and 1730s, the Franciscan missionaries of Zacatecas and the governors of Nuevo León combined their efforts to seek a diplomatic, military, and cultural resolution to the ongoing crisis on the eastern frontier. At the very least, all concerned hoped to establish safe routes from Nuevo León to the Gulf Coast and to reduce the level of Indian attacks on the communities of Nuevo León.[3] Ultimately, they hoped to convert the region's Indians and bring them into the colonial sphere.

In 1729, Governor Pedro de Sarabia and Fray Juan de Losada, accompanied by a force of four militia companies, traveled east from Linares on a diplomatic and religious mission into the Sierra Tamaulipas. Their efforts combined war, gift diplomacy, and proselytization. Losada, who had worked closely with Francisco Barbadillo, now sought to create the kinds of communities that already existed in Nuevo León in the unsettled lands to the east. The hostile Indians of the Sierra Tamaulipas were not innocent of Spanish culture or methods. In fact, their leaders were generally referred to as "*muy ladino*" and they were widely known by Hispanicized names or nicknames. They knew a great deal about the Spanish, but they were not fond of them. The entry of armed Spaniards into Tamaulipas drew immediate attacks from local Indian nations. The Spanish were confronted with growing enemy ranks as Indian war leaders gathered larger coalitions to oppose them.[4]

In the period of attacks and reprisals that followed, Sarabia and Losada employed Indian intermediaries to negotiate with the hostile war leaders who now spoke for a multitude of smaller tribes. The Spanish methods were sometimes

---

[3] The ferocity of Indian attacks in the 1730s is attested to in the April to August 1735 correspondence bound with the Fernández de Jáuregui Urrutia report.
[4] The following account of the work of Seravia and Losada comes from AGN Historia, vol. 30.

conciliatory, but at other times harsh. Sarabia and Losada at first focused on three of the major Indian leaders who currently commanded coalitions of tribes: Pajarito, Marcos, and Pedro Botello. The Spanish were not above taking women and children as hostages in an attempt to bring Indian leaders to terms. In fact, it was this tactic that yielded the first strategic breakthrough. Governor Sarabia's soldiers surprised an Indian camp and took Pajarito's wife, Anastasia, captive. Soldiers shackled Anastasia and brought her to Juan de Losada in chains. Over the days that followed, the missionary baptized Anastasia and persuaded her to help bring her husband and his men into the Christian camp. In this way, Anastasia helped to suspend hostilities and open negotiations between the Spanish and their Indian adversaries. Soon all of the major war leaders in the area accepted baptism and, in some fashion, acknowledged the rule of the king of Spain.[5]

We can consider this series of negotiations through a number of different lenses while acknowledging that the Spanish and Indian parties may have understood these encounters differently. Despite the likely cultural and linguistic differences, we should not assume that these encounters were completely baffling to the participants.[6] All parties were speaking a common language; the Spanish and Indian leaders were already known to each other (at least by reputation); and the nomads, though not yet members of religious congregations, were familiar with missions, missionaries, and the idea of baptism. The Spaniards and Indians had some notion of each other's military hierarchy; and because of this, they were able to make reciprocal gestures of respect, to conduct trade, and to negotiate alliances. José de Escandón believed that the Indians of Tamaulipas had *capitanes* and *cavos* who had operational control of *escuadras* of Indian fighters, forming a mirror image of his own Indian and Spanish command chains. Though he may not have understood the details of their social organization he was close enough to understanding the military hierarchy of his adversaries and to have respectful diplomatic exchanges.[7]

Ultimately, it was a shared understanding of the equivalence between the commensurate strata in the two hierarchies that permitted the Spanish system to subsume the Indian one. The recruitment of Anastasia and Pajarito led to negotiations with even more powerful Indian leaders. Soon Marcos, who claimed to lead more than half a dozen Indian nations, accepted baptism and swore allegiance to the crown as a "Christian Knight." Pedro Botello, who claimed to speak for twenty-six Indian nations, followed suit, becoming a Christian and a subject of the king, and accepting military service under Nuevo León's Miguel Cantú.

[5] AGN Historia 30, exp. 15, fols. 201–14.

[6] Brooks, *Captives and Cousins*, and Barr, *Peace Came in the Form of a Woman*, have argued convincingly that Spanish and indigenous warriors in New Mexico developed a shared honor culture based on combat and captive taking, in which their gestures of war and diplomacy were mutually intelligible.

[7] Escandón's report to the Audiencia of Mexico, AGS Secretaría de Guerra 7032, fols. 14–17.

The Indian leaders soon became at least nominal Christian vassals of Spain. Despite these celebrated missionary and military successes, the new Christian vassals of the Sierra Tamaulipas were far from the sedentary subjects that Spanish viceroys long hoped would people the north. These Indian nations were mobile kinship groups who acknowledged leaders like Botello only in times of crisis. The rest of the time they followed their food supply in seasonal cycles and consulted no authority outside their group. Though they were willing, and perhaps even eager, to accept baptism, they at first had little interest in settling in permanent mission-towns. In fact, it does not appear that Losada or the Neoleonés leader expected the Indians to settle immediately in sedentary communities.[8] Instead, they hoped for a mutually beneficial agreement for safe passage and trade between Nuevo León and the Gulf.

During the administration of Governor Fernández de Jáuregui Urrutia (1735–1740), Losada continued to work on behalf of Spain's spiritual and material objectives in the Mountains of Tamaulipas. Losada and Jáuregui understood the limits of their personal power and the necessity of winning the cooperation of military actors within the colonial sphere and of negotiating peace agreements with the Indian leaders outside it. Working inside the colonial order, the two men organized a *junta* of Neoleonés leaders to plan for the security of the eastern frontier and to help launch new mission settlements in Tamaulipas. This group included four ex-governors, Nuevo León's major military commanders, and its *alcaldes mayores*. Reaching beyond the colonial sphere, Losada arranged a conference involving seventeen heads of Indian nations, the *alcalde mayor* of Linares, and Governor Jáuregui. Most important to the governor and Losada was the conclusion of an agreement that would permit safe passage for Spaniards through Nuevo Santander to the best source of salt extraction on the Gulf. A substantial part of Nuevo León's subsistence came from cattle, and thus the scarcity of salt for curing and preserving meats was a matter of vital economic concern. The Sierra Tamaulipas lay between Nuevo León and its most promising supply of salt, but the mountains had heretofore been all but impassable due to Indian attacks. At the invitation of Governor Jáuregui, the Indian leaders Pedro Botello and Juan Antonio made their way to Monterrey on horses provided by Losada to negotiate the terms of the eastern salt trade. A mutually beneficial agreement soon emerged. The Spanish soldier and entrepreneur Miguel Cantú would lead convoys from Nuevo León to the coast under the protection of eastern Indians commanded by Botello and Juan Antonio.[9]

---

[8] The cumulative agreements of the 1730s were recorded by Nuevo León's governor, Pedro de Barrio Junco y Espriella, in 1741. They show that early trade and safe passage agreements led to alliances, and eventually to agreements by which Indians of the hill country worked, at least seasonally, on Spanish lands at the edges of Nuevo León. Agreements executed by Dn. Pedro de Barrio Junco y Espriella, Benson MSS: Salce Arredondo Papers, no. 36.

[9] Some of the new vassals of the Sierra Tamaulipas remained vassals and trade partners until the time of the full-scale colonization of Nuevo Santander, Joseph Antonio Fernández de Jáuregui Urrutia, *Descripción del Nuevo Reino de León, 1735–1740* (Monterrey, Mexico: ITESM, 1964), 13.

So it was that in the early eighteenth century many Indian nations of Tamaulipas became a part of the economic and diplomatic universe of New Spain. The colonial peoples of Nuevo León and the uncolonized populations of future Nuevo Santander had forged a common system of communication and exchange. Yet, the internal political life of its Indian bands was largely untouched. Only with the export of the mission-town model to Nuevo Santander would the political and cultural lives of these seminomadic peoples merge with those of the colonial populations.

GATEWAY TOWNS AND MOTHER COLONIES

The strategic location of several Nuevo León towns made them vital both to the defense of the realm and to all future colonization projects. From the 1730s to the 1750s, a number of military and political leaders from Nuevo León planned colonizing ventures in neighboring territories. These men viewed Nuevo León as both the model and the logistical center for the new settlements. One such leader was Antonio Ladrón de Guevara, a wealthy and influential military commander and landowner. In the long course of his career Ladrón de Guevara served in a variety of military and civil posts, but he left his greatest mark upon the region through his efforts to colonize Nuevo Santander (today's Tamaulipas). His reports and correspondence constantly meditated on the shortcomings of the colonial system and proposed new methods for settling Texas and the Huasteca from existing bases in the New Kingdom of León.[10]

Ladrón de Guevara's writing catalogs the resources and leadership structures of the region's major settlements. His description of the Valley of Pilón reveals some of the changes that had occurred since the seventeenth century, and which propelled the inhabitants' commitment to further colonization. Ladrón de Guevara tells us that in the mid 1750s Pilón was situated in the midst of an "active frontier" and still a site of ongoing conversion (*viva conversión*) for newly arrived Indians. However, its Spanish community was no longer just a sparsely populated collection of ranches. In addition to cattle ranching, the valley was now well irrigated with *acequias*, and produced abundant crops of grain and sugar. An *alcalde mayor* governed the valley, and Franciscan missionaries cared for both Spanish residents and the Indians of the two missions-towns.[11] Between the 1720s and 1750s Nuevo León's military elite proposed and executed a series of colonial ventures into surrounding lands. These plans were informed by past experience in Nuevo León, and sought to replicate the most successful elements of its mission-towns. Antonio Ladrón de Guevara was one of the most important architects Nuevo León's colonization projects. He carried out a series of visits within Nuevo León and in the unsettled territories in order to determine the best methods of future colonization.[12]

---

[10] For biographical information on Ladrón de Guevara, see the editor's introduction to Ladrón de Guevara, *Noticias de los poblados*.

[11] Ladrón de Guevara, 28–31.

[12] Ladrón de Guevara, 16–18; Fernández de Jáuregui Urrutia, *Description of Nuevo León*, 17.

Ladrón de Guevara viewed the inhabitants of the mission-towns of the New Kingdom of León as elements in a strategic system that could be redeployed to respond to changing conditions. His chief concern was to gain control of Texas and the Huasteca while drawing nomads into the mission system. Tlaxcalans served with Ladrón de Guevara in his expeditions to the east, and they figured prominently in his colonization schemes. Within the Kingdom, Tlaxcalans helped to locate and retrieve bands of "apostates" while continuing their tutelary role in the pueblos. In his 1756 correspondence with Franciscan leaders, Ladrón de Guevara reported several transfers of populations that affected the Valley of Pilón. Pelones from the Divina Pastora mission (a part of the Guadalupe settlement) were transferred to Purificación. At the same time, the small number of Tlaxcalans at Purificación and Concepción (presumably small due to Tlaxcalan participation in new colonial foundations) moved to Guadalupe where they were joined by redeployed Tlaxcalans from other mission-towns in the New Kingdom of León.[13] In Ladrón de Guevarra's generation, Tlaxcalans were a more important element of regional defense than the small numbers of royal soldiers deployed to frontier posts. Like Spanish elites, Tlaxcalans served the crown while serving themselves. They were willing to move in response to strategic necessity, provided that the new sites served their own material interests.

The communities of Nuevo Léon were utilized in the new colonization projects in several ways. Some, such as Pilón, Monterrey, and Guadalupe, provided settlers, provisions, and equipment. Others had additional functions as points of departure and strategic gateways to the new territories. In the Valley of Pilón, both the Tlaxcalan mission-towns and the Spanish populations were crucial to the new settlement schemes.[14] The population and productivity of Pilón was such that Ladrón de Guevara chose it as one of the staging grounds for colonizing Tamaulipas. Its *alcalde mayor* and *capitán a guerra*, Pedro Barrera, raised troops and gathered supplies to establish settlements in the new colony. The communities under his purvey provided a promising model for the new colonizing venture, pointing the way toward towns that could grow and prosper as they attracted new populations. Purificación and Concepción contained Tlaxcalans as well as a mixed population from various Chichimec nations; all

---

[13] Records of this transfer of populations have sometimes misled historians into believing that there ceased to be a Tlaxcalan community in the Pilón missions. This impression is perhaps reinforced by the fact Nicolás de LaFora's 1766–1768 survey of the region's settlements makes no mention of a Tlaxcalan presence there. Purificación and Concepción appear in his list of missions, but not in his list of *pueblos de tlaxcaltecas*. Nonetheless, the parish records for the Valley of Pilón demonstrate that more than a third of the population of Purificación and Concepción was made up of Tlaxcalans, see Martínez Perales, 20; on the 1766–1768 expedition of Rubí, see Nicolás de Lafora, *Relacion del viaje que hizo a los presidios internos situados en la frontera de America septentrional*, ed. Vito Alessio Robles (Mexico City: Pedro Robredo, 1939), 250.

[14] Cavazos Garza has emphasized the breadth of participation in the colonization of Nuevo Santander by the populations of the major communities of Nuevo León in *Breve historia de Nuevo León*, chap. 12.

were served by Franciscan missionaries. The rate of Chichimec settlement during this period was significant. The population brought into Concepción under Capitán Santiago of the Guachichiles alone amounted to 250 individuals. The two Indian pueblos neighbored Spanish estates, and the whole valley was surrounded and perforated by unincorporated Indian populations. Ladrón de Guevara tells us that Pilón was surrounded by Nazas, Narices, and Pelones; and that, even within the valley, Indians of these nations could be found camped between all of the Spanish estates.[15] Places like Pilón were still themselves frontier areas, but they had evolved relatively stable relationships among a variety of ethnic communities. The institutional structures and cultural knowledge of these Neoleonés communities would be a great asset in the settlement of neighboring regions.

The new colonizing ventures of the eighteenth century all built outward from a strategic system established in the previous century. From a military perspective, San Cristóbal de los Hualahuises (in the east of Nuevo León), San Miguel de Aguayo (in the north), and San Antonio de los Llanos (in the southeast) all served the kingdom in the same way. San Miguel guarded the northern point of entry into Nuevo León and protected colonial settlements from the Apaches. San Cristóbal and San Antonio guarded an eastern entry to Nuevo León from the nomads of Nuevo Santander. Historically, San Cristóbal and its neighboring Spanish town of Linares had been the point of departure for slave raids into the coastal region that is today Tamaulipas. In 1688, the founder of the Spanish settlement of Linares still described himself as the "captain of the forces of the frontier mission of San Cristóbal."[16]

A map of the Río Bravo and Río Conchas basins produced for the governor of Nuevo León in the 1730s labels all lands to the east of Linares as "uninhabited country as far as the coast"; this was the land that would become Nuevo Santander.[17] Though the Franciscan order began evangelizing from the coast in the early seventeenth century, colonial settlement of Nuevo Santander did not begin in earnest until the 1747 expedition of José de Escandón created twenty-two towns between Linares and the Gulf.[18] The settlement of new lands was accomplished through a partnership between Spanish military elites and the

[15] Ladrón de Guevara, 6–29, and appended correspondence: Carta al reverendo padre comisario General fray José Antonio de Oliva, 1756, 49–50; Carta á Antonio de Oliva, 1757; Carta a José Antonio de Oliva, 1756, 65; Carta á Antonio de Oliva, 1756, 69–70; Carta á José Antonio de Oliva, 1756, 81–83; Carta á Fray José Antonio de Oliva, 1757, 73–74; Consulta al excelentísimo señor virrey hecha por el sargento mayor don Antonio Ladrón de Guevara sobre establecimiento de una compañía de soldados en las misiones de su comando [1750s], 87–91.

[16] 16 Apr. 1688, AMM Protocolos, vol. 22, exp. 15, fol. 8.

[17] "Copia del mapa que envió el gobernador en 1736." Pedro Gómez Danés, *Las Misiones de Purificación y Concepción*, 42.

[18] Israel Cavazos Garza, *Breve historia de Nuevo León*; Portillo Valdez y Gómez Danés, *La Evangelización del Noreste* (Monterrey, Mexico: Arquidiocesis de Monterrey, Mexico, 2001), 12–15; Hubert J. Miller, *José de Escandón: Colonizer of Nuevo Santander* (Edinburg, TX: New Santander Press, 1980).

Tlaxcalan and acculturated Chichimec population of San Miguel de Aguayo, San Cristóbal, and the Valley of Pilón. In many instances, families from these communities helped to found the new frontier pueblos.[19]

San Antonio de los Llanos was one of the many *repúblicas de indios* reorganized by Francisco Barbadillo that played a role in later colonization. In 1715 Barbadillo sent a mixed force of Spanish soldiers and Indian archers under the command of Capitán Juan Guerra Cañamar and accompanied by Fray Juan de Losada to suppress Indian nations still at large in the area. He then resettled some of the former nomads in San Antonio de los Llanos and Río Blanco. As in other parts of the kingdom, Barbadillo sought to end cycles of Indian labor exploitation and rebellion in the south of Nuevo León. The reconstituted pueblo of San Antonio de los Llanos was to be a mix of Tlaxcalans and Chichimecs under *cabildo* governance. To eliminate conflicts with neighboring Spanish ranchers, the pueblo was given significant land rights, and its missionary was empowered as the legal and administrative intermediary to the outside economy, tabulating and regulating the community's cattle herds. Even before Barbadillo's intervention, the town had a successful record of integrating northern nations. The Janambres, who were described as a great threat to regional peace in the chronicles of the 1670s, were considered model Indians by Barbadillo's time. He offered the "valiant Janambres" of San Antonio as an example of the successes of the new mission-pueblo system.[20]

In the 1720s, the Tlaxcalans of San Antonio de los Llanos served after the fashion of their ancestors as a frontier garrison to contain attacks from the Indians of the Sierra Tamaulipas. San Antonio and its sister colony of Tlaxcalans at San Cristóbal de Hualahuises guarded the same frontier. In 1720s, both colonies found their numbers insufficient to arrest the rising tide of attacks. Their response to the crisis demonstrates that the Tlaxcalan pueblos still maintained communications with each other, their ancestral government at Tlaxcala, and the viceroyalty. The leaders of San Cristóbal and San Antonio discussed the strategic crisis and decided to petition Tlaxcala for a new wave of settlers. Both the Tlaxcalan and viceregal governments agreed in principle to settle new Tlaxcalan families under the same terms as those offered to the 1591 colonists. The city of Tlaxcala insisted that the viceroyalty foot the bill as it had done two centuries before. The viceroy and his *junta* agreed to do so, but explained that the project would have to wait until enough funds were available. It is unclear when, or if, these funds ever came through.[21]

---

[19] The first missionary activity in the region began in the sixteenth century under Fr. Andrés de Olmos, but thereafter missionary activities were sporadic, small in scale, and rarely reached farther north than the Río Pánuco, Joaquín Meade, Notes on the Franciscans in the Huasteca Region of Mexico, in *The Franciscan Missions of Northern Mexico*, 33–40.

[20] Chronicle of Fernando Sánchez reproduced in Alonso de León, Juan Bautista Chapa, Gral. Fernando Sánchez de Zamora, *Historia de Nuevo León*, notas de Israel Cavazos Garza (Monterrey, Mexico: Ayuntamiento de Monterrey, 1980), 234–41; Barbadillo, 20 Feb. 1715, AGI Audiencia de Guadalajara 166, fols. 42–45; AGN Tierras 3044, exp. 4, fols. 1–15.

[21] Jan. 1725, AMM Civil 53, exp. 26, fol. 4.

Renewed plans for Tlaxcalan frontier colonies provoked new discussions on the mission-towns' land regime. A set of instructions issued by Viceroy Casafuerte to the New Kingdom of León described the land system as it operated under the Barbadillo settlements: for the first two years, each new colony would be worked in common by the Tlaxcalans and Chichimecs. Missionaries held supplies in trust for the community, distributing provisions to the Indians every eight days. The draft animals were community property, and the *acequias* and reservoirs were built and maintained by the community.[22] The Tlaxcalans resisted this system, and in 1725 demanded legal recognition of individual family plots. Francisco Barbadillo, having returned to his post in Mexico City, eventually agreed. The resulting decision, articulated by Viceroy Casafuerte, referred not just to Tlaxcalans but also to other "civilized" Indians – perhaps Mexica and Otomí: "this decision will have to be universal for all the Tlaxcalan Indians and whatever other ones of all the pueblos that are not Chichimecs."[23]

The Janambres, who had seemed inassimilable sixty years before, had since become rural laborers largely integrated into the colonial system. In 1732 Fray Losada described them as the *"peones de aquel valle,"* and noted that they provided a military force to carry out operations against enemy Indians in the mountains of la Malinche. In this capacity, they fulfilled what previously had been a Tlaxcalan role of defending the community, settling new groups, and modeling colonial agricultural practices. Losada's use of the term *peón* to describe the Janambre laborers suggests that they did not possess the individual property rights of their Tlaxcalan neighbors, but it does indicate their level of incorporation in the local economy. Newly settled tribes were clearly subordinate to the Tlaxcalans, who occupied a higher rung in the colonial hierarchy.[24]

In the 1740s, the colonial map of the Northeast was changing, and with it the military and economic context of San Antonio de los Llanos. The governors of Nueva Vizcaya and the Nuevo Reyno de León were setting their sights on the Gulf Coast. Competing plans abounded for the opening of roads, the pacification of enemy tribes, and the establishment of new colonies between the current frontiers of the New Kingdom of León and existing or anticipated Gulf ports. Don Antonio Ladrón de Guevara, as *alcalde mayor* of San Antonio, was one of the leading voices for this new project of colonization. In 1739, he described the Río Blanco-San Antonio *alcaldía* with an eye toward his future settlement plans. He reported that both were served by a Franciscan friar, and both were promising producers of wool and grain, but that they were also perched on the edge of a dangerous frontier. Beyond the eastern boundaries of the jurisdiction lay a land inhabited by *"indios bárbaros"* from numerous nations.[25] Two years later, the new governor of the New Kingdom of León, Pedro de Barrio Noriega Junco y Espriella,

---

[22] Marqués de Casafuerte, 20 Nov. 1725, AMM Civil 53, exp. 26, fol. 4, also reproduced in Zavala, *Entradas.*

[23] 1725 AMM Civil 53, exp. 126, fol. 4.

[24] AGN Historia 30, exp. 15, fols. 201–14.

[25] Ladrón de Guevara, 201.

made a visit of inspection to San Antonio de los Llanos. He described the town as having three elements: Spanish, Tlaxcalan, and Chichimec. It was a community founded for the Tlaxcalan tutelage of Janambres, but now it provided additional assets to the crown. He described the area as being rich in natural resources, and as the "best location in this kingdom" owing to its agricultural riches and its position along a good route to Tampico. He attributed the weaknesses of the community to relentless attacks from the Indians to the east. He proposed transforming the area by creating two presidios (which did not come to pass) and by linking it to a chain of new roads and colonies through Tamaulipas (which did).[26]

Following the vast eastward colonization efforts of 1748, San Antonio de los Llanos was soon considered the westernmost community of Nuevo Santander rather than the final stop on the eastern fringe of the Nuevo Reino de León. Sometimes now referred to as Santo Domingo de los Ojos, the mission-town continued to function as a site for the resettlement and acculturation of new groups of displaced *bárbaros*.

TEXAS

Nuevo León served, in the mid eighteenth century, as the staging ground for expeditions to the east, north, and west. By the 1730s, Nuevo León had become a military and administrative center on an expanding frontier. Its composite military, based on the cooperation of separate ethnically defined forces and armed colonies of citizen-soldiers, was seen as a model that could be profitably exported to neighboring regions still dominated by mobile Chichimecs. New communities were established in three directions from Nuevo León: across the Río Grande in the province of Texas, far to the north along the Río Grande, and to the east of Nuevo León in the new coastal province of Nuevo Santander. All three regions would draw upon the Neoleonés model.

In the 1680s and 1690s, Alonso de Léon carried out the first Neoleonés forays into Texas in the hopes of containing the advance of French settlements along the Gulf Coast. Tlaxcalan soldiers, serving as diplomats, scouts, and translators, were crucial to these efforts.[27] In the 1680s one such Tlaxcalan, Agustín de la Cruz, went forth on a preliminary mission to attract allies among Indians of Texas and thus reduce the incidents of nomadic attacks on Spanish outposts. In the midst of these efforts, de la Cruz encountered a Frenchman who had once been a member of the la Salle expedition but had since taken up residence among the Indians of Texas. De la Cruz informed Alonso de León who promptly launched an expedition into Texas and employed de la Cruz as his guide and translator.

Alonso de León had both military and missionary ambitions in Texas, and he was aided in these efforts by Fr. Damián Massanet who established the

[26] Pedro de Barrio Junco y Espriella, 4 Jan. 1741, Benson Collection, University of Texas, Austin (hereafter Benson), Salce Arredondo Collection, no. 36.

[27] Alonso de León, chaps. 2–3; Eduardo Enrique Ríos, *Fray Margil de Jesús: Apóstol de América*, segunda edicion (Mexico: Editorial Jus, 1955); Alessio Robles, *Coahuila y Texas*, 332–47.

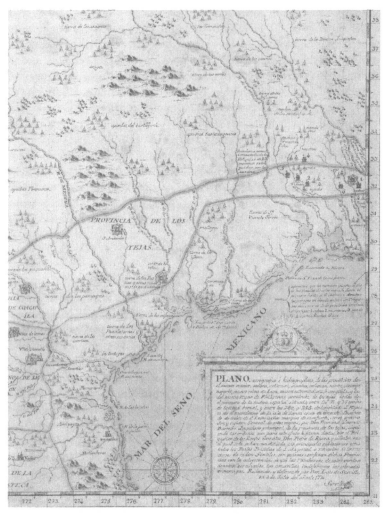

FIGURE 6. A detail from the 1727 Álvaro Barreiro map showing early settlements in Texas ("Plano corografico de los dos reynos de Nueva Estremadura o Coaguila, y el nuevo de León ...," British Museum, Additional MS. 17,650.b)

earliest Texas missions. These first communities did not thrive, however, and most were abandoned by 1693. A decade later, Nuevo León began to formalize and strengthen its Tlaxcalan-Chichimec mission-towns and to export these institutions to Texas with greater success.[28] In the early eighteenth century, once again concerned about the French threat, the Spanish founded new towns in Texas – this time in the east near Nacogdoches, and in the west at the site of

---

[28] Enrique Ríos, *Fray Margil de Jesús*, chap. 14.

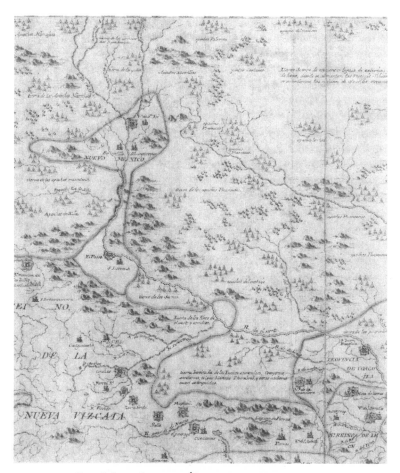

FIGURE 7. Detail from the 1727 Álvarez Barreiro map showing the area of the upper Río Grande that would be a focus of strategic settlement in the mid eighteenth century. ("Plano corografico de los dos reynos de Nueva Estremadura o Coaguila, y el nuevo de León . . .," British Museum, Additional MS. 17,650.b)

modern San Antonio. Tlaxcalans and Tlaxcalan institutions were a vital part of this colonization project. The people and supplies for the Texas settlements were moved through the Tlaxcalan communities at Saltillo and Boca de Leones. The Tlaxcalans of San Esteban de Saltillo were in charge of much of the transport and the defense of supply lines that bound old Tlaxcalan settlements to new ones.[29]

---

[29] Alessio Robles, *Coahuila y Texas*, 460. A description of this convoy system occurs in a letter of Dn. Juan de Sierra, 17 June 1722, AGI Audiencia de Guadalajara 166, fol. 243. Boca de Leones continued to be a logistical center for Franciscan evangelization of Texas into the nineteenth century, AGI Audiencia de Guadalajara 587. In the 1790s, one of the Nacogdoches settlements is referred to as the Pueblo de Nra. Sra. del Pilón, suggesting that Tlaxcalans or Spaniards of the

The success of Tlaxcalans as frontier soldiers and settlers made them desirable partners for the settlement of Texas. However, with Tlaxcalans deployed to strategic points throughout New Spain's many frontier areas, their numbers were not equal to the task. The Marqués de San Miguel de Aguayo established a number of new military and missionary posts in his expedition to Texas in 1721, but he was soon convinced that Tlaxcalan colonizers were needed to hold down the territory and instruct the local Indian populations. When their numbers proved insufficient, other civilized settlers were recruited to fulfill the same function.

San Miguel de Aguayo's plan called for a multiethnic settlement program in Texas that resembled that of Nuevo León, but on a much larger scale. He proposed a vastly expanded San Antonio, whose population would be bolstered with 200 Tlaxcalan settlers and 200 settlers (or settler families) from Galicia, Cuba, and the Canary Islands. The terms offered to the settlers resembled those of the 1590 Tlaxcalan charters. The crown would provide their transport, tools, supplies, and arms. Each family head would receive a land grant, and he and his descendants would be elevated to the rank of *hidalgo*. That this was an attempt to replicate the past success of the Tlaxcalan model is obvious. In this case, however, the project was burdened with unforeseen difficulties. It proved impossible to mobilize the desired number of Tlaxcalan and overseas settlers. The group of Canary Islanders, which in the end amounted to only fifty-five individuals, did not reach its destination until 1731, and few of the other populations arrived at all. The majority of the early inhabitants of San Antonio would be Indian. Though the scale of the settlement fell short of expectations, it did retain important structural elements of the Nuevo León mission-towns. The area of San Antonio was evolving as a complex of ethnically distinct barrios, each of which cultivated its own lands, instructed newly arrived groups, and contributed to regional defense. Unlike many of the communities farther to the south, San Antonio also had a presidio and a force of professional soldiers.[30]

Not all of the Texas settlements followed the Tlaxcalan model, but it was the Tlaxcalan model that proved most effective. Missionaries attempted to create some freestanding *conversiones* to minister to nomadic tribes – that is, missions to northern Indians that did not employ civilized Indians settlers. The most ambitious (or reckless) of these attempts was a mission to the Apaches. In 1756 a group of Apaches requested that a Franciscan missionary be sent to their area. The result was the creation of Mission Santa Cruz de San Sabá – a

---

Valley of Pilón may have made up a portion of the original population, 7 Jan. 1794, Archivo del Arzobispado (hereafter AAM), Monterrey, Mexico: Libro de Govierno del Obispo, 1792–1830. The San Antonio de Béjar area included a number of Spanish and Indian colonial settlements. Unless otherwise noted, I use the place name inclusively.

[30] The presidio was established 1718 with thirty-five soldiers and six families; it supported efforts of three missions from the Queretaro college and one from the Zacatecas college, Jones, 42–52; Escandón, xxxviii. The population was composed largely of local Indian groups according to María del Carmen Velázquez, *Tres Estudios Sobre las Provincias Internas*, 48; Alessio Robles, *Coahuila y Texas*, 470–1; Enrique Ríos, 178–83.

settlement that gave temporary hope to those anticipating the eventual conversion and settlement of the Apaches. These hopes were dashed in 1758 when the enemy Comanches attacked and destroyed the Apache community, killing its Spanish missionaries.[31]

The massacre at San Sabá triggered a strong reaction from the colonial government, and the leaders of Texas and Nuevo León soon gathered a large force to retaliate against the Comanches. The composition of this army demonstrates the extent to which the Neoleonés model of military cooperation between Tlaxcalans, Chichimecs, and Spaniards had taken hold. The army was assembled of 139 presidial soldiers, 241 non-Indian militiamen, 30 Tlaxcalan militiamen, and 90 Indian militiamen from other nations. Though largely unsuccessful in its short-term objectives, the scale and structure of the army suggest the growing strength of the colonial community's defenses. For a time, all hopes of converting the Apache were abandoned, but the multiethnic army composed of Spaniards and a variety of non-Spanish peoples remained the standard structure for Texas.[32]

To strengthen local defenses and regional military coordination, Texas paired royal presidios with Tlaxcalan-style militia towns. The structure of San Agustín Ahumada, established in 1756, is typical of communities built on this model. It included a presidio of thirty professional soldiers who worked in partnership with a neighboring town of twenty-five Spanish settlers and twenty-five Tlaxcalans from San Esteban de Saltillo. Its religious affairs were managed by a missionary from the Franciscan college of Guadalupe de Zacatecas. By the 1760s, the complex of settlements that comprised larger San Antonio de Béjar had created the sort of large-scale, multiethnic militias that were emerging during the same period in the provinces to the south. The area's Spanish population provided fifty militiamen (and its Indian pueblos, with a combined population of around 800) were able to field 100 archers.[33]

The Texas colonies experienced many reversals of fortune in the eighteenth century, but the colonies clustered around San Antonio were a success by most standards. They bound together a wide variety of local and settler populations, they irrigated and cultivated productive farmland, and they supplied a fighting force that, when augmented and coordinated by presidial soldiers, was adequate to local and regional defense. Like their counterparts in Nuevo León, the San Antonio mission-towns served, over a long period of time, as sites of acculturation and civic incorporation for successive waves of northern Indians who settled in their midst.

---

[31] Weber, *Spanish Frontier*, 186–91. Several struggling missions from the Colegio de Santa Cruz to the Apaches already existed at the time of San Sabá's foundation. However, judging from an official visit conducted in 1751, they were already on the way to collapse, "Carta de Fray Juan Hernández, 1751," Instituto Nacional de Antropología e Historia, Mexico City (hereafter INAH) Fondo Franciscano, vol. 145.

[32] Alessio Robles, *Coahuila y Texas*, 521.

[33] Lafora, 208–10.

THE UPPER RÍO GRANDE[34]

In the late eighteenth century, leaders from Monterrey and Saltillo were both involved in attempts to colonize the upper Río Grande and thus address the seemingly interminable attacks from the Gran Apachería. There, as elsewhere in the north, colonies were designed to combine civilized Indian and Spanish settlers with local Indians. As in the earlier history of Nuevo León, much of the land of the upper Río Grande was deeded to Spanish elites who did not fulfill all the intended terms of settlement. Now, following the path established in Nuevo León, some of these lands were expropriated and used to establish Indian communities with pueblo governments. This policy was aided by the Bourbon strategy of combining the functions of presidios with those of trading posts, so as to attract mobile bands into the planned communities.

The presidio of Carrizal, planned in 1759 and 1760 for the security of the zone between the Río Grande and Conchos, typifies the settlements of the period. The design of this community closely imitated Francisco Barbadillo's colonies of 1715. Dn. Antonio Mendoza Castellano, the governor of Nueva Vizcaya, expropriated lands from the hacienda of Carrizal for the town. On this land he established a mix of settlers from older colonies and Chichimecs from neighboring haciendas, missions communities, and autonomous *rancherías*. The settlers were both Spaniards and Indians, and they were accompanied by two missionaries. This was a town for citizen-soldiers. Mendoza Castellano described the status of the settlers in his instructions for the new colony:

> Justices shall be named from among them, the same *vecinos* that may be most apt and interested in the establishment and growth [of the colony]. . . . [A]ll the settlers to whom land has been distributed must be armed and equipped, forming, according to what their numbers permit, one or more Militia Companies in each one of the populations that reaches 50 *vecinos* or two or three squadrons in order that these *vecinos* may enjoy the rights and privileges of settlers in the first years.[35]

These communities were a part of regional military planning. To carry out large-scale campaigns, northern governors convened multiethnic *juntas de guerra*,

---

[34] Texas and Nuevo Santander (as Tamaulipas) continue to exist as recognizable units of political geography. The third area of settlement discussed in this chapter, the Upper Río Grande, is more difficult to visualize as a coherent region. It is perhaps best to think of Nuevo León as one island of colonial control and New Mexico as another. A vast expanse of territory between them was very difficult to control despite the fact that the Río Grande connected them. One strategic focus of mid-century military planners was the general area of the confluence of the Río Grande and Río Conchos, in which they would eventually build the presidio towns of Junta de Rios and Carrizal. See Griffen, *Apaches at War and Peace: The Janos Presidio, 1750–1858.* Throughout this chapter, I use "upper" and "lower" to indicate the position of settlements on the Río Grande relative to the towns in Nuevo León. I hope this will not be a source of confusion to reader for whom "upper Río Grande" means New Mexico. Readers also should take note that the Río Conchos of the Junta de Rios zone is entirely different from the Río Conchas that appears in the discussions of eastern Nuevo León and the settlement of Nuevo Santander.

[35] AGI Audiencia de Guadalajara 327, fol. 55.

which included the ranking captains of the Spanish towns and presidios, leaders of Spanish and Indian militias, and the leaders of bands of *indios amigos*. While the settlement program continued to work toward a cultural and administrative synthesis, military pragmatism demanded the cooperation of all existing armed bands under leaders who could be called on to defend the colonial community against dangerous tribes and bandits.

Lists recording the names and origins of settlers for the upper Río Grande reveal the demographic composition of the new colonies. The standard design was a fifty-family community of citizen-soldier-farmers. The heads of families were Spaniards, Tlaxcalans, or other *gente de razón*. Naming patterns among the wives, however, suggest that even this founder-population included some recently Christianized Indians. To these core communities were soon added locally recruited Chichimec settlers.[36]

The Tlaxcalans had a stake in many of the communities of Texas and the upper Río Grande. They served as settlers, soldiers, guides, translators, and purveyors of goods. Tlaxcalan populations were linked by chains of communication and authority both to Spanish elites and to the other communities of the Tlaxcalan diaspora. Documents from the Tlaxcalan mother colony of San Esteban de Saltillo record the participation of Tlaxcalan soldiers in the punitive raids at San Sabá and name Purificación, Concepción, Guadalupe, and San Miguel de Aguayo as colonies established and maintained "to suppress the hostilities of the barbarous Indians" that lay beyond them.[37] The defense of Boca de Leones was partly in the hands of Tlaxcalans, whose strategic colony of San Miguel de Aguayo had the same mixed Tlaxcalan-Chichimec structure as Purificación and Concepción.[38] The fact that Tlaxcalans guarded Boca de Leones, and that Tlaxcalans from as far away as Saltillo were sent to the aid of Texas missions, suggests that their colonies in Nuevo León coordinated responses to military threats.[39] Tlaxcalan communities were both a model for Spanish colonial projects and active partners in those colonial ventures.

---

[36] Writings of Antonio Mendoza Castellano, capt.-gen. of Nueva Vizcaya, 1759–1760, AGI Audiencia de Guadalajara 327, fols. 1–82. During the period, "de la Cruz" was a common surname for recently baptized Indians; it was shared by a number of women with no other apparent familial relationship.

[37] Fray Joseph Antonio Lazo, 14 May 1760, *San Esteban de Tlaxcala: documentos*, 159.

[38] The Tlaxcalan colony of San Miguel de Aguayo was paired with the Chichimec community of Santa María de los Dolores, Adams, "At the Lion's Mouth," 329–32.

[39] Thus a reassignment of part of the Tlaxcalans from Pilón to Guadalupe in the 1750s may have fit into a broader project of redeploying Tlaxcalan militias to the periphery and relocating less reliable Chichimecs to the interior. For an overview of the military difficulties of the north in the seventeenth and eighteenth centuries, see Luis Aboites Aguilar, "Nómadas y sedentarios en el norte de México: elementos para una periodización," in *Nómadas y sedentarios*, 277–97. On the military crisis of the 1770s and the role of San Miguel de Aguayo, see Adams, "At the Lion's Mouth," 324–46; on Apache and Comanche incursions and on San Sabá, see Pedro Angeles Jiménez, "Entre Apaches y Comanches: algunos aspectos de la evangelización franciscana y la política imperial en la misión de San Sabá," *Nómadas y sedentarios*, 419–37.

PLANTING MULTIETHNIC GOVERNMENTS

Most of the provinces of New Spain's northern frontier were settled piecemeal through a series of independent ventures, but Nuevo Santander was an exception. It was colonized in the 1740s and 1750s in the most systematic settlement project since the original Tlaxcalan colonies of 1590. In the first two decades of the eighteenth century, missionaries worked hard to win conversions in the Sierra Tamaulipas, and Neoleonés military commanders carried out a number of operations aimed at negotiating a safer eastern frontier and a corridor of safe passage to the coast. Ongoing attacks from the Sierra Tamaulipas commanded the attention of military planners. Meanwhile the success of early missionary and diplomatic overtures pointed to opportunities for conciliation and peaceful colonization.

In the 1730s, three northern leaders competed for a royal charter to carry out the settlement of Tamaulipas: Narciso Barquín de Montequesta (a settler on the southern fringes of Tamaulipas), José Antonio Fernández de Jáuregui y Urrutia (the governor of Nuevo León), and Antonio Ladrón de Guevara (a wealthy rancher from Nuevo León). The three contenders presented the viceroy and *junta de guerra* with detailed proposals for an invasion and settlement of the region. They made exploratory trips to the region, made diplomatic contacts with Indian leaders, and sought out the natural resources that would make the venture profitable.[40] In the most extensive of the exploratory missions, Ladrón de Guevara made provisional agreements with Chichimec chieftains, awarding them Spanish military titles. In the battle for royal favor, he even brought a delegation of these Chichimec notables to Mexico City to speak with the *junta de guerra* and add credibility to his arguments.[41]

The three proposals shared most of the same basic strategies: early military operations would be followed by the establishment of Indian and Spanish settlements; the salt trade and mining operations would come next, hopefully recouping the expenses of the conquest. It was Ladrón de Guevara's plan that in 1734 won royal approval. His proposal stood out among those of his peers in several respects: first, it was extremely ambitious in that it called for the construction of dozens of settlements simultaneously; second, it was economical for the crown, in that it relied on self-funded militiamen and Indian allies; and finally, it was heavily informed by past experience in Nuevo León. Ladrón de Guevara studied the successes and failures of previous settlements and decided that the Tlaxcalan-Chichimec model of armed settlements was both the most

[40] On the colonization of Nuevo Santander, see Pedro Fidel de Lejarza, *Conquista Espiritual del Nuevo Santander* (Madrid: Instituto Santo Toribio de Mogrovejo, 1948); Miller, *José de Escandón: Colonizer of Nuevo Santander*; Jones, *Los Paisanos*, chap. 3; Octavio Herrera, *Breve historia de Tamaulipas* (Mexico: Colegio de México, 1999).

[41] "Carta de Don Antonio Ladrón de Guevara al Reverendisimo Padre Comisario General Fray José Antonio de Oliva, en el año de 1759," in documents from the Real Academy de la Historia de Madrid recorded by David Alberto Cossio, 105–6.

effective and the most profitable approach. Though the Ladrón de Guevara plan became official policy in 1739, its execution would have to wait more than a decade.[42]

In 1748, the plan was finally set in motion with the principal military command awarded to José de Escandón. Escandón was a career military officer who had been stationed in the mining regions of the interior and at coastal fortresses on the Gulf. He was now appointed commander of the conquest and the first governor of the colony of Nuevo Santander. The scale of the colonizing effort was impressive. Escandón arranged for six different groups of soldier-settlers originating from Coahuila, Nuevo León, Texas, and the Gulf Coast to enter Nuevo Santander by different routes. This initial wave of settlers included more than 700 armed men and their families as well as "civilized Indians" and the "*indios amigos*" who were recruited for the venture. From 1749 to 1755, Escandón's followers established more than two dozen towns and a viable network of routes for trade and communication between them.[43]

Nuevo León's system of interdependent Tlaxcalan, Spanish and Chichimec communities was the basis of the new settlements in Tamaulipas. Tlaxcalans from Nuevo León took part in many such ventures; so did populations that had been instructed and influenced by Tlaxcalans. By the mid eighteenth century, the success of the Tlaxcalan-Chichimec mission-towns of Nuevo León provided colonial governments with a broader population of "civilized" Indians to draw upon. In addition to the Tlaxcalans, many settled and incorporated Chichimecs served the traditional Tlaxcalan function of providing defense, creating irrigated agriculture, and recruiting and instructing nomadic Indians. Thus, many of the Tamaulipas pueblos began as intentional aggregations of barrios belonging to newly settled local Indians and "*gente de razón*" – a group that included Tlaxcalans, Chichimecs who had attained Tlaxcalan status, and (in some places) armed black or mulatto settlers from the Gulf Coast.[44]

José de Escandón lobbied for and received broad powers for the settlement of Nuevo Santander. As in Nuevo León, the military and civil commands were unified – in this case based on the argument that, as citizen-soldiers, many of inhabitants of Nuevo Santander were logically under military jurisdiction.[45]

---

[42] These proposals survive in a mix of published and unpublished forms. See Don Antonio Ladrón de Guevara, *Noticias*; Fernández de Jáuregui Urrutia, *Description of Nuevo León*; José de Escandón, *General State of the Settlements Made by D. José de Escandón*, trans. Edna Brown (Mexico City: National Printers, 1993); and as reviewed in the 1795 brief of Félix María de Calleja AGS Secretaría de Guerra 7027, exp. 1, fols. 8–9. The three full proposals are contained in AGS Secretaría de Guerra 7032, exp. 1.

[43] In 1755 the new province had twenty-four pueblos containing 8,989 "personas de varias castas" and 3,443 "Indios gentiles en misiones inmediatas y agregadas a los mismos pueblos," AGS Secretaría de Guerra 6966, fol. 268.

[44] Mulatto settlers fulfilling the same function appear in the description of Pilón and de la Mota in the 1740 correspondence between governor and viceroy, Fernández de Jáuregui Urrutia, 90.

[45] "[W]ith the assignment of royal lands to the militiamen and settlers [*milicianos y pobladores*] by only conceding to them the privileges that as soldiers they are exempt from the ordinary juris-diction, and only subject to the Capitan General and his respective subordinate chiefs that have

Escandón arrived in Nuevo Santander as the head of the military and civil hierarchy. Despite this fact, the construction of civil society required negotiations between several distinct political communities. The design of Nuevo Santander's institutions made the sharpest distinctions between three broad groups: people who took part in colonial political economy (Spaniards, mestizos, mulattos, and "civilized Indians"), those within the colony but not yet brought into political life (the Indian residents of the *vivas conversiones*), and the enemy outsiders (for the most part Apaches of the lower Río Grande).[46]

Nuevo Santander followed the most successful models in Nuevo León. This continuity was a matter of policy and of habit: *policy* because Ladrón de Guevara and Escandón studied and reapplied the successes of the Neoleonés communities, and *habit* because many of the settlers came from those same Neoleonés populations. The town of Camargo, located on the south bank of the Río Grande, was one of the early colonies that set the pattern for further settlement. In 1748 a large group of settlers departed Nuevo León's Villa of Cerralvo for the lands to the east. Taking with them weapons, tools, and flocks, they crossed into the territories of Nuevo Santander and established the town of Camargo. A surviving map of the settlement shows a town plan of twelve blocks, each block being divided into sixteen individual properties. Land was set aside for a church and for a plaza that would be used to drill the local militia. Soon the Spanish settlement attracted to it Indians from five nations. In the early days of the colony, the Indian population grew rapidly. Even as the settled Indians began constructing a church, other as-of-yet unbaptized groups settled on the fringes of the emerging town.[47]

From the beginning, Nuevo Santander was designed to incorporate all of the area's populations into colonial political life. It borrowed from the Neoleonés system in which Tlaxcalans instructed Chichimecs, and in which Chichimecs, once acculturated, attracted other tribes into the settlements.[48] The royal charter for the colony recognized the preexisting governments of the local Indian nations and sought to incorporate them into the colony by offering their leaders official titles and offering their populations land rights in the new agricultural communities. It also recognized that civilized Indians like the Tlaxcalans of Nuevo León would arrive under the authority of their own legally constituted *pueblos de indios*. The charter instructed the governor to

> arrange the missions and their synods in the whole colony and in the new
> settlements so that they may carry on, giving to each instructions for the actions

zealously offered to defend the new Missions at their own expense," 27 Apr. 1727, AGS Secretaría de Guerra 7032, exp 1, fol. 11.

[46] Report to the Audiencia of Mexico, AGS Secretaría de Guerra 7032, exp 1, fols. 5, 11. Though the term *Apachería* usually has been applied to a region to the north and west controlled by Apaches, military planners also confronted a second population of Apaches near the mouth of the Río Grande.

[47] Miller, 15–16, 29–30; Lejarza 155–7, 169.

[48] Escandón expected the first citizen soldiers to attract local Indians, beginning a chain settlement process, report to the Audiencia of Mexico, 27 Apr. 1727, AGS 7032, exp. 1, fol. 11.

and practices that they ought to undertake in order that with Indians added and congregated you may make use of the abilities of the missionaries ... you may make distributions of land assigned to each settlement arranging it according to the merits of each settler and his abilities ... giving equally the corresponding amount to the Indians that join themselves to those settlements ... in the new colony they need not follow the rules prescribed by the laws for the *nuevas conversiones de indios* because that population has been formed from cities ... though they may have their own particular government by means of their captains and lesser governors [*governadorcillos*].[49]

In Nuevo León, a similar cultural map had evolved over time, with each group negotiating over the terms of political inclusion. In Nuevo Santander, policy makers began with the assumption that neighboring groups of different ethnic and cultural backgrounds would converge in the formation of larger political communities.

In 1748 and 1749, viceregal military commanders, accompanied by missionaries, regular soldiers, and Neoleonés settler-militiamen, moved through Nuevo Santander recruiting new Indian allies and negotiating with them to create new joint communities. The commanders implicitly recognized two sources of political authority, one imperial and the other quasi-democratic. Indian populations became a part of the Spanish political universe when their leaders accepted Spanish titles under the crown. However, the Spanish considered Indian leaders legitimate only when they were elected by their own populations. José de Escandón described one example of this political process as follows:

The *capitanes principales* among them, toward the end of ending the influx of their atrocious former abuses, presented themselves to me by means of said Guevara; they have accompanied me for more than a month with some of their people, and coming together among them, they asked me to settle in a place called las Ciénagas de Cavallero.... I gave them clothing, I gave the title of Capitan to him whom they elected.[50]

As in the previous settlements of Nuevo León, the Chichimecs of the Tamaulipas who accepted this type of political incorporation were then settled beside agricultural peoples and issued several years of provisions and tools by the missionaries and *protectors*. The mission-town represented a negotiated convergence of political authority. The political legitimacy of indigenous leaders and of the crown was simultaneously confirmed in this form of local government.

The Tlaxcalans had long been vital intermediaries in joining indigenous and Spanish political structures. Pedro de Nava would later reflect on the success of Neoleonés Tlaxcalans in transforming Chichimecs into productive subjects. He noted that, when transplanted from one environment to another, "Tlaxcalans retain their inherited fidelity and good inclinations," and that "the Gualaguises

---

[49] "From Cédula de la Provincia sobre la población de la colonia de Nuevo Santander ..." 29 Mar. 1763, "Buen Retiro" in Lejarza, 125.

[50] Escandón's report to the Audiencia of Mexico, AGS 7032, exp. 1, fols. 11, 34.

and Borrados, well instructed in catechism and the Spanish language, imitate them in everything, [becoming] diligent, hard-working and obedient." He saw less pleasant outcomes for Chichimecs deprived of Tlaxcalan guidance: "the other Indians are perverse for having always lived in complete liberty ... [They are] lazy wanderers without religion, giving themselves barbarously to all manner of vice and destroying the peace with the robbery and murder that they have committed, and continue to commit, in the New Kingdom [of León] and the bordering province of Santander." Fortunately, from the perspective of colonial governance, Tlaxcalan influence was capable of spreading far beyond the Tlaxcalan population.[51]

There were never enough Tlaxcalans to plant them as cultural tutors in every colony. Consequently, in Nuevo Santander the model of the Tlaxcalan-Chichimec mission-towns was often perpetuated and adapted using populations of acculturated Chichimecs, mestizos, *pardos*, or even Spaniards in the usual role of Tlaxcalans. Most of Nuevo Santander's new towns were designed from the start to have a composite population of several ethnicities. For a colony to function and survive, its members needed to be able to produce the majority of their subsistence goods and to provide some level of autonomous military security. The typical town combined populations that already practiced sedentary agriculture with some who did not. Likewise, it mixed vulnerable populations with those already integrated into the regional military system. While Tlaxcalans were an important part of the settler population throughout the northeastern frontier, they constituted a smaller portion of the population in Nuevo Santander where it was the Tlaxcalan *system*, more than the Tlaxcalans *themselves*, that exerted a decisive influence.

The earliest colonies in Nuevo Santander demonstrate the use of both Tlaxcalans and other settler populations. The provisional capital was initially ruled by José de Escandón and peopled by a dozen professional soldiers and seventy settler families.[52] The soldiers were a company from Boca de Leones, and thus likely to have been partly or wholly Tlaxcalan. However, this use of Tlaxcalan soldiers was not as common in Nuevo Santander as in Nuevo León and Coahuila. More typical was the case of San Juan de Horcasitas, which began as a military post under Captain José Antonio Oyanvides. It was originally populated by eleven professional soldiers, fifty settler families, and seventy Huasteco Indians who were granted land adjoining that of the settlers.[53] Like

[51] "Misiones del Nuevo Reyno de León Pertenecientes a la Intendencia de Sn. Luis Potosí separrado de la Comandancia General de las Provincias Internas y sujetos al virreynato," AGS Secretaría de Guerra 6966, fol. 259.

[52] San Miguel de Aguayo, whose militiamen helped to guard Boca de Leones, had a population of 200 Tlaxcalan families just a few years before. A substantial number seem to have been distributed to the new colonies in Tamaulipas, Coahuila, and Texas in this period. Fernández de Jáuregui Urrutia shows that Boca de Leones had a Tlaxcalan squadron (p. 29) and 200 affiliated families (p. 251).

[53] Report of José de Escandón to the Audiencia of Mexico (1748–1749), fol. 23.

an old Tlaxcalan mission-town, Horcasitas was intended as a tutelary colony to bring the newly incorporated Indian population into civic life – in this case, with all the settlers assuming the traditional Tlaxcalan role. Soon Horcasitas began to acquire Indian satellite communities after the fashion of Nuevo León's pueblos. The leader of a group of Palaguecos, who entered into negotiation with town leaders, was issued a staff and greatcoat as badges of offices; then his people were given title to nearby lands. The Palaguecos were just one of several groups that entered local civic life by this mechanism. By 1749 Horcasitas was composed of three central barrios, one of *gente de razón*, one of Huastecos, and one of Olivos, with the additional Palagueco satellite a few miles beyond.[54]

In the late colonial period, Nuevo Santander contained many Indians who had mastered the Tlaxcalan modes and idioms of citizenship. In 1804, José Miguel Valli, an Indian leader from the community of San Joachín del Monte, petitioned both the governor and the bishop of Mexico over several local concerns. He represented himself as a "married Christian Indian" and a "Governor, *natural* and *vecino* of the Pintos congregated at the Mission San Joaquín del Monte." He provided documentation to demonstrate that he was the legitimate governor of three nations (Pintos, Comecrudas, and Tejones) and that he had been confirmed in this office by a grant of authority from a Spanish *alcalde mayor*. He also presented judicial records to prove his faithful practice of Christianity. His petition sought to further legitimate his authority and, at the same time, secure his people's place in the colonial order of Nuevo Santander by attaching them to the institutions of the town of Reynosa and by certifying their land claims. Ultimately, José Miguel Valli wanted his people to receive visits from a missionary, to gain legal representation through a *protector*, and to collect rents from the lands they had customarily occupied. Clearly, Valli was no stranger to the rules of the game under Spanish law. Though the colonization of Nuevo Santander began later than that of Nuevo León, it followed a similar political process and created the same types of acculturated Chichimec leaders – Indians fully conversant in colonial law and politics.[55]

Mestizos and mulattos were more important in the early phase of colonizing Nuevo Santander than they had been in Nuevo León. Nuevo Santander was colonized from several directions and thus drew into its colonies different populations. Colonizers entering from the Gulf side were supplied and manned from Tampico, Veracruz, and even Campeche. Those port cities included significant populations of African descent. In the area of Nuevo Santander nearest Tampico, José de Escandón also encountered preexisting communities of free blacks who had already entered the area and begun to intermarry with local Indians. In 1749 Captain Juan Pérez brought *pardo* soldiers from Tampico to help secure the routes between new settlements. Spanish, Indian, and *pardo* forces cooperated to establish the nearby town of Altamira, and to secure the Pass of the Metate, which guarded access to Altamira and was a vital point of regional defense. At the pass,

[54] Fidel de Lejarza, *Conquista Espiritual del Nuevo Santander*, 109.
[55] 1809 Congregación San Joachin del Monte, Nuevo Santander, AGN Misiones 11, fol. 77.

a group of *pardo* soldiers and Indian allies cooperated with Spanish military commanders to construct and man a fortification that would hold the area against hostile Indians. This same combination of Spaniards, *pardos*, and Indian allies would form the basis of the local population in the years that followed.[56] Several black and mulatto communities that were the nucleus of later Nuevo Santander towns were created on the initiative of their own founders. Spanish administrators later noted that these mulatto communities considered themselves *villas* despite lacking any legitimate founding charter.[57] In other words, free blacks and mulattos formed communities whose governments operated like *pueblos de indios* or Spanish *villas*. Like so many Chichimecs who edged their way toward Tlaxcalan status, these *pardo* communities built themselves into the military and civil system of the viceroyalty.

In the second half of the eighteenth century, Nuevo León exerted a powerful influence on the new colonies it helped to establish to its north, east, and west. In one sense, Nuevo León served as an intermediary between the center and the periphery of New Spain – a place through which Spanish and Nahua institutions were transmitted into more distant Indian realms. However, the new colonies owed as much to their Neoleonés handmaidens as to their distant progenitors in central New Spain. The new towns in the Junta de Ríos zone, Texas, and Nuevo Santander were closely modeled on the multiethnic, symbiotic systems of Nuevo León. Community partnerships that evolved over time in Nuevo León were planted by design, and from the outset, in the new frontier towns.

These late colonies also had distinctive traits not found in Nuevo León. The success of the Tlaxcalan-Chichimec system bred imitation and adaptation. New colonies used a variety of non-European "civilized" populations to fulfill the Tlaxcalan role. These later colonies were also a product of a different time. While Bourbon planners learned from and imitated the Tlaxcalan settler garrisons, they also sought to integrate them into a more uniform military system. The presidio towns of the late eighteenth century were modeled on Tlaxcalan frontier colonies, but they were also built into a military bureaucracy. Late colonies combined the old traits of Tlaxcalan vassal communities with the new notion of citizenship implicit in Bourbon militia systems.

---

[56] Escandón, AGS 7032, exp. 1, fols. 7, 11, 23.

[57] The customary recognition of nonchartered *pardo* communities is noted in AGS Secretaría de Guerra 6966, exp. 69, fol. 281, though the acknowledgment of this state of affairs is made amid critical remarks about the corrupting effects of these "infected castes."

5

War and Citizenship

A great army did not conquer this empire; it was done with the help of the Tlaxcalans and progressively with that of all the Indians of New Spain that contributed to its welcome collapse. The chief conquistador never refused the peaces they offered him: he took advantage of the faithful conduct of his true friends.

–Instructions of the Conde de Gálvez to Comandante Ugarte y Loyola, 1786[1]

It should be an axiom in these lands that the condition of soldiers should be, as much as possible, united to that of a citizen, the same person undertaking both.

–Félix María Calleja's report to the viceroy, 1795[2]

FIGURE 8. In the late eighteenth and early nineteenth centuries, military strategists such as Ramón de Murillo continued to design fortifications, equipment, and command structures for professional soldiers; but the numbers and impact of regulars would remain small relative to the far greater number of militiamen and Indian allies. (Ramón Murillo, "Diseño de uniforme de las fuerzas de Caballería. Soldado de Cuera," Archivo General de Indias: MP-Uniformes, 81)

A vast population on the scale of Mexico's can exist as a political community only inasmuch as its members share a common notion of themselves as citizens. Members of small communities may be linked by personal acquaintance and may recognize each other by sight, but the members of a nation are connected by

---

[1] AGS Secretaría de Guerra 7041, exp. 8, fol. 155.
[2] AGS Secretaría de Guerra 7027, exp. 1, fol. 8 (string-bound).

a shared imagination of a much larger community.[3] Militias have several important political properties in this respect. They express membership in the community, they model social hierarchies, and they demonstrate the connections between political power and the monopoly of force. This chapter explores the principles of political inclusion expressed by changing rules of eligibility for military service during the late eighteenth century. It also describes the formation of regional identities based on the aggregation of local military units, and the expression of political beliefs through the appointment or election of military officers. Finally, it illustrates the ways that preexisting features of Indian and Spanish military citizenship converged with Bourbon notions of governance in the Provincias Internas.

In the north of New Spain, the introduction of new regional and national militias, beginning in the 1760s, exerted a crucial influence on state formation and citizenship. The integration of local military units into standardized armies, for the first time, created a set of lateral civic relationships between men of different localities. Structurally, these militias expressed the equivalence of citizens from different communities within a larger body. When assembled for inspection or deployment, these soldiers from separate ethnic enclaves for the first time experienced ties of citizenship as a perceptible fact. Musters and mobilizations also demonstrated to the participants that the real military power of the region resided in its citizens.[4]

In order to understand eighteenth-century citizenship, we must consider the individual's relationship to local, regional, and imperial institutions. Through most of the colonial period, the inhabitants of New Spain's northeastern frontier experienced citizenship primarily in local terms. Full members of a community were *vecinos*, and they participated in public life as electors of Indian *cabildos*, church officers, and urban *ayuntamientos*. These local political roles expressed horizontal ties that bound together the immediate community. There were strong democratic elements in this local political culture, but no electoral processes reached beyond the bounds of a given residential community. At the extralocal level, most political relationships were hierarchical. *Vecinos* voted as members of a local community, but they also petitioned the crown as members of an imperial one. Before the law, people appeared as subjects, and when

---

[3] The historiography of "imagined communities," Anderson, *Imagined Communities*. The application of Anderson's model to national independence movements in Latin America has been challenged and modified by Latin Americanists. A wide variety of voices on the subject may be found in Castro-Klarén and Chase, eds., *Beyond Imagined Communities*.

[4] José Cuello's research on late eighteenth-century Bourbon administrative penetration on the northeastern frontier helps us to see that growing administrative oversight during these years meant imperial politics exerted more influence on daily life in the north. His analysis of regional political alignment during the Hidalgo period considers the relationship between taxation and rebellion. My argument, in this chapter and the next, focuses on Bourbon militias and their role in defining membership in the community and polity. Cuello, "The Economic Impact of the Bourbon Reforms," 301–23.

rendering military service, they termed themselves vassals of the king. Colonial citizenship could be conceived of in two ways: as local and fraternal, or as imperial and hierarchical. Beginning in the 1760s, new militia systems began to bridge these two notions of citizenship.

EARLY MILITARY SYSTEMS

At the beginning of the seventeenth century, the northeastern frontier did not have a centrally coordinated military system. Struggles against external Indian nations were carried out by separate forces whose legitimacy was tied to the viceregal government, but whose men and resources were local. The earliest Spanish commanders went north bearing commissions that granted them the authority to establish mines and settlements and to wage "just wars" against any barbarians who attacked them or obstructed missionary activity.

Though perpetually faced with the same threats from hostile northern Indians, the colonial order in Nuevo León adjusted its military system several times in the seventeenth and eighteenth centuries, responding in part to local conditions and in part to imperial policy. The earliest military system was essentially feudal, and the recruitment and command of the conquering forces were personal. Spanish adventurers were licensed by the crown to conduct *entradas*, military offensives that conferred a grant of *encomienda* over conquered Indians. In the north, Spanish conquistadors commanded mixed forces of Spaniards and allied Indian warriors from the time of the Chichimec wars.[5] The first governors (or captains-general) of Nuevo León were part of a patron-client chain of command, holding their power in grant from the king and dispensing commands and appointments to the *alcaldías mayores*. In the seventeenth century, a small number of royal troops guarded strategic points, but local militias were the backbone of the military system.[6] Thus, the cooperation between Nuevo León's Tlaxcalan and Spanish militias was central to the defense of the north.

Governor Martín de Zavala (1625–1664) presided over the first sustained military and civil government in the New Kingdom of León. In Zavala's time, we can point to three types of colonial forces: Tlaxcalan militiamen drawn from the Tlaxcalan-Chichimec pueblos, Spanish militiamen drawn from the haciendas, and a small number of professional soldiers stationed at presidios. Zavala's presidio system was limited to two wooden structures, one at Cadereyta and the other at Cerralvo, each with less than two dozen soldiers. The presidios were headed by men who, like the governor, were both chief magistrates and

---

[5] The first northern presidios were constructed to guard the Zacatecas road in the Chichimec wars. Weber, *Spanish Frontier*, 212. Military cooperation between Tlaxcalans and northern tribes probably first occurred when Guachichiles fought beside Tlaxcalans in 1590s, Frye, "The Native Peoples of Northeastern Mexico," 109.

[6] Roberto Mario Salmon, *Indian Revolts in Northern New Spain*, 25–99; Weber, *The Spanish Frontier*, 213.

commanding officers. Their presidial companies were very small and far from points of supply or assistance.[7]

Large haciendas and Tlaxcalan pueblos both provided military service on the frontier. Just as all Tlaxcalan heads of household were armed for local defense, so too were Spanish landholding families. Early land rights were conditioned on the legal obligation of heads of households to maintain horses, weapons, and supplies in preparation for military emergencies. Spanish *vecinos* were armed at their own expense, and they were required, when summoned, to arrive ready for duty and carrying fifteen to twenty days of rations.[8]

New Spain retained a set of ancient political traditions regarding the symbolic separation of military and political authority. The Roman tradition sought to insulate politics from war by distinguishing between the peacetime and wartime powers of magistrates and by forbidding the activation of military commands within the imperial city. Nuevo León followed the same tradition at a local level. *Vecinos* summoned for war remained in the legal state of civilians until assembled outside the boundaries of the town. Once drawn up in a group and assembled more than half a league from town, the civilians became a royal cavalry. Just as Rome distinguished between the civil and military characteristics of citizenship, so did Nuevo León. A presidio commander, acting in his civil capacity, was a *justicia mayor*; acting in his military capacity, he became a *capitán*.[9] In a practical sense, the routine possession of dual military and civil offices meant that both forms of authority usually were concentrated in the same hands and, furthermore, that rising leaders could parley one sort of authority into the other.

In the seventeenth century, formally commissioned military officers like the governor or presidio captains coordinated heterogeneous groups of militiamen and allies. Tlaxcalans and Spaniards along with friendly Chichimecs (*indios amigos*) cooperated in joint campaigns and shared the spoils of war. Indian governors were able to mobilize their communities of Indian *vecinos* either autonomously or at the request of Spanish magistrates. With the exception of the small number of men in the presidial companies, there was no standing force, nor was there a uniform militia system at an extralocal level. In Tlaxcalan communities, the governor was generally the chief of civil government and chief military commander.[10]

---

[7] Juan Díez de la Calle, "Descubrimiento, población y pacificación del Nuevo Reyno de León," BNE MSS 3026 Noticias Sacrales y Reales ... 1653, fols. 216–21.

[8] Testimony of Villalobos, AGI Audiencia de Guadalajara 173, Expediente sobre Nicolás Villalobos, *protector de indios*, unnumbered string-bound bundle, signed by D. Nicolás de Villalobos, 6 May 1727.

[9] Testimony of Villalobos, AGI Audiencia de Guadalajara 173.

[10] In the 1730s Fernández de Jáuregui Urrutia noted that the normal way of summoning forces was for the frontier *alcaldes* to rouse armed settlers for retaliatory raids; he criticizes the slow response time. Fernández de Jáuregui Urrutia to viceroy, 12 June 1738, in Fernández de Jáuregui Urrutia, *Description of Nuevo León, Mexico*, 80–1.

In the early eighteenth century, Francisco Barbadillo reformed the administration of frontier defenses, aiming to reduce the level of conflict between colonial peoples and nomads, and to create tighter coordination among Nuevo León's armed groups. He retained most seventeenth-century assumptions about the relationship between the crown's Spanish and Indian soldiers but gave them a clearer administrative articulation. Barbadillo recognized the *mayordomos* of haciendas as the official commanders of small defense forces, and he capitalized on the tradition of Tlaxcalan-Spanish military cooperation. He recognized the transmission of Tlaxcalan military citizenship from Gran Tlaxcala to San Esteban and ultimately to the daughter colonies of Nuevo León, and he made it a priority to provide a steady supply of gunpowder to the Tlaxcalan arcabusiers. He also advocated, but did not fully implement, the use of flying companies, which were linked to the presidios but carried out ongoing patrols between Nuevo Léon's Spanish and Indian communities. To Barbadillo, the terms of *vecindad* were similar for Spaniards and Tlaxcalans – without arms and a mount, a man could not be considered a *vecino*.[11]

Tlaxcalan-Spanish cooperation was nowhere so pronounced as in the north of Nuevo León. In 1723, Barbadillo established the Spanish presidio of Boca de Leones near the existing Tlaxcalan colony of San Miguel de Aguayo. The two armed settlements would have a symbiotic military relationship for the next century. Though the forms of military citizenship enjoyed by Spaniards and Tlaxcalans were codified from the first days of colonization, the political and military status of other cooperating Indian groups evolved more often by custom than by law. From the outset, the colonizers had made use of alliances and ad hoc military ventures with *indios amigos*.

Barbadillo redefined settled Chichimec warriors as Indian militiamen rather than simply *indios amigos*. He abolished obsolete rules forbidding non-Tlaxcalan Indians from owning horses, and he recognized groups of Chichimec archers as town guards and night watchmen. In the Tlaxcalan-Chichimec pueblo of San Miguel/San Antonio, the colonial government recognized an official body of Tlaxcalan arcabusiers and another of Alasapa archers. Barbadillo's plans for permanent fortresses were limited to the two existing presidios and the new one at

---

[11] On arms and citizenship, 9 May 1719, Decreto, Mexico, AGI Guadalajara 166, fol. 185; on Tlaxcalan governments and their military function in Nuevo León, Pedimento de los Indios de el Pilón [1726] AGI Audiencia de Guadalajara 173 and Memorial de los Indios de la Conzepcion [1725] AGI Audiencia de Guadalajara 173, fols. 11–12; on rules regarding horses and arms, Carta del lic. Francisco de Barbadillo Vitoria alcalde de corte de la Audiencia de México, 6 Aug. 1717, AGI Audiencia de Guadalajara 166, fol. 154; on the foundation of San Miguel de Aguayo, letter of Sargento Dn. Pedro de las Fuentes, 28 June 1721, AGI Audiencia de Guadalajara 166, fol. 201; on Tlaxcalan arcabusiers, Carta de Blas de la Garza to Barbadillo, 1 May 1720, AGI Audiencia de Guadalajara 166, fol. 192; on the military role of hacienda *mayordomos*, Representación que hizieron los criadores de ganado de el Nuevo Reyno de León [1725], AGI Audiencia de Guadalajara 173.

Boca de Leones. His force of regulars amounted to only a few dozen men, but the entire military resources of the New Kingdom, which included Spanish land-owners, Tlaxcalans, and Chichimecs, were more substantial. His approach to regional defense was to better coordinate separate community-based military forces without blending them into a uniform body.[12]

REGIONAL AND PROTO-NATIONAL MILITIAS

Problems with banditry and hostile nomads were perennial in the northeast. However, in the mid eighteenth century, two new concerns began to influence strategic planning: competition with other European powers and fear of coordi-nated regional rebellions. The success of the English and Anglo-Americans in the Seven Years' War, along with the ongoing threats from nomadic Indians, con-vinced strategists that the current military forces in the north were insufficient.

Between the time of the accession of Carlos III in 1759 and the outbreak of revolutionary conflicts in 1810, the security of northern New Spain became an even higher priority for the Spanish monarchy. The period was characterized by attempts to extend and regularize royal administration. It was also a period of frequent reversals in policy, and of conflicts and changes in jurisdictions and leadership. Crown reforms of regional administration were often launched, only to be altered again prior to full implementation. Royal strategists were troubled by the following problems: the high cost of maintaining northern missions and presidios, the long-term failure of those systems to protect subjects' lives and property, the inability to settle and incorporate new waves of nomadic enemies (most notably Comanches and Apaches), and the inability to control costs while gathering revenues from the region. Most schemes for addressing these problems recommended some version of the following: using uniform parish administra-tion to replace the previous mix of secular and regular jurisdictions; creating a regional militia system to replace smaller ad hoc or customary groups; replacing insular presidios with new military communities that would merge the functions of presidios, missions, and trading posts; abandoning attempts to fully incorpo-rate the most dangerous nomads; and relying on trade monopolies rather than individual taxation for revenue. In practice, none of the new institutions was built from the ground up; instead, the new policies redefined the relationships between existing institutions. For instance, to "secularize" a mission typically meant that the Franciscan missionary began sending reports to the bishop. The new presidial trade policy, at times, meant merely regularizing trade where contraband trade already existed. Creating militias was sometimes just a matter of granting formal titles to existing armed groups and their leaders. Yet, this was also a time in which more people of all castes were armed, drilled, and

---

[12] On the established functions of San Miguel and Boca de Leones, see the acts and correspondence of Barbadillo, 1717–1723, AGI Audiencia de Guadalajara 166, fols. 177–227; on the functions of Chichimec archers, carta del lic. Francisco de Barbadillo Vitoria . . ., 6 Aug. 1717, AGI Audiencia de Guadalajara 166, fols. 141–76.

recognized as citizen-soldiers. These militias, along with the new language and accounting practices of public administration, began to integrate local *vecindad* into a broader notion of national and imperial citizenship.[13]

Beginning in the 1760s, New Spain's military systems were reformed in order to yield the kind of vast conscription forces that already had come to dominate European warfare. In 1766, Spanish Inspector General Juan de Villalba presented to the king his program for the creation of a new militia system in New Spain. The plan fit neatly with prevailing notions of Bourbon administration, but it also was rooted in older Spanish and classical notions of empire. The result was a system that included strong meritocratic features while preserving traditional kinds of officer commissions based on birth and wealth. Mixing the language of feudalism and that of classical governance, Villalba promised that Mexico would have a vast new militia of *"nobles republicanos"* and "king's vassals." To Villalba, Mexico City was the cradle of New Spain, and the site at which the ruling families of the New World and the Old had been joined: "the nobility and gentry which exist in Mexico [City] is large, very distinguished, and comes from the Great Houses of Spain ... [From the] remaining descendants of the Emperors and Kings and Caciques that were pagans have been made Great Spanish Houses." In Roman language, and following a Roman logic, Villalba argued that the whole society, both Indian and Spanish, should be bound together by military service. Yet he argued that commanders should be appointed based on the historic hierarchies within their own cultural groups. He thought it a particularly poor idea that a militia system be constructed "without distinction between noble and plebe (*plebeyo*), or master and servant, treating all with equal honor." His scheme was rooted in the belief that an underlying hierarchy of birth transcended that of nationality. Through this logic, European and New World societies could be bound together as parallel hierarchies in the service of the Spanish crown.[14]

In an attempt to assess and maximize the manpower of the entire society, Villalba categorized the population based on each man's fitness for military service. In the first category he placed "robust young men"; in the second, widowers and married men without children; and in the third, married men with children. He also categorized the population by each man's utility in the economic sphere; for instance, he noted the indispensability of maintaining a certain number of farmers in the fields while others fought. These two methods of categorizing the male population became the bases for a proposed national conscription that would be carried out by drawing lots. This, in many ways, prefigured the mass armies of the Napoleonic period. Villalba, however, was uncomfortable with a system of appointments that did not recognize distinctions

---

[13] On the structures of the Provincias Internas, see Vizcaya Canales, *En los albores de la independencia* and del Carmen Velázquez, *Tres Estudios Sobre las Provincias Internas;* on related administrative practices in Spain, Anthony H. Hull, *Charles III and the Revival of Spain* (Washington, DC: University Press, 1980).

[14] BNE MSS 3650 Papeles de Asuntos Militaries y Conspiraciones, fols. 1–18.

of birth. His theory of natural leadership was rooted in European social hier-archies, but it also recognized the social distinctions that existed among Indians.

Villalba's notion of parallel Indian and Spanish hierarchies was rooted in his understanding of the historic origins of colonial government. To Villalba, Spain's mandate to rule the lands of New Spain derived from Cortés's absorp-tion of the indigenous Mexican hierarchy into the Spanish one. He observed that Mexico City was the "Metropolis and Capital of North America before the advent of the Catholic faith" and "in its paganism was the court, site, and throne of the emperors." He reasoned that, consequently, it remained, by its nature, the capital of New Spain. Even though that throne was now in the hands of Spanish kings, the change in ultimate leadership in no way dissolved the natural, preex-isting hierarchy. Not only did Villalba demand the maintenance of separate white and *pardo* forces, but he also opposed the disruption of historic indige-nous hierarchies and the mixing of elite Indians with other inhabitants of the realm. Most distasteful to him was the prospect that militia and conscription lists would be mixed in such a way that "Nobles would be made equal to blacks, along with their servants and plebes (*plebeyos*)." Villalba's solution was that *sargentos mayores* would conduct a census and draw up appropriate lists of separate, ethnically bounded militias, each of which would preserve appropriate internal cultural hierarchies. In Spanish towns he surveyed the legitimate Spanish population. In *pueblos de indios* he recorded the number of humble Indians and the number of *gente de razón*. The command hierarchies descended from *capitán* to *teniente*, *subteniente*, *sargento*, and common soldier. Common soldiers and *sargentos* might be drawn from the humbler ranks of *vecinos*, but *subtenientes*, *tenientes*, and *capitanes* were men who enjoyed the status of "don."[15]

Villalba looked forward to a time in which the whole population of New Spain would be organized for war and placed under a uniform system of commandants general. In many places such as Mexico City and San Luis Potosí, however, the formation of local, ad hoc military organizations preceded his orders, and the organizers continued to ignore many of their particulars. Villalba's ideas about national organization might be new, but they relied on existing populations – populations whose local leaders had, long before, created their own customs for military organization.[16]

The plan for new militias was still in its infancy when a crisis in San Luis Potosí demanded a rapid and decidedly less structured mass mobilization.[17] In 1767 resentment over mining conditions created an unexpected cross-caste

---

[15] BNE MSS 3650 Papeles de Asuntos Militaries y Conspiraciones, fols. 1–18.
[16] BNE MSS 3650 Papeles de Asuntos Militaries y Conspiraciones, fols. 1–18.
[17] William B. Taylor and Christon I. Archer have both commented on the 1767 rebellion as a moment that highlights a new (or uncomprehending) attitude by Bourbon administrators toward the interethnic political alliances. Archer, *The Army in Bourbon Mexico*, 85–94; William B. Taylor, *Drinking Homicide and Rebellion* (Stanford, CA: Stanford University Press, 1979), 122–3.

rebellion. Miners of various ethnic admixtures joined with discontented Indian groups to make common cause against the authorities of San Luis Potosí. The crisis completely overwhelmed the area's limited standing force, and provoked the rapid formation of a regional militia from the urban populations of the city of San Luis Potosí and from dozens of smaller communities. Faced with a large cross-caste rebellion, San Luis Potosí wisely formed the largest possible cross-caste militia army. After the crisis had passed, the militiamen expected a civic status commensurate with their military responsibilities. Thus began a long process of negotiation over how this mixed force would conform to the new national system. In the late 1760s, leading members of the militias gained a permanent source of wages and status when they became city guards of San Luis Potosí. Other militiamen (especially those of more humble origins) continued to proclaim their membership in the old militia, despite the fact that it remained unmobilized and did not conform to the new continental system.[18]

The 1767 rebellion combined internal and external threats to the stability of colonial society. This fastened the attention of policy makers on the expansion of the militia system and the defense of settlements from both invasion and rebellion. Broader coalitions of enemies demanded a broader coalition of colonial militiamen. A Spanish landowner described his father's response to the 1767 rebellion thus:

> In the year 1767 in the months of May, June and July ... there rose up simultaneously the people of the mines and Indians of the pueblos and the mobs of the royal city of Guadalcazar, the mountain of San Pedro, and the pueblos of San Nicolás and San Sebastián del Venado, and the valley of San Francisco, whose object was robbery and all manner of insults. ... He responded with said company, with their hunting servants, hacienda workers, and other individuals that convened in growing numbers and offered the needed help to contain the insolence of the rebels, and he paid them from his pocket.[19]

Here we see the ways that a paid militia system and the officer commissions of major landowners rested on a common foundation of local patronage. Ad hoc militias, called together by wealthy notables in response to emergencies, were expanded to face the greater scale of regional conflict. Soon they would be subsumed by a broader bureaucracy of national militias.

THE GÁLVEZ ERA: VISIONS OF HISTORY AND THE ARMY OF THE FUTURE

The late Bourbon administrators who reshaped the military systems of the north were not men from the region. Most were peninsular Spaniards sent, in part, to study conditions in the north and, in part, to change them. They were

---

[18] Prontuario para ... las Milicias del Reyno de Nueva España, 20 Jan. 1772, BNE MSS 18745, no. 28; AGS Secretaría de Guerra 7002, exp. 1, fols. 1, 38.

[19] Méritos de Dn. Juan José María de Mora y Luna Pérez Calderón Conde de Santa María de Guadalupe del Peñasco, Secretaría de Guerra, AGS 7002, exp. 1, fol. 45.

concerned both with questions of routine annual administration and with broader questions about the history and future of Spanish Empire in the north. They entered the scene after two centuries of Spanish efforts in the region, and they sought to retool administrative systems in light of past successes and failures. José de Gálvez set the general agenda for the changes to colonial military administration that would take place in the final half-century of colonial rule. Gálvez organized all the northern frontier provinces into a jurisdiction called the Provincias Internas and placed them under a single military commander. He ordered a shift in long-term strategy, abandoning the defenses of many of New Spain's forward positions, and retreating to a clearer line of defense. He also counseled a shift in military practice, urging commanders to focus on trade-based diplomacy and the cultivation of alliances with friendly nomads.[20]

Between 1765 and 1771 José de Gálvez served the crown as a special visitor charged with the reform of royal administration in the New World. In the north of New Spain, his agents, the Marqués de Rubí and the military engineer Nicolás de Lafora, carried out a vast tour of inspection between 1766 and 1768. Rubí was very clear about the nature of the military threat in the north and the vulnerabilities of the current system. The nomads of the north (especially the Apaches) were excellent horsemen and archers. Worse still, they could travel vast distances in small groups, attack without warning, and disappear without a trace. They had no central commands or concentrated populations to attack. Rubí considered the current presidial defenses almost useless; they were both expensive and ineffective. The presidios were spaced at such distant intervals that hostile Indians could pass between them at will. The soldiers, he claimed, saw little gain in leaving their presidios to pursue the enemy. Gálvez planned to close the northernmost presidios and pull back to a more modest and defensible frontier, along which presidios would be more closely and regularly spaced. Lafora, Rubí, and Gálvez considered the current presidio system a failure, but they saw much potential for improved defense of the region by the colonies' own inhabitants. Militias, not presidios, were the real key to their plans. Lafora sometimes dismissed presidios as a waste of money even while praising the military value of neighboring towns. Towns paid for themselves while fielding larger forces.[21] Real security lay in the settlement of a larger population in the north.

Lafora was keenly aware of the military and settlement functions performed by Tlaxcalans. His report noted twelve Tlaxcalan colonies in northeastern

---

[20] On the Gálvez reforms, see Luis Navarro García, *La política americana de José de Gálvez según su "Discurso y reflexiones de un vasallo"* (Málaga: Algazara, 1998).

[21] For instance, Lafora recommended the closure of the presidio of Monclova, which had been central to regional military planning, dismissing its salaries and expenses as a waste of money. It was the *vecinos* of the area, not the soldiers, in which he took an interest. He noted healthy communities of Spaniards, mestizos, and mulattos in neighboring settlements. Nicolás de Lafora, *Relación*, 178–82.

frontier zones. Lafora described their crucial role in the foundation of Saltillo and its daughter colonies:

> San Esteban de Tlaxcala is inhabited by pure Tlaxcalan Indians that founded it in the conquest of this country, and despite having sent out various colonies to form Parras, the Alamo, Monclova, Boca de Leones and some seven others, its population numbers three thousand people governed by a Spanish *protector* and a governor of their nation dependent on the viceroyalty of Mexico and administered by a cleric of San Francisco who is their priest[.] They are very civilized *ladinos* that possess the best fields and orchards.[22]

Presidios were only one tool (and at that time, a poor one) for defending the frontier. Even while Bourbon administrators reformed the presidio system, they contemplated the effectiveness and future applications of the Tlaxcalan military colony.

To bind together the military forces of the north, Gálvez and Rubí recommended the formation of a unified northern administration (the Provincias Internas) that, for military purposes, would subsume the existing provincial governments. In 1782, Teodoro de Croix, a royal inspector of troops, produced a comprehensive report on military administration in New Spain with the same ends in mind. Like Rubí and Gálvez, de Croix took a long view of the history of the north. His reports to the crown on the administration of the region focused on the following question: Why were the early conquistadors so successful in conquering the center of Mexico? And why were subsequent generations of Spaniards so unsuccessful in conquering and controlling the north? His answer would help to define the practices of the Provincias Internas.[23]

De Croix believed that the triumphs of the sixteenth century were attributable to superior European weapons, the use of cavalry, effective alliances with Indians, and, above all else, the element of surprise. In that fortunate epoch, "the old conquistadors fought against peoples that had never seen horses or firearms, but the Apaches, the Comanches, and the other Indians of the north ride them with skill ... their lances and arrows they use without pause and with inconceivable accuracy." In the center of Mexico, many of the sedentary populations were disarmed at the time of conquest and successfully incorporated into a peaceful colonial order. In the north it proved impossible to deprive the nomads of arms and mounts, just as it was impossible to reduce the most dangerous tribes to permanent settlement. De Croix acknowledged that many of the settlements of the past had been a success and noted that existing policies might have been sufficient were it not for the more recent and more serious confrontation with the Apaches and Comanches.[24]

---

[22] LaFora, *Relación*, 173.

[23] Informe sobre el estado de las Provincias Internas por su comandante Teodoro de Croix, 23 Apr.1782, AGI Audiencia de Guadalajara 253, fols. 5–6.

[24] De Croix, 23 Apr. 1782, AGI Guadalajara 253, fols. 5–6.

To de Croix, presidios were important, but insufficient, to the task of defending the north. He noted that at present the presidios were barely capable of defending themselves, much less of defending other colonial communities. De Croix advocated a two-part military system in which presidios would become logistical centers for coordinating much larger regional defense forces composed of local militia companies. Under this system, not only would the presidios be protecting towns, but the militias also would be "reinforcing the presidios with *compañías volantes*, and *piquetes*, and *dragones* [light cavalry, infantry, and dragoons]." He envisioned several lines of defense: the first of presidials and the rest of citizen-soldiers who would reinforce the frontiers of the province, contribute *piquetes* and *dragones*, and establish a second wall of military colonies. In keeping with the old Tlaxcalan mission-town model, these new military colonies would be populated by Spaniards, civilized Indians, and newly acculturated Indian populations. He advocated the replication of the Tlaxcalan-Spanish-Chichimec settlement model (already widespread in the area of Monclova) in new sites along the Río Grande.[25]

The strategy sketched out by José de Gálvez did not just sit on a shelf gathering dust. A digest of his recommendations was issued to de Croix and to the other commanders who succeeded him in the Provincias Internas. These commanders continued to address the problems of the north within the Gálvez paradigm, adding to and refining his analysis of regional strategy. Like de Croix, Gálvez was constantly returning to the question of which techniques of the great sixteenth-century conquistadors could, or could not, be profitably translated to the northern frontier. The Tlaxcalans were central to his understanding of the sixteenth-century conquest, and their example exerted an important influence on his plans for the future. In the instructions Gálvez issued to his commanders, we find the following historical lesson on the conquest of the Aztecs: "a great army did not conquer this empire; it was done with the help of the Tlaxcalans and progressively with that of all the Indians of New Spain who contributed to its welcome collapse. The chief conquistador [Cortés] never refused the peaces they offered him: he took advantage of the faithful conduct of his true friends." Gálvez pointed out that all periods of Spanish success in the Americas were attributable to this Tlaxcalan (or Roman) strategy of expansion by alliance and confederation; leaders who abandoned this principle did so at their own risk.[26]

Gálvez was concerned by both the failure of recent military efforts in the northeast and their inefficiency; it was not just that there were too few troops, but that they were using the wrong diplomatic and military strategies. He noted that a small number of men had defeated the Aztecs and that, as recently as 1729, the northern frontier was guarded by only 734 men. In his day the crown was

[25] De Croix, AGI Audiencia de Guadalajara 243, títulos 44, 836, 774. This idea is echoed by Gálvez, who spoke of the Tlaxcalans of the Monclova area as the "owners" of five mixed-population settlements and the model for the new Río Grande sites, AGS Secretaría de Guerra 6966, Copia del Informe ... de 1784 sobre las misiones del Reyno de Nueva España, 170.

[26] Instructions issued to Dn. Jacobo Ugarte, 1786, AGS Secretaría de Guerra 7041, exp. 8, fol. 155.

committing more men and more money, but with worse results. Gálvez concluded that traditional military methods were no longer effective because the enemy had changed. In the sixteenth century, Spain faced two kinds of Indians: the civilized Indians of central Mexico, who could be integrated into the empire, and the uncivilized Indians of the north – people innocent of Spanish society, weapons, and tactics. The latter were once "innocent people, like those of today in California," but contact and experience had long since changed them. Now the Apaches and Comanches were excellent horsemen and archers and were well schooled in Spanish practices. The Indians' exposure to firearms was such that they no longer feared them, and their bows were, in practice, more dangerous than guns.[27]

Gálvez concluded that, at least in the near future, battlefield victory over the Apaches was impossible. Setting that objective aside, he focused on reducing the effects of Apache raids by eliminating their causes. He believed that the root causes of these attacks were material scarcity and Spanish vulnerability. Historically, the Apache lived on hunting. Now that the Spanish filled the north with cattle ranching, the nomads could only survive by two means: by stealing from the Spanish or by trading with them. Gálvez argued that increasing trade and gifts to the Indians was a safer and less expensive method than war. He acknowledged that a century of deceit and opportunism by both nomadic and Spanish war leaders left little room for trust in good-faith diplomacy. The north would need a kind of *realpolitik* that dealt in material goods and force. If the Spanish continued to seek pitched battles, Apache warriors (who kept their women, children, and supplies safe in concealed settlements) could forever evade the Spanish while continuing their incessant raids. Always pragmatic, Gálvez was willing to abandon purely military strategies for modes of commerce and diplomacy that could be undertaken at less expense.[28]

The Gálvez strategy called for larger defensive militias within the colonial sphere, new strategic settlements of citizen-soldiers, a defensive line of presidios to separate colonial lands from those of the nomads, and a new system of gift diplomacy and strategic alliances. He hoped to make war less profitable than peace for the Apaches and to make security both possible and affordable for the crown through his new system of "incessant war, opportunistic peace, and reciprocal commerce."[29]

In 1772 Spain began the reform of militias in the Provincias Internas and throughout New Spain. The *Reglamento y Instrucción* of 1772, issued by Viceroy Antonio Bucareli y Ursua, defined official policy from 1772 to 1794.[30]

[27] AGS Secretaría de Guerra 7041, exp. 1, fol. 4, arts. 26–8, 33–7; on archers: "the use of these arms [muskets] by the Indians is not more dangerous than that of arrows, due to their agility and skill in firing them ... this doesn't happen with firearms, which require time to reload and charge, their being able to attain fewer shots of a bullet than of an arrow ... ," AGS Secretaría de Guerra 7041, exp. 1, fol. 4, arts. 76–9.

[28] AGS Secretaría de Guerra 7041, exp. 1, fol. 4, arts. 40–50; exp. 1, fol. 26.

[29] AGS Secretaría de Guerra 7041, exp. 1, fol. 3.

[30] AGS Secretaría de Guerra 7039, exp. 8.

The new system built on several existing ones. It drew upon the militias of 1766–1767, on the old presidial system, and on the Tlaxcalan system of armed mission-towns. Gálvez cited the "tumults of the year 1767" as one of the motives for these reforms; but the reforms were also influenced by the Rubí-Lafora recommendations on the retrenchment and fortification of the presidial line. Presidios were to be built, closed, or moved in order to create a uniform chain of thirteen presidios at forty-league intervals, creating a defensive line from the Atlantic to the Pacific. Twenty professional soldiers were to staff each presidio, but this force of 260 men was only a small part of the new military system; its core was the militia. Gálvez drew up plans for a militia of 26,000 men in New Spain. These soldiers would serve at their own expense, paying for arms, uniforms, and supplies that would be distributed by the crown.[31]

Both the scale and structure of New Spain's emerging mass militias had important implications for political life. At its base, the organization was built from the country's existing social units. Militia companies would still come from Indian pueblos and rural haciendas, but they also would come from the most basic social units of urban society. In cities, many militia units would be defined as *"milicias urbanas de comercio"* – companies formed from trade-based *gremios* (guilds). Thus, beginning in the 1770s there emerged a popular consciousness, among all those groups, of membership in a national system. Military planners imagined that at full wartime strength, New Spain would have 26,000 men under arms. This force comprised twenty-six regiments, each regiment ten companies, and each company one hundred men (though in subsequent practice, companies usually had between twenty-five and fifty men). From the militia lists, we can see that each regiment included companies defined by membership in local Indian communities, hacienda residence, or urban trades. Assembling a regiment meant placing companies of Tlaxcalans, Chichimecs, ranch hands, merchants, butchers, and blacksmiths all side by side. This system preserved an old notion of society as consisting of symbiotic corporate structures, but it also shaped a new notion of universal citizenship. Companies were of different cultural, ethnic, and vocational types, but they were formally equivalent within the military hierarchy. When drilled and assembled together, they demonstrated to participants the composition of New Spain's male citizenry.[32]

Mission-towns were one of the cultural units at the base of the militia system. The new colonies of the upper Río Grande and Nuevo Santander were intentional replications of the Tlaxcalan garrison town system. Often begun with a group of fifty founding *vecinos*, they were created on the same scale as militia companies and were enrolled as militia companies. Thus, in some cases, the body

[31] Prontuario para … las Milicias del Reyno de Nueva España, 20 Jan. 1772, BNE MSS 18745, no. 28; Carmen Velázquez, *Tres estudios sobre las Provinicas Internas*, 62.
[32] Prontuario para … las Milicias del Reyno de Nueva España, 20 Jan. 1772, BNE MSS 18745, no. 28.

of *vecinos* of a town was formally and functionally coextensive with the local militia.[33]

For Bourbon administrators, the regularization of jurisdictions was always a guiding priority. It was thought, perhaps rightly, that record keeping, taxation, defense, and public order could all be improved by rendering military, economic, and political boundaries coterminous. This ideal was hard to achieve in practice – as witnessed by the awkward layering of administration in the northeast where the provincial governments, the intendancy of San Luis Potosí, and the archdiocese of Monterrey overlapped in a peculiar fashion. Locally, however, royal administrators made progress toward establishing parishes as the basic unit of spiritual administration, and militia companies as the basic unit of military administration. Increasingly, an established, landholding male head of household – Indian or Spanish – would have viewed himself as a *vecino*, militiaman, and parishioner of the same geographical and human community. Each of these institutions (town, parish, and militia company) became a vehicle for social and political inclusion.[34]

In the 1780s, the church hierarchy and military hierarchy cooperated to integrate what formerly had been separate local institutions. In 1781, Pope Pius VI issued *Breve Apostólico y Estatutos Generales para la erección y govierno de las custodias de misiones Franciscanos en las Provincias Internas*. The order addresses a set of problem conditions that the church and civil hierarchy feared in the north. It feared, on one hand, clerical exploitation of Indian labor. On the other hand, it feared that opportunistic Indians, mestizos, and even Spaniards would wander from community to community, consuming resources but not paying proper taxes or clerical fees. Many *indios* and *gente de razón* had become *vagos* or *forasteros*, falling between the cracks of too loose a system. The pope's new order sought not only to fix the membership of northern peoples in specific communities, but also to more clearly define the authority and membership of local clerics in larger ecclesiastical administrations. The order still acknowledged the difference between *nuevas conversiones* and parishes, but urged the transformation of the former to the latter whenever possible. Whether in a parish or a *conversión*, the local cleric was to fulfill the role of community priest and to carry out the same administrative functions: recording baptisms, masses, church expenditures, and all financial transactions involving community funds (those of the *cofradías, pías menores*, and *limosnas perpetuas*).[35]

---

[33] AGI Audiencia de Guadalajara 327, fols. 1–47.

[34] For a discussion of how colonial jurisdictions overlapped in the same physical space, see Gerhard, *The North Frontier of New Spain*, 10–21, 344–57.

[35] Pope Pius VI, *Breve apostólico de Pió Sexto y Estatutos Generales para la Erección y Gobierno de las Custodias de Misioneros Franciscanos Observantes de Propaganda Fide en las Provincias Internas de Nueva España* (Joachin Ibarra, Impresor de Cámara de SM, 1781). On forasteros, see Ann Wightman, *Indigenous Migration and Social Change: The Forasteros of Cuzco* (Durham, NC: Duke, 1990).

The papal order also shows how the political processes of church institutions paralleled those in the lay world. It required that all Franciscans be connected to a clear hierarchy of ever-larger jurisdictions (*vicaros/hospicios*, *definidores*, *custodios* and chapter presidencies). Many of the official appointments in this hierarchy were accomplished through an electoral process. As was the case in many political communities of the day, participation in church elections was dictated by one's category of membership: humble missionaries held only a passive vote, while the superior level of administrators held an "active voice."[36]

Church administrators and royal administrators in the 1780s were focused on the goal of turning communities of newly converted Indians into Indian towns. This meant that newer populations of Indians should be baptized, settled, and instructed in Christianity and agriculture. In religious terms, the Indians should become parishioners; in political terms, their communities should become *pueblos de indios* led by Indian *cabildos*. The stated goal of the Franciscan order, working throughout the north, was "to advance the missions, making them into pueblos ... not only toward the good republican government of the Indians, [but also] introducing among them the order of families and obedience to their superiors and putting in their emerging or infant settlements agriculture and the civilized arts, and all possible commerce, with which they may be bound together and unified."[37] The settled Indian communities were to become towns with their own elected governments and with a shared stake in the economic productivity and security of the region.

The new Bourbon militia systems, in defining membership and designating community and regional leaders, created an important political model that was shared by soldiers of all castes. Elections of several sorts already existed in northern colonial society, but the election of militia officers now connected a local political process to a universal regional body. A hierarchy with elected elements existed in the church and in *pueblos de indios*, as well as in large colonial cities with *ayuntamientos*, but the election of company commanders, at least by a uniform process, was a new phenomenon. The militia enrollment records for the 1770s show that enlistment levels were based on a universal census, and that companies were defined by ethnicity and trade. The company officers were drawn from amongst each group's local membership. Sometimes through voting and sometimes through the drawing of lots, militiamen became officers. In this way, the armed citizenry of the north was joined together in a common militia system that was rooted in organic local communities that recognized the principle of electoral leadership.[38]

---

[36] Pope Pius VI, *Breve apostólico ... 1781.*

[37] Antonio de las Reyes, "Expediente sobre el Plan para arreglar el Govierno espiritual de Pueblos y Misiones en las Provincias," AGI Audienca de Guadalajara 586, exp. 3, fols. 105–14.

[38] Prontuario para conocimiento del estado en que se hallan las Milicias del Reyno de Nueva España, 20 Jan. 1772, BNE, MSS 18745, fol. 28.

AN EMPIRE OF YEOMAN FARMERS?

In the final decades of the eighteenth century, the colonial government was sometimes uneasy about the relationship between multicaste militias and political power on the northern frontier. Since the uprising of 1767, leaders had been left with a fear of cross-caste rebellion and with the precedent of a large multicaste militia system. The crisis of the 1760s had brought into being two regiments of militiamen: the regiment of San Luis and the regiment of San Carlos – both headquartered at San Luis Potosí. These were the largest forces ever created in the region, and a tremendous military asset, but they also created doubts in the minds of military planners. Spanish leaders wondered whether it was best to have the largest possible force, or actually safer to have a smaller force composed only of *castas limpias*. This was the question faced by Nemesio Salcedo who was charged with the reorganization of the region's militias in the 1790s. He followed the trend of reducing the official rolls of the active militia and narrowing its demographic scope. The original force of the 1760s was to have 3,441 men, but this proved unmanageably large. In 1788, a proposal was introduced to reduce the active force to 1,139 men, keeping an additional 1,906 as reserve forces. In 1797, Salcedo further reduced the active force to 696. Salcedo had several ways of categorizing and understanding the population of the northeast. He counted the population by household, and he expected that the security of the region would require one militiaman for each six families. The population included Spaniards, Indians, mulattos (*pardos*), and a growing number of other mixed-caste inhabitants. He considered the last of these to be the least reliable. Salcedo's principal critique of the old regiments was that more than half of their members were *castas*. Balancing his fears of Apache attacks against his fears of *casta* rebellion, Salcedo arrived at what he considered a practical compromise. The new regiments would be small and made up exclusively of men from "*familias de castas limpias*," but a larger multiethnic force would be held in reserve, so that "in case of a major emergency, there will be on hand the rest of the castes of people that are common in the provinces of San Luis Potosí [the intendancy], and from which the greater number from the disbanded Legion was composed."[39] The compromise is an interesting one. It retained the idea that the entire society could be gathered under arms, while at the same time enforcing a distinction in status between the old members of the northern, colonial society – the Spanish, Tlaxcalans, and acculturated Chichimecs – and the populations of mixed ancestry.[40]

Salcedo retained the idea of a military draft, which was to be carried out at a local level by drawing lots. He also retained the notion that some command positions were elective. He worried that too many layers of incomplete reforms of the northeastern forces had created confusion over the membership of companies, and over who held legitimate commands. Higher commissions went only

[39] AGS Secretaría de Guerra 7002, exp. 1, fol. 38.
[40] AGS Secretaría de Guerra 7002, exp. 1.

to men of high birth who could finance part of the army, but more humble posts remained elective. The composite system of militias under San Luis Potosí describes many of the complexities of late colonial society. It was a corporate society in which Spaniards and Indians had a more clearly defined position than people of mixed ancestry. Power at the highest echelons was determined by elite ancestry and wealth, and yet local governance had strong democratic features. At some level, all men capable of bearing arms were a part of this militarized society.

In 1795, Salcedo carried out an administrative review of northern troops that must have been a striking illustration of the structure of the emerging Bourbon state. He called for the assembly of all the soldiers, of all types, drawn from the *naturales y vecinos* of the whole kingdom residing in the intendancy, so that he might determine the actual troop levels, proper salaries, and legitimate *fueros* of the whole population.[41]

The formation of imperial militias, of necessity, involved a new level of sophistication in counting and categorizing the region's inhabitants. On paper, the militia system established by Viceroy Bucareli in 1772 lasted until 1794. As this discussion of the period makes clear, however, the execution of the 1772 plan was far from perfect, and regional leaders were constantly tinkering with its details. In the 1790s the overhaul of the militia system was a high priority, but its execution kept changing hands between the intendant of San Luis Potosí (Félix María Calleja), the commanders general of the Provincias Internas, and the state governors. In 1795, Calleja was in the midst of a general inspection of all forces in Nuevo León when he was called to attend to urgent military matters in Nuevo Santander. He turned the task over to Governor Simón de Herrera who produced a thorough written report.

Like Salcedo, Herrera knew that in times of crisis he would need to mobilize much of the Indian and mixed-caste population, but he also feared the consequences of keeping them perpetually armed and drilled. Whenever possible, Herrera thought it safest for the activated militias to be Spanish. His 1797 report to the crown explained: "I remit to your Excellency the [report on the] state of the whole population that I have formed for the enlistment of militias – it does not include Indians, mulattos, or other castes, because there is a sufficient number of Spaniards to complete it." Herrera and Salcedo began with the notion that the government must count the entire population to be defended, determine the total number of men capable of bearing arms, and then determine the number of militiamen needed. Herrera found that there were 13,600 families of *castas limpias*. Of this population, 2,892 men were of proper age, health, and fitness to bear arms; and 1,842 youths were capable of attending the soldiers and reloading their weapons. From these numbers, he created a provincial regiment of fifteen companies and 1,556 men – men who were responsible for maintaining their own weapons at their own expense. In other words, his plan enabled the

---

[41] AGS Secretaría de Guerra 7002, exp. 1, fol. 9.

creation of an all-Spanish peacetime militia, but only by enrolling more than half of the able-bodied adult male population! Each of the fifteen companies came from a geographical catchment that corresponded to existing jurisdictions for *valles, ciudades*, or *reales de minas*. The soldiers in each company were qualified by their age, their fitness, and by their ability to supply their own equipment. Sergeants were in all cases experienced soldiers (*veteranos*). These *veteranos* were distinguished by their experience in frontier warfare and were counted upon to organize and train the local forces. They were, in a sense, missionaries for the creation of a universal militia society.[42]

The records for the provinces and the intendancy for this period link the issues of citizenship, taxation, and military service. The state of Nuevo León was, in many respects, a military organization. Its head was both a civil governor and a general; its lesser magistrates had dual responsibilities as civil leaders and captains of valleys and mining towns. The military records describe militiamen as both vassals (*vasallos*) of the crown and as citizens of their local communities. Residents of the larger cities of Linares and Monterrey were referred to as *ciudadanos*; residents of the *valles* and *reales* as *vecinos*. All such men were householders, landowners, and heads of families. To call them vassals is not far from the mark, given that they were granted the military *fuero* in return for their service in battle as self-funded warriors.[43]

In laying out a system of provincial Spanish militias, Calleja and Herrera were not dispensing with the region's Indian forces. During the same period in which the Spanish militias were reformed, Spanish commanders continued to work with Tlaxcalan and Chichimec soldiers and with the mixed-caste militiamen of San Luis Potosí and Nuevo Santander. They also made alliances with outside *indios amigos* in an attempt to fend off attacks by the Apaches. Calleja and Herrera were willing to call upon these auxiliary forces in times of emergency. They also noted in their reports to the crown that while the core of each Spanish company was Spanish, additional nonwhite soldiers could be enrolled at any time to fill out the ranks. It appears that one of the goals of the Bourbon commanders was to create a reliable chain of command linking Spain to local commanders. In the service of this goal, they wanted an officer corps that was in its higher echelons composed of peninsular Spaniards and, at its base, composed of creoles. The Spanish militiamen were the backbone of a larger system that ultimately included as many indigenous militiamen as European ones.[44]

Since the time of Francisco Barbadillo, royal officials had often lamented the long-term effects of Nuevo León's early land grants on the development of the region's economy and military. Barbadillo was concerned that the enormous early land grants, given to a small number of Spanish families, had deprived Indians of productive lands and also retarded the rate of settlement by Spaniards

---

[42] AGS Secretaría de Guerra 7039, exp. 7, 8.

[43] AGS Secretaría de Guerra 7002, exp. 1, fol. 40; exp. 4, fols. 40, 43; exp. 1, fol. 44, map [Mp y D-Xi-13].

[44] AGS Secretaría de Guerra 7002, exp. 1, fol. 38.

from the center of New Spain. He emphasized that the frontier could be controlled only if a sufficiently large colonial economy could be planted on northern
lands. Toward this end, he seized lands from several large Spanish estates to
create the second wave of Tlaxcalan-Chichimec pueblos. Barbadillo wanted to
lay the foundation for a much larger population of armed farmers and ranchers –
both Indian and Spanish – who could serve as soldiers to defend their
communities.[45]

At the beginning of the nineteenth century, Spanish leaders believed that the
underlying problem faced by Barbadillo remained unsolved: the north lacked a
sufficient population to provide for its own defense. Following the Louisiana
Purchase, they marveled at the pace of U.S. settlement in frontier areas to the
north. In analyzing New Spain's military failures, they reached some of the same
conclusions as Barbadillo: the north must be populated quickly with a citizenry
ready to defend the land from attacks by nomads, Anglo-Americans, or other
Europeans. With elite estates occupying the best lands, and in some cases
measuring more than 300 leagues, the prospects were poor for attracting colonists. An 1805 report commissioned by the crown counseled both royal subsidies and small land grants to anyone willing to settle upon, cultivate, and defend
the lands of the north.[46] The report noted that the core provinces of New
Spain had a population 5,321,877, but that the entire Provincias Internas was
home to only 442,847 settled inhabitants. The result was a swath of northern
provinces that were economically backward and difficult to defend. In their
dream of populating the north with citizen-soldiers, Spanish administrators
were inspired by both Anglo-American and Roman models. The author of the
1805 report noted that an orderly and more egalitarian settlement of the north
might incorporate and acculturate troublemakers and former Indian enemies.
He argued that

> Rome came to be the ruler of the whole world, and the policy of its foundation
> was none other than the admission of all those trouble-makers who didn't fit in
> their own kingdoms, assigning them lands and granting them proportional
> honors, according to the circumstances, populating well the colonies they
> acquired through conquests; and if this worked in those remote times, why
> should we not apply it to our fine part of the Spanish Empire?[47]

The report argued for the continuation and acceleration of some of the methods
employed by Barbadillo. It foresaw a time when all arable land would be

---

[45] On the problems of large land grants, Barbadillo, 20 Sept. 1715, AGI Audiencia de Guadalajara
166, fols. 20–24. This notion that New Spain must emulate U.S. settlement practices to populate
the frontier was shared by Manuel Salcedo and Texas Governor Miguel de Lardizabal y Uribe.
Salcedo toured the United States and studied its model. He recommended to Ladizabal y Uribe the
use of American-style trading posts followed by settlers. This failing, he feared an inevitable
demographic absorption of Texas by the United States. Comunicacíon de dn. Manuel Salcedo a
Miguel de Lardizabal y Uribe ..., 15 Nov. 1809, BNE 18636, no. 28.

[46] BNE MSS 19709.

[47] BNE MSS 19709, no. 37, fol. 3.

brought under cultivation, and when the hill country would sustain vast herds of sheep and cattle for the textile mills and tanneries of growing cities. Like Barbadillo's system, this one was ethnically inclusive. Along with a hierarchy of Spanish jurisdictions, it planned for the growth of the Indian economy under the oversight of *subdelegados*, priests, and the *cabildos* of the *repúblicas de indios*. The planners for the Provincias Internas expected that, beside the settled populations, the "barbarous Indians that border them, whose continuous attacks they must today resist, will little by little be affected and accustomed to trade with the educated and civilized peoples by whom, it is to be believed, they will be settled."[48]

NORTHERN CITIZENSHIP IN AN AGE OF REVOLUTIONARY VIOLENCE

The period between the outbreak of the Hidalgo Rebellion and the conclusion of Mexican national independence was a turbulent time in northeastern New Spain. Institutions were formed and dissolved in rapid succession while control of Spain and New Spain was never long in the same hands. Amid the chaos, however, important and lasting changes to regional political culture took place. Both locally and regionally colonial institutions and colonial citizens were integrated into an emergent modern state. This evolution took place *not in spite of* the surrounding violence and institutional disruption, *but because of* them.

Before descending into the details, it is helpful to map out the major turning points in this period of revolutionary conflict. This era of instability began in northern New Spain, as in the rest of Latin America, when Napoleon occupied Spain and forced the abdication of the royal family. Between 1808 and 1814 the relationship between Spain and New Spain was confused by the absence of the king and by the contest between Napoleonic and Spanish nationalist governments. In Mexico itself, struggles over the control of the capital city were soon overshadowed by the revolutionary threat posed by Miguel Hidalgo. Hidalgo and his followers won a series of early battles, and the viceroyalty called upon the soldiers of the northeast for aid. It was at this point that the crisis came to the northeastern frontier.

We may roughly periodise the changing allegiances of the northeast as follows. From October 1810 to January 1811, the provinces mobilized all available military forces to defend the viceroyalty. In this time of crisis, however, much power devolved to local authorities and to humble military officers who soon sided with the insurgents. From January to March 1811, the militias and local leaders of Nuevo León supported Hidalgo. Local governments, war councils, and even company commanders made most immediate decisions because the region lacked a functional chain of command linking the soldier to the state. When the

---

[48] BNE MSS 19709, no. 37, fol. 3.

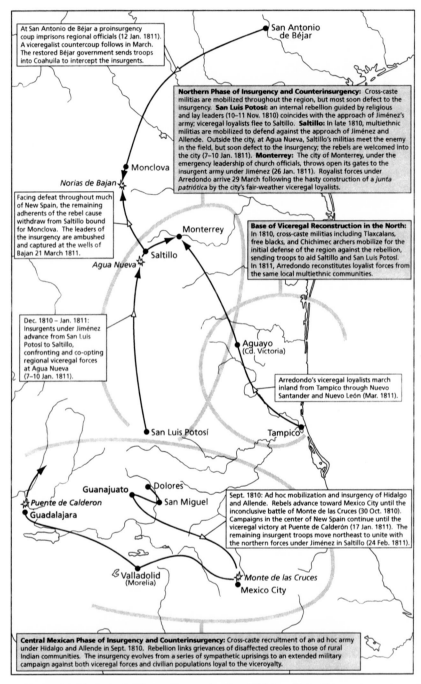

At San Antonio de Béjar a proinsurgency coup imprisons regional officials (12 Jan. 1811). A viceregalist countercoup follows in March. The restored Béjar government sends troops into Coahuila to intercept the insurgents.

Northern Phase of Insurgency and Counterinsurgency: Cross-caste militias are mobilized throughout the region, but most soon defect to the insurgency. **San Luis Potosí:** an internal rebellion guided by religious and lay leaders (10–11 Nov. 1810) coincides with the approach of Jiménez's army; viceregal loyalists flee to Saltillo. **Saltillo:** In late 1810, multiethnic militias are mobilized to defend against the approach of Jiménez and Allende. Outside the city, at Agua Nueva, Saltillo's militias meet the enemy in the field, but soon defect to the insurgency; the rebels are welcomed into the city (7–10 Jan. 1811). **Monterrey:** The city of Monterrey, under the emergency leadership of church officials, throws open its gates to the insurgent army under Jiménez (26 Jan. 1811). Royalist forces under Arredondo arrive 29 March following the hasty construction of a *junta patriótica* by the city's fair-weather viceregal loyalists.

Facing defeat throughout much of New Spain, the remaining adherents of the rebel cause withdraw from Saltillo bound for Monclova. The leaders of the insurgency are ambushed and captured at the wells of Bajan 21 March 1811.

Base of Viceregal Reconstruction in the North: In 1810, cross-caste militias including Tlaxcalans, free blacks, and Chichimec archers mobilize for the initial defense of the region against the rebellion, sending troops to aid Saltillo and San Luis Potosí. In 1811, Arredondo reconstitutes loyalist forces from the same local multiethnic communities.

Dec. 1810 – Jan. 1811: Insurgents under Jiménez advance from San Luis Potosí to Saltillo, confronting and co-opting regional viceregal forces at Agua Nueva (7–10 Jan. 1811).

Arredondo's viceregal loyalists march inland from Tampico through Nuevo Santander and Nuevo León (Mar. 1811).

Sept. 1810: Ad hoc mobilization and insurgency of Hidalgo and Allende. Rebels advance toward Mexico City until the inconclusive battle of Monte de las Cruces (30 Oct. 1810). Campaigns in the center of New Spain continue until the viceregal victory at Puente de Calderón (17 Jan. 1811). The remaining insurgent troops move northeast to unite with the northern forces under Jiménez in Saltillo (24 Feb. 1811).

Central Mexican Phase of Insurgency and Counterinsurgency: Cross-caste recruitment of an ad hoc army under Hidalgo and Allende in Sept. 1810. Rebellion links grievances of disaffected creoles to those of rural Indian communities. The insurgency evolves from a series of sympathetic uprisings to an extended military campaign against both viceregal forces and civilian populations loyal to the viceroyalty.

San Antonio de Béjar

Monclova

Norias de Bajan

Monterrey

Agua Nueva   Saltillo

Aguayo (Cd. Victoria)

San Luis Potosí   Tampico

Guanajuato   Dolores
Puente de Calderon   San Miguel
Guadalajara

Valladolid (Morelia)   Monte de las Cruces
Mexico City

MAP 3. Multiethnic Military Forces in the Hidalgo Rebellion, 1810–1811 (Map commissioned from Cox Cartographic Limited)

leaders of the insurrections were captured in Coahuila, the northeastern leaders changed sides once again, proclaiming for the viceroy and concealing their recent involvement in the rebellion. Local notables, who had recently supported the insurgency, were able to survive the political upset by reconfiguring their insurrectionary *juntas* as new *juntas patrióticas*. These organizations proclaimed their allegiance to the viceroy and denounced the rebellion. From October 1812 to November 1814, the Constitution of Cádiz was applied to Nuevo León, validating strong local governments and creating the first provincial assembly. In 1814, following the collapse of the Napoleonic empire, King Ferdinand VII was restored to the Spanish throne. He immediately repudiated the constitution, disrupting the newly established political institutions in New Spain.

In the four-year period from the arrival of Hidalgo's armies to the revocation of the Constitution of Cádiz, the following general trends prevailed: an increase in the number of men under arms; greater lateral political ties among ethnic communities; and strengthened institutional expressions of regional political power and representation. From 1815 to 1820, the viceroyalty would attempt to reconstruct many of the legal and political conditions that had existed in the eighteenth century, but this proved difficult. In Nuevo León the influences of Hidalgo and of the Constitution of Cádiz, along with the profound effects of expanding militia systems, would continue to shape political culture until the Constitution of Cádiz was restored in 1820.

Between the outbreak of the Hidalgo Rebellion in 1810 and the creation of new state constitutions in 1826, every element of the north's political and military systems was tested by crisis. Both village-level political systems with deep roots in the colonial period and the new militia systems of the late Bourbon period would define the region's response to that era's revolutionary forces. The Hidalgo Rebellion and consequent vice-regal restoration caused a near complete collapse of large-scale administrative systems in New Spain. In 1810 and 1811, small militia units and local governing *juntas* assumed independent control over land, men, and resources, and conducted independent negotiations with insurgent and viceregal commanders. While political bonds were strongest at the local level, the region encompassed by the militias of the Provincias Internas Orientales also developed statelike characteristics in this period. The political commitments of the northeast do not seem to have been driven by revolutionary ideologies, and yet the Hidalgo period had revolutionary consequences. The process of military mobilization, negotiation between opposing armies, and the autonomous reconstruction of local governments set powerful democratic precedents.[49]

---

[49] My perspective on the psychology of political violence on the northeastern frontier is, in many respects, consistent with the descriptions of political culture that have been put forward by William B. Taylor in his study of colonial rebellion (*Drinking, Homicide and Rebellion*), and by Eric Van Young in his study of the independence period (*The Other Rebellion*). The subjects of my research, like those of Taylor and Van Young, responded more to immediate circumstances than

In discussing the vicissitudes of local and colonial government in the 1810s, the general crisis of authority in the Spanish world must always be borne in mind. Between the time of the Napoleonic invasion of 1808 and the restoration of Ferdinand VII in 1814, it was by no means obvious who held legitimate sovereignty in Spain, and thus in New Spain. In 1810, both the viceroy of Mexico City and Miguel Hidalgo represented themselves as the legitimate defenders of Catholicism and the royal family. When news of the Hidalgo Rebellion reached the northeastern frontier, many military commanders stalled for time because it was not at all clear who had the better claims of legitimacy, who would prevail on the battlefield, or how the populations of the north would react. Local *cabildos* and state governors had every motivation to mobilize troops and prepare for war, but also every reason to keep the troops close to home and in defensive positions.

The most striking feature of the insurrectionary period in the northeast is how little blood was shed. San Luis Potosí, Coahuila, Nuevo Santander, and Texas all changed hands from viceroyalty to insurgency and back again with little loss of life. The entire region was committed more to its internal welfare than to any of the ideological claims presented by the viceroyalty or the insurgent leadership. The people of the northeast were defenders of the faith and the Spanish Crown, but their other institutional loyalties were conditional.

The north's frontier peoples were, first and foremost, citizens of their local communities and of the region. The broader allegiances of the northeast followed the prevailing winds. The region followed the viceroy when his fortunes were ascendant and Hidalgo and Allende when their star was rising. Generally speaking, the cities and towns of these provinces were "conquered," not in pitched battles, but by desertion, negotiation, realignments, and surrenders. As the insurgent armies advanced northward, the local population sought means of conciliation. In November of 1810, the population of San Luis Potosí threw open its gates to the rebels. In December, most of the northern militias defected to the insurgency, and in January, Monterrey welcomed the insurgent commanders. A coup carried out by one faction of Texan leaders imprisoned many of the province's military and civil leaders and bound the state to the insurgency. A few months later, the northeast reversed its allegiances. Following the capture of insurrectionary leaders in March of 1811, Texans carried out a counter coup, Monterrey proclaimed for the viceroy, and San Luis Potosí and Saltillo returned to the fold. The people of the north were clearly pragmatists

to long-term ideological commitments. I concur with both in understanding the political violence of the period as continuing to operate within a Catholic, monarchical worldview. However, I also believe that the encounter between mass conscription armies and large volunteer forces caused local participants to reinterpret themselves as members of a broader imagined community. Thus, though these militiamen did not enter the Hidalgo movement for ideological reasons, their participation had a radical, democratizing effect. These findings are generally compatible with the description of political identity formation in Guerrero proposed by Peter Guardino, *Peasants, Politics, and the Formation of Mexico's National State.*

who had no love of lost causes. They valued their lives and livelihoods above any ideological crusade.[50]

After Hidalgo issued his famous call for rebellion in Dolores on 16 September 1810, news of the movement traveled with remarkable speed. In only four days, word reached Monterrey; by the end of the month, word had reached Texas and Nuevo Santander. The news spread through both official and unofficial channels. Viceregal officials sent dispatches ordering military mobilizations and requisitioning supplies. Yet at the same time, they feared that informal contacts between men of different regions were fomenting rebellion. In the northeast, it proved impossible to separate these two forms of communication. The Hidalgo Uprising began as Saltillo was conducting its annual fair – an event that supplied much of the commerce between central New Spain and the northeast. Soldiers from as far away as Texas purchased their supplies there, and many presidios were virtually abandoned while the fair was open. Northern military commanders claimed that propagandists at the fair were spreading rebellion though it is just as plausible that mere news of the uprising fanned regional resistance as soldiers and merchants left the fair and disseminated the rumors far and wide.

In the beginning of November, rebel armies approached San Luis Potosí but were spared a battle for the city by the complicity of several local leaders. A group of conspirators, led in part by clergymen Juan Villerias and Juan Nepomuceno Camaño, freed political prisoners, seized the armory, and armed the town's many rebel sympathizers. They then declared for the insurgency and welcomed the rebel armies.[51] Surprised by the rapid advance of the insurgency, many of the inhabitants of the wealthy mining towns to the north of San Luis

---

[50] The following general summary of events draws on these sources: Cavazos Garza, *Breve historia*, chap. 16; Alessio Robles, *Coahuila y Texas*, chap. 43; Luis Navarro García, *Las Provincias Internas en el siglo XIX* (Seville: Escuela de Estudios Hispano-Americanos, 1965), 45–74; Vizcaya Canales, *En los albores de la independencia*, chap. 1; Ricardo Covarrubias, *Los gobernantes de Nuevo León, 1585–1961* (Monterrey: 1961), 45–50. The story of smaller communities and individual military units comes largely from my own archival research and is cited in the course of the chapter. Though the above sources are generally reliable, I take issue with the claim of Covarrubias that, while other Indians joined the insurgency, "los indios tlaxcaltecas, siempre fueron fieles al gobierno virreinal y participaron con las huestes realistas." I suspect Covarrubias here generalizes on the basis of Tlaxcalan behavior in the center of New Spain without reviewing sufficient specific documentation from the north. In order for his claim to be correct with respecto to Nuevo León, one would have to assume that Tlaxcalans, as individuals, detached themselves from their larger military units leaving little documentary residue. I concur with Covarrubias that Tlaxcalans usually perceived themselves as royalists, but in this case, they seem to have sided with the rest of Neoleonés communities in perceiving Hidalgo's armies as the defenders of church and crown. Archer's research on supposed Tlaxcalan conspiracies demonstrates that the loyalty of Tlaxcalan colonies to the viceregal chain of command was not a foregone conclusion for Spanish administrators in the early nineteenth century. Archer, *The Army in Bourbon Mexico*, 99–100.

[51] "Queretaro año 1811 sumaria formada contra el Presbitero Br Dn Juan Nepomuceno Camaño por indiccios en la Insurrección de San Luis Potosí ... infidencia #1642," BNE MSS 3650 Papeles de Asuntos Militares y Conspiraciones, exp. 9, fol. 90. Note that the BNE catalogs this defendant's name as Caamano, while the contents of the document spell his name Camaño.

Potosí (Venado, Real Catorce, Charcas, and Matehuala) fled with all portable wealth to Saltillo. The city of Saltillo soon became the focus of insurgent and viceregal military strategy. Royalist commanders moved money and men from Monclova to Saltillo. Meanwhile, the forces at Saltillo, commanded by Coahuila's governor Antonio Cordero, awaited the arrival of further support from Nuevo León. The insurgents under Mariano Jiménez amassed an ever-larger army a few miles from Saltillo as workers fleeing nearby haciendas and military deserters from Nuevo Santander flocked to his camp.

Just south of Saltillo at the hacienda of Agua Nueva, the two armies took up positions in anticipation of a battle that would determine possession of Saltillo. Both the composition and the conduct of the two armies tell us a great deal about the changes taking place in the region. The opposing armies massed near Saltillo were undoubtedly the largest number of armed men ever assembled at any one time and place in the history of the region. In fact, it may have been the largest number of people assembled for any purpose. The several thousand insurgents led by Mariano Jiménez were people of varied origins: Indians, mestizos, and creoles who had flocked to the movement as Hidalgo's armies moved through the center-north of New Spain. Cordero's viceregal forces were organized around a small core of professional soldiers from the presidio of Monclova, but they were joined by men from other northern presidios and *pueblos de indios*, and by militiamen from Coahuila, Nuevo Léon, and Nuevo Santander. Cordero commanded about 700 men when his position at Aguanueva was at its strongest. However, beginning in the last days of December and culminating on 7 January 1811, his soldiers abandoned him. Insurgents imprisoned Cordero and occupied Saltillo.

Let us consider how this insurgent victory may have appeared to the participants. Both armies were led by commanders who claimed to be fighting on behalf of the crown. Jiménez's men brandished images of the Virgin of Guadalupe and also proclaimed themselves champions of the nation and enemies of the French and their Spanish collaborators. Songs, poems, and sermons proclaiming their cause had been circulating through the region for several months. The insurgents spoke as a nation, and the composition of their army illustrated the composition of that nation. They were an assortment of regulars, militiamen, and irregulars of kinds from a variety of regions and ethnic extractions – some dressed in uniforms and some dressed in their customary clothing. Cordero's followers were fewer in number and would have more closely resembled a regular army. They were presidial soldiers and militiamen with some measure of formal hierarchy and experience in drills and in fights with the region's nomads. Yet, the men were probably as varied in origin as Hidalgo's men. Their numbers included companies of Spanish dragoons, Tlaxcalan cavalry, and Indian archer corps from Nuevo Santander. The idea that the northeastern provinces formed a coherent administrative unit had existed for decades, but the political bonds connecting the region's constituent communities were now illustrated more clearly than ever before. The northern forces were, in fact, the northern citizenry under arms. The militia units were capable of acting independently or in concert; and at this moment, in the absence of a clear and legitimate political superstructure, they were capable of deciding whether to fight, negotiate, or withdraw. The northern militiamen and insurgent army stood poised on the brink of battle for several days. Then the northerners, acting on their own authority, voted with their feet. They had been sent to suppress the insurgency, but they joined it instead.

In March 1811, the fortunes of the rebels and royalists reversed once again. Hidalgo and many of the other rebel leaders were betrayed and captured in Coahuila just as a new loyalist force was entering the region from Nuevo Santander. In a few days, the prospects for the rebellion appeared dead. Monterrey quickly made amends with loyalist commanders, and the leaders of smaller towns followed suit. Governor Santa María, who had helped to bring Nuevo León into the rebel camp, was tried for treason. Most of the lesser leaders, however, escaped prosecution and remained influential in local politics. The leadership class of Nuevo León was so thoroughly complicit in the rebellion that any serious attempt to purge the ranks would have risked a collapse of public administration.

General Joaquín de Arredondo, representing the viceroyalty and Spain's governing *junta*, began the reconquest of Nuevo Santander and Nuevo León by moving inland from Tampico toward Monterrey. Facing little resistance, he entered the city and made it, once again, the headquarters for the Provincias Internas Orientales. For Arredondo, suppressing the armed insurgency was a difficult but attainable objective. However, regaining full political control over the region was another matter entirely. Following the capture of Hidalgo and Allende, local governments that had supported the insurgency quickly reconfigured themselves as *juntas patrióticas*, proclaiming their loyalty to the viceroyalty. Thus, when Arredondo arrived in Monterrey, he was welcomed by a locally elected *Junta Patriótica* that included former collaborators who now claimed to support Arredondo and the viceroyalty.[52] The *junta* claimed to have broad authority over the city of Monterrey and even over the larger province of Nuevo León. The conquering general had no enemy to oppose, but he was confronted with a collection of local governments that expected a high level of autonomy and refused to cooperate with many of his instructions. Arrendondo, who needed all the help he could get, had no choice but to court the favor of local leaders who had just recently cooperated with the insurgency.

The persistence of violent conflict in the region ensured that the association between military service and political participation remained strong in the years following the capture of Hidalgo. Though the northeast was no longer at the center of New Spain's revolutionary struggles, the fear of revolution remained ever present in the minds of strategists. Morelos fought on in the center and south of New Spain until his capture in 1815; Guerrero fought on until national independence in 1821. In May 1814, the new *diputación provincial* in

---

[52] These reconfigurations of the *ayuntamiento* and the underlying continuity in leadership are observable in the resolutions of 1 Jan., 1 Apr., and 20 Jan. 1811 in *Actas del Ayuntamiento de Monterrey, vol.* III, 1776–1821 (Monterrey, 2006).

Monterrey was forced to pay what amounted to extortion money to a large body of soldiers in Saltillo in order to persuade them to demobilize.[53] That summer, Arredondo warned his superiors that governance was still "paralyzed in certain places by popular movements."[54] The tumults of the Hidalgo period encouraged incursions by Comanches, Apaches, and other northern tribes, who continued to raid the area in the years that followed.[55] Under the circumstances, northern leaders remained in constant fear of outside Indian attacks while still fretting that those communities whose leaders were only nominally loyalist might revert to rebellion.[56]

Under these circumstances of political and military instability, the armed citizen remained the functional foundation of civil society. The *juntas patrióticas*, which had assumed control of many communities in the power vacuum created by the collapse of the Hidalgo Rebellion, continued to thrive as local political and military organizations. The formation and expansion of these organizations continued in the years that followed. In the spring of 1814, Linares described itself as an armed populace, noting the importance of maintaining a militia at the constant disposal of the *ayuntamiento*. In the summer of 1814 a group of 75 men formed a new "company of patriots" in the city of Monterrey. On the upper Río Grande and in Texas, Indian attacks continued and Anglo-American invasion threatened.[57] There, missionaries and military commanders agreed as to the practical link between citizenship and military service. Petitioning the crown from his post at the presidio of the Río Grande, a Franciscan friar urged the placement of more settlers to strengthen the northern militia system. He urged that all settlers be armed and asked the crown to supply additional firearms to those who lacked them "in order that your majesty may count each *vecino* a soldier that aids in the defense of the others."[58]

The second half of the eighteenth century witnessed many changes and variations in the militia systems of the northeastern frontier, but the underlying trends are clear. The entire population was being counted, categorized, and organized for war. At the local level, all the preexisting relations within ethnically and geographically defined communities persisted, but new connections were now forged between those old communities. The role of provincial governments with respect to the Provincias Internas and the relationship between governors,

---

[53] 10 May 1814, "Acta de instalación de la Diputación Provincial," AGI Audiencia de Guadalajara 297.

[54] 2 June 1814, Arredondo, AGI Guadalajara Audiencia de Guadalajara 297.

[55] 7 Sept. 1814, Arredondo to Miguel de Lardizabal y Uribe, AGI Audiencia de Guadalajara 297.

[56] 2 Jan. 1814, Bonavía, AGI Audiencia de Guadalajara 297.

[57] The correspondence of northern governors in the first decade of the nineteenth century demonstrates the extent to which fear of Anglo-American settlement practices had begun to influence policy. Real and imagined Anglo-American plots were constantly on the minds of colonial administrators. Comunicación de Dn Manuel Salcedo [governor of Texas] to Miguel de Lardizabal y Uribe ..., 15 Nov. 1809, BNE MSS 18636, no. 28.

[58] 21 Aug. 1816, Manuel Goyom, Presidio Rió Grande, AGI Audiencia de Guadalajara 409.

commandants general, and intendants were the source of much change and administrative confusion. Regardless of the administrative arrangement at any given moment, however, one change in the political culture was firmly established: all armed *vecinos* of a locality became armed citizens of the state and region, connected to each other by standardized titles, the ritual of military exercises, and the administrative structures of the national militia system.

On one hand, the Bourbon leadership accelerated frontier settlement and the incorporation of new populations; on the other hand, it bounded these projects. Apaches (and usually Comanches as well) were now considered the ultimate and permanent cultural other. The purpose of the strengthened line of presidios was to mark a less ambitious boundary between civilized and uncivilized spheres. At the same time, however, the colonial government redoubled its efforts to settle and people Nuevo Santander, the existing sites in Texas, and the upper Río Grande. As the line between the Apache and colonial spheres grew sharper, the ethnic boundaries within the colonial community grew weaker.

Despite all the shifts in administrative systems, the Gálvez reforms were not a revolution in Neoleonés understandings of the relationship among the Spanish, Tlaxcalan, and Chichimec populations. Regional defense had always involved diplomacy with nomadic tribes through gifts and trade, and military expeditions that combined Spanish and Indian forces.[59] Though the reign of Carlos III is associated with standardization of royal administration, it would be a mistake to assume that the Gálvez militia displaced the military organizations that preceded it. Both the administrative correspondence and the details of military action in Nuevo León suggest that the Tlaxcalan mission-town system remained indispensable. After 1787, the Tlaxcalan forces were a part of the General Command through their *protectors*. This rearticulated the command structure, but it did not change the basic set of assumptions that connected the Tlaxcalan towns to the crown.[60]

Though much about the Tlaxcalan communities remained the same, their context was rapidly changing. At one time, their privilege and obligation to maintain horses and arms had distinguished them from other ethnic communities and secured their status. Likewise, their function in the creation of armed agricultural mission-towns had been distinctive. Now the Tlaxcalans had a great deal of company. Presidios began to take on the function of mission-towns. Spaniards assumed the role of Tlaxcalan colonists, and many Indian and mixed-caste men (now armed and mounted) formed local military companies. The population was growing, and Tlaxcalan citizenship was quickly merging with a sort of proto-national citizenship. In some ways, Tlaxcalans were the original architects of the system, but their numbers and their influence relative to the growing population were waning.

In the early nineteenth century, simultaneous political instability in Spain and in New Spain created a great deal of confusion over political legitimacy and

[59] Weber, *Bárbaros*, 178–220; Weber, *The Spanish Frontier*, 230–31.
[60] Sheridan Prieto, "'Indios madrineros,'" 44.

constitutional systems. It is tempting to pass over this chaotic period, turning quickly from descriptions of colonial government to the constitutional systems of the early independent republic; but passing over this period lightly comes at a great cost to our understanding of how ideas about the state and citizenship evolved at the local and regional levels. The collision of conflicting political systems in this era disrupted centralized authority, permitted the dissemination of new political ideologies, and allowed local leaders to apply selectively any of the institutional principles then in circulation.

The great irony of the period is that both the forces of rebellion and reaction contributed to the democratization of the region's political culture and the emergence of casteless citizenship. Hidalgo's followers are usually correctly understood as representing egalitarian forces in New Spain. They fought on behalf of Indians, mestizos, and creoles against peninsular privilege and against slavery. To meet the challenge of Hidalgo's enormous citizen armies, the vice-royalty was forced to mobilize the broadest possible citizen militias. In a system that had always linked military participation with political power, this meant a vast expansion of political participation. In the power vacuum created by institutional collapse, militia leaders governed the areas in which they commanded. In Nuevo León, the militias mobilized first for the viceroyalty and then switched allegiances to support Hidalgo. Even when they returned to the loyalist camp, militias became the source of military power undergirding the *ad hoc juntas patrióticas* that managed the political transition.

One powerful trend in the first decades of the nineteenth century was the formation of a regional political identity that bound together the inhabitants of the northeastern provinces of New Spain. In the late colonial period, the intendancy of San Luis Potosí and the Provincias Internas Orientales began to describe the militiamen of the region as belonging to an organization that extended beyond the bounds of their individual towns or provinces. From 1812 to 1814, this regional militia organization took on a second life as a political jurisdiction. The Constitution of Cádiz called for the election of *diputaciones provinciales*. On the northeastern frontier, the new provincial deputation would draw from Coahuila, Nuevo León, Texas, and Nuevo Santander to create a regional legislature in Monterrey. What was once a military district became a political one.[61] The regional application of the Constitution of Cádiz mixed elected and appointed instruments of governance. Governors, *corregidores*, and other magistrates were appointed from above, while municipal *ayuntamientos* and the regional *diputación provincial* were elected from below.[62]

---

[61] May–June 1814, Copias de varias ordenes expedidas por la Diputación Provincial a los Governadores y Ayuntamientos de las quatro Provincias de Oriente, AGI Audiencia de Guadalajara 297.

[62] 27 May 1814 correspondence of Arredondo and 23 June *decreto*, AGI Audiencia de Guadalajara 297.

The decade that followed the *Grito de Dolores* was dominated by violence and by institutional and ideological confusion over conflicting constitutional systems. On the northeastern frontier, this period had several lasting effects. The activation of the regional militias and their decisive role in subsequent political decisions reinforced the link between military service and citizenship. Frequent collapses in imperial authority strengthened the importance of local citizenship. At the same time, however, the military apparatus of the regional militias and military *juntas* often served as the de facto state. Thus, the armed citizens of the northeastern provinces came to understand their shared membership in a military and political organization.

The conjunction of these military experiences with the advent of the Constitution of Cádiz was politically transformative. The same soldiers who twice determined the allegiances of the region by "voting with their feet" were now enfranchised under the Constitution of Cádiz as citizens of a broader Spanish world. Similar forces were at work in the relationship between ethnic communities. During the military crises of the period, armies were assembled from barrio-based companies, demonstrating the civic equivalence of local groups within the greater whole. In the new armies, as in the region's emerging municipalities, ethnic communities could be seen as interdependent and equivalent. When the Constitution of Cádiz propounded the principle of casteless citizenship, northeastern New Spain assimilated the message in regional terms. Local Indian populations, as soldiers and as landholders, like their Spanish counterparts, sought to retain historic privileges while grasping new constitutional prerogatives. Consequently, there emerged a civic culture that operated in two political languages, one colonial and the other republican. This broader political lexicon more fully accommodated the real political and economic relationships of the north – a place in which, on one hand, the history of Spanish and Indian republics' service to the crown remained culturally relevant, but which, on the other hand, was inhabited by a growing mestizo population, unable to represent itself in the language of colonial citizenship. The political speech of the independence period continued to draw a boundary around the community of citizens, distinguishing them, as always, from barbarians, but now also from foreigners and from ideological enemies of the state.

6

Modern Towns and Casteless Citizens

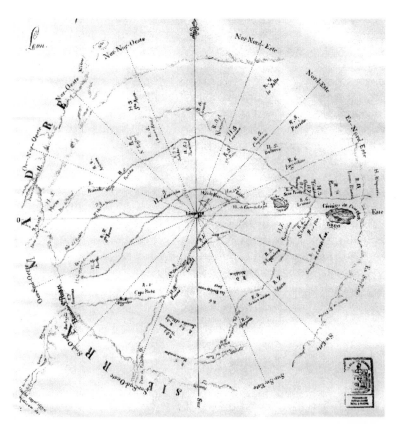

FIGURE 9. This 1841 map shows the *partido* of Linares under the system of *departamentos* and *partidos* imposed by Santa Ana in an attempt to suppress older regional networks of authority. ("Mapa del partido de la ciudad de Linares del departamento de Nuevo León, 1841," Archivo General del Estado de Nuevo León)

The formation of the Mexican state must be viewed both in terms of imagined communities and in terms of concrete, perceptible ones. At the local level, the new constitutional order of the nineteenth century combined the members of separate ethnic pueblos into larger municipalities. This legal transformation was accompanied by a physical one: surveying streets and properties, laying stones for new civic buildings, cutting roads through farms, placing new boundary stones between reapportioned fields, building new homes on new lots, and conscripting laborers for public works. The Mexican Constitution of 1824 replaced colonial definitions of citizenship with republican ones; and like the Constitution of Cádiz, it articulated a new casteless notion of citizenship in which the terms *español* and *indio* lost all legal functions.[1] From this point forward, the inhabitants of Mexico became *ciudadanos republicanos* of the nation and *vecinos* of a municipality.[2] The most basic political units of the new state were no longer the civic islands of *pueblos de indios* and *pueblos de españoles*, but larger and more inclusive Mexican *municipios*. In binding together communities of Spaniards, Tlaxcalans, and northern Indians, emergent municipalities of northern Mexico represented both a new republican system and the culmination of an old colonial project.

VECINOS AND MILITIAMEN IN THE VALLEY OF PILÓN

News of the Hidalgo Rebellion reached Nuevo León in the last days of September 1810. For a time, Pilón, like other valleys in Nuevo León, regarded the rebellion from a distance. As local and provincial leaders mobilized the population for war, local people weighed conflicting political claims and the merits of competing rumors. However, in January 1811, the residents of Pilón no longer had this luxury – the conflict came to them. Pilón found itself between two loci of revolutionary upset: Saltillo and Monterrey. At the end of 1810, the insurgent army, retreating from defeats in central Mexico, had regrouped near Saltillo under the command of Mariano Jiménez. Widespread defections from the loyalist camp led first to rebel victory on the battlefield, and afterward to the

---

[1] On notions of local and national citizenship in the history of Spanish America, see Tamar Herzog, *Defining Nations;* on local state formation in Mexico, see Peter Guardino's *In the Time of Liberty: Popular Political Culture in Oaxaca, 1750–1850* (Durham, NC: Duke, 2005), and collection of essays comprising Joseph and Nugent, eds., *Everyday Forms of State Formation.*

[2] Guardino's central argument treats Mexican state formation; for his discussion of the origins of municipalities and notions of citizenship in relation to ethnicity, see *Peasants, Politics, and the Formation of Mexico's Modern State*, 76–79. The legal incorporation of the municipalities of Nuevo León was a consequence of national politics in the era of Mexican Independence, but most of the local outcomes were determined by existing relationships among local populations. Guardino's study of Guerrero illustrates the ways in which preexisting constituencies continued long-standing local conflicts through the new, national politics of the early nineteenth century. He suggests that local political actors, in pursuit of local aims, shaped the national political culture of Mexico. However, as he acknowledges, the situation of Guerrero was unusual because its local leaders found themselves in the center of the transformative military conflicts of the age (pp. 1–14); for the origin of the "imagined communities" debate, see Anderson, *Imagined Communities.*

capitulation of Saltillo. Overnight, the fortunes of the contending forces reversed. Seeing the writing on the wall, Nuevo León's governor, Manuel de Santa María, quietly joined the insurgency. He left the governorship in the hands of another newly minted revolutionary, and rushed to Pilón to rally support for the emerging rebel government. The locals, keen to be on the winning side of the war, embraced the cause, freed a large group of rebel prisoners of war, and proclaimed themselves in favor of independence. A few months later, when the Hidalgo movement collapsed, the leaders of Pilón had a great deal of explaining to do. Jiménez soon reconquered the north for the viceroyalty, and the *vecinos* of Pilón did their best to reorganize themselves as a loyalist government and to obscure their previous involvement in the rebellion. By January 1812, the leading citizens of the valley were representing themselves as a faithful *junta governadora.*[3]

From 1810 to 1812, the disruption of institutions in the New Kingdom of León laid bare many of the underlying power relationships between the different elements of the population. Local leaders organized governing *juntas* that reflected a simple political calculus: people with military power and financial resources at their disposal got representation. In Pilón, the constitutional relationship between the Spanish *villa* and the two *pueblos de indios* was at first unclear. In March 1812, Antonio López Fonseca was consolidating his authority as *subdelegado* of the Valley of Pilón and leading armed patrols, both to defend the area from external attack and to suppress what he described as a rising tide of drunkenness and robbery within the valley. Groups of Indians reportedly ignored the boundaries between Indian and Spanish lands, drank riotously, and engaged in crime.[4] Yet, even in this period of improvised government and security, López Fonseca was hesitant to overstep the limits of his authority with respect to the *pueblos de indios*. In order to avoid a juridical and practical blunder, he wrote to the Monterrey *junta* asking whether he held legal authority over Purificación and Concepción.[5]

The *protector* of the two *pueblos de indios*, Pedro Borrego, raised similar questions in December. Unable to control the disorders among the valley Indians, his concerns were both legal and pragmatic. Recently, the whipping of

---

[3] Their efforts were so successful that few documentary records of Pilón's political history in the first half of 1811 survive. Records were disrupted after the fact by anxious rebel collaborators, but also during the crisis by loyalists. Some viceregal loyalists fled the area when Pilón declared independence, taking with them the valley's paper records. In 1812, the new *alcalde* noted that he lacked most of the previous year's records for Purificación and Concepción because his predecessor had fled to Veracruz during the insurrection, carrying off the documents. Most of Pilón's leading *vecinos* sided with the independence movement in January 1811; a year later, they had a shared interest in obscuring all records of the intervening events. 15 Oct. 1814, Arredondo, AGI 297, Duplicados de los Comandantes Generales de las Provincias Internas, 1808–1814, exp. 13; 27 Jan. 1812, AGENL Correspondencia de Alcaldes, Montemorelos, box 1.

[4] [No date; context and location indicates 1812], AGENL Correspondencia de Alcaldes, Montemorelos 1812–1821, box 1.

[5] 7 Mar. 1812, AGENL, Correspondencia de Alcaldes, Montemorelos 1812–1821, box 1.

an Indian offender by Spanish authorities had been interrupted when a messenger arrived with directions from the Indian *cabildo* countermanding the punishment. Borrego wrote to Domingo Ballesteros asking for the authority to punish Indian offenders, while at the same time warning that Pilón currently had too few soldiers to do so. The answer from Ballesteros was unambiguous: the *protector* has no such authority to punish the Indians. He informed Borrego that the determination of guilt and punishment of Purificación and Concepción's Indians remained in the hands of their own governors. Higher authorities continued to uphold the legitimacy of Indian governments amid the confusion over constitutional systems.[6]

Though royalists had regained control of the cities of Nuevo León by the beginning of 1812, the effects of civil war lingered. Fighting between the newly reconstituted authorities and bands of rebels continued sporadically in the region, merging with the violence surrounding the Mina invasion in 1817.[7] In 1812, the most obdurate of the rebels in the area near the Valley of Pilón was a man named Miguel del Valle.[8] In January, Antonio López Fonseca, *subdelegado* of Pilón, summarized the dire situation to his superiors in Monterrey's *junta governadora*: an epidemic was sweeping through the region, causing a desperate shortage of labor; meanwhile, the military resources at his disposal were insufficient to defend the community against constant attacks by groups he characterized as bandits, rebel Indians, and deserters. The *vecinos'* control of the area was so weak that, when they had the good fortune to capture some of the offenders, a new wave attacked, freeing the captives from jail. The *subdelegado* begged for military support, but the kingdom's resources were stretched very thin. Sargento don Cristóval de León, in command of the local militia, struggled to fend off the attacks, but had little success against Miguel del Valle and his fellow "deserter" Gil Saucedo.[9]

It is not easy to identify all of the bands that were attacking Pilón in 1812. The formal leaders of the valley thought of them as deserters and bandits, but one man's deserter-bandit is another man's patriot. Most who fought on the side of the insurrection in 1811 were soldiers and militiamen who had deserted to the rebel cause. When the governments of Monterrey and Saltillo returned to the

---

[6] 30 Dec. 1812, AGENL Correspondencia de Alcaldes, Montemorelos 1812–1821, box 1.

[7] Spanish republican revolutionary Francisco Javier Mina, in cooperation with José Teresa de Mier y Noriega, attempted to spark a Mexican independence movement with a small invasion of Gulf Coast. Mina landed in April of 1817, but failed to trigger a widespread movement. He was captured in November.

[8] From Vicente Antonio López Fonseca to the pres. y vocal de la junta governadora [n.d], AGENL Correspondencia de Alcaldes, Montemorelos 1812–1821, box 1.

[9] 16 Jan. 1812, AGENL Correspondencia de Alcaldes, Montemorelos 1812–1821, box 1. On López Fonseca's assumption of office after Ballesteros, 13 Feb. 1812 AGENL Correspondencia de Alcaldes, Montemorelos 1812–1821, box 1. Jailbreaks were a frequent occurrence in this period. This is less surprising than it might at first seem, since, at least as of March 1812 and probably much later, the building in question was a "shack ('*jacal*') that serves as a jail," López Fonseca to Esquivel, 7 Mar. 1712, AGENL Correspondencia de Alcaldes, Montemorelos 1812–1821, box 1.

royalist fold, these soldiers lost their link to civic authority. In effect, nearly all those fighting for independence would have been considered deserters. In Nuevo León, Indian attackers had historically been considered rebels (*sublevados*) or bandits. There was little distinction in the use of the two terms, since the main objective of most Indian raids was to seize cattle. Many of the roving bands of 1812 were former residents of the *pueblos de indios* who had joined the insurrection.

At this moment of crisis, alliances in the valley were not neatly determined by caste. Both the forces defending the valley and those attacking it were a mix of Indian and Spanish irregulars. The population of the region was in flux as a mixture of refugees, deserters, active partisans, opportunists, and criminals traveled the roads. In January 1812, López Fonseca articulated a policy of interrogating any stranger who arrived in the valley.[10] Pilón's leaders seem to have instituted a system of internal passports as a means of controlling the situation. From armed travelers, they demanded documentation of militia membership; from unarmed Indian travelers, they demanded documentation of their place of residence and their freedom from debt. It seems that many hacienda workers thought it an opportune moment to leave their debts behind them and strike out on the road. If discovered by Pilón's patrols, they usually were whipped. The question of military affiliation in a period of highly irregular command hierarchies was harder to resolve. Most militia leaders in Pilón were personally acquainted with the commanders in neighboring valleys, making it an easy matter to verify a soldier's status with a letter of passage.

Determining the status of soldiers from outside the region was not as easy. Historically, Tlaxcalans had served in military campaigns far from home, and this continued to be the case during the Hidalgo Rebellion. In July 1812, López Fonseca and his men encountered an armed soldier passing through the valley. When they demanded his letter of passage, the man produced a document signed by Dionicio Samora, the Tlaxcalan governor of Boca de Leones, identifying him as Capitán Comandante de Armas Juan Cristóval Baca. Baca claimed he had been taken prisoner by the Apaches, but was now returning to the city of Monterrey. Unsure about how to proceed, López Fonseca disarmed the soldier but permitted him to continue on his way to the capital, while at the same time dispatching a message to the Monterrey government inquiring about the authenticity of the passport.[11] Larger groups of armed men, encountering each other on the highways, reportedly proclaimed their allegiances by shouting either "¡Viva Mexico!" or "¡Viva España!" When a royalist traveler from Parras misjudged the alignment of some Indians on the road though Pilón, he found himself threatened with a whipping for invoking Spain rather than Mexico.[12]

---

[10] 27 Jan. 1812, AGENL Correspondencia de Alcaldes, Montemorelos 1812–1821, box 1.

[11] 23 July 1812, AGENL Correspondencia de Alcaldes, Montemorelos 1812–1821.

[12] Dec. 1812, Correspondence of Pedro José Borrego Capitán José Domingo Ballesteros, AGENL Correspondencia de Alcaldes, Montemorelos 1812–1821, box 1.

What it meant to be a royalist or a rebel was not always clear. Both Hidalgo and the viceregal authorities had proclaimed their loyalty to the royal family. Meanwhile, communications came to New Spain from both the Napoleonic government and the Cádiz government. Under the circumstances, the *vecinos* of Pilón chose a cautious path. They formed their own government and military unit, invoking traditional sources of authority and focusing on local security. In January 1812, Antonio López Fonseca sent a plea for aid to the viceregal military; he begged for the deployment of some regular soldiers to Pilón, noting that bandits could currently enter and leave the valley unopposed, taking what they wished and springing prisoners from jail. He lamented that the valley had only a militia to protect it.[13] Yet, there was nothing unusual about this state of affairs. Pilón rarely had regular troops. Its military system *was* the militia. In March 1813, a group of twenty-four men, headed by Pedro Borrego and describing themselves as "*vecinos republicanos*" and "*fieles vasallos*" of the deceased king, formed what they called a "*compañía patriótica*" – a militia that gathered arms and mounts for local defense.[14] In a period of violence and contested political authority, this group of men was effectively the military, the police, and the broker of any agreement over the political alignments of the valley.

Though many Indians fled from the *pueblos de indios* in 1811, the pueblos and their governments continued to function.[15] In 1812 Indian and Spanish leaders reached a basic, functional consensus on the relationship between the valley communities. In July, Joseph Domingo Ballesteros described the elements of his local government (one which would soon become a *partido* under the Cádiz Constitution): it consisted of himself (the executive and military commander), six *vecinos*, the governors of Concepción and Purificación, and the local military commander, Sargento Cristóbal de León. Thus, while both the Indian and Spanish communities were internally self-governing, some matters clearly required the deliberation of all parties. In this larger *junta*, Indian governors spoke on behalf of their *cabildos*.[16] As in times past, rebels who failed to negotiate a group settlement found themselves in a much worse situation than those who did. In June 1812, Captain Juan José de los Santos took thirty-two captives in the valley of Labradores. López Fonseca, who issued a report on these events, used the term *piezas* to describe the captives, a wording which strongly suggests that the prisoners were to be enslaved. López Fonseca received the

---

[13] 16 Jan. 1812, AGENL Correspondencia de Alcaldes, Montemorelos 1812–1821, box 1.

[14] 3 Mar. 1813, AGENL Correspondencia de Alcaldes, Montemorelos 1812–1821, box 1.

[15] This claim is based on extant documents that reference other lost documents from the pueblo, 27 Jan. 1812, AGENL Correspondencia de Alcaldes, Montemorelos 1812–1821, box 1.

[16] The ad hoc composition of this government comes through in Ballesteros's decription of his accession to office: "I have been placed in possession of the administration of justice for this *partido*, this action being executed with only the support of six *vecinos*, the governors of the missions, and some plebs, lacking the attendance of the rest of the subjects that compose the republic," Ballesteros to vocal secretario Nuñoz de Esquivel, Pilón, 14 July 1812, AGENL Correspondencia de Alcaldes, Montemorelos 1812–1821, box 1.

thirty-two men in Pilón, noting that they were now "placed at the disposal of the *junta governadora*." Only nine of the captives were identified as insurgent soldiers, which raises the possibility that in the confusion of institutional authority, some opportunists were returning to traditional patterns of slave raiding.

When viewed in the context of Pilón's long history of Spanish-Indian alliances and of Indian flight, rebellion, and resettlement, the events of 1812 conform to a familiar eighteenth-century pattern. The most successful local military campaigns against the bandit-rebels were carried out by a mixed force of Indians and Spaniards under the command of Spanish *vecino* José Joaquín Barbosa and the Indian governor of Purificación, Juan José de la Sana.[17] As was generally the case in the previous century, Indian rebels who retained their unity and negotiated a settlement were able to enter (or reenter) colonial society as free members of a *pueblo de indios*. Barbosa's team entered into negotiations that secured the settlement of one group of rebels in Purificación. In another amnesty agreement, a group of five Indian rebel leaders approached the colonial soldiers, asking for quarter on behalf of their followers. Pedro Borrego's report on the surrender describes a negotiation firmly rooted in the discourse of the old mission-town system. The Indians asked to be settled in Concepción and made subjects of its governor. In return, they offered to lay down their arms proclaiming themselves "vassals of our Sovereign Fernando VII and in his absence to the Supreme Junta of the Regency." They presented their bows and arrows, crossed themselves, repented of their sins, invoked the grace of Christ, and asked that they be given religious instruction.[18] Barbosa and Sana collaborated to capture another rebel group that had concealed itself in an arroyo near Pilón. This group of insurgents included former members of the *cabildo* of Guadalupe. They too asked for quarter, turning over their muskets and requesting settlement in Purificación with a pledge of total obedience to its leaders.[19] Sometimes Indian bands were able to arrive in the pueblos without attracting the notice of the patrols on the roads. Under these circumstances, they were able to negotiate directly with local priests or *cabildos*, as was the case with six rebel Indians who reentered the missions after establishing communications with Fray Justo Rojo and Pilón's *cura* Rafael de la Garza.[20]

Under the new Cádiz Constitution, Pilón's population was redefined as an urban municipality, which entitled it to a full *ayuntamiento*. At the beginning of 1813, Pilón's Spanish *vecinos* and Indian communities elected their respective leaders, and in the process reaffirmed most of the elements of the colonial pact between them. The Spanish *vecinos* rearticulated the social contract of their

---

[17] [No date, location and context indicate 1812] AGENL Correspondencia de Alcaldes, Montemorelos 1812–1821, box 1.

[18] 11 Nov. 1812, AGENL Correspondencia de Alcaldes, Montemorelos 1812–1821, box 1.

[19] Barbosa to the president of the Junta Governadora, [n.d.] 1812, AGENL Correspondencia de Alcaldes, Montemorelos, 1812–1821, box 1.

[20] Rojo to Garza, 28 [month illegible] 1812 and 11 Nov. 1812, AGENL Correspondencia de Alcaldes, Montemorelos, 1812–1821, box 1.

community, emphasizing the links between landholding, military service, and citizenship. In the second decade of the nineteenth century, Pilón was the second-largest population in the New Kingdom of León, but the number of *vecinos* that participated in elections and in the constitutional deliberations of the day was never more than a few dozen. In March 1813, the twenty-four active *vecinos* of Pilón, describing themselves as *fieles vasallos* and *vecinos republicanos*, announced the formation of a *compañía patriótica* and the collection of arms and mounts in order to contribute a strengthened civil defense force to the kingdom.[21] In some respects, the valley saw a return to preinsurrection normalcy. Pedro Borrego with his armed and landholding *vecinos* governed the Spanish population, while Governor Juan Matías Oyenvides ruled Concepción. The Spanish and indigenous communities contributed to the common defense and, as the rental revenues of the *pueblos de indios* show, both communities were willing to make binding contracts over land and water rights to their mutual satisfaction.[22]

In May 1814, the Ayuntamiento of Pilón had much to celebrate: the valley had been elevated to the status of *municipio*, and a new *diputación provincial* was soon to be established in nearby Monterrey.[23] But the path to the new constitutional order would prove a tortuous one. The de facto leader in Pilón during times of turmoil was usually the owner of its largest estate, the hacienda Nuestra Señora de la Regla. While elections were ordered under the new constitution, the estate's owner, Pedro Joseph Ballesteros, served as interim *alcalde*.[24] However, unbeknownst to the locals, by the time the *ayuntamiento* learned of the plans for the new *municipio* and *diputación*, the restored king had already suspended the constitution from the other side of the Atlantic. This left the status of current officeholders in question. Despite some pointed inquiries from the commandant general of the Provincias Internas, the Ayuntamiento of Pilón remained in office at least through the summer of 1814.[25]

In 1821, at the moment of Mexican Independence, Pilón was linked to national politics largely through its military relationship with Saltillo.[26] By then, the center of revolutionary conflict in Mexico had moved far from Nuevo León, and the region's military concerns focused, once again, on defense

[21] 3 Mar. 1813, AGENL Correspondencia de Alcaldes, Montemorelos 1812–1821, box 1.

[22] It is not clear whether in 1813 both *pueblos de indios* shared a common governor. In 1813 Purificación took in 235 pesos in rents, and Concepción 159, [n.d.] AGENL Correspondencia de Alcaldes, Montemorelos 1812–1821, box 1.

[23] 1814 Pilón, Bancroft MSS 74/159, file 54; AGI Audiencia de Guadalajara 297.

[24] Bancroft MSS 74/159, file 46 announces the provisional appointment of Pedro José Ballesteros as Alcalde of Pilón, 22 Jan. 1814.

[25] The members of the first *ayuntamiento* were José Bernardino Cantú, Pedro de Llano, Juan Bautista de Arizpe, and José León Lobo.

[26] The region remained nominally royalist for five months following the announcement of the Plan of Iguala. Saltillo and San Estaban declared for independence (1 July 1812) before Monterrey. Arredondo mobilized troops from Monterrey to deploy against Saltillo, but rapid desertions to the other side persuaded him to capitulate to independence, Navarro García, *Las provincias internas*, 131–2.

against Indian attacks.[27] When Nuevo León joined Mexico in declaring national independence, the Pilón militia changed its name, but not its structure or function. In 1821 it was rechartered as the *Valle de Pilón Milicia Nacional Local de Ynfantería y Caballería.*[28] Continuity in leadership, and the fact that it was alternately called the *"Compañía Patriótica de Ynfanteria,"* shows that it was understood to be a continuation of the old *compañía patriótica.* A more complete charter document explains that its purposes were to aid the Army of the Three Guarantees, to defend Pilón, and to maintain the "normal interior tranquility of the pueblo."[29] Like the *ayuntamiento,* the officer corps of the militia seems to have been elected by a limited male franchise.[30] The militia was to be under the civilian control of the *ayuntamiento,* though, in point of fact, the individuals comprising the civilian and military leadership overlapped. Some militiamen continued to claim military exemptions from civil courts and imprisonment, but the appointment and direction of the local militia remained in the hands of the civilian *ayuntamiento.*[31] In 1826, under the new federal and state constitutions, the militia persisted as the principal defense force in the Valley of Pilón. A local armory held its weapons and supplies. A successor organization to the *Junta Patriótica,* the *"Junta de la Sociedad Patriótica de Amigos del País de este Distrito de Montemorelos,"* was elected by the members of the *ayuntamiento.*[32]

Late Bourbon-era militias had included both *indios* and *españoles,* but the two groups served in separate militia companies. Thus regiments were integrated, but companies were not. The new militia records, in keeping with the new legal language of Mexico, make no mention of caste. However, local and institutional memory of the old system persisted. Just as members of ex-missions retained property rights relating to their previous status, so too did members of the old Indian militias retain status based on previous service. In 1826, the

---

[27] Correspondence between Pilón and Saltillo shows regional cooperation for funding and arming troops to defend against Indian bands, 28 Sept. 1821, AGENL Correspondencia de Alcaldes, Montemorelos 1812–1821, box 1.

[28] 3 Dec. 1821, AGENL Correspondencia de Alcaldes, Montemorelos 1812–1821, box 1.

[29] 3 Dec. 1821, 17 Dec. 1821, 24 Dec. 1821, AGENL Correspondencia de Alcaldes, Montemorelos 1812–1821, box 1.

[30] The Spanish term *elejido* can indicate an election or appointment from above, making it at times difficult to distinguish between the two processes on the basis of the documents. However, in case of the 1821 commissions, the document has exactly the same appearance and format as the record for the *ayuntamiento* election. Both appear to show either election from small electorates or a two-stage election in which a smaller group of notables made the final appointments, 24 Dec. 1821, AGENL Correspondencia de Alcaldes, Montemorelos 1812–1821.

[31] In 1824 the *alcalde* of Pilón complained that he had been disobeyed and insulted by a drunken militia soldier. This he offers as an illustration of why Pilón, which currently had no military jail, needed the authority to detain soldiers in civilian jail, 13 Sept. 1826, AGENL Correspondencia de Alcaldes, Montemorelos 1821–1826, box 2.

[32] In the years immediately following independence, *ciudadano* seems to have remained an honorary, rather than universal, term for valley residents. In early elections the names of high office-holders were preceded by the letter "C," replacing the title of "Don," which was by then legally suspect, 27 June 1826, AGENL Correspondencia de Alcaldes, Montemorelos 1821–1826, box 2.

Ayuntamiento of Montemorelos announced a six-month period in which all Indians "who fought for the liberty of the Nation" might put forward claims.[33] Thus it appears that the members of these disbanded units received compensation and pensions for past expenditures and service.

Through all the tumult of the early nineteenth century, one local institution bound together the men of the separate communities of the Valley of Pilón: the militia. Though the names and legal descriptions of local militia units changed in response to the broader political environment, the local body continued to exist with roughly the same membership and purpose. It kept the peace in the valley, suppressed banditry, defended against rogue Indian bands, and periodically combined with other regular and irregular forces to protect the larger population of the region. Regardless of the valley's relationship to royalist or revolutionary movements, the militia retained these qualities. As a civic institution, the militia helped to define male citizenship and political culture. Militia leaders were selected through a process that combined election and appointment, mirroring similar processes in the old Spanish *ayuntamientos* and Indian *cabildos* as well as in the emerging republican systems of the post-Cádiz state. In tranquil times, militias may have conformed to the well-ordered regional systems engineered by late Bourbon administrators. In times of crises, however, when long chains of command collapsed, militias could be formed, reshaped, or redeployed autonomously. The civilian twin of the militia was the *Junta Patriótica*, a spontaneously formed valley government. Often the leaders of the two bodies were the same men. In times of acute constitutional crisis, the *juntas* and militias functioned largely without administrative oversight. For reasons of necessity, more than ideology, they took on republican qualities.

LOYALTY, CASTE, AND THE CONSTITUTION OF CÁDIZ

In Europe, the French Revolution gave rise to an era in which political beliefs became a test of loyalty and citizenship.[34] French political thought, though it was considered dangerous and subversive, was at the same time appropriated into Spanish political culture. The resulting mixture of political discourses found its way into the conflicts in New Spain. Thus we find supporters of the viceregal government touting their "defense of liberty" even while suppressing what they considered dangerous French thought. French political writing was banned in New Spain, and agents of French subversion were widely feared. The 1809 correspondence between the Supreme Junta in Spain and Nemesio Salcedo, commander of the Provincias Internas, reflects the widespread fear over French ideologies. The Junta, in a moment of optimism, described how it had "succeeded gloriously in the peninsula by our glorious Catholic arms against the perfidious and execrable,

---

[33] Acta no. 37, 1826, AGENL Correspondencia de Alcaldes, Montemorelos 1821–1826, box 2.

[34] On evolving European notions of citizenship in the years surrounding the French revolution and their ideological, cultural, and symbolic elements, see Sahlins, *Unnaturally French*, and Lynn Hunt, *Politics, Culture, and Class in the French Revolution* (Berkeley: U.C. Berkeley, 1986).

monstrous, horrible, and detestable tyrant of humanity Napoleon Bonaparte."
That same spring, Salcedo celebrated the loyalty of northern subjects to the crown,
and their willingness to fund the peninsular war; but he also expressed his fear that
French agents were spreading revolutionary doctrines in the region.[35]

The upheavals of 1810 and 1811 infused all discussions of civic life with the
question of loyalty. In preceding centuries, Spaniards of the north had bolstered
their claims of civic standing with records of service to the crown, and their
fundamental loyalty to the viceregal government was never at issue. However,
the political landscape changed with the eruption of the Hidalgo Revolt. From that
point forward, one's allegiance, beliefs, and fidelity to a chain of command became
important litmus tests for citizenship. In July of 1812, following the suppression of
the Hidalgo Rebellion, the viceroy ordered provincial governments to draw up lists
not only of insurgents and collaborators, but also of virtuous subjects who had
served the crown in this time of crisis. When the region's elites were subjected to
investigations, they usually accumulated large bodies of notarized documents,
seeking to demonstrate their loyalty. This was a time when political scores were
settled, and also a time in which citizenship was articulated in new terms. For the
first time the *vasallos* and *ciudadanos* of the north were called upon to demonstrate
membership in the polity as defined by political beliefs and affiliations.

Some men sought to distinguish themselves in the eyes of their superiors by
demonstrating their record of patriotic service during the rebellion. Others could
only hope to make their ties to the rebels less obvious. One group of viceregal
loyalists from the town of Laredo had stuck to its guns even when the soldiers of
the presidio went over to the rebellion. They and a group of "*paisanos* and
amigos" from Texas documented their tenacity as well as the loyalty of other
soldiers and clergymen who continued to support the Mexico City government.
Men with dubious records usually sought to disassociate themselves from the
events of the rebellion. Don Andrés de Imaz Altoaguirre who resided in Nuevo
León at the time of the Hidalgo Rebellion smoothed over his place in the events
of the period, offering documentation of his detachment from public life. His
notarized record of merits included the claim that "according to the testimony of
the bishop . . . he did not mix himself in the public disputes and lived closed in his
home; he is respected by the *cabildo* and viewed as a supporter of peace."[36]

In the past, it had gone without saying in the region that the clergy were
faithful subjects of the "two majesties," crown and church. Clergymen, in
applying for benefices or seeking election as bishops, sought to demonstrate
their history of accomplishments in the service of the church, but there was no
need to test or demonstrate their fundamental loyalty.[37] The Hidalgo Rebellion

---

[35] La Carta Acordada de ese Real y Supremo Consejo ...," 29 May 1829, AGI Audiencia de
Guadalajara 297 Duplicados del Comandante General de las Provincias Internas, 1808–1814.

[36] "Exercicios literarios, meritos y servicios del Doctor Don Andres de Imas y Alto laGuirre," AGI
Audiencia de Guadalaja 409.

[37] The only exception is the period of Jesuit expulsions in the 1760s, though in that case it was the
collective order, not the individual, that came under suspicion.

changed the political landscape for the region's clergy. They were courted by opposing armed camps and in several cases exerted an important political influence on the course of the rebellion. Across New Spain, the revolutionary clergymen Hidalgo and Morelos were widely celebrated and feared.[38] In San Luis Potosí, clergymen were leaders of the city's internal revolution in November 1810; and in Monterrey the region's bishop helped to orchestrate the city's alignment with the rebellion and to finance the rebel armies. Fr. Juan de Salazar, as part of the rebel armies, was blamed for the robbery of the royal treasury at Laredo.[39] Meanwhile, the loyalty of Guadalupe's Franciscan friar was questioned, while that of Monterrey's Franciscan *comisario* was lauded.[40]

After the capture of Hidalgo, several clergymen were investigated for participation in revolutionary conspiracies. San Luis Potosí's Fray Villerias helped to spark the urban revolt by releasing from jail, arming, and funding rebels. His accomplice, Presbítero Juan Nepomuceno Camaño, was sentenced to ten years of imprisonment for involvement in the rebellion. Camaño's actions, utterances, and beliefs were all at issue in his trial, and his poetry and sermons received special attention. Some of his nationalist writing was entered as evidence, including a sonnet that criticized the current wave of *peninsulares* lording over New Spain. In a verse most damaging to his case, Camaño lamented that Spaniards "Depart from Spain poor and lost/Greed makes them very impatient/ They abandon their fathers, brothers and relatives/abandon their country ... poor devils who make themselves owners of businesses, governments, and fortunes/And are the possessors of our kingdom."[41]

While Camaño fought charges of treason, clergymen who remained loyal to the viceregal government advanced their careers on the strength of their records of fidelity. When Monterrey returned to the viceregal fold, the city's clergy were quick to bury all records of collaboration with the rebellion and to document their fidelity to the central government. Fr. Antonio Manuel de Alamo, who served as the *comisario* of missions in Nuevo León, proclaimed his loyalty in an 1811 record of merit. He reminded his superiors that he had fortified the Franciscan convent against the rebels and sheltered peninsular Spaniards from attack. Summarizing his political commitments, del Alamo recalled "the honor of having been one of the best vassals of Your Majesty at all times, especially in the disgraceful insurrection of this kingdom in which your *cura* never ceased his

---

[38] For subtly different assessments of the centrality of clergymen and religion to rebellion in the Hidalgo and Independence periods, see Brading, *The First America*, chap. 26; William B. Taylor, *Magistrates of the Sacred*, 449–71; Brian F. Connaughton, *Clerical Ideology in a Revolutionary Age* (Calgary: University of Calgary, 2003), chap. 3.

[39] Reports of Dn. Andrés de Imaz y Altolaguirre [recounting events of 1811], 5 July 1816, AGI Audiencia de Guadalajara 409.

[40] Arredondo's claim that the *cabildo* funded the armies of Jiménez appears in "Acta de instalación de la Diputación Provincial ...," 15 Oct. 1814, AGI Audiencia de Guadalajara 297.

[41] "Sumaria formada contra el Presbítero Dn Juan Nepomuceno Camaano [sic] por indicios en la Insurrección de San Luis Potosí ... infidencia #1642," Querétaro [1811], BNE, MSS 3650 Papeles y Asuntos Militares y Conspiraciones, exp. 9, fol. 90.

public exhortations and proclamations to sustain these pueblos in the obedience owed to Your Majesty sometimes as preachers and sometimes as soldiers." A soldier, writing in support of del Alamo, proclaimed that the friar and other loyal citizens had risked their lives in the "defense of liberty."[42]

Tlaxcalans are often maligned in modern, popular memory, first as collaborators in the Spanish conquest, and second as perpetual royalist reactionaries.[43] There is some truth behind this image. Tlaxcalans invested centuries of effort in cultivating and defending their status as favored vassals within the Spanish Empire. They often advanced their interests by siding with the crown against domestic enemies in New Spain. The early decades of the nineteenth century, however, were a complicated time. It was seldom clear which of the contending armies were the true servants of the crown. Gran Tlaxcala remained prudently aligned with the viceroyalty during the Hidalgo Rebellion.[44] In the years that followed, its leaders reminded viceregal officials of their role in putting down "the most impolitic and barbarous insurrection yet to occur in this beautiful and flourishing kingdom."[45] The Hidalgo Rebellion superimposed loyalty to the king and hostility toward peninsular Spaniards. The Constitution of Cádiz defined Spanishness as a matter of loyalty and belief rather than ethnicity. At times, Indians in the northeast struggled against the terms of the Constitution of Cádiz, seeking to retain the privileges of Indian citizens. At other times, Indians (Tlaxcalans among them) expressed their political identity through a new language of universal citizenship. The Tlaxcalans, who had always been quick to master Spanish legal theory and legal language, adapted immediately to this new political landscape.

In Nuevo León, the Tlaxcalans' role in the Hidalgo period was complex. Tlaxcalan militias were some of the first to mobilize in response to the threat of insurrection; however, their changing loyalties in 1810 and 1811 followed those of the region's military leadership, not of the viceroyalty. When the leaders of Monterrey and Pilón went over to the insurgency, the region's Tlaxcalans followed suit. The Tlaxcalan forces avoided outright conflict with Spanish forces regardless of their formal alignments, and they were quick to sense changes in the prevailing winds. On 1 April 1811, the insurgent governor Santiago de Villareal resigned, turning power over to Monterrey's newly reformed viceregal *junta gobernadora*. The first military force to pronounce itself for the *junta* was a group of twenty-three Tlaxcalan soldiers from the neighboring community of Guadalupe, who called themselves "faithful knights of Guadalupe of Tlaxcala."[46] It would be most accurate to say that that the Tlaxcalans of

---

[42] Memorial de Fr. Antonio Manuel del Alamo (1815), AGI Audiencia de Guadalajara 409, exp. 12.

[43] The myth of persistant Tlaxcalan culpability in the Spanish conquest is familiar to many modern readers through Elena Garro's short story, "La culpa es de los tlaxcaltecas," *Cuentos Mexicanos inolvidables*, ed. Edmundo Valadés (Mexico: Asociación Nacional de Libreros, 1994).

[44] Ricardo Rendón Garcini, *Breve historia de Tlaxcala* (Mexico: Colegio de Mexico, 1996), 65–67.

[45] AGI Audiencia de Guadalajara, Duplicados del Commandante General de las Provincias Internas, 1808–1814, signed by the "Siempre Leal Ciudad de Tlascala," 19 Sept. 1812.

[46] Vizcaya Canales, 187–93.

Nuevo León, like the province's other local political communities, sought to cast their lot with the winning side. Their rapid response to changing circumstances suggests a high level of military readiness, and their pragmatic shifts in alignment indicate an attitude of calculated self-interest that matched that of other Indian and Spanish communities.

In 1812, the Cortes of Cádiz, which included a representative for Gran Tlaxcala and one from the Provincias Internas Orientales, promulgated a new constitution for the entire Spanish world. The aims of the constitution were, if anything, more revolutionary than those of Hidalgo. The Constitution of Cádiz rendered all Spaniards and Indians – regardless of their place of residence, in the New World or the Old – formally equivalent as citizens of the empire. It also reenvisioned the hierarchy of governance. A ladder of political representation would rise upward by degrees of indirect representation from the distant fringes of the Americas to the legislature of a new constitutional monarchy in Spain. In 1810, Hidalgo had addressed his followers, no matter how humble, as citizens of a nation. Now the government of Spain began to address the people of New Spain in similar terms. In 1813 public functionaries of the Provincias Internas received a message addressed to all the subjects of Spain in the New World. The 1 January message spoke to them all as *ciudadanos* and celebrated the "costly sacrifices like those made by the Spanish peoples of both hemispheres to resist the tyrant of Europe [Napoleon]." The message then sketched out the hierarchy of jurisdictions that linked local *municipios* to the central government in Spain.[47] All communities with populations of more than 1,000 would participate directly in elections for *ayuntamientos*, and indirectly in elections of the *diputación provincial*. As New Spain implemented the instructions of the Spanish Cortes, each community went through the experience of redefining its electorate and its relationship to the state.[48]

From the outset, the ideology of the Constitution of Cádiz was hotly debated among the leaders of northern New Spain. Some perceived the abolition of legal castes as emancipating Indians from legal disabilities; others believed that it justly deprived them of unfair privileges. There also were great difficulties of implementation. In November 1812, the bishop of Monterrey received word that the *juntas provinciales* should partition and distribute the lands of each pueblo's Indian commons to the individual *vecinos*. Ten months later, the regional governments still were unable to execute the policy. The bishop accepted the order in principle, but explained that "to our disgrace we have still not been able to suppress the remaining insurgent groups that, despite the

---

[47] Proclamation from the Congreso Nacional, 1 Jan. 1813, AGI Audiencia de Guadalajara 409.

[48] My findings on the long-term influences of the Constitution of Cádiz on the political culture of the north are compatible with the perspective on New World revolutions expressed by both Mario Rodríguez and Jaime Rodíquez O., though I give far greater weight to the influence of preexisting political communities on the integration of distinct ethnic groups as Mexican citizens. Mario Rodríguez, *The Cádiz Experiment in Central America, 1808–1826* (Berkeley: U.C. Berkeley, 1978); Jaime Rodríguez O., *The Independence of Spanish America.*

encouragement of our troops always beating them, continue the great obstinacy of their cruelty and looting."[49] These gaps between official policy and implementation were common throughout the greater northern frontier. For example, at the emerging administrative headquarters for the Provincias Internas in Durango, northern commanders struggled to arrive at an exact practical application of the new casteless citizenship. The leaders of the Provincias Internas acknowledged the abolition of *mita* (a form of forced labor rotation already uncommon in the region), along with all forms of corporate labor among the Indians, without resolving more complex legal questions that arose in the transition from corporate to liberal citizenship.[50]

Applying the Constitution of Cádiz across the north's various caste communities was no easy matter. Generally speaking, the region's inhabitants were happy to accept new forms of privilege and political representation offered by the constitution, but they were loath to relinquish traditional privileges or dissolve existing institutions. Monterrey elites sought to protect the symbolic status and political authority of their *ayuntamiento* when it conflicted with the new powers assigned to the provincial deputation.[51] The same was true of Indian communities long accustomed to ruling themselves through local *cabildos*. In 1814, northern military commanders were all too aware that the stability of the new regime required the assent of Indian communities. Bernardo Bonavía, commandant general for the western provinces, recommended that his peers work hard to persuade Indian leaders of the legitimacy of the new government. He feared that if he failed, the region could again slip into anarchy. However, he, like the leaders of the eastern provinces, faced a major obstacle to the implementation of the constitution: Indian communities continued to insist on the election of their own separate *cabildos*.[52] Nor was the power of these *cabildos* merely symbolic. In 1814, Arredondo complained that he was unable to compel the Indian *cabildos* to comply with some of his orders. He claimed that under Spanish law he had possessed the authority to draw funds from Indian treasuries since the summer of 1812, but that in the two years since then, this had proved impossible.[53]

49 [Primo Feliciano Marín de Porras] Bishop of Monterrey, 11 Sept. 1813, AGI Guadalajara 409.
50 Durango 17 May 1813, AGI 409. The document also expresses the opinion that "the Indians ... enjoy exemptions and privileges that the rest of the Spanish don't have ... they live freely, work as little as possible, know no other necessities than those of the moment. Many rent out their lands so as not to have to cultivate them themselves, and if they have orchards ... they have no special industry and the zeal of the priests and justices is not enough to change them ... only the women work hard." It suggests that the new system of universal citizenship and private property will break through their apathy and isolation, rendering them more productive.
51 On this constitutional struggle between Arredondo, the Ayuntamiento of Monterrey, and local authorities, AGI Audiencia de Guadalajara 297, "Duplicados de Comandantes Generales de las Provincias Internas, 1808–1814: Arredondo to Cordero," 5 Feb. 1814, "Al Alcalde Constitucional ...," 24 Feb. 1824; Arredondo 2 June 1814; "Reservado al Ayuntamiento del Valle del Pilón," 25 May 1814; contestación, 27 May 1814; "Acta de instalación de la Diputación Provincial," 10 May 1814.
52 Copy of 2 Jan. 1814 letter of Bonavía, AGI Audiencia de Guadalajara 297.
53 Arredondo, 15 Sept. 1814 Monterrey, AGI Audiencia de Guadalajara 297.

The implementation of the constitution took place amid political upsets in Spain and revolutionary violence in Mexico. The environment defies simple political categorization. During the Hidalgo Uprising, all parties in northeastern Mexico were avowedly fighting on behalf of King Fernando and against the French, but they defined this struggle in very different ways. Hidalgo's followers fought for their own constitutional order, while the institutional military fought first on behalf of old-regime governance and later on behalf of the system expressed in the Constitution of Cádiz. When King Fernando repudiated the constitution in 1814, northern commander Joaquín de Arredondo was saddled with the unpleasant task of suspending the recently instituted organs of constitutional governance. The King's orders instructed him to dissolve all local *ayuntamientos* that did not exist before May 1812 and to dissolve the *diputación provincial*. The delegates elected for the 1815 session of the *diputación provincial* were to be deprived of office, and the delegates now en route to the Cortes were to be suspended and turned back.[54]

In Mexico Hidalgo had been defeated, and in Spain the king had been restored, but the democratizing forces unleashed between 1808 and 1814 in both peninsular and colonial society were not easily reversed. In practice, the very processes of rebellion and restoration only strengthened the trend toward civic inclusion. When General Arredondo began his reconquest of the Provincias Internas for the crown, he was opposed by enormous militias that had gone over to Hidalgo. He responded in kind by raising a force of 1,300 men as he marched from Nuevo Santander to Texas. Given the desperate military circumstances, Arredondo was happy to enlist anyone he could find; and his army, though large, was by his own admission an unruly mob composed of "many without discipline and in the most miserable state." The militias that first opposed Hidalgo, and then joined him, drew from the broadest population in the history of the region. It appears that the troops raised by Arredondo to suppress them were men even more marginal to the economic and political establishment. Each step in the conflict widened and democratized the scope of conflict.[55]

A TOWN OF BRICKS AND MORTAR, STICKS AND MUD

Tlaxcalan-Chichimec pueblos and their neighboring Spanish *villas* were the original components of the colonial state in the northeast.[56] From them, the

[54] Arredondo to crown, 7 Sept. 1814, AGI Audiencia de Guadalajara 297, Duplicados de Comandantes Generales de las Provincias Internas, 1808–1814, Arredondo to crown, 7 Sept. 1814.

[55] On Arredondo's campaign, Arredondo to Spain, 15 Oct. 1814, AGI Audiencia de Guadalajara 297, exp. 13. My thinking on the group psychology of expanding conflicts is informed by the scope of conflict theory developed in E. E. Schattschneider, *The Semisoverign People* (New York: Holt, Rinehart, Winston, 1960).

[56] On barrio structures and Indian governance in the urban environment, see Dana Velasco Murillo, "The Creation of Indigenous Leadership in a Spanish Town: Zacatecas, Mexico, 1609–1752," *Ethnohistory* 56, no. 4 (Fall 2009), 669–97, and *Los indios y las ciudades de Nueva España*, ed. Felipe Castro Gutiérrez (Mexico: UNAM, 2010).

structures of the new Mexican Republic were assembled. Indian pueblos entered the municipal system of republican Mexico in one of two ways: they were either transformed into autonomous municipalities, or fused with Spanish towns.[57] Plans for the construction of the new towns usually began well before national independence and were propelled, in part, by the temporary application of the Constitution of Cádiz.[58] Yet these projects were not completed until long after national independence.[59]

The first institution to incorporate all the residents of the Valley of Pilón was the Parish of San Mateo. Prior to 1793, the valley's Indian pueblos and the Spanish town were separate spheres in the eyes of the church. With the secularization of the missions, the three valley communities were redefined as a parish. In practice, this was a change more in bookkeeping than in the conduct of local religious life. The Franciscan friars of the mission churches continued to administer the sacraments to their separate congregations of Indians, while the *cura* of Pilón discharged his functions from the parish church of San Mateo. Nonetheless, this parish now included people of all castes, an early precedent for the creation of an integrated civic community. In 1805 word reached Pilón of the royal order to liquidate assets (including agricultural land) belonging to *cofradías* and other church institutions, such as the *obras pías* accounts. However, the order exempted those organizations whose membership was exclusively Indian.[60] Accounts for Purificación and Concepción in 1809 indicate

57 Though no previous publications have taken on the general question of municipal formation and state formation in Nuevo León, several studies of individual communities have helped pave the way by addressing Tlaxcalan relationships to other indigenous peoples and exploring their influnce on developing towns: On Bustamante, Adams, "At the Lion's Mouth," 324–46, and Butzer, *Historia social*; on Guadalupe, Cavazos Garza, *Ciudad Guadalupe*; on Montemorelos, Martínez Perales, *Montemorelos, Nuevo León*, and Cantú, *Origen de la Ciudad de Montemorelos*; on Hualahuises, Nevarez Pequeño, *Villa San Cristóbal Hualahuises*.

58 The creation of rational, geometric cities was a persistent aspiration of northern settlers. This urban ideal was invoked across several centuries at moments of institutional transition or reform. One cannot easily pin down the origins of the urban grid characteristic of northern town plans. Dora P. Crouch, Daniel J. Garr, and Axel Mundigo's *Spanish Planning in North America* (Cambridge: M.I.T., 1982) challenges the notion that the Latin American town grid is a simple exportation of Iberian urban forms. They propose that the late colonial cities of Spanish North America are rooted in Renaissance ideas of order rather than traditional Spanish practice. However, the underlying geometrical regularities of Tlaxcalan-Chichimec mission-towns may owe as much to the norms of urban life in the Nahua *altepetl*. Lockhart describes Nahua norms about urban structure that are compatible with the ordering of social space found in Renaissance urban plans, *The Nahuas*, chaps. 2–3.

59 The best published explanation of the creation of the city of Montemorelos is contained in Martínez Perales's recent *Montemorelos, Nuevo León*. Martínez Perales begins this narrative with a discussion of the recognition of San Mateo de Pilón as a municipality in 1814 under the newly applied Spanish Constitution of 1812; see also Cantú, *Origen de la Ciudad de Montemorelos*. The Bancroft Library also possesses a large body of correspondence from the office of Pilón's chief functionaries through much of the nineteenth century. The materials span from 1805 to 1865 with very few substantial interruptions save the period from 1806 to 1814. Some of the documentation for these years remains in the AGENL.

60 1805 Pilón, Bancroft 74/159, file 38.

that the community institutions of these mission-towns were permitted to continue unaltered.[61]

Beginning in 1805, the influential Spaniards of the Valley of Pilón began discussing a project they generally referred to as the "extension of the pueblo." In the simplest sense, it would mean expanding the residential district around the parish church of San Mateo de Pilón, which was currently surrounded on all sides by properties deeded to Purificación and to several Spanish estates. Any expansion of the village, of necessity, involved the land and water interests of the mission, the haciendas, and the church (which possessed their own shares of these resources).[62] This proposed redistricting raised political and jurisdictional questions about the relationship between the parish, the *pueblo de indios*, and the growing town. In the long run, it also would raise questions about how jurisdictions would be defined in reference to the inhabitants' caste and place of residence.[63]

In 1815, Pilón's first *ayuntamiento* was elected under the new constitution (the valley had previously been led by a *subdelegado* or *teniente* appointed by the governors of Nuevo León), and its members immediately set about planning an expanded city grid. Between 1815 and 1820, the valley lacked a legally constituted *ayuntamiento*, but this proved less of an obstacle than one might imagine. Spanish residents of the New Kingdom of León were long accustomed to the formation of ad hoc organizations to address local problems. Emergency *juntas* were commonly assembled to respond to military crises, epidemic disease, and famine. Effectively, Pilón did have an *ayuntamiento* during these years, but under a different name. The planning *junta* of roughly two dozen *vecinos*, in cooperation with the *subdelegado*, set the agenda for the urban development plan and delegated specific responsibilities to individuals serving in roles such as treasurer or *síndico*.

When the constitution was rescinded later in 1815, Pilón formally complied with the order to dissolve its *ayuntamiento*. However, the *vecinos* continued to pursue their new urban plan through a committee of notables that looked suspiciously like the *ayuntamiento* of the year before. As the plans for urbanization moved forward, the power of the office of *procurador* (or "*síndico procurador*") expanded proportionally. *Procurador* was a peculiar post in the Valley of Pilón, and one that reflected the continuing influence of Pilón's largest hacienda. From the beginning of the discussions over the expansion of the urban

---

[61] 9 Feb. 1809 accounts for Purificación and Concepción, AGENL Corresondencia de Alcaldes, Montemorelos 1812–1821 – note that this one-year fragment from the state archive of Nuevo León belongs to the same series as the Bancroft ledgers from which it was presumably separated.

[62] The November 1802 correspondence shows that the parish church of Pilón also operated its own sugar mill. AGENL Correspondencia de Alcaldes, Montemorelos 1812–1821, box 1.

[63] Discussions of the annexation of Indian and hacienda lands to the town began against the backdrop of the royal decrees of 1805, which threatened elements of the corporate economy. On the political properties of the Consolidación de Vales Reales, see Margaret Chowning, "The Consolidación de Vales Reales in the Bishopric of Michoacan," *Hispanic American Historical Review* 69, no. 3 (Aug. 1989), 451–78.

core, it was understood that the land for the existing town had originated from the lands of the Nuestra Señora de la Regla estate. Pedro José Ballesteros, who owned the estate at the time of the urban expansion, first entered into negotiations through his own *mayordomo*, who is termed the "*síndico.*" In surveying the town, the *síndico* was charged with most procedural decisions regarding boundaries and populations, and even served as the auditor of elections. On 2 May 1815, Subdelegado Froilan de Mier Noriega announced the election results and the new plan for the city of San Mateo de Pilón. In the emerging public health language of the day, he promised that the new city would be planted on higher ground farther from the river, and planned with broad streets so that the population might "enjoy better ventilation and achieve better health." The first step in the project was a land survey carried out by the *procurador*; it noted all existing properties, their boundaries, and the productivity of each plot. Then the construction of the city would begin.[64] As late as 1820 (when the constitution was restored), a group of sixteen *vecinos republicanos* functioned as the active citizenry of the town, empowering five local notables to define and distribute the properties for the new town site.[65]

Pilón's period of transition from a valley made up of three separate territorial entities (San Mateo, Purificación, and Concepción) to a municipality under one set of legal systems began with a set of plans sketched out in 1815, and culminated in the execution of those plans (though somewhat modified by intervening constitutional changes) in 1826. In 1815 and 1816, the leading *vecinos* of Pilón sketched out a new map of the town, incorporating both private Spanish lands and lands from the *pueblos de indios*. From 1816 to 1820, valley residents argued over land and water rights, and over public rights-of-way. The planning body of leading Spanish citizens became the most powerful institution in the valley in part because of its members' ability to place private resources at the disposal of the project. Committee members negotiated with each other over boundaries and land allotments and over the contributions each would be assessed for the construction of the new church and urban grid.

The scale of Pilón's new public works exceeded any previous community effort. Until this point, the valley's shared public infrastructure had been limited to its irrigation system. The *acequias*, which supplied water from the Pilón River to valley farms, were periodically extended, and existing channels required regular maintenance to prevent accumulated silt from clogging them. The arbitration of disputes involving water rights (measured in days and hours of flow), and of maintenance obligations, had always been central issues in community governance. The new town would require labor for the construction and

[64] "Copia del oficio de Dn. Froilan de Mier Noriega que en el año pasado de 1815 dirigió al subdelegado que fue D. Vicente Paras relativo al Procurador y Población de este Valle del Pilón [original date 2 May 1815]." This document is filed with the 1826 municipal incorporation records, AGENL Correspondencia de Alcaldes, Montemorelos 1812–1821, box 1.

[65] 10 July 1820, AGENL Correspondencia de Alcaldes, Montemorelos, caja 2, 1826 – note that this document is misfiled amongst later materials from 1826.

maintenance of additional *acequias* and the new grid of streets. The 1816 plan called for the construction of sixteen urban blocks, a plaza, a church, *casas reales*, and a stretch of road passing through the valley and connecting it with two other towns. The money, equipment, and labor came from the valley residents. The planning *junta* decided how much its individual members would contribute to the new town in land, cash, and labor. The labor came in the form of dependent workers residing on hacienda lands who were loaned to the construction projects for a specified period of time. Each hacienda owner was assessed a number or workers proportional to the size of his estate. In other words, the actual digging of channels, clearing of roads, and transport of construction materials were carried out by laborers bound in some sense to the mandates of their employers. In describing these labor allotments, an 1820 resolution states that each *vecino* shall submit a "proportional share ... of carts, oxen and peons."[66]

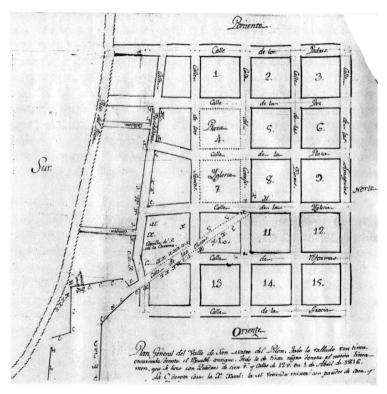

FIGURE 10. The original color manuscript of this 1816 urban plan for the town of Pilón labeled with red ink all the unnumbered blocks as well as block 10. The accompanying text identified this zone (along with the other bank of the river) as belonging to the former Tlaxclan-Chichimec *repúblicas* of Purificación and Concepcíon. (Archivo General del Estado de Nuevo León: Correspondencia de los Primeros Alcaldes, Montemorelos)

[66] 13 Aug. 1820, AGENL Correspondencia de Alcaldes, Montemorelos, caja 2, 1826.

In 1820, the plans of the *vecinos* and the fortunes of the nation converged. As local government moved forward with the incremental fusion of the Spanish *villa* and Indian pueblos, the Riego Revolt in Spain forced the king to restore the Constitution of Cádiz, thereby again dissolving the legal basis for separate Indian and Spanish republics in the Valley of Pilón. In 1820, San Mateo de Pilón was recognized as a municipality and the *ayuntamiento* was restored. In the meantime, the town's major landowners had continued to plan and survey for the new town grid. Thus, the 1825 proclamation of Montemorelos as a municipality was really no more than a confirmation of existing political arrangements and an affirmation of the symbolic connection between the community and the new, independent nation. The basic plan for the new city, along with the debates and conflicts that it engendered, was already clearly defined in 1820, well before the 1821 declaration of Mexican Independence, the promulgation of Mexico's 1824 Constitution, or the creation of Nuevo León's 1825 Constitution.

In the 1820s, the population and economy of the valley were growing. The leading Spanish residents of the Valley of Pilón, and in particular José Domingo Ballesteros, envisioned an expanded role for municipal government in building infrastructure and boosting economic productivity. The *ayuntamiento* created a uniform standard of water rents in the valley under which a standard-sized plot of land was entitled to a ten-day ration of water. Along with a new interurban road and the new grid of urban streets, Montemorelos began constructing bridges across the river Pilón, connecting the barrio of the ex-pueblo of Concepción with the rest of the municipality. The local government even carried out an experiment to see if flax would grow in the area – a sort of state-sponsored economic development plan that would have made any late Bourbon administrator proud.[67]

Public health, along with infrastructure improvement, provided an important rationale for administrative integration of the valley communities. The first plans for the urban expansion, drafted in 1815 and 1816, were justified by their authors, in part, as a means to create better ventilation and flood control to protect the citizens from epidemic disease and loss of property. At times, these justifications may have been a Trojan horse for the seizure of pueblo lands, but they also responded to serious local problems. The 1825 resolutions of the *ayuntamiento* repeated earlier commitments to public sanitation and the opening of streets while adding plans to provide food and medicine to the sick and destitute.[68] Measures for public health, of necessity, involved the entire valley, and their advent often preceded other policies that would integrate the governance of the three valley communities.

---

[67] 16 Dec. 1826, 30 Sept. 1826, and 26 Oct. 1826, Ayuntamiento de Montemorelos, AGENL Corespondencia de Alcaldes, Montemorelos.

[68] 2 May 1815, AGENL Corespondencia de Alcaldes, Montemorelos, box 2: 1821–1826 (this was originally part of documentation collected in 1826); 26 May 1816, AGENL Correspondencia de Alcaldes, Montemorelos, caja 2, 1826; 1825 Pilón documents relating to public health and safety, Bancroft MSS 74/159, files 121, 123, 124, 126.

Perhaps the most ambitious element of the urban plan of 1816 was the new parish church. Over time, efforts to construct this church defined membership in the valley community in the broadest terms. The 1816 plan set aside a plot of land for the church facing the plaza. The parish church, as a corporate entity, was also allocated land and water rights in the new town, which would generate revenues for its operations in perpetuity.[69] While these revenues, along with clerical fees, might fund the eventual operations of the parish, the construction project itself would require vast financial and labor levies from the entire community. The *junta* that planned the new town comprised only twenty-three or twenty-four individuals. We might think of these influential men as the active citizens of the valley. The subscription list of *vecinos* contributing for the construction of the new church runs to six pages. This larger group of parishioners was, effectively, the entire passive citizenry of Pilón.[70] The following year, the governor of Nuevo León approved the church construction project, and the leaders of Pilón named a special treasurer to manage collections and disbursements.[71] The construction got underway in 1820.[72]

There is no sign that the birth of the Ayuntamiento of Pilón meant the death or immediate decline of the *cabildos* of Purificación and Concepción.[73] Nor was there any interruption in the functions of the Indian *cabildos* between 1815 and 1820. Despite López Fonseca's earlier proposal to transfer populations from Purificación to Concepción in order to accommodate the urban expansion, the original maps of the urban grid indicate only a partial annexation of pueblo lands by the Spanish town. Not only did both pueblos remain essentially intact, but they also received new populations. In 1817 several new groups of Chichimecs settled in both pueblos, swearing to be good Christians and faithful vassals of the Spanish crown.[74] In December 1820, the first *alcalde* of Pilón, Justo Pastor Ibarra, wrote to Governor Bruno Barrera in Monterrey in an attempt to sort out the status of the valley's three communities under the restored Constitution of Cádiz. Pastor Ibarra noted that it was the usual time for Indian *cabildo* elections, but asked whether the *cabildos* were supposed to continue under the new system. The answer from the governor was unequivocal: the pueblos should hold the elections and the *cabildos* should continue to operate in

---

[69] López Fonseca to Barrera, 6 May 1816, AGENL Correspondencia de Alcaldes, Montemorelos, caja 2, 1826.

[70] The subscription list is dated only with the year 1816, but may have been attached originally to the 6 May document.

[71] López Fonseca and Cantú to Barrera, 17 Feb. 1816, AGENL Correspondencia de Alcaldes, Montemorelos, caja 2.

[72] Records for that year show the requisition of carts, draft animals, and thirty workers for the project, 10 July 1820, AGENL Correspondencia de Alcaldes, Montemorelos, caja 2, 1826.

[73] 30 Dec. 1820, Ibarra to Barrera and 2 Jan. 1821 Barrera to Ibarra, AGENL Correspondendencia de Alcaldes, Montemorelos 1812–1821, box 1.

[74] Pedro Borrego to the *vocales* of the governing junta, 27 Nov. 1817, AGENL Correspondencia de Alcaldes, Montemorelos, box 1.

their accustomed manner. The elections went forward as usual, and a new Spanish *protector* was named at the request of the two communities.

DIVIDING THE COMMONS

One of the simplest generalizations about the changes between the colonial and modern economy of Mexico is that collective Indian landholding was replaced with individual private landholding. This generalization is useful, but also potentially misleading. The economy of the colonial-era Indian pueblos combined elements of family landholding with collective landholding. Furthermore, in republican Mexico, local communities often retained significant corporate land and water rights. In other words, the colonial pueblo was closer to a liberal economy, and the mid-nineteenth-century municipality farther from a liberal economy, than is commonly assumed. Nonetheless, the constitutional changes of the early nineteenth century required a significant legal rearticulation of the rules of property.

The Mexican Constitution of 1824 and the Nuevo León state constitution of 1825 reaffirmed the dismantling of castes and *repúblicas* mandated by the 1820 restoration of the Constitution of Cádiz. Acting on this principle, the Congreso Constituyente of Nuevo León ordered the distribution of the lands and waters of the "ex-missions of Purificación and Concepción" to the individual residents of those communities.[75] The 1826 and 1827 acts of the Congress explained how this allotment would take place: surveyors would recheck the boundaries of each ex-mission and mark the *solares* that would be the basis of the new real estate titles. The "corporation," made up of the families that were formerly enrolled members of the pueblos, would now be described as a body of shareholders (*accionistas*). Each shareholder then would be issued an official, stamped document validating his family's claim to a portion of the land and water of the community.[76] Thus, one might say that although the landed commune of each mission would cease to exist on paper, the members of the community and their property would still be bound together, taking on a new life as a community of shareholding residents.[77] Lands were to be assigned a cash value and rendered transactable. In truth, though, the pueblo system was only being legally rearticulated, not destroyed. Two thirds of each village's lands were to be partitioned and distributed as private plots, but the other third was to be retained as

[75] "Memoria por duplicado con que la Municipalidad de la ciudad de Monte Morelos da cuenta al governador del Estado ..." 14 Jan. 1826. Note the shift in terminology: the word *misión* had usually been used to describe the activities, land, and structures belonging to the church within the "pueblos" of Purificación and Concepción. For some reason, the term *ex-misión* was, from around this time, applied to the entire land-area of each former *pueblo de indios*.

[76] Resolutions of the Ayuntamiento of Montemorelos, 1826–1827, no. 69, AGENL Correspondencia de los Alcaldes de Nuevo León, 1821–1826, box 2.

[77] I owe a debt of gratitude to two fellow researchers at the Archivo General del Estado de Nuevo León who directed my attention to this type of documentation in the summer of 2005: María Gabriela Márquez Rodríguez and Raul García Flores.

property of the municipality and would generate revenue for the ongoing operations of local government. Even the lands under private title were to be reckoned more the property of a family than of an individual.[78]

In Nuestra Señora de Guadalupe, preparations for the privatization of lands began in 1825, but the policy was not fully executed until 1837. Guadalupe was a town peopled by the descendants of Tlaxcalan and Chichimec settlers, neither of whom immediately lost their former identities. Even at the time of the land distributions, seventeen years after the Mexican constitution abandoned the legal categories of Indian and Spaniard, the Ayuntamiento of Guadalupe continued to count its Tlaxcalan and Chichimec inhabitants separately, and it and took measures to ensure that no aspect of the land distributions would incite conflict between the two groups. In planning and surveying, the *ayuntamiento* frequently reemphasized that Tlaxcalan and Chichimec families would receive equal shares of village resources.[79]

The members of the ex–*pueblo de indios* were now legally described as shareholders (*accionistas*). It appears that there was an exact equivalence between the identity of *accionistas* and that of *vecinos* in the nascent municipality of Guadalupe. An *accionista* was typically an indigenous, literate, male head of household. An 1835 list of Tlaxcalan land title recipients in Guadalupe comprises 112 male family heads, 52 widows, and 29 orphans (whose lands were administered in trust). The patterns of land tenure in this community tell us a great deal about prevailing definitions of local citizenship. Every person who was issued a share of the lands of Guadalupe could be described as a *vecino* of the town, an Indian, and the head of a household. The basic civic unit was not the individual, but the family.[80]

The equitable distribution of land and water was the most important civic issue in minds of the Neoleonés *vecinos*. Their fear of preferential distribution is reflected in both state and local policy. A series of state ordinances of 1831 outline the proper steps to be taken in the reallocation of land from the

---

[78] This 20 July 1825 resolution outlining the process of land distribution is summarized in an 8 Nov. 1831 document that is unbound but cataloged with "Espediente del Reparto de tierras y aguas hecho entre los naturales del Pueblo de Guadalupe, Año 1837," AGENL L 26/391. The same process of distribution is illustrated in the documents for the town of Rió Blanco contained in AGENL CL 21/345.

[79] The equal distribution of plots to Tlaxcalans and Chichimecs is made clear in documents 15 Nov. 1831 and 5 Nov. 1831 in AGENL L 26/391, which distinguishes between "Tlascaltecas" and "indigenas." The duration of these disputes is illustrated by the whole scope of the materials contained in AGENL L 26/391 covering the period from 1825 to 1837. It appears that the assumption of land titles by the 196 legitimate *accionistas* did not begin until 14 Nov. 1836, according to a document of that date in "Espediente del reparto de tierras ... 1837," AGENL L 26/391.

[80] The AGENL materials include a series of censes for Guadalupe: 19 Nov. 1832 "lista de tlaxcaltecas cavecas de familias ..."; 19 Nov. 1832 "lista de vecinas del pueblo ..."; 19 Nov. 1832 "lista de los Tlaxcaltecas huerfanos"; 20 Apr. 1835 "lista de los Tlaxcaltecas Cavezas de Familia ..."; 10 Apr. 1835 "lista de las vecinas Tlaxcaltecas ..."; 20 Apr. 1845 "lista de huerfanos de Tlaxcaltecas ..." AGENL L 26/391.

commons. After setting aside one third of the pueblo property for each town's *ejido*, the local *ayuntamiento* was to survey and catalog the remaining land. Three types of land were comprehended by the new system: urban home and garden lots (*solares*), farm plots, and more distant pastures for livestock (*agostaderos*). A survey of lands produced a map of the municipality noting the cash value of every farm plot. A concurrent census rendered a list of household heads eligible to receive lands. To ensure a fair process and to create shares of equal value, both *escribanos* and *síndicos* scrutinized the maps. In the end, family plots were assigned by drawing lots under the supervision of the specially appointed *juez de reparto*. Families were entitled to lands based on birth and conduct. A proper recipient was a "natural" (a native) of the pueblo who had worked the land continuously. Families long absent from their lands were not eligible for land claims, and families recently absent were required to return to their lands within three years or cede their rights them.[81]

In the 1820s, the biggest source of controversy and conflict in Pilón was not elections or constitutional law, but road construction. Though Pilón's planning *juntas* had been drafting maps of the new city's *solares* and streets since 1815, the most heated conflicts began in 1821 when work crews began clearing roads to make the physical city match the lines on the map. Typically, the new roads were drawn through lands currently under cultivation. This resulted in almost comical legal complaints in which the same patches of soil were referred to by the residents as "fields" and by the *ayuntamiento* as "roads." In March 1821, Antonio López Fonseca and the members of the *ayuntamiento* ordered that the "filthy and shameful *jacales*" that were obstructing the "streets" be cleared immediately.[82] Pilón's leaders complained to the Monterrey government that the town's new streets were choked with *jacales*. They explained that the city needed room to house its growing population; they also requested a verification of the existing boundary with Purificación and the cession of more of its lands to the city.[83] It is not hard to read between the lines: the new grid included lands within the boundaries of Purificación, and the surveyors were attempting to cut streets through the home sites and fields of Purificación residents who refused to budge. Now the town hoped the provincial governor could be persuaded to intervene on its behalf and permit further municipal annexations of the Indians' pueblo lands. It was no easy matter to make a legal determination in this conflict.

Land surveys always were a contentious process. At the state level, the privatization of titles was ordered in 1825, and it was confirmed the following year by the Montemorelos Ayuntamiento. At some point in 1826, the

[81] Consecutive maps indicating the division of lands for Guadalupe are included in AGENL 26/391, p. 171 and pp. 256–8; on the reservation of lands as an *ejido* to fund local government, 8 Nov. 1831, AGENL 26/391; on the exclusion on the requirement of ongoing cultivation for land claims, 5 Nov. 1831, AGENL 26/391; role of *juez de reparto* appears in the text surrounding the above-mentioned maps.

[82] 24 Mar. 1821, AGENL Correspondencia de Alcaldes, Montemorelos, caja 2, 1826.

[83] From the leaders of Pilón to Gaspar, AGENL Correspondencia de Alcaldes, Montemorelos, caja 2, 1826 [contents indicate composition after 20 Mar. 1821].

ayuntamiento, recognizing the legal complexities of the situation, ordered a temporary halt to the distributions.[84] Several surveyors were hard at work marking the new streets and *acequias*, though they often suffered criticism from interested parties. The earliest surveys had been performed by the *síndicos procuradores* of the *ayuntamiento*, but in 1826 the Purificación and Concepción accounts show the Indian communities paid out substantial sums to land surveyors.[85] The arrangement suggests that both the ex-missions and the town were willing to pay handsomely in order to make sure their interests were not overlooked. The surveys were declared completed in June.[86]

Along with debating whether plots of land were fields or streets, the Spanish town and the Indians of Purificación argued over a group of buildings that the *ayuntamiento* derided as "*jacales* and a house that they call the convent of the *barrio* of Purificación." It seems that by the beginning of August, Indian appeals to higher authorities had spared the land and buildings from the land distribution scheme.[87] Tlaxcalan and Chichimec road construction litigants also won a partial victory when the town accepted the principle that the shareholders of Purificación should be compensated for these eminent domain appropriations.[88] At the same time, renters on pueblo lands, happy with their long-standing agreements over land and water rates, exacted an agreement from the *ayuntamiento* for the preservation of the same water rates under the municipality.[89] The earlier colonial *pueblos de indios* should not be imagined as uniform populations consisting exclusively of Indians who farmed the land in common and on equal terms. Many *pueblos de indios* held a very large area of arable land relative to their populations. Consequently, rental of land and waters to outsiders was a common practice. Thus, these legal disputes over the distribution of mission lands involved not just the land rights of Indians from the pueblos, but also suits from long-term renters anxious to preserve customary rates.

There are signs that the Tlaxcalans continued to exist as a distinct residential community and interest group within this broader pool of shareholders. In local disputes of 1826, the Barrio de Purificación was described as

---

[84] The order to suspend distributions appears in the numbered resolutions of the acts of the Ayuntamiento of Montemoreles of the year 1826 as no. 47, but lacks a date, AGENL Correspondencia de Alcaldes, Montemorelos, box 2: 1821–1826.

[85] To the Gov. Ballesteros from the Ayuntamiento of Montemorelos, 18 Mar. 1826; 20 July 1826. Surveyors Albino and Exiquio Silva were paid 200 pesos. Albino Altuna's relationship to the project was complex: he was in the employ of the missions as a surveyor, but also an interested party, given that his own land bordered Indian pueblo lands, AGENL Correspondencia de Alcaldes, Montemorelos, box 2: 1821–1826 – doc. date 18 Apr. 1826.

[86] AGENL Correspondencia de Alcaldes, Montemorelos, box 2: 1821–1826 – doc date 5 June 1826.

[87] 31 Aug. 1826, resolution of the Ayuntamiento no. 195. This entry refers to the 4 August order from Monterrey to leave the property intact.

[88] 31 Aug. 1826, resolution of the Ayuntamiento no. 196, box 2: 1821–1826.

[89] Note that water rents were paid in cash or in labor. Both Indians and non-Indians before and after the urban expansion often paid their dues by constructing or clearing *acequias*: "los ciudadanos Domingo fuentes y Juan Marcos de la Zerda," 5 June 1826, AGENL Correspondencia de Alcaldes, Montemorelos, box 2: 1821–1826.

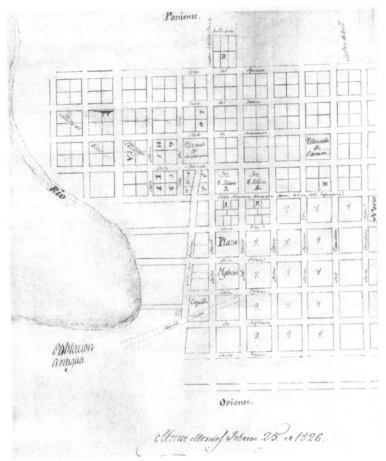

FIGURE 11. The 1826 plan for the city of Montemorelos demonstrates the realization of
the 1816 plan, and also indicates the location of the integrated *pueblos de indios* partly
within the town grid and partly along the river banks. (Archivo General del Estado de
Nuevo León: Correspondencia de los Primeros Alcaldes, Montemorelos)

containing *"indígenas y tlaxcaltecas,"* who were parties in agreements over
water rights.[90] The records make clear that both political communities were
empowered to make combined or separate agreements. For instance, in 1826
the Tlaxcalans, as a body, negotiated a ten-year concession from the
Ayuntamiento of Montemorelos to operate a regional trade fair.[91]

---

[90] 10 Aug. 1826, Ayuntamiento de Montemorelos, AGENL Correspondencia de los Alcaldes de
Nuevo León, 1821–1826, box 2.
[91] 1826 Resolutions of the Ayuntamiento of Montemorelos, no. 113, AGENL Correspondencia de
los Alcaldes de Nuevo León, 1821–1826, box 2.

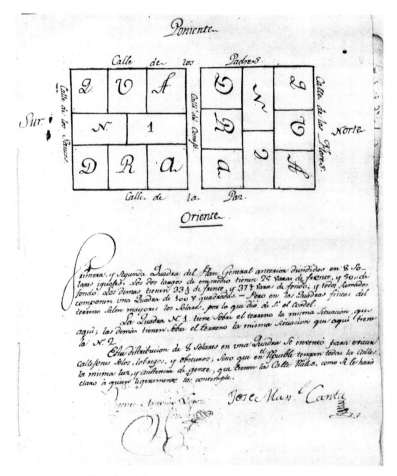

FIGURE 12. This detail from the 1826 Montemorelos urban plan shows two model blocks (also visible in Fig. 11) designed to illustrate how existing properties could be brought into conformity with the new standards for urban space. (Archivo General del Estado de Nuevo León: Correspondencia de los Primeros Alcaldes, Montemorelos)

Since early in the eighteenth century, Spanish observers had pointed out that Tlaxcalan farmers primarily worked their own family plots, but also worked a specified number of days on the common lands, thereby funding community expenditures.[92] The authors of the mission-town system had hoped that after a period of adjustment, newly settled Chichimecs would conform to the Tlaxcalan

---

[92] Israel Cavazos Garza describes Nuevo León's Indian pueblos, including Tlaxcalan pueblos, as structured around communal landholding. Until the time of national independence, *Breve historia de Nuevo León*, 41–43. The documents consulted in this chapter suggest a mix of collective and individual economic relationships both before and after independence.

pattern of land tenure, and it appears that many did.[93] Tlaxcalans and long-settled Chichimecs held family plots in trust from the pueblo and worked some number of days for the commons. From the former came their subsistence; from the latter their contributions to the festivals, church ornaments, social welfare, and emergency funds.[94] Meanwhile, substantial parts of the lands within the mission boundaries were worked by outsiders, whose rents contributed to the welfare of the Indian communities.[95] All of these factors produced a process of land privatization that was slow, complex, and involved the interests of every sector of the valley's population.

In all of these legal struggles and business dealings, the government of the *pueblo de indios* continued to exist as a *cabildo*, which administered a common fund on behalf of the shareholders. Between 1826 and 1830, the *fondo de Concepción* and the *fondo de Purificación* received compensation on behalf of the Tlaxcalans and Chichimecs of Purificación, issued water shares for the *accionistas* of both ex-mission communities, took in water rents, and managed the construction of new *acequias*.[96] The transfer of some resources from Purificación to Concepción accounts suggests that some residents of the former community moved to the other side of the river as part of the property exchanges taking place with the city.[97] Still, the aggregate record of agreements and disputes suggests that most of the members of the ex-missions remained on the land that they had always occupied.

In many respects, the municipal land system of the ex–*pueblos de indios* was the same as that of the original Tlaxcalan *pueblos de indios*. In the Tlaxcalan *pueblos de indios*, the family was the fundamental unit for labor and land-holding. All families lived in a surveyed solar, worked a surveyed set of family fields, and contributed labor to the common fields that sustained the local treasury. Before and after independence, land was effectively family capital. However, in the years after independence it became transactable property that might be bought or sold. Water was never an entirely private resource. Water was a finite, shared resource, and its delivery to fields by means of *acequias* required shared labor for both construction and maintenance. Both before and after independence, water rights were linked to land rights, but these rights were

---

[93] See Chapters 2 and 3.

[94] This system is described in principle in the Barbadillo reforms (see Chapter 3) and is observable in practice in account books from the *pueblos de indios* such as "Cuenta del Avío dado a los hijos de la misión de Concepción," 1795–1800, Bancroft MSS 74/159, file 2.

[95] The accounting for Concepción in 1795 demonstrates how this worked. Rents owed to the community by outsiders appear as credits in the community treasury that were then redeemed for goods through the *protector*, 12 Nov. 1795 accounts of goods distributed to Concepción, Bancroft MSS 74/159.

[96] 31 Jan. 1826; 30 Sept. 1826 water contract; 30 Oct. agreement on water and new *acequias*, 5 Dec. 1826 list of *accionistas* with water shares; 1826–1827 acts of Montemorelos Ayuntamiento, resolution no. 69, Correspondencia de Alcaldes, Montemorelos, box 2: 1821–1826.

[97] 25 Mar. 1826, AGENL Correspondencia de Alcaldes, Montemorelos, box 2: 1821–1826.

carefully delimited. The business of distributing, rationing, and charging rents for water was already a part of customary village practices.[98]

CIVIC MEMBERSHIP AND INTEGRATION

The Constitution of Cádiz aimed to abolish the distinction between Indian and Spaniard, but this is not the sort of political transformation that is accomplished with the stroke of a pen. In the civil sphere, Indian and Spanish political life merged through formal and informal mechanisms. The mixed-caste population had expanded greatly in the late colonial period, and people of all kinds circulated and intermarried regardless of any official designs. Long-standing demographic trends favored a transition to a more integrated society. Separate Indian and Spanish populations were now increasingly accompanied by mestizos who became parishioners and *vecinos* of Spanish towns.

The integration of communities took place as a result of both corporate and individual interaction. In religious life, clergymen served a variety of communities linked to a single parish church. Thus, constituent missions, towns, and *visitas* were all culturally connected. In military life, Indian and Spanish communities raised separate militias, but then placed them under the unified commands of *alcaldes mayores* and later *subdelegados*. The old system of the separate *repúblicas* still described part of the political economy of the region in the 1810s and 1820s, but the new constitutional notion of casteless citizenship provided a means of describing and incorporating the substantial population of mixed ancestry.

Because regional governments applying the Constitution of Cádiz ceased to categorize populations by ethnicity, it is sometimes difficult to analyze the ethnic makeup of the population of New Spain in the years after 1812. Thankfully, some church officials continued to tally populations according to the traditional ethnic categories. A church census for 1814 provides some clues as to how demographic integration might have matched the civic integration envisioned by the constitution. The existing bishopric of Monterrey corresponded geographically to the new *diputación provincial* – an area comprising Nuevo León, Nuevo Santander, Coahuila, and Texas. This permits us to study the caste composition of a political district that technically did not recognize caste. The bishop reported that the region's population included roughly 51,000 Spaniards and 37,000 Indians. However, nearly as many people were of mixed ancestry – roughly 36,000 mestizos and 37,000 "of other castes."[99] In other words, regardless of colonial legal theory, a large portion of the population lay outside the two republics.

The Constitution of Cádiz advocated a change in civic culture already made inevitable by demographic forces. The people of the region were intermarrying

---

[98] The *reparto* documents generally refer to the distribution of "*tierras y aguas*," but water rights required the ongoing payment of rents.

[99] 28 Dec. 1814, AGI Audiencia de Guadalajara 409.

and interbreeding at such a rate that the old legal boundaries between castes could not long survive. The bishop of Monterrey remarked that

> In the kingdom of Nuevo León the relationship between the different *calidades* of the population is also more varied than in other places. While the class of Spaniards is superior to everyone else, taken in isolation, the class of mestizos is almost equal to that of Indians; one notices that they and the Spaniards inter-mingle much more than in the other provinces ... and one notes the absence of certain rivalries that are harmful in politics and economics.[100]

It appears that in Nuevo León, a social process of caste synthesis that had begun long before was now converging with the legal conditions of the Constitution of Cádiz. Just as Tlaxcalan communities had aggregated and incorporated north-ern tribes, so too had formal and informal unions between Indians and Spaniards produced a large population of mixed-caste individuals who lived among Spaniards and shared their customs. Furthermore, by 1814, nearly all of the Indians inhabiting colonial lands had been brought into the community of Christians and colonial subjects. In the population of more than 37,000 Indians, the census found just over 1,100 neophytes. This is to say that the settled Indian population was baptized, Christianized, and to a considerable degree accultu-rated to colonial norms. The Tlaxcalan-Chichimec mission-town model, which had been employed throughout the region, had produced colonial subjects according to its design. These colonial subjects were now positioned to become citizens in the new constitutional empire.

The bishop of Monterrey's comment implies that the case of Nuevo León was exceptional, but this was not so. Other discussions in the diocesan records indicate that Nuevo Santander was experiencing the same erosion of caste boundaries. Indians moved into Spanish communities and drew upon the services of their priests; meanwhile non-Indians took up residence on Indian lands and joined their spiritual communities. In the 1790s, the bishop found it necessary to appoint two sets of priests and ecclesiastical judges for communities with large populations of both *indios* and *gente de razón*.[101] The census records are not complete for every community, but they are extensive enough to give us a clear notion of which Indian and Spanish towns were closely connected to each other.[102]

Two facts about the demographic record are most striking: the expansion of the population considered Spanish and *casta*, and the proximity and uniform administrative connections between Indian and Spanish communities through-out the colony. The structure of political life in Nuevo Santander was designed on the basis of interdependent and self-governing Spanish and Indian commun-ities. However, this state of affairs was understood as transitional – a means by which to create a colonial system in which integrated production and

---

[100] 28 Dec. 1814, AGI Audiencia de Guadalajara 409.
[101] AAM: Libro de Govierno del Obispo, 1792–1830: 18 Nov. 1793.
[102] The operational connections between the diocesan and missionary college system are clearly illustrated for Nuevo Santander in AGN Misiones 11.

governance would eventually prevail. In the 1760s, much of the land held in community by Indian mission-towns was distributed as private property to Indian families. This process continued (with some reversals) to the end of the eighteenth century. The result was an economy in which the boundary between Indian and Spanish land was less and less important. During those same years, the secularization of church administration meant that missionaries ministered to both Spaniards and Indians and reported to both their missionary colleges and to the bishop. These administrative changes seem to have matched changes in the social experience. The rapid growth of mixed-caste peoples as local citizens and parishioners suggests both intermarriage and mobility.[103]

Intermarriage was only one of many reasons that residential segregation was breaking down in the Valley of Pilón. At the beginning of the nineteenth century, the boundaries between the valley's communities were already somewhat porous: members of the *pueblos de indios* drew wages working on haciendas; outsiders were employed to tend the Indians' herds; and the missions rented out land and water to Spanish *vecinos*. Thus, there was a significant gap between the legal theory of separate republics and customary practice. A late colonial governor of Nuevo León noted that "neither the King nor his subordinates permit, without the knowledge of this government, the rental to Spaniards or other castes of the lands that are assigned to the *pueblos*, assuring, whenever possible, that these same natives cultivate and benefit from them." In practice, however, the rental of pueblo lands to outsiders was a major part of the valley's economy. A set of 1816 rental records, audited by the *protector*, indicates that in that year Purificación made forty-four rental agreements and Concepción ten. The list of renters' names is accompanied by a list of dependents, suggesting that the outsiders often made their homes on the lands of the *pueblo de indios*. If this is the case, then there were eighteen nonmember families living inside the bounds of the pueblos as renters. Social elites in the Spanish *villa* seem to have augmented their personal lands with land rentals from the Indian communities. The list of contracts for 1816 includes seven renters with the honorific "don" before their names, including the clergyman "señor cura dn. Clemente Arocha."[104]

The late colonial history of San Miguel de Aguayo illustrates both the corporate and individual mechanisms of integration. In San Miguel, Tlaxcalans and Alasapas of the mid eighteenth century had both separate and shared structures of governance, and they cooperated with each other in regional defense. Yet each community was a jealous defender of its own land and water rights. The result was a clear but permeable boundary between the two barrios. The Alasapas

---

[103] AGS Secretaría de Guerra 6966, exp. 69, charts following fols. 278 and 321.

[104] "Lista de los Arrendatorios y sus arrimados que hay en este pueblo de N.S. de la Purificación cuias rentas se cobran en el 1 de enero de 1817"; "Lista de los Arrendatarios de hay en este Pueblo de N.S. de la Concepción en este año de 1816 cuias rentas se cobran en el 1 de enero 1819," AGENL Correspondencia Montemorelos, box 1. On the exchange of goods and peoples accross these legal boundaries, see Magnus Mörner, *La Corona española y los foráneos en los pueblos de indios de América* (Madrid: Ediciones de Cultura Hispanica, 1999).

drew new Indian settlers of other ethnicities into their barrio, while the Tlaxcalan community also prospered, gaining in numbers and in military and economic strength. In the second half of the century, however, the Alasapa population shrank relative to the Tlaxcalan population. It appears that while many Alasapas were "becoming Tlaxcalan" in a political sense, the community also was becoming Tlaxcalan in a demographic sense. Elisabeth Butzer's study of San Miguel uses parish records to estimate the rates of Tlaxcalan exogamy. Between 1760 and 1820, her numbers show high rates of Tlaxcalan marriage to mestizos and Alasapas (as well as a significant number of marriages to Spaniards). In a town of between 200 and 300 Tlaxcalan families, the parish recorded 104 exogamous marriages between 1790 and 1820.[105] Thus, it is very likely that much of the decline in the recorded Chichimec population of San Antonio after mid century was the result of mixed Tlaxcalan-Chichimec families identifying themselves as Tlaxcalan. Just as in the case of Saltillo and San Esteban, the twin communities of San Miguel and San Antonio were originally divided at the shared cultural center of the church and along the axis of a common water source. In the early eighteenth century, this was a clear cultural boundary, but by the time of independence it was of less consequence.

The persistence of many of the cultural traits of the former Tlaxcalan military colony remained strong into the republican era. San Miguel (and later Bustamante) retained strong martial and religious traditions from the past. The same families that had defended against Apache raids in the eighteenth century were mobilized as citizen militias in 1810 to defend against Hidalgo. Between 1817 and 1820, the town still fielded 100 soldiers, and its contributions to the ongoing defense against Comanches and Apaches continued throughout the nineteenth century.[106] The local cult surrounding the image of el Señor de Tlaxcala remained strong. In 1854, when drought afflicted Bustamante, the image was once again taken in procession from the church to the fields in the hopes that the town's spiritual *protector* might bring rain. The crowds that followed him were composed of local people, many descended from original Tlaxcalan colonists, and many from Alasapas who had remade themselves, first as Tlaxcalans and later as Mexicans. Bustamante was in some ways unlike the Valley of Pilón. In Pilón, the informal residential boundaries between the Tlaxcalan and Borrado sphere on one hand, and the *nueva conversión barrios* on the other, persisted far beyond the moment of national independence. In Bustamante, the boundaries grew weaker far sooner. Intermarriage and late-eighteenth-century shifts in ethnic self-identification created a more porous membrane between San Antonio and San Miguel. The Chichimecs had effectively joined themselves to the Tlaxcalans before independence. The town, thus formed, now crossed into the republican period as a single, uniform municipality.

[105] Butzer, 186–95.
[106] Adams, "At the Lion's Mouth," 341–45.

San Esteban de Saltillo, the mother colony for most northeastern Tlaxcalan pueblos, had always played an important role in articulating the relationship between Tlaxcalans and the crown. In 1814 San Esteban had a population of approximately 5,000 individuals. Its leaders, invoking the Constitution of Cádiz, asked for recognition of the town's *ayuntamiento*. The documents exchanged between San Esteban and the *diputación provincial* in Monterrey demonstrate the emergence of a new shared language of republican citizenship in the region. The *diputación* recognized that its mandate came "through your electors ... in order to assure our liberty and rights." Legitimacy rested on the consent of the population, and the deputation's avowedly utilitarian aim was "the foundation of happiness in the whole nation." The proclamations of the *diputación* described a Spanish Empire composed of many nations, and each nation composed of many individual citizens – a polity in which "we are all part of this larger body." These documents redefined all loyal subjects of the crown and constitution as Spaniards, tying together "the free man and the free system of the Spanish constitution." In this worldview, both the ethnic Spaniards of Saltillo and the Tlaxcalans of San Esteban were Spanish citizens – at least, all those who, by belief and conduct, aligned themselves with the political system. The *diputación* did draw a line of exclusion between citizens and noncitizens, but this was a distinction based on loyalty and political ideology, not caste. Quoting from the Constitution of Cádiz, it warned that anyone who rejects the government of the province or of the constitutional monarchy is not worthy of "the name of a Spaniard" – "he shall lose his job, salary and honors and be expelled from the territory of the nation."[107]

Integrating Spanish and Indian republics provoked complex negotiations over membership in new political communities or the retention of membership in old ones. In the midst of Pilón's municipal integration, Antonio López Fonseca, a supporter of the expansion plan, made two very different sorts of arguments for loosening the protections on Indian land in 1816. On one hand, he argued within the logic of the original colonial system that, due to illegal immigration and intermarriage, the claims of the communities as *pueblos de indios* were no longer completely valid. Employing a different tactic, he argued on the basis of economic utility that the Chichimecs were underutilizing the land and thus should not be allowed to retain their land rights in perpetuity. Both arguments appear side-by-side in his proposal to expand the *villa* into the lands of Purificación:

> It would bring great honor to the general [the provincial governor] and great benefit to the state of the *vecinos* of this valley if they were to undertake the creation of this *villa*.... . The *Pueblo* of Purificación has no more than two legitimate Indians and those that are reputedly Tlaxcalans are castas and

---

[107] 12 May 1814, Monterrey, AGI Audiencia de Guadalajara 297. On the political language of legitimacy and national union, see Brian F. Connaughton, "Conjuring the Body Politic from the Corpus Mysticum: The Post-Independent Pursuit of Public Opinion in Mexico, 1821–1854," *Americas* 55, no. 3 (Jan. 1999).

could be accommodated in the *villa* giving them surveyed lands [illegible sign] like the others. And those who do not wish it may move to Concepción, which has sufficient lands. Until now they have maintained themselves on rents from the renters, contrary to the Laws of the Sovereign that the lands given them by the King they must work themselves, and not rent to the Spanish.[108]

In other words, legitimate Indian caste status was determined by blood, but land-use rights were conditioned on productivity. The Tlaxcalans were a distinct case because their agricultural productivity was unquestioned. Apparently, a full-blooded Tlaxcalan, under the López Fonseca plan, could either choose the legal status and concomitant land rights of an Indian (on the south side of the river), or pass into the Spanish system, accepting lands and a housing site as a Spanish *vecino* (on the north side of the river).[109]

Along with heredity, birthplace, and residence, a person's conduct was a crucial determinant of political membership in the community, particularly when revolutionary upheavals undermined administrative hierarchies and put local allegiances to the test. In Nuevo León, property holding had always been an element of citizenship. In the colonial period, the citizen was defined by Christian conduct, family, and service. Though the republican era swept away the notion that political status was heritable, conduct and wealth remained central to civil standing. In 1826, Hualahuises compiled an official list of local malefactors in what might be termed a civil purge. Eight men were formally stigmatized as lazy habitual drunkards and adulterers. Officeholding required citizenship, and citizenship was conditioned on economic productivity and good conduct. The local magistrates of the day were consistently referred to as "citizens" (as in "*alcalde ciudadano*"), while those who transgressed community standards of good conduct were excluded and blacklisted.[110]

Individual naturalization seems to have been common in practice, but was less clearly defined under the law. In the fall of 1816, Subdelegado Antonio López Fonseca described a case of individual naturalization as part of what he understood to be a dangerous social phenomenon. Ten years before, José de la Cruz, an Indian from Horcasitas who had married a woman from San Miguel del Grande, resettled his family in Concepción. In 1815 the family made plans to leave the pueblo, but *subdelegado* Vicente Parras (López Fonseca's predecessor) forbade the family's departure. Now the son of José de la Cruz wished to marry a woman from outside the community and move to her residence. López Fonseca decided to consult with the Monterrey government on the case, but first he provided an overview of how naturalization and cross-jurisdictional marriages

---

[108] López Fonseca to Interim Governor Bruno Barrera, 7 Dec. 1816.

[109] Martínez Baracs has noted the prevalence of *mestizaje* even among the elites of Gran Tlaxcala. Martínez Baracs, *Un Gobierno de Indios*, 23.

[110] Among those stigmatized in the proscription list of 1826 is Antonio Leal, a local military officer accused of raping a local Pame woman three years before. List of malefactors of 1826 included in 9 Oct. 1827 document, AGENL Correspondencia de los Primeros Alcaldes, Hualahuises, 1825–1830, box 2; on the previous criminal accusation, 11 Jan. 1823, AMM Correspondencia, vol. 1, exp. 30.

had been handled in the past. He noted that "in the *pueblos de indios* of Pilón marrying people from outside has been permitted," and in this sense "they do not keep to the formalities of the *Recopilación de Leyes* which forbids it." This and the practice of renting lands to Spaniards had allowed the pueblo to grow, but at a cost: "the lands that the king has given them to cultivate they rent to Spaniards and other castes. And they are paid rents, obtaining through this the gathering of people to their *pueblos* to augment them without maintaining order." The result was an increasingly chaotic civic life. López Fonseca claimed the unregulated *fandangos* and dances, in which the participants arrived armed, were a source of drunkenness, violence, and subsequent litigation.[111] The system of separate ethnic republics was unraveling with consequences unforeseen even by the most forward-thinking officials.

In this atmosphere of blurred boundaries and deteriorating social regulation, both Spanish elites and Indian *cabildos* fought to define the terms of community membership. They invoked standards based not just on birth and residence, but also on conduct. Free citizens were people entitled to participate in political affairs, and also entitled to travel freely between communities. The passports demanded of Indian travelers were used both to distinguish bandits from legitimate travelers and to identify debt fugitives. Passports also contained information about past residence and heredity that would allow Indian *cabildos* to distinguish those with legitimate membership claims from unaffiliated wanderers seeking to siphon wealth from the commons. In these documents, we see the terms under which a legitimate member of an Indian pueblo might return after a period of wage labor. In one such passport, the hacienda owner attests that "Hilario, Indian of that Mission [Concepción] with his wife and another Indian widow named Gerrarda, sister of the other Indian of the Mission of Concepción ... having completed the agreed term for me may return." The implications of the document are clear. Indebted workers and workers under contract were not free to leave the haciendas; furthermore, *pueblos de indios* were not obliged to admit unenrolled Indians.[112]

According to the thinking of the time, an indebted worker was not a free civic actor, and because of this, the debt status of workers was often hotly contested. *Subdelegados* demanded evidence of freedom from debt whenever Indians changed their community of residence; but at the same time, they required that landowners making claims on laborers produce contracts and accounting records to prove a legitimate debt had not been liquidated. In November 1816, one of Pilón's *hacendados*, Don Pedro Falcón, demanded the seizure and return

---

[111] López Fonseca to Bruno Barrera, 4 Oct. 1816, AGENL Correspondencia, Montemorelos, 1812–1821, box 1.

[112] Ballesteros to Barrera, 29 Feb. 1817, AGENL Correspondencia, Montemorelos, 1812–1821, box 1. Passports were not only required of Indians laborers. A month later, López Fonseca examined the passports of a Spanish family of rank who supplied documentation of its origins and destination, as well as proof that its members were "bien nacido." López Fonseca to Barrera, 7 Mar. 1816, AGENL Correspondencia Montemorelos, 1812–1821, box 1.

of Anastacio Marcos de Castro, an Indian worker whom he claimed still owed a debt. *Protector de indios* and *subdelegado* Antonio López Fonseca heard the complaint from Falcón and, determining that Pedro Falcón was an *indio de razón*, conducted an interview. First, López Fonseca determined that Marcos de Castro was a member of a distant *pueblo de indios* (Encarnación in Aguascalientes), and that he had worked on the lands of Falcón for two months before leaving to seek employment elsewhere. Second, he demanded to see the books of debts and wages from the hacienda, which he eventually received over the "frivolous protests" of Falcón. Apparently unimpressed by Falcón's documentation, the *protector* permitted de Castro to seek employment elsewhere. The following month, in a similar case, López Fonseca ruled in favor of a landowner and against an indebted Indian.[113] Such cases make it clear that the local magistrates were not merely rubber-stamping a system of debt-peonage; they were rendering case-by-case judgments on contract disputes.

RULERS AND VOTERS

The local political integration of caste communities was a long historical process. However, the disruption and reconstruction of political systems in the greater independence period accelerated this process and gave it a far clearer legal articulation. In the colonial period, multiethnic *pueblos de indios* often employed mixed representation in elective councils. The nineteenth century saw the first application of this principle to institutions that included Spaniards.

The most striking recognition of corporate integration emerged in the early nineteenth century during the suppression of the Hidalgo Rebellion. In 1811, when Joachín de Arredondo invaded Nuevo Santander to reassert viceregal authority, he quickly reestablished loyal and functional local governments. The system he instituted had to take count of the fact that the demographic reality of Nuevo Santander no longer matched the early colonial notion of separate civic spheres for Indians and Spaniards. Communities legally defined as Spanish *villas* now contained many non-Spaniards; meanwhile, the Indian pueblos had become the home to many mixed-caste and Spanish people. Arredondo's practical solution was to recognize this state of affairs by creating a system of mixed representation in local government. He proposed that each *villa* should have three *cabildo* leaders – two Indian, and the third a *persona de razón*. Pueblos would be headed by two judges, one *"persona de razón"* and one from the population of *indios y castas*. These forms of mixed representation resemble those of Nuevo León's Tlaxcalan-Chichimec mission-towns where a Tlaxcalan governor presided over a *cabildo* with a predetermined balance of Tlaxcalan and Chichimec *regidores*. However, the Neoleonés system sought to preserve a corporate synthesis based on the cooperation of distinct ethnic barrios. Arredondo, in contrast, sought to break down this inherited political

---

[113] López Fonseca to Bruno Barrera, 13 Nov. 1816, López Fonseca to Bruno Barrera, 26 Dec. 1816, AGENL Correspondencia, Montemorelos, 1812–1821, box 1.

geography. One of his stated goals in introducing the new form of proportional representation was to undermine the power of the "captains of the companies of each neighborhood." Neighborhood captains, whose power was linked historically to their Indian nations of origin and currently to local militia organizations, were a dangerous source of local power.

Arredondo hoped to blend the political interests of multiple ethnic constituencies, and to dissipate conflicts by co-opting communities as groups of individuals, not as distinct corporate organizations. In this way, Arredondo's policies anticipated those that would accompany the Constitution of Cádiz. By the second decade of the nineteenth century, several social and political forces would have converging effects. Demographic change, the Hidalgo Revolt's egalitarian message, the disruption of institutions, the Cádiz Constitution, and the pragmatic reforms of Arredondo all furthered the trend toward more fluid boundaries between castes, and toward a more individual and less corporate mode of political participation. This binding together of peoples, which had begun within the mission-town system, now accelerated. Despite all these changes, many of the historically rooted social units survived. Nuevo León and its daughter colonies in Nuevo Santander, Texas, and Coahuila still retained local subcommunities and local structures of leadership derived from the earliest pacts between Spaniards, Tlaxcalans, and Chichimec nations.

In Nuevo Santander, the coastal community of Altamira, with its combination of Spanish, Indian, and black populations, remained a stable political entity and a powerful military presence throughout the colonial period.[114] The original settlement was made up of Spaniards, free blacks, and Indians. Later, a satellite community called Nuestra Señora de las Caldas added an additional population of Anacac Indians and *castas*.[115] Like the valleys of Nuevo León, Altamira maintained parallel caste-based governments, though there was more blurring of the demographic and jurisdictional line between them. On the eve of the Hidalgo Revolt, the town's parallel Indian and Spanish hierarchies were joined in the person of a village magistrate. He oversaw both a Spanish officer in charge of a Spanish militia, and an Indian governor in charge of an Indian archery corps.[116] In the wake of the Hidalgo invasion, Altamira remained a vital element of regional security, supplying a paid corps of Indian archers who took to the field beside Spanish (and probably *casta*) cavalry and infantry.[117]

In Nuevo Santander, some Indians retained their own governments as members of *pueblos de indios*; others blended into the growing urban population of *gente de razón* and participated in Spanish institutions. There are some indications that the colony even evolved its own distinctive system of power-sharing governments with mixed representation from neighboring ethnic communities.

---

[114] On black militiamen in the colonial order, see Ben Vinson, *Bearing Arms for His Majesty: The Free-Colored Militia in Colonial Mexico* (Stanford, CA: Stanford University Press, 2001).

[115] AGS 6966 Secretaría de Guerra, fol. 278.

[116] 1810 Altamira, AGN Provincias Internas 240, exp. 19, fol. 289.

[117] AGN: Provincias Internas 240, exp. 19, fols. 223–30, 289.

Several populations of "civilized" Indians and blacks served in the traditional Tlaxcalan role, but these groups were not as committed to maintaining exclusive ethnic privileges as were the Tlaxcalans of Nuevo León. In Nuevo Santander, there was a very important distinction of status and power between those peoples considered barbarous and those considered civilized, but this distinction was not based on rigid hereditary identities. Unlike Tlaxcalans, the civilized Indians and free blacks of Nuevo Santander could not point to an ancestral bond connecting them to the original conquest of Mexico, nor did they have ties of patronage connecting them to Mexico City. Status was based on their cultural characteristics and on the economic and military functions of the current generation, rather than on the contributions of their ancestors.

A similar process of political integration took place in the area of San Antonio de los Llanos and the neighboring Indian pueblo of Santa María de los Angeles. At least until 1830, and perhaps even after that, the Indians of Río Blanco were still governed by their own *cabildo* and governor, and joined with a non-Indian community through a mixed governing body like the one employed in Tamaulipas.[118] An 1829 document records the election of a new *cabildo* and governor by "half of the *cabildo*, and the rest of the Indios of Río Blanco ... by secret ballot [*voz secreta*]." The reference to "half the *cabildo*" is somewhat confusing. It may indicate the type of mixed governing body that existed in Nuevo Santander at the eve of the independence period – one in which representatives of Indian and non-Indian communities were included according to a fixed quota. In most other respects, Río Blanco preserved the characteristics of a Barbadillo-style mission-town well after independence. A surviving book of accounts covering the years 1827–1831 shows that the Chichimec lands of Río Blanco were managed in much the same way as the *nueva conversión* lands of Pilón and Hualahuises. Río Blanco's *cura ministro de doctrina* audited incomes and expenditures, recording the productivity of croplands and herds and mediating fiscal relations with the outer economy. In 1831 the state government ordered the privatization of all land and water rights for a specified list of mission-towns, among them Santa María de los Angeles de Río Blanco.[119]

During the years of the suspension of the Constitution of Cádiz, electoral processes continued in accordance with the *pueblos de indios* system. In 1816 normal *cabildo* elections were held in the two *pueblos de indios* in the Valley of Pilón. The election records help to clarify the composite political structure that bound together the Tlaxcalan and northern populations. Each mission had its own governor and *cabildo*. Each pueblo's government consisted of a governor, an *alcalde* for the Tlaxcalans, an *alcalde* for the *indios de la nueva conversión*, a *regidor*, and a *fiscal*. Thus the valley was divided between Spanish and Indian communities; the Indian community was composed of two separate pueblos, and each pueblo was divided into two distinct Tlaxcalan and Chichimec halves.

---

[118] AGN: Provincias Internas 240, exp. 11, fols. 156–60.

[119] AMM CL-21/345: "Vecinos de Rio Blanco, piden se les reparta las tierras y aguas del pueblo de Santa Maria de los Angles 1831."

The latest available mission records for Concepción and Purificación refer to their inhabitants merely as "*los hijos de la misión*" or "*los hijos del pueblo*," using the two terms interchangeably and without reference to more specific ethnic identities.[120]

In the summer of 1821, when national independence was affirmed by treaty, northern leaders sought to cement the terms of the 1820 constitution. In September, Pilón's leadership asserted that the community was still entitled to an *ayuntamiento*. In December, the standing officers held elections for the next year's *ayuntamiento* and issued commissions for the militia. The *ayuntamiento* elected for "the first year of the independence of this empire consisted of two *alcaldes*, eight *regidores*, and two *procuradores*." Many of the names are recognizable as belonging to the same group of landowners that had dominated local councils since before the Hidalgo Revolt. The *ayuntamiento* included two representatives from the Ballesteros family and one from the Cantú family, and the list of militia commanders included a member of the Dávila family.[121]

The leading families remained in control of most northern communities. However, the early independence period also witnessed a major expansion of the electoral franchise. The 1822 election returns from the valley of la Mota described universal (presumably adult male) suffrage and indirect *cabildo* election: "Together, all its resident citizens of all classes and castes" voted for a smaller body of electors, who then selected an *ayuntamiento* comprising an *alcalde*, six *regidores*, and a *síndico procurador*.[122] The la Mota example indicates that the elements of the Constitution of Cádiz calling for the enfranchisement of all Indians and Spaniards was, in fact, being applied in the area's local elections. It might lead us to expect that the inhabitants of the Valley of Pilón were combined into one indivisible electorate, but this was not the case. At every transition in constitutional systems, the Indians of Purificación and

---

[120] Since only two of the offices in each *cabildo* are identified as Tlaxcalan or *nueva conversión* posts, one can't be certain of the rules of eligibility or selection for the other offices. However, given that the names of all officeholders, save those of the *nueva conversión*, are preceded by the honorific "don," it seems likely that all except the two *alcaldes de los de nueva conversión* were Tlaxcalans. "Lista de los Yndividuos que han salido electos para los empleos de la República en los Pueblos de Purificación y Concepción del Valle de Pilon," 30 Nov. 1816. AGENL Correspondencia, Montemorelos 1812–1821, box 1. Ciro R. Cantú has reconstructed some of the history of municipal consolidation through legislative and legal records. He maintains that both the Tlaxcalan and *nueva conversión* populations of the Pilón mission continued under the communal land system until the *nueva conversión* Indians petitioned for a partition and distribution of mission lands as private plots under the new Mexican *Ley de Reparto* of 1825, Cantú, 145–46.

[121] 15 Sept. 1821, AGENL Correspondencia de Alcaldes, Montemorelos 1812–1821, box 1. The document's use of the plural "*cabildos*" to describe the elective bodies appears to recognize the ongoing election of separate *cabildos* in the *pueblos de indios*; 3 Dec. 1821, AGENL Correspondencia de Alcaldes, Montemorelos 1812–1821, box 1; 17 Dec. 1821, AGENL Correspondencia de Alcaldes, Montemorelos 1812–1821, box 1; 24 Dec. 1821 description of militia in Pilón, 3 Dec. 1821 document accompanying militia rolls, AGENL Correspondencia de Alcaldes, Montemorelos 1812–1821, box 1.

[122] 30 Nov. 1816, AGENL Correspondencia de Alcaldes, Montemorelos, 1812–1821, box 1; 24 Dec. 1822, AGENL Correspondencia de los Alcaldes Primeros, Hualahuises 1790–1824.

Concepción were able to exact guarantees from the local and provincial government that their separate elective *cabildos* would continue to operate.[123] Indians
remained in separate political communities under their own governments. The
case of de la Mota, however, demonstrates that Indians and mestizos who were
not enrolled in the *pueblos de indios*, and who were instead residents of the
town, became voting *vecinos* along with their Spanish neighbors.

Though increasingly outnumbered and physically surrounded by other populations, the pueblo communities remained culturally and geographically intact.
Pilón's population grew from a few thousand in the 1760s to several times that in
the early nineteenth century. In 1768 Pilón's parish priest recorded that the
pueblo amounted to 622 families. The census of 1824 found the municipality
of San Mateo to have 12,282 inhabitants;[124] the Montemorelos census records
for 1837 and 1838 show 14,566 and 15,020, respectively.[125] It is clear that the
influx of new Spanish and mestizo immigrants was outpacing the Indian community's natural rate of increase. Yet, the pueblo *cabildos*, in one form or
another, survived for a time.

Even after the disappearance of the Indian *cabildos* from the public record,
other local offices appear to have preserved Indian community governance. The
1838 census for the *partido* of Montemorelos (a jurisdiction encompassing the
three neighboring valleys of Pilón, China, and la Mota) permits us to see how
new government systems integrated preexisting populations. The census used
three categories for describing the inhabited land: *barrios, haciendas*, and *ranchos*. It broke down the population by geographical districts, each headed by a
"*juez encargado*."[126] The urban core ("*dentro de la ciudad*") of Montemorelos
was divided into quadrants, with the population of each recorded in aggregate.
The agricultural population outside the urban core was divided into the same
sort of political units, and the number of people inhabiting each constituent piece
of property was noted. A *juez* typically administered an area with several
hundred inhabitants living on *ranchos* and, in some cases, haciendas. If the
position of *juez* was elective, as it appears to have been, then the populace of
the districts of Purificación and Concepción retained a form of direct local
representation.[127] Not surprisingly, at least one of the two *jueces* presiding
over the ex-mission barrios was the descendent of Tlaxcalan governors.[128]

---

[123] Correspondence between the Spanish authorities of Pilón and Monterrey confirm this arrange-
ment in 1816, 1821, and even in 1825 after the creation of the new state and national
Constitutions. Monterrey to Pilón, 2 Jan. 1821, AGENL Correspondence; Arredondo in
Monterrey to Pilón 3 Jan. 1825.

[124] Martínez Perales, 20.

[125] Bancroft MSS 74/159, file 201.

[126] All the census information that follows is drawn from "Censo de la poblacion de esta ciudad de
Montemorelos," Bancroft MSS 74/159m file 201.

[127] "Censo de la poblacion de esta ciudad de Montemorelos," Bancroft MSS 74/159m file 201.

[128] See later explanation of the Oyenvides family history.

The book of records for the Indian town of San Cristóbal de los Hualahuises offers an appropriate metaphor for the social and economic transitions in the era surrounding national independence. The initial pages record the quotidian management of the *pueblo de indios* from the 1790s to 1809; a turn of the page reveals the municipal records of the town from 1826 to 1848.[129] This battered volume, with its frustrating lacuna, is not unlike the larger narrative of independence: it suggests disruption and erasure, but also continuity and incremental change. The institutional transformations of the independence period were significant. However, many of the fundamental features of local life endured: residential geography, religious organizations, and the composition of the local leadership class. A larger population and a new administrative superstructure grew over a set of civic forms established long before. A process of incremental civic integration set in motion by the mission-town system continued well into the nineteenth century.

The constitutional changes of the 1820s had important effects at the local level, but they should not be overstated. Most of the transformations that led to the modern municipality were already underway in the first two decades of the nineteenth century. By then, San Cristóbal de los Hualahuises possessed many of the political systems of the later municipality: it was led by an elective council, and it collected revenues for the maintenance of the commons and the church, administered a treasury, and paid salaries to officeholders Its *cabildo* often described itself as an *ayuntamiento*, and its leader as the *presidente municipal* or *alcalde ciudadano*. In fact, the structure and responsibilities of the late colonial Indian government were more like those of Nuevo León's later municipalities than they were like the government of contemporary Spanish towns. Many features of this colonial pueblo endured in the years after independence.[130]

The male population of Hualahuises was always much larger than the electoral franchise. In the colonial period there was a sharp distinction between *vecinos*, who were heads of households, and other non-enfranchised inhabitants, who were considered dependents of households or mere wanderers. In 1836 the municipal government of Hualahuises produced a census of the citizenry. It

---

[129] The observations that follow are drawn from the San Cristóbal de los Hualahuises Mission inventory and accounts and the municipal records that appear at the end of the volume. There is a substantial elision in the record between 1809 and 1826, but matching water marks on the leaves suggest that this part of the volume was not assembled from separate ledgers. The official charter of municipal incorporation for Hualahuises is dated 1828 ("se concede al pueblo de San Cristóbal la denominación de Villa San Cristóbal Hualahises," 20 Mar. 1828, in Nevarez Pequeño, *Villa San Cristóbal Hualahuises*); however, the Bancroft manuscripts demonstrate that the municipal government was already function according to the same structure in 1826.

[130] Guardino notes that in the 1820s, Indian villages had more experience with elections and councils than did their neighbors in Spanish towns, *Peasants, Politics and the Formation of Mexico's National State*, 92–93. On the history of democratic processes, see also Luís Chávez Orozco, *Las Instituciones democráticas de los indígenas mexicanos en la época colonial* (Mexico City: Instituto de Investigaciones Indigenistas, 1943).

defined the classes of citizenship based on tax bracket, and thus ultimately on class. The humblest citizens were those who paid a one percent tax, a second group paid double the normal contribution, and a third paid enough to be considered active citizens for the purposes of elections.[131] This system matched a new national, liberal political discourse based on class rather than caste or ethnic community. However, the barrio-level organizations referenced in local documents from Nuevo León suggest the persistence of a parallel political universe that preserved some elements of the corporate society of the colonial past under the umbrella of the new municipalities.[132]

Alongside the new national political culture, many old colonial structures endured. The religious life of ex–*pueblos de indios* retained many of the institutional characteristics of the colonial period: *Cofradías* still appear in records from the 1830s, as do community funds for poor relief and for education. Despite mobility, intermarriage, and seismic changes to the surrounding constitutional structures, some vestigial caste-based communities remained. However, they now functioned within much larger civic systems that gave no heed to the old ethnic *repúblicas*. In the Valley of Pilón, the election records of 1848–1849 reveal the preservation of a colonial-era political microgeography within the modern municipality of Montemorelos. The records show that the center of the *municipio* still comprised four urban barrios and the periphery eighteen additional districts.[133] These boundaries conform to the older settlement patterns of Tlaxcalans, Spaniards, and Chichimecs, and to the later system of barrio representation. Community organizations such as schools continued to reflect the identity of their locations.[134] Confraternities continued to provide a means by which barrio-based religious observances were joined together at the parish level, regardless of changes in national church-state relations.[135]

The local histories of the early nineteenth century reveal a convergence between national, municipal, and individual action. Military service and new constitutional structures bound together people across ever greater distances as citizens of an emerging nation. They were people who belonged to communities shaped by a long history of corporate, multiethnic synthesis. However, by working, trading, renting, and marrying across local ethnic boundaries, they

---

[131] Bancroft MSS 75/53, 1836. Though local history shaped implementation, this categorization of classes as citizens was, of course, occasioned by the effects of the recently issued *Siete Leyes*. Michael Costeloe, "Federalism to Centralism in Mexico: The Conservative Case for Change." *Americas* 45, no. 2 (1988), 173–85.

[132] In Tlaxcala, the notion of active citizenship expressed as membership in the body of vocales is noted in Martínez Baracs, *Un Gobierno de indios*, chap. 8.

[133] Bancroft MSS 74/159, files 284 and 286.

[134] Bancroft MSS 74/159, files 160, 161, 175–77, 184–87, 191, 195–99, 202.

[135] Despite national legislation hostile to confraternities, we see the birth (or rebirth) of a parish confraternity in Montemorelos as late as 1857. Bancroft MSS 74/159, file 478.

and their ancestors had also set in motion forms of individual integration more suited to the political order of the modern state. The towns of the nineteenth century inherited both histories. Generation after generation, Chichimecs had become colonial Indians, and colonial Indians who were ever more like Tlaxcalans. In the end, the world of the Tlaxcalans and the world of the Spaniards collapsed into each other, integrating the varied peoples who had found a home in both.

Conclusion

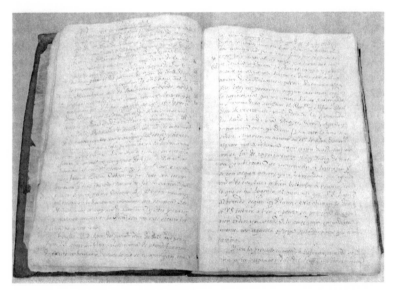

FIGURE 13. Mission-town records, like this one from San Cristóbal de los Hualahuises, recorded the transition from *cabildo* governance under the colonial *republicas* to municipal governance under the independent Mexican government. (Bancroft Manuscripts 76/53)

The modern Mexican nation was built on a political culture that emerged from the interethnic compacts of its colonial predecessor. For three centuries, the colonial *república de indios* was the most important institution in bridging cultures and integrating them within a larger polity. In the past, historians often have erred in assuming that *repúblicas de indios* were wholly Spanish institutions, invented and controlled by missionaries and colonial magistrates, or, conversely, that Indian villages were insular communities preserved intact from pre-Columbian antiquity. In truth, New Spain was a collection of constituent ethnic republics bound together by regional economic and military ties and by alliances with a larger European empire. The *repúblicas de indios* of New Spain's northern frontier came from two political genealogies, one Iberian and the other Nahua. They arose from naturally occurring parallels between the two social orders, and functioned thanks to the successful ongoing translation of political ideas between cultures. New Spain, like old Spain, was a successful political organism that evolved and prospered because of its ability to incorporate new populations and to confirm local liberties and individual authority under a shared monarchy.

Although past generations of colonial Latin American historians focused on conquest and conversion, a more recent generation has been fixated on the notion of resistance – especially in terms of class, race, and gender. The earlier paradigm might lead us to imagine colonization as the erasure of indigenous culture. The latter paradigm tempts us to understand political life almost exclusively as a form of structural conflict. A historical obsession with questions of individual agency has opened our eyes to the fascinating variety of personal experience and free choice in past ages, but it also has often left us without satisfying conclusions on a larger sociological scale. The research behind this book has persuaded me that Spanish colonial society was a coherent and functional political system, and one which laid the groundwork for modern multiethnic states.

The principal objective of this book is not to debunk existing narratives or to discredit our accustomed vocabulary. Instead it aims to present an alternative description of the development of imperial and early republican citizenship that is more firmly rooted in the early history of New Spain. Close attention to the details of local civic behavior and regional political formations (both in my research and in that of many other scholars) has begun to reveal a set of coherent practices and ideologies that were crucial to the operations of a global, multiethnic empire: the mutual recognition of political hierarchies across cultures, complementary exercise of local and imperial citizenship, and the flexible negotiation of cross-cultural alliances.

Over the long colonial period, there was great consistency in the ways that individuals advanced and defended their social status and material interests. Spaniards, Tlaxcalans, and Chichimecs sought first to cultivate and preserve their personal authority within their separate cultural spheres. A Spaniard's lineage and record of merit established his place in a social hierarchy, bolstered his claims over property, and justified his freedom of action. Tlaxcalan society had its own notions of nobility, accumulated merit, and social capital. The Tlaxcalans' Chichimec neighbors also recognized distinctions based on birth and merit. When ambitious individuals from different ethnic communities interacted, they relied both on their status within their respective communities and on their ability to translate and rearticulate that status in the shared civic language of the day.

This shared civic language was initially that of Hapsburg Europe. The Hapsburg Empire, with its enormous scale, multiethnic composition, and its great variety of local governance, was a highly adaptable political organism. On its periphery, the exercise of power was indirect, leaving many opportunities for smaller clients to retain a high level of autonomy while still benefiting from imperial patronage. Though the idea of Tlaxcalans serving as vassals to a German-Iberian crown may at first seem odd, it should not seem so. The Hapsburg family's vassals included not just Belgians, Germans, and Iberians, but also Magyars and Canary Islanders. Political and military symbiosis, not cultural uniformity, was the rule of the empire.

In the Americas, central Mexico stands out as the Hapsburg Empire's most successful early project of political integration. It was there that many of the hybrid institutions of Latin America first developed: the integration of Spanish and indigenous military systems, the legal theory of the *pueblo de indios*, the customs of *cabildo* governance, and the hybrid Christian institutions that bound culture and governance together. This central Mexican model of community within the larger empire became the favored model of viceregal New Spain. This book has focused on the specific application of what I call the "Tlaxcalan model" to state formation on New Spain's northern frontier. In truth, though, this diplomatic apparatus, which wove together multiple ethnic states into a larger polity, was not merely Tlaxcalan or Iberian; it was a pragmatic system that was common throughought the early modern colonial world.

New Spain's political culture was quite different from that of the modern liberal nation-state; and yet, in Mexico, the latter grew out of the former. Modern citizenship entails two modes of social inclusion: one within the immediate, perceptible sphere of daily life in local communities, and the other within the larger "imagined community" of the nation. Today, we use the term "Mexican citizens" to describe a group of individuals who are formally equivalent before the law and who are members of a municipality, a state, and the Mexican nation. They are distinguished from noncitizens by geographical boundaries and by a legal system that describes foreigners as nonparticipants, and Mexicans as participants, in political life. Generally speaking, this is also what was meant by "citizens" in the mid nineteenth century, but it is markedly different from the definition of citizenship in the early colonial period. This book has sought to explain the connection between the two.

In one sense, we may describe the origins of the Mexican citizen and the Mexican nation by retelling the events of 1821, by describing the constitutional system of 1824, and by narrating the subsequent upsets and revisions of that political system throughout the nineteenth century – but this would explain only a set of institutional processes. Nations and citizenship have a cultural basis in addition to a legal one. In cultural terms, Mexican independence from the Spanish empire required a shift in the individual's understanding of his relationship to his local community and to higher political authority. The colonial citizen experienced lateral political ties to the other *vecinos* of his town, as well as vertical political ties to a hierarchy culminating in the person of the king. His formal, civic connection to the *vecinos* of other towns and regions was mediated through his political and religious superiors. In contrast, the emergent Mexican citizen experienced lateral ties to fellow citizens across the nation that replaced his sense of connection to the imperial hierarchy. This shift in thinking required that he perceive himself as a member of a municipality that subsumed the ethnic republics of the past.

The immediate conditions that occasioned this shift in thinking were the multiple crises of authority generated by the Napoleonic wars, the Constitution of Cádiz, and the Hidalgo Rebellion. Yet this shift was possible only because long-term cultural processes had created the necessary psychological and social conditions. Seventeenth-century Tlaxcalans and Franciscans laid deep foundations for regional political life by creating networks of colonies that shared common material interests and cultural practices. Functioning as sites of ongoing recruitment and civic integration for Chichimecs, these communities set the pattern for continuous organic growth of the colonial civic sphere. From the mid eighteenth century, regional militias bound together the members of the Tlaxcalan-Chichimec pueblos with the region's non-Indian populations. The system of Franciscan missionary colleges that brought scattered populations under the umbrella of the order were, over time, functionally integrated with the region's emerging diocesan organization. Here, as in the militias, multiple Indian populations along with the Spanish and mestizo populations entered into a shared regional community. Growing towns that subsumed preexisting ethnic communities evolved a common religious life rooted in seasonal ritual observances, devotion to pilgrimage sites, charitable contributions, and collective labor – all carried out through local councils and *cofradías*. The time of national independence may appear, from our distant vantage point, a moment of revolutionary liberal individualism, but it also manifested the integrative power of corporate social organizations to build regional and national communities.

Modern Mexican citizenship is rooted in two older forms of colonial citizenship: that of the vassal and that of the *vecino*, the former imperial and the latter local in character. Both forms of citizenship were, in the colonial period, exercised in two parallel political realms defined by ethnicity: the *república de indios* and the *república de españoles*. This book has presented the history of Mexican state formation by describing, first, the creation of Spanish and Indian colonial communities and, second, their integration as Mexican municipalities. Much of this book examines the mechanisms by which Tlaxcalans exported the *república de indios* to the northern frontier, incorporating Indian groups that previously lay outside the colonial sphere. This is the story of how Chichimecs became like Tlaxcalans and entered into the political life of the empire. It is also the story of how the civic and military lives of Tlaxcalans, Chichimecs, Spaniards, and *castas* grew together, creating a sense of regional solidarity and of membership in a Mexican community of citizen-soldiers.

One might compress and simplify this narrative as follows. Tlaxcalans and Spaniards colonized the northern frontier. Both Spaniards and Tlaxcalans drew Chichimecs into their economic systems, but only the Tlaxcalan pueblos incorporated them into their political systems. The Tlaxcalan-Chichimec towns produced colonial Indian citizens who considered themselves *vecinos* of their mission-towns and armed vassals of the king. The military and economic realities of the northern frontier demanded close cooperation between Spanish and

Indian communities. This cooperation prefigured and eased the application of Bourbon military systems to the north. Soon the multiethnic forces of the region were incorporated into vastly expanded militia systems with a far broader geographical sweep.

The final decades of the colonial period brought to the frontier new political ideas and new forces of group psychology: the revolutionary notions of liberal, impersonal citizenship articulated in the Constitution of Cádiz; and the visceral, democratizing experience of confrontations between vast popular armies in the Hidalgo Revolt. In this period, the scale of lateral political ties was vastly expanded, and the political culture of the local multiethnic Indian republics was extended and generalized to embrace the idea of a regional and national multiethnic citizenry. In the northeast, the municipalities that became the fundamental building block of Mexican political life were formed out of the elements inherited from the early Tlaxcalan-Spanish pact, but now rearticulated in a new European language of liberal citizenship.

In the nineteenth century, Mexico separated itself from the Spanish empire. However, national independence by no means erased the political culture that had evolved over the three previous centuries. Though Mexicans were no longer vassals of the king, they remained citizens of towns and citizens of states and regions whose relationship to the capital was still shaped by the old colonial order. The link between military service and political participation remained strong in the century of intermittent warfare that followed independence. The Mexican state may have officially repudiated the older system of ethnic republics and caste-based citizenship, but the fingerprints of those previous systems are still plainly visible in the local political geographies and local political processes of the modern state. An honest assessment of the long history of colonial citizenship points clearly toward an unexpected truth: the new nation of Mexico was as much a fulfillment of colonial ambitions as a repudiation of them. Nahua *principales*, Franciscan missionaries, and Spanish military commanders created the mechanisms of local autonomy and regional interdependence that would eventually provide the structures of the Mexican state. The translation of political ideas and hierarchies between the Spanish and indigenous worlds had, by the nineteenth century, produced a shared language of citizenship and a new kind of citizen.

THE LAST OF THE TLAXCALAN NOBILITY

The Oyenvides family of the Valley of Pilón was Tlaxcalan nobility, and in the early nineteenth century, they retained significant land rights and political influence in the community of Purificación. Don Juan Matías Oyenvides was among the governors of Purificación and Cándido Oyenvides among its *principales*.[1] In the late 1820s, the members of the Oyenvides family were the most obstinate of ex-mission residents in resisting the new urban plan. In 1826, after

---

[1] Undated document, but contents indicate Feb. 1813, AGENL Correspondencia de Alcaldes, Montemorelos 1812–1821, box 1; 4 Jan. 1826, AGENL Correspondencia de Alcaldes, box 2.

all the other *accionistas* of Purificación had arrived at settlements with the municipality, Jesús Oyenvides was still fighting the construction of a road between Montemorelos and Guajuco that would cut through his lands. At times, he denied the legal existence of the route, pointing out that what the village called roads he considered fields and arroyos; at other times, he held out for monetary compensation. The Spanish *vecinos* complained that the matter had been resolved "since last year by agreement of that *ayuntamiento* with the knowledge and help of the indígenas y Tlascaltecas." But Oyenvides rallied his neighbors to the cause, temporarily disrupting negotiations between town and *accionistas*. By summertime, Oyenvides and his allies were reportedly "maliciously" planting their crops on the strip of land that had been marked by the town surveyors as a road. Still fearing for his land and his pocketbook, Oyenvides appealed to a higher authority. In November, the state government ordered the municipality to compensate Oyenvides for the crops that would be lost to the new road.[2]

Jesús Oyenvides seems to have lost no political capital in the land disputes of 1826. In 1837, long after the integration of the pueblo into the municipality, we find him leading the community of the "Barrio de Purificación" as its *juez encargado*.[3] Oyenvides's title of nobility carried no weight in the new Mexican republic, but his position in the community did. Having exhausted the possibilities of colonial political language, men like Oyenvides carved out a niche for themselves in the new municipal system.

Changing the lexicon of citizenship and ethnicity does not change the underlying demography or history of a town. Perhaps the greatest irony of the new municipal system was that, though the national and state constitutions theoretically eliminated caste, the process of privatizing Indian lands required a careful reckoning of heredity and ethnic identity. By proving descent from enrolled members of the Indian pueblos, residents of the Valley of Pilón could make claims on the resources distributed from the privatized commons or receive payments as part of the compensation agreements between the municipality and the *accionistas*.

While many elements of pueblo government were dismantled under the municipal system, some social welfare functions were preserved. Impoverished members of the community, and those unable to work due to age or infirmity, had once been supported with subsidies from the *cabildo*. Under the new land regime, farm plots were set aside as rental properties that would generate revenues to support the poor and infirm.[4] The presence of widows, orphans,

---

[2] 1 Aug., 10 Aug., 21 Nov. 1826, AGENL Correspondencia de Alcaldes, Montemorelos 1821–1826, box 2.

[3] Bancroft MSS 74/159, file 201.

[4] Resolution no. 71, 1826–1827 Resolutions of the state government regarding Montemorelos (undated numbered resolutions from the two-year session), AGENL Correspondencia de Alcaldes, Montemorelos 1821–1826, box 2. The new municipal government of Pilón also assumed social welfare responsibilities in the valley, subscribing a fund to provide food and medicine to the

and families that had intermarried with nonpueblo members made charity and
land distribution claims difficult to adjudicate. In 1826, Tlaxcalan orphans were
each awarded a standard share of the lands and waters. The *cabildo* provided
them with tutors and appointed guardians for the administration of the lands
until the titleholders reached adulthood.[5] Predictably, this measure generated
years of legal disputes over legitimacy and trusteeship.

In the early nineteenth century, intermarriage was blurring the line between
Indian and non-Indian populations. The land disbursements, which rearticulated the connection between property and ethnicity, provoked more legal
wrangling over birth, marriage, and inheritance. Another equally litigious member of the Oyenvides clan brought before the courts several difficult questions
regarding marriage, residence, and land claims. María Brígida Oyenvides, the
daughter of a Tlaxcalan *principal*, was born in the pueblo of Purificación. Upon
reaching adulthood, she married outside the community, taking up residence
with her husband on lands rented from Purificación. When Oyenvides learned
that Purificación's lands were to be partitioned and privatized, she demanded a
standard share. Her husband Antonio petitioned on her behalf to the governor
and Ayuntamiento of Nuevo León. In what was essentially a class-action suit,
they asked that equal shares be granted to everyone who could claim direct
descent from the Tlaxcalan pueblo.[6] The Oyenvides family was not willing to
give an inch in local conflicts, but they were willing and able to adapt their tactics
to succeed within the new legal regime.

In the nearby town of Hualahuises, *vecinos* came through the revolutionary
period with a new language of citizenship added to the old one. After 1820, there
was no longer a legal basis for distinctions of caste, but individuals still belonged
to concrete ethnic communties. At least in this first generation, there survived a
clear memory of the inhabitants' past identities. In some respects, the formal
abolition of caste may not have been a great shock to the people of Hualahuises.
It had long been their practice to redefine recently settled Indians as "former
barbarians" as soon as they acquired the cultural traits of the larger community.
Around 1800, one group of "new conversion" Chichimecs was elevated to the
status of "*antiguos borrados*." That is, they were transformed from *indios
bárbaros* to pueblo Indians in the eyes of the community. Twenty years later,
they and their children ceased to be Indian *vecinos* and became instead casteless
citizens.[7]

poor while attempting to stamp out vagrancy, Bancroft MSS 74/152, files 124 and 126. The
municipal programs differed significantly from those of the old *pueblos de indios* in that virtually
all revenue came from voluntary contributions, 16 Nov. 1826, AGENL Correspondencia de
Alcaldes, Montemorelos 1821–1826, box 2.
[5] 10 Mar. 1826, AGENL Correspondencia de Alcaldes, Montemorelos 1821–1826, box 2.
[6] 11 Jan. 1826, Correspondencia de Alcaldes, Montemorelos 1821–1826, box 2.
[7] This influx of additional Chichimecs is visible in the mission-town census numbers. Between 1802
and 1804, the Chichimec population of San Cristóbal more than doubled. Thereafter, the newcomers were distinguished from the "*antiguos borrados*" as Indians of the "*nueva conversión*,"
Bancroft MSS 75/53.

In 1822, the last *protector de indios* for San Cristóbal, José Antonio de Villalón, resigned his office. He did so not because he believed the constitution had made his position irrelevant, but because he believed the process of cultural tutelage was now complete: even the latest waves of Chichimecs were fully integrated into local economic and civic systems. In his letter of resignation, Villalón explained to his superiors that an educated and literate descendent of the Chichimec *conversión* was now an elected deputy representing the municipality of Hualahuises. Villalón contended that under the circumstances, a Spanish intermediary between the Indians and the state was no longer necessary. In the eyes of the ex-*protector* and those of his peers in the government, a long cultural process had come to fruition: they believed that centuries of missionization and settlement had made barbaric Indians into civilized ones, and civilized Indians into fully vested citizens of the new republic.[8] What Villalón witnessed in San Cristóbal also came to pass along much of the northern frontier: by the 1840s, the last of the pueblo Chichimecs ceased to be considered Chichimecs, and the last of the Tlaxcalan conquistadors laid down their coats of arms.

[8] 21 June 1822, AMM Correspondencia, vol. 10, exp. 43.

Archival Collections and Abbreviations Used in Citations

MEXICO

Archivo del Arzobispado de Monterrey, Monterrey, Nuevo León (AAM)
Archivo General de la Nación, Mexico City (AGN)
Archivo General del Estado de Nuevo León, Monterrey (AGENL)
Archivo Municipal de Monterrey, Monterrey, Nuevo León (AMM)
Instituto Nacional de Antropología e Historia, Mexico City (INAH)

SPAIN

Archivo General de Indias, Seville (AGI)
Archivo General de Simancas, Simancas (AGS)
Archivo Histórico Nacional de España, Madrid (AHNE)
Biblioteca Nacional de España, Madrid (BNE)

UNITED STATES

Bancroft Library, Berkeley, California (Bancroft)
Benson Collection, University of Texas, Austin (Benson)
De Golyer Library, Southern Methodist University, Dallas (De Golyer)

Bibliography

Aboites Aguilar, Luis. "Nómadas y sedentarios en el norte de México: elementos para una periodización." In *Nómadas y sedentarios*, ed. Marie-Areti Hers. Mexico City: UNAM, 2000.

Acosta, José de. *Natural and Moral History of the Indies*, ed. Jane E. Mangan. Trans. Frances López-Morillas. Durham, NC: Duke, 2002 [1590].

Actas del Ayuntamiento de Monterrey, ed. Israel Cavazos Garza. Monterrey, Mexico: Ayuntamiento de Monterrey, 2006.

Adams, David B. *Las colonias tlaxcaltecas de Coahuila y Nuevo León en la Nueva España: un aspecto de la colonización del norte de México*. Saltillo, Mexico: Archivo Municipal de Saltillo, 1991.

"Embattled Borderland: Northern Nuevo León and the Indios Bárbaros, 1686–1870," *Southwestern Historical Quarterly* 95, no. 2 (1991): 205–20.

"Borderland Communities in Conflict: San Esteban, and the Struggle for Municipal Autonomy, 1591–1838," *Locus* 6, no. 1 (1993).

"At the Lion's Mouth: San Miguel de Aguayo in the Defense of Nuevo León, 1686–1820," *Colonial Latin American Historical Review* 9, no. 3 (2000): 324–46.

Adelman, Jeremy. "From Borderlands to Borders: Empires, Nation-States, and the Peoples in between in North American History," *American Historical Review* (June 1999): 814–41.

Aguirre Beltrán, Gonzalo. *Formas de gobierno indígena*. Mexico City: Intituto Nacional Indigenista, 1981 [1953].

Alberto Cossío, David. *Historia de Nuevo León*. Monterrey, Mexico: Consejo de Educación Publica en el Estado, 1924.

Alden, Dauril. *The Making of an Enterprise: The Society of Jesus in Portugal, Its Empire, and Beyond, 1540–1750*. Stanford, CA: Stanford University Press, 1996.

Alessio Robles, Vito. *Bibliografía de Coahuila, histórica y geográfica*. Mexico: Secretaria de relaciones exteriores, 1927.

Francisco Urdiñola y el norte de la Nueva España. Mexico: Imprenta Mundial, 1931.

Coahuila y Texas en la Epoca Colonial, 2d ed. Mexico City: Editorial Porrúa, 1978.

Alvarez, Salvador. "Agricultores de paz y cazadores-recolectores de guerra: los tobosos de al cuenca del Río Concho en la Nueva Vizcaya." In *Nómadas y sedentarios*, ed. Marie-Areti Hers. Mexico City: UNAM, 2000.

Anderson, Benedict. *Imagined Communities: Reflections on the Origin, and Spread of Nationalism*, rev. ed. London: Verso, 1991.

Anderson, Gary Clayton. *The Indian Southwest, 1580–1830: Ethnogenesis and Reinvention*. Norman: University of Oklahoma, 1999.

Angeles Jiménez, Pedro. "Entre Apaches y Comanches: algunos aspectos de la evangelización franciscana y la política imperial en la Misión de San Sabá." In *Nómadas y sedentarios en el Noreste de México: Homenaje a Beatriz Braniff*, ed. Marie-Areti Hers, et al. Mexico City: UNAM, 2000.

Archer, Christon I. *The Army in Bourbon Mexico, 1760–1810*. Albuquerque: University of New Mexico, 1977.

   ed. *The Birth of Modern Mexico 1780–1824*. Lanham, MD: Rowman and Littlefield, 2003.

Ares Queija, Berta and Serge Gruzinski, ed. *Entre dos mundos: fronteras culturales y agentes mediadores*. Seville: CSIC, 1997.

Assadourian, Carlos Sempat, "Memoriales de fray Gerónimo de Mendieta," *Historia Mexicana*, 37, no. 3 (1988).

Asselbergs, Florine. *Conquered Conquistadors: The Lienzo of Quauhquechollan: A Nahua Vision of the Conquest of Mexico*. Seville: Escuela de Estudios Hispano-Americanos, 1997.

Astrain, Antonio. *Jesuitas, guaranís y encomenderos: historia de La Compañía de Jesús en Paraguay*. Asunción: Centro de Estudios Paraguayos, 1996.

Baber, R. Jovita. "Native Litigiousness, Cultural Change and the Spanish Legal System in Tlaxcala, New Spain (1580–1640)," *Political and Legal Anthropology Review* 24, no. 2 (2001): 94–106.

   "Empire, Indians and the Negotiation for Status in the City of Tlaxcala." In *Negotiation with Domination: Colonial New Spain's Indian Pueblos Confront the Spanish State*. Comp. Ethelia Ruíz Medrano and Susan Kellogg. Boulder: University Press of Colorado, 2009.

Bailey, Lynn Robinson. *Indian Slave Trade in the Southwest: A Study of Slavetaking and Traffic of Indian Captives*. Los Angeles: Westernlore, 1966.

Bakewell, Peter. *Silver Mining and Society in Colonial Mexico: Zacatecas, 1546–1700*. New York: Cambridge, 1971.

   A History of Latin America: 1450 to the Present. Oxford: Blackwell, 1997.

Bargalleni, Clara. "Representations of Conversion: Sixteenth-Century Architecture." In *The Word Made Image*. Ed. Jonathan Brown Boston: Isabella Stewart Gardner Museum, 1998.

Barr, Juliana. *Peace Came in the Form of a Woman: Indians and Spaniards in the Texas Borderlands*. Chapel Hill: University of North Carolina Press, 2007.

Bateman, Rebecca, B. "Africans and Indians: A Comparative Study of the Black Carib and Black Seminole," *Ethnohistory* 37, no. 1 (Winter 1990): 1–24.

Bautista Chapa, Juan. "Historia de Nuevo León de 1650 a 1690." In *Historia de Nuevo León, notas de Israel Cavazos Garza*. Monterrey, Mexico: Ayuntamiento de Monterrey, 1980 [17th century].

Bazan de León de Vaquero, Beatriz. *Crónica de Montemorelos Nuevo León*. Santa Catarina, Mexico: Editorial Nogales, 2003.

Benavides, Adan, Jr. "Loss by Division: The Commandancy General Archive of the Eastern Interior Provinces," *Quarterly Review of Inter-American Cultural History* 43, no. 2 (1986): 203–19.

Benjamin, Thomas A. *Atlantic History: Europeans, Africans, Indians and Their Shared History, 1400–1900*. New York: Cambridge University, 2009.

Bennett, Herman L. *Africans in Colonial Mexico: Absolutism, Christianity, and Afro-Creole Consciousness, 1570–1640.* Bloomington: University of Indiana, 2003.

Benson, Nettie Lee, ed. *Mexico and the Spanish Cortes, 1810–1822.* Austin: University of Texas, 1966.

Bhabha, Homi K. *The Location of Culture.* New York: Routledge, 1994.

Bireley, Robert. *The Refashioning of Catholicism, 1450–1700: A Reassessment of the Counter Reformation.* Washington, DC: Catholic University, 1999.

Blackburn, Carole. *Harvest of Souls: The Jesuit Mission and Colonialism in North America, 1632–1650.* Montreal: McGill-Queen's University, 2000.

Block, David. *Mission Culture on the Upper Amazon: Native Tradition, Jesuit Enterprise, and Secular Policy in Moxos, 1660–1880.* Lincoln: University of Nebraska, 1994.

Bolton, Herbert and Thomas Marshall. *The Colonization of North America, 1492–1787.* New York: Macmillan, 1920.

Boone, Elizabeth Hill and Walter D. Mignolo. *Writing without Words: Alternative Literacies in Mesoamerica.* Durham, NC: Duke, 1994.

Boyer, Christopher R. *Becoming Campesinos: Politics, Identity, and Agrarian Struggle in Postrevolutionary Michoacán, 1920–1935.* Stanford, CA: Stanford University Press, 2003.

Boyle, Susan Calafate. *Comerciantes, Arrieros, y Peones: The Hispanos and the Santa Fe Trade.* Washington, DC: National Park Service, 1994.

Brading, David A. *The First America: The Spanish Monarchy, Creole Patriots, and the Liberal State, 1492–1867.* Cambridge, U.K.: Cambridge, 1991.

Miners and Merchants in Bourbon Mexico, 1763–1810. Cambridge: Cambridge, 1991.

Mexican Phoenix: Our Lady of Guadalupe, Image and Tradition across Five Centuries. Cambridge, U.K.: Cambridge, 2001.

Bringas de Manzaneda y Encinas, Diego Miguel. *Friar Bringas Reports to the King: Methods of Indoctrination on the Frontier of New Spain in 1796–1797.* Trans. Daniel S. Matson and Bernard L. Fontana. Tucson: University of Arizona, 1977.

Brooks, James F. *Captives and Cousins: Slavery, Kinship, and Community in the Southwest Borderlands.* Chapel Hill: University of North Carolina, 2002.

Brotherston, Gordon and Ana Gallegos. "El Lienzo de Tlaxcala y el Manuscrito de Grasgow," *Estudios de Cultura Náhuatl* 20 (1990).

Butzer, Elisabeth. *Historia social de una comunidad tlaxcalteca: San Miguel de Aguayo* (Bustamante, N. L., 1686–1820). Saltillo, Mexico: Archivo Municipal de Saltillo, 2001.

Cañizares-Esguerra, Jorge. *How to Write the History of the New World: Histories, Epistemologies, and Identities in the Eighteenth-Century Atlantic World.* Stanford, CA: Stanford University Press, 2001.

Cantú, Ciro R. "Don José María Paras Ballesteros primer gobernador constitucional de Nuevo León," *Humanitas* [México] 12 (1971): 277–323.

"Don Juan Manuel Muñoz de Villavicencio, Gobernador del Nuevo Reino de León," *Humanitas* [Mexico] 16 (1975): 439–48.

"El gobernador Manuel de Santa María y los insurgentes en el valle del Pilón, la guerra de independencia," *Humanitas* [Mexico] 17 (1976): 427–40.

Origen de la ciudad de Montemorelos: síntesis de una investigación histórica. Montemorelos: Universidad Autónoma de Nuevo León, 2002.

Carillo Cázares, Alberto. *El debate sobre la Guerra Chichimeca, 1531–1585: derecho y política en la Nueva España.* Zamorra, Michoacán: El Colegio de Michoacán, 2000.

Carmen Velázquez, María del. *Tres estudios sobre las Provincias Internas de Nueva España.* Mexico City: Colegio de México, 1979.

Carrasco, Davíd, ed. *The Oxford Encyclopedia of Mesoamerican Cultures: The Civilizations of Mexico and Central America*. New York: Oxford University, 2001.

Castro-Klarén, Sarah and John Charles Chase, eds. *Beyond Imagined Communities: Reading, and Writing the Nation*. Baltimore: Johns Hopkins, 2003.

Cavazos Garza, Israel. "Incursiones de los indios ... en el noreste de México durante el siglo XIX," *Humanitas*, no. 4 (1964): 343–56.

"El municipio de General Escobedo," *Humanitas* [Mexico] 13 (1972): 263–71.

"Matehuala, jurisdicción del Nuevo Reino de León (1638–1718)," *Humanitas* [Mexico] 14 (1973): 433–56.

Muy Ilustre Ayuntamiento de Monterrey, 1596–1996. Monterrey, Mexico: Municipio de Monterrey, 1980.

El lic. Francisco Barbadillo Vitoria: fundador de Guadalupe, Nuevo León. Monterrey, Mexico: UANL, 1991.

Breve historia de Nuevo León. Mexico: Colegio de México, 1994.

Escritores de Nuevo León: diccionario biográfico. Monterrey, Mexico: UANL 1996.

Nuevo Reino de León y Monterrey: a través de 3,000 documentos (un síntesis) del Ramo Civil del Archivo Municipal de La Ciudad, 1598–1705. Monterrey, Mexico: Congresso del Estado de Nuevo León, 1998.

Ciudad Guadalupe, Nuevo León en la historia y en la crónica. Monterrey, Mexico: UANL, 2000.

Chance, John K. *Conquest of the Sierra: Spaniards and Indians in Colonial Oaxaca*. Norman: University of Oklahoma, 1989.

"The Barrios of Colonial Tecali: Patronage, Kinship, and Territorial Relations in a Central Mexican Community," *Ethnology* 35, no. 2 (1996): 107–39.

"The Caciques of Tecali: Class and Ethnic Identity in Late Colonial Mexico," *Hispanic American Historical Review* 76, no. 3 (Aug. 1996): 475–502.

"Mesoamerica's Ethnographic Past," *Ethnohistory* 43, no. 3 (1996): 379–403.

"The Noble House in Colonial Puebla, Mexico: Descent, Inheritance, and the Nahua Tradition," *American Anthropologist* 102, no. 3 (2000): 485–502.

Chance, John K. and William B. Taylor. "Cofradías and Cargos: An Historical Perspective on the Meoamerican Civil-Religious Hierarchy," *American Ethnologist* 12, no. 1 (Feb. 1985): 1–26.

Chávez, John. *Beyond Nations: Evolving Homelands in the North Atlantic World, 1400–2000*. New York: Cambridge, 2009.

Chevalier, Francois. *La formación de los grandes latifundios en México*. Mexico City, 1956.

Chomsky, Aviva and Aldo Lauria-Santiago, eds. *Identity and Struggle at the Margins of the Nation-State: The Laboring Peoples of Central America and the Hispanic Caribbean*. Durham, NC: Duke, 1998.

Chowning, Margaret. "The Consolidación de Vales Reales in the Bishopric of Michoacán," *Hispanic American Historical Review* 69, no. 3 (1989): 451–78.

Christian, William. *Local Religion in Sixteenth-Century Spain*. Princeton, NJ: Princeton University, 1981.

Person and God in a Spanish Valley. Princeton, NJ: Princeton University, 1989.

Clendinnen, Inga. "Ways to the Sacred: Reconstructing Religion in Sixteenth-Century Mexico," *History and Anthropology* 5 (1990): 105–41.

Coleman, David. *Creating Christian Granada: Society and Religious Culture in an Old-World Frontier City*. Ithaca, NY: Cornell, 2003.

Comerford, Kathleen and Hilmar M. Pabel. *Early Modern Catholicisms: Essays in Honour of John W. O'Malley*. Toronto: University of Toronto, 2002.

Connaughton, Brian. "Conjuring the Body Politic from the Corpus Mysticum: The Post-Independence Pursuit of Public Opinion in Mexico, 1821–1854," *Americas* 55, no. 3 (1999): 459–80.

Clerical Ideology in a Revolutionary Age. Calgary: University of Calgary, 2003.

Cortés, Hernán. *Letters from Mexico.* Trans. A. R. Pagden. New York: Grossman, 1971.

Cosentino, Delia Annunziata. "Landscapes of Lineage: Nahua Pictorial Genealogies of Early Colonial Tlaxcala, Mexico." Ph.D Dissertation, U.C.L.A., 2002.

Costeloe, Michael. "Federalism to Centralism in Mexico: The Conservative Case for Change," *Americas* 45, no. 2 (1988): 173–85.

Cramaussel, Chantal. "De como los españoles clasificaban a los indios: naciones y encomiendas en la Nueva Vizcaya central." In *Nómadas y sedentarios*, ed. Marie-Areti Hers. Mexico City: UNAM, 2000.

Crouch, Dora P., Danile J. Garr and Azel Mundigo. *Spanish Planning in North America.* Cambridge, MA: M.I.T., 1982.

Cuadriello, Jaime, ed. *El origen del Reino de La Nueva España, 1680–1750.* Mexico: Instituto de Investigaciones Estéticas, 1999.

Las Glorias de la república de Tlaxcala: o la conciencia como imagen sublime. Mexico: UNAM, 2004.

Cuellar Bernal, Rene. "Los Tlaxcaltecas En Nuevo León." In *Estudios de Historia del Noreste.* Monterrey, Mexico: Sociedad Neuvoleonesa de Historia, Geografía y Estadística, 1972.

Cuello, José. "The Economic Impact of the Bourbon Reforms and the Late Colonial Crisis of Empire at the Local Level: The Case of Saltillo, 1777–1817," *Americas* 44, no. 3 (1988): 307–24.

"The Persistence of Indian Slavery and Encomienda in the Northeast of Colonial Mexico, 1577–1723," *Journal of Social History* 21, no. 4 (1988): 683–700.

El Noreste y Saltillo en la historia colonial de Mexico. Saltillo, Mexico: Archivo Municipal de Saltillo, 1990.

Cushner, Nicolas P. *Jesuit Ranches and the Agrarian Development of Colonial Argentina.* Albany, NY: S.U.N.Y., 1983.

Cutter, Charles R. *The Protector de Indios in Colonial New Mexico, 1659–1821.* Albuquerque: University of New Mexico, 1986.

The Legal Culture of Northern New Spain, 1700–1810. Albuquerque: University of New Mexico, 1995.

Dandalet, Thomas. *Spanish Rome, 1500–1700.* New Haven, CT: Yale, 2001.

Daniels, Christine and Michael Kennedy, eds. *Negotiated Empires: Centers, and Peripheries in the Americas, 1500–1820.* New York: Routledge, 2002.

Dávila Aguirre, José de Jesus. *La Colonización tlaxcalteca y su influencia en el noreste de la Nueva España.* Coahuila, México: Colegio Coahuilense de Investigaciones Históricas, 1977.

Dávila Cabrera, Patricio. "La frontera noreste de mesoamerica: un puente cultural hacia el Mississippi." In *Nómadas y sedentarios*, ed. Marie-Areti Hers, et al. Mexico City: UNAM, 2000.

Dávila del Bosque, Ildefonso. *Los cabildos tlaxcaltecas: ayuntamientos del pueblo de San Esteban de la Nueva Tlaxcala desde su establecimiento hasta su fusión con la villa del Saltillo.* Saltillo, México: Archivo Municipal de Saltillo, 2000.

Deagan, Kathleen. "Colonial Transformation: Euro-American Cultural Genesis in the Early Spanish American Colonies," *Journal of Anthropological Research* 52, no. 2 (1996).

Deeds, Susan M. "Land Tenure Patterns in Northern New Spain," *Americas* 41, no. 4 (1985): 446–61.

"First Generation Rebellions in Seventeenth-Century Nueva Vizcaya." In *Native Resistance and the Pax Colonial in New Spain*, ed. Susan Schroeder. Lincoln: University of Nebraska, 1998.

Defiance and Deference in Colonial Mexico: Indians under Spanish Rule in Nueva Vizcaya. Austin: University of Texas Press, 2003.

DeLay, Brian. *War of a Thousand Deserts: Indian Raids and the U.S. Mexican War*. New Haven, CT: Yale, 2008.

Díaz Balsera, Viviana. "A Judeo-Christian Tlaloc or a Nahua Yahweh? Domination, Hybridity, and Continuity in the Nahua Evangelization Theater," *Colonial Latin American Historical Review* 10 (2001): 209–28.

Diccionario Porrúa de historia, biografía, y geografía de México, 5th ed. Mexico: Editorial Porrua, 1986.

Diccionario universal de historia y geografía. Mexico, Imp. J. M. Andrade y Escalante, 1856.

Driver, Harold E. and Wilhelmine Driver. *Ethnography and Acculturation of the Chichimeca-Jonaz of Northeast Mexico*. Bloomington: Indiana University, 1963.

Ducey, Michael T. *A Nation of Village: Riot and Rebellion in the Mexican Huasteca, 1750–1850*. Tucson: University of Arizona, 2004.

Early, James. *The Colonial Architecture of Mexico*. Albuquerque: University of New Mexico, 1994.

Presidio, Mission, and Pueblo: Spanish Architecture and Urbanism in the United States. Dallas, TX: Southern Methodist University, 2004.

Eastman, Scott. "Ya no hay Atlántico, ya no hay dos continentes: regionalismo e identidad nacional durante la Guerra de Independencia en Nueva España," *Tiempos de América* 12 (2005): 153–66.

Elliott, John. *Imperial Spain, 1469–1716*. New York: Pelican, 1970.

The Old World and the New, 1492–1650. Cambridge: Cambridge, 1970.

Spain and Its World: Selected Essays. New Haven, CT: Yale, 1989.

Spanish Imperialism and Political Imagination: Studies in European and Spanish-American Social and Political Theory, 1513–1830. New Haven, CT: Yale, 1990.

Empires of the Atlantic World: Britain and Spain in America, 1492–1830. New Haven, CT: Yale, 2006.

Escalante Arce, Pedro de Antonio. *Los Tlaxcaltecas en Centro América*. San Salvador: Biblioteca de Historia Salvadoreña, 2001.

Escandón, José de. *Estado general de las fundaciones hechas por D. José de Escandón*. Mexico: AGN, 1929.

La Sierra Gorda y el Nuevo Santander. Santander, Spain, 1985 [18th century].

General State of the Settlements Made by D. José de Escandón. Trans. Edna Brown. Mexico City: National Printers, 1993 [18th century].

Farago, Claire, ed. *Reframing the Renaissance: Visual Culture in Europe and Latin America, 450–1650*. New Haven, CT: Yale, 1995.

Farriss, Nancy M. *Maya Society Under Colonial Rule: The Collective Enterprise of Survival*. Princeton, NJ: Princeton University, 1985.

Fernández Areu, Ismael. *La lingüística y el habla de Monterrey*. Monterrey, Mexico: Archivo General del Estado de Nuevo León, 1995.

Fernández de Jáuregui Urrutia, Joseph Antonio. *Descripción del Nuevo Reino de León, 1735–1740*. Monterrey, Mexico: ITESM, 1964 [1735–1740].

Fisher, Andrew B. and Matthew D. O'Hara. *Imperial Subjects: Race and Identity in Colonial Latin America*. Durham, NC: Duke, 2009.

Florescano, Enrique and Margarita Menegus. "La época de las reformas borbónicas y el crecimiento económico (1750–1808)." In *Historia General de México*. Ed. Daniel Cosío Villegas et al. Mexico City: Colegio de Mexico, 2000, 363–430.

Foley, Neil. *The White Scourge: Mexicans, Blacks, and Poor Whites in Texas Cotton Culture*. Berkeley: U.C. Berkeley, 1997.

Fortson, Robert, et al. *Los gobernantes de Nuevo León*. Mexico City: Fortson and Cia, 1990.

Frye, David. *Indians into Mexicans: History and Identity in a Mexican Town*. Austin: University of Texas, 1996.

"The Native Peoples of Northeastern Mexico." In *Cambridge History of Native Peoples of the Americas*, vol. II, eds. Richard E. Adams and Murdo J. Macleod. New York: Cambridge, 2000.

"Pame." In *The Oxford Encyclopedia of Mesoamerican Cultures*, ed. Davíd Carrasco. New York: Oxford, 2001.

Galante, Mirian. "La revolución hispana a debate: lecturas recientes sobre la influencia del proceso gaditano en México," *Revista complutense de historia de América* 33 (2007): 93–112.

García Flores, Raul. *Formación de la sociedad mestiza y la estructura de castas en el noreste: el caso de Linares*. Monterrey, México: Archivo General del Estado de Nuevo León, 1996.

"También aca hubo Pames: Nuevo León, 1770–1830," *Actas* 2, no. 3 (2003).

Garrett, David T. *Shadows of Empire: The Indian Nobility of Cusco, 1750–1825*. New York: Cambridge, 2005.

"'His Majesty's Most Loyal Vassals': The Indian Nobility and Túpac Amaru," *Hispanic American Historical Review* 84, no. 4 (2004): 576–617.

Garza Guajardo, Gustavo. *Las cabeceras municipales de Nuevo León: fundadores, nombres, decretos*. Monterrey, Mexico: UANL, 1986.

Gerhard, Peter. *Colonial New Spain, 1519–1786: Historical Notes on the Evolution of Minor Political Jurisdictions*. Washington, DC: Library of Congress, 1967.

A Guide to the Historical Geography of New Spain, rev. ed. Norman: University of Oklahoma, 1993.

The North Frontier of New Spain, rev. ed. Norman: University of Oklahoma, 1993.

Gibbon, Edward. *The Decline and Fall of the Roman Empire*. New York: Random House, n.d. (1787).

Gibson, Charles. *Tlaxcala in the Sixteenth Century*. New Haven, CT: Yale, 1955.

The Aztecs under Spanish Rule. Stanford, CA: Stanford University Press, 1964.

Gillespie, Jeanne Lou. "Saints and Warriors: The 'Lienzo de Tlaxcala' and the Conquest of Tenochtitlán." Ph.D Dissertation, Arizona State, 1994.

Gómez Canedo, Lino. "Misiones del Colegio de Pachuca en el Obispado del Nuevo Reino de León," *Humanitas* [Mexico] 13 (1972): 409–53.

Gómez Danés, Pedro. *Las misiones de Purificación y Concepción*. Monterrey, Mexico: UANL, 1995.

Negros y mulatos en el Nuevo Reino de León, 1600–1795. Monterrey, Mexico: Archivo General Del Estado, 1996.

San Cristóbal de Gulaguises: haciendas, ranchos y encomiendas, siglo xviii. Monterrey, Mexico: Archivo General del Estado de Nuevo León, 1999.

Gonzáles, Hector. *Siglo y medio de cultura neoleonesa*. Monterrey, Mexico: Biblioteca de Monterrey, 1993.

Gosner, Kevin. "Las élites indígenas en los altos de Chiapas, 1524–1714," *Historia Mexicana*, 33, no. 4 (1984).

"Caciques and Conversion: Juan Atonal and the Struggle for Legitimacy in Post-Conquest Chiapas," *Americas* 49, no. 2 (Oct. 1992): 115–29.

Gradie, Charlotte M. "Chichimec." In *Oxford Encyclopedia of Mesoamerican Culture*, ed. Davíd Carrasco. New York: Oxford, 2001.

"Discovering the Chichimecas," *Americas* 51, no. 1 (1994): 67–88.

The Tepehuán Revolt of 1616: Militarism, Evangelism, and Colonialism in Seventeenth-Century Nueva Vizcaya. Salt Lake City: University of Utah, 2000.

Grafton, Anthony. *New Worlds, Ancient Texts: The Power of Tradition and the Shock of Discovery*. Cambridge: Harvard, 1995.

Green, Stanley C. *The Mexican Republic: The First Decade, 1823–1832*. Pittsburgh: University of Pittsburgh, 1987.

Greene, Jack P. "Atlantic Empires: The Network of Trade and Revolution, 1712–1826," *International History Review* 6, no. 4 (1984): 507–69.

Greer, Allan and Jodi Bilinkoff, eds. *Colonial Saints: Discovering the Holy in the Americas*. New York: Routledge, 2003.

Griffen, William B. *Indian Assimilation in the Franciscan Areas of Nueva Vizcaya*. Tuscon: University of Arizona, 1979.

Apaches at War and Peace: The Janos Presidio, 1750–1858. Albuquerque: University of New Mexico, 1988.

Utmost Good Faith: Patterns of Apache-Mexican Hostilities in Northern Chihuahua Border Warfare, 1821–1848. Albuquerque: University of New Mexico Press, 1988.

Griffith, James S. *Beliefs and Holy Places: A Spiritual Geography of the Pimería Alta*. Tucson: University of Arizona, 1992.

Griffiths, Nicholas and Fernando Cervantes. *Spiritual Encounters: Interactions between Christianity and Native Religions in Colonial America*. Lincoln: University of Nebraska, 1999.

Groubart, Karen B. "The Creolization of the New World: Local Forms of Identification in Urban Colonial Peru, 1560–1640," *Hispanic American Historial Review* 89, no. 3: 471–99.

Gruzinski, Serge. *Painting the Conquest: The Mexican Indians and the European Renaissance*. Paris: UNESCO, 1992.

The Conquest of Mexico: The Incorporation of Indian Societies into the Western World, 16th–18th Centuries. Cambridge, U.K.: Cambridge, 1993.

Images at War: Mexico from Columbus to Blade Runner (1492–2019). Trans. Heather MacLean. Durham, NC: Duke, 2001.

Guardino, Peter. *Peasants, Politics, and the Formation of Mexico's Modern State: Guerrero, 1800–1857*. Stanford, CA: Stanford University Press, 1996.

In the Time of Liberty: Popular Political Culture in Oaxaca, 1750–1850. Durham, NC: Duke, 2005.

Guía general de los archivos estatales y municipales de México, series Archivos estatales y municipales de México, vol. 1. Mexico City, 1988.

Guy, Donna J. and Thomas E. Sheridan, eds. *Contested Ground: Comparative Frontiers on the Northern, and Southern Edges of the Spanish Empire*. Tucson: University of Arizona, 1998.

Hackel, Steven W. *Children of Coyote, Missionaries of Saint Francis: Indian-Spanish Relations in Colonial California, 1769–1850*. Chapel Hill: University of North Carolina Press, 2005.

Hämäläinen, Pekka. *The Comanche Empire*. New Haven, CT: Yale, 2008.

Hanke, Lewis. *The Spanish Struggle for Justice in the Conquest of America*. Dallas, TX: SMU, 2002.

Haskett, Robert. *Visions of Paradise: Primordial Titles and Mesoamerican History in Cuernavaca*. Norman: University of Oklahoma, 2005.

Herrera, Octavio. *Breve historia de Tamaulipas*. Mexico City: Colegio de Mexico, 1999.

Hers, Marie-Areti, et al., ed. *Nómadas y sedentarios en el norte de México: Homenaje a Beatriz Braniff*. Mexico City: UNAM, 2000.

Herzog, Tamar. *Defining Nations: Immigrants and Citizens in Early Modern Spain, and Spanish America*. New Haven, CT: Yale, 2003.

Horn, Rebecca. *Postconquest Coyoacan. Nahua-Spanish Relatioins in Central Mexico, 1519–1650*. Stanford, CA: Stanford University Press, 1997.

Hoyo, Eugenio del. *Historia del Nuevo Reino de León (1577–1723)*. Monterrey, Mexico: ITESM, 1972 [documents].

   Esclavitud y encomienda en el Nuevo Reino de León, siglos xvi y xvii. Monterrey, Mexico: Gobierno del Estado, AGENL, 1985.

   Indios, frailes y encomenderos en el Nuevo Reino de León, siglos xvii y xviii. Monterrey, Mexico: Archivo General del Estado de Nuevo León, 1985.

   Señores de ganado: Nuevo Reino de León, siglo xvii. Monterrey, Mexico: Gobierno del Estado, AGENL, 1987.

Hsia, Ronnie Po-Chia. *The World of Catholic Renewal*. Cambridge, U.K.: Cambridge University, 1997.

Hull, Anthony H. *Charles III and the Revival of Spain*. Washington, DC: University Press, 1980.

Hunt, Lynn. *Politics, Culture, and Class in the French Revolution*. Berkeley: U.C. Berkeley, 1986.

Hurtado, Albert L. "Parkmanizing the Spanish Borderlands: Bolton, Turner, and the Historians' World," *Western Historical Quarterly* 26, no. 2 (Summer 1995): 149–67.

Ignatiev, Noel. *How the Irish Became White*. New York: Routledge, 1995.

Iriarte, Francisco. *Franciscan History: The Three Orders of St. Francis of Assisi*. Trans. Patricia Ross. Chicago: Franciscan Herald Press, 1982.

Jáuregui, Luis. "El Plan de Casa Mata y el federalismo en Nuevo León, 1823," *Secuencia* [Mexico] 50 (2001): 140–67.

John, Elizabeth. *Storms Brewed in Other Men's Worlds: The Confrontation of Indians, Spanish, and French in the Southwest, 1540–1795*. College Station: Texas A&M, 1975.

Jones, Okah L. *Los Paisanos: Spanish Settlers on the Northern Frontier of New Spain*. Norman: University of Oklahoma, 1979.

Joseph, Gil and David Nugent, eds. *Everyday Forms of State Formation*. Durham, NC: Duke, 1994.

Junco y Espriella, Don Pedro de Barrio. *Visita general del Nuevo Reino de León por el Governador Don Pedro de Barrio Junco y Espriella en 1754*. Monterrey, Mexico: UANL, 1979 [1754].

Kagan, Richard. *Urban Images of the Hispanic World, 1493–1793*. New Haven, CT: Yale, 2000.

Kagan, Richard and Geoffrey Parker, eds. *Spain, Europe, and the Atlantic World*. Cambridge, U.K.: Cambridge University, 1995.

Kamen, Henry. *How Spain Became a World Power, 1493–1763*. New York: Penguin, 2002.

Katzew, Ilona. *Casta Paintings: Images of Race in Eighteenth-Century Mexico*. New Haven, CT: Yale, 2004.

Kellog, Susan. *Law and the Transformation of Aztec Culture, 1500–1700.* Norman: University of Okahoma, 1995.

Kellog, Susan and Norma Angélica Castillo Palma. "Conflict and Cohabitation between Afro-Mexicans and Nahuas in Central Mexico." In *Beyond Black and Red: African-Native Relations in Colonial Latin America,* ed. Matthew Restall. Albuquerque: University of New Mexico Press, 2005.

Kellog, Susan and Matthew Restall, eds. *Dead Giveaways: Colonial Testaments of Spanish America.* Salt Lake City: University of Utah Press, 1998.

Kicza, John E. *Resilient Cultures: America's Native Peoples Confront European Colonization, 1500–1800.* Upper Saddle River, NJ: Prentice Hall, 2003.

Klein, Herbert S. "The Colored Militia of Cuba 1568–1868," *Caribbean Studies* 6, no. 2 (1966): 17–27.

Knight, Alan. "Peasants into Patriots: Thoughts on the Making of the Mexican Nation," *Mexican Studies/Estudios Mexicanos* 10, no. 1 (1994).

Kranz, Travis Barton. "The Tlaxcalan Conquest Pictorials: The Role of Images in Influencing Colonial Policy in Sixteenth-Century Mexico." Ph.D Dissertation, UCLA, 2001.

Kubler, George. *Mexican Art and Architecture in the Sixteenth Century.* Westport, CT: Greenwood, 1972.

Kupper, Karen. *Indians and English: Facing off in North America.* Ithaca, NY: Cornell, 2000.

Ladrón de Guevara, Antonio. *Noticias de los poblados del Nuevo Reino de León (1738).* Monterrey, Mexico: ITESM, 1969.

Lafaye, Jacques. *Quetzalcóatl and Guadalupe: The Formation of Mexican National Consciousness, 1531–1813.* Chicago: University of Chicago, 1976.

Lafora, Nicolás de. *Relación del viaje que hizo a los presidios internos situados en la frontera de América septentrional.* Mexico City: Pedro Robredo, 1939.

Landers, Jane. "Black Community and Culture in the Southeastern Borderlands," *Journal of the Early Republic* 18, no. 1 (Spring 1998): 117–34.

"Gracia Real de Santa Teresa de Mose: A Free Black Town in Spanish Colonial Florida," *American Historical Review* 95, no. 1 (Feb. 1990): 9–30.

Lang, James. *Conquest and Commerce: Spain and England in the Americas.* New York: Academic Press, 1975.

Las Casas, Bartolomé de. *Defense of the Indians.* Trans. Stafford Poole. DeKalb, IL: Northern Illinois University, 1974 [1552].

Leal Ríos, Armando. *Linares: ayer y hoy.* Monterrey, Mexico: UANL, 1989.

Linares: cuidad en llamas. Monterrey, Mexico: UANL, 1999.

Linares: capital de Nuevo León. Monterrey, Mexico: UANL, 2001.

Lear, John. *Workers, Neighbors, and Citizens: The Revolution in Mexico City.* Lincoln: University of Nebraska, 2001.

Lejarza, Pedro Fidel de. *Conquista espiritual del Nuevo Santander.* Madrid: Instituto Santo Toribio de Mogrovejo, 1948.

Lempériere, Annick. "¿Nación moderna o república barroca? Mexico, 1823–1857." In *Inventando la nación: Iberoamerica, siglo xix,* eds. Francois-Xavier Guerra and Monica Quijada. Mexico City: Fondo de Cultura Económica, 2003.

León, Alonso de, Juan Bautista Chapa, and Fernando Sanchez de Zamora. *Historia de Nuevo León, con noticias sobre Coahuila, Tamaulipas, Texas y Nuevo Mexico, siglo xvii, notas de Israel Cavazos Garza.* Monterrey, Mexico: Ayuntamiento de Monterrey, 1980 [17th century].

León Garza, Rodolfo de. *Fray Servando: vida y obra*. Monterrey, Mexico: Fondo Editorial Nuevo León, 1993.

León Portilla, Miguel. *The Broken Spears: The Aztec Account of the Conquest of Mexico*. Trans. Alberto Beltrán. Boston: Beacon, 1962.

Lightfoot, Kent. *Indians, Missionaries, and Merchants: The Legacy of Colonial Encounters on the California Frontiers*. Berkeley: U.C. Berkeley, 2004.

Liss, Peggy K. *Atlantic Empires: Networks of Trade and Revolution, 1713–1826*. Baltimore: Johns Hopkins, 1983.

Lockhart, James, Frances Berden, and Arthur J. O. Anderson, eds. *The Tlaxcalan Actas: A Compendium of the Records of the Cabildo of Tlaxcala, 1545–1627*. Salt Lake City: University of Utah, 1986.

   The Nahuas after Spanish Conquest: A Social and Cultural History of the Indians of Central Mexico, Sixteenth through Eighteenth Centuries. Stanford, CA: Stanford University Press, 1992.

   We People Here: Nahatl Accounts of the Conquest of Mexico. Berkeley: University of California, 1993.

Lomnitz, Claudio. *Deep Mexico, Silent Mexico: An Anthropology of Nationalism*. Minneapolis: University of Minnesota, 2001.

López-Alves, Fernando. *State Formation and Democracy in Latin America, 1810–1900*. Durham, NC: Duke, 2000.

López Sarrelangue, Delfina Esmeralda. *La Nobleza Indígena de Pátzcuaro en la Época Virreinal*. Mexico City: UNAM, 1965.

Losada, Juan. *Cuaderno de visita de los conventos y misiones del Nuevo Reino de León (Mayo 1739)*, ed. Eugenio del Hoyo. Monterrey, Mexico: ITESM, 1970.

Loyola, Rosy and Carlos E. Ruiz Abreu. *Fuentes documentales coloniales para la historia de Nuevo León*. Mexico City: Archivo General de la Nación, 1999.

Lupher, David. *Romans in the New World: Classical Models in Sixteenth Century Spanish America*. Ann Arbor: University of Michigan, 2003.

Lynch, John. *Spain under the Hapsburgs*. Oxford: Basil Blackwell, 1981.

   Bourbon Spain, 1700–1808. Oxford: Basil Blackwell, 1989.

MacCormack, Sabine. *On the Wings of Time: Rome, the Incas, Spain and Peru*. Princeton, NJ: Princeton University, 2007.

Madero Quiroga, Adalberto Arturo. *Nuevo León a través de sus constituciones*. Nuevo León: Congreso del Estado, 1998.

Martínez, Patricia. "The 'Noble Tlaxcalans': Race and Ethnicity in Northeastern New Spain, 1770–1810." Ph.D Dissertation, U.T. Austin, 2004.

Martínez Baracs, Andrea. "Colonizaciones tlaxcaltecas," *Historia Mexicana* 49, no. 2 (1993): 195–250.

   Un Gobierno de Indios: Tlaxcala, 1519–1750. Mexico City: CIESAS, 2008.

Martínez Perales, José de Jesús. *Montemorelos, Nuevo León*. Monterrey, Mexico: Congreso del Estado de Nuevo León, 2003.

Martínez Serna, José Gabriel. "Vineyards in the Desert: The Jesuits and the Rise and Decline of an Indian Town in New Spain's Northeastern Borderlands." Ph.D Dissertation, Southern Methodist University, 2009.

Matthew, Laura, "El náhuatl y la identidad mexicana en la Guatemala colonial," *Mesoamerica* 40 (2000): 41–68.

Matthew, Laura and Michel R. Oudijk. *Indian Conquistadors: Indigenous Allies in the Conquest of Mesoamerica*. Norman: University of Oklahoma, 2007.

Meade, Joaquín. "Índice general del Ramo de Provincias Internas existente en el Archivo General de la Nación," *Boletín del Archivo General de La Nación* [Mexico] 31, no. 1 (1960): 117–34.

"Notes on the Franciscans in the Huasteca Region of Mexico." In *The Franciscan Missions of Northern Mexico*, ed. Thomas E. Sheridan. Mexico: Editorial Jus, 1991.

Medina, Jose Toribio. *Historia del Tribunal del Santo Oficio de la Inquisición en Mexico*. San Angel, Mexico: Consejo Nacional para la Cultura y las Artes, 1991 [1852–1930].

Melville, Elinor G. K. *A Plague of Sheep: Environmental Consequences of the Conquest of Mexico*. Cambridge and New York: Cambridge University Press, 1994.

Melvin, Karen. "Urban Religions: Mendicant Orders in New Spain's Cities, 1570–1800." Ph.D Dissertation, U.C. Berkeley, 2005.

Mendinueta, Pedro Fermín de. *Indian and Mission Affairs in New Mexico, 1773*. Santa Fe, NM: Stagecoach Press, 1965.

Merrill, William L. "Nueva Vizcaya al final de la epoca colonial." In *Nómadas y sedentarios*, ed. Marie-Areti Hers, et al. Mexico City: UNAM, 2000.

Metcalf, Alida, *Go-Betweens and the Colonization of Brazil, 1500–1600*. Austin: University of Texas, 2005.

Miguel Bringas, Father Diego Miguel. *Friar Bringas Reports to the King: Methods of Indoctrination on the Frontier of New Spain in 1796–97*. Trans. Bernard L. Fontana. Tucson: University of Arizona, 1977.

Miller, Hubert J. *José de Escandón: Colonizer of Nuevo Santander*. Edinburg, TX: New Santander Press, 1980.

Mills, Kenneth and Anthony Grafton, eds., *Conversion: Old Worlds and New*. Rochester, NY: University of Rochester Press, 2003.

Montemayor Hernandez, Andrés. "La congrega o encomienda en el Nuevo Reino de León desde finales del siglo xvi hasta el siglo xvii," *Humanitas* [Mexico] 11 (1970): 539–75.

Historia de Monterrey, Monterrey, 1971.

ed. *La Congrega: Nuevo Reino de León, Siglos XVI-XVIII*. Monterrey, Mexico: Cuadernos del Archivo, 1990.

Moorhead, Max L. *The Apache Frontier in Northern New Spain, 1769–1791*. Norman: University of Oklahoma, 1968.

Morales, Francisco, ed. *Franciscan Presence in the Americas: Essays on the Activities of the Franciscan Friares in the Americas, 1492–1900*. Potomac, MD: Academcy of American Franciscan History, 1983.

Mörner, Magnus. *La Corona española y los foráneos en los pueblos de indios de América*. Madrid: Ediciones de Cultura Hispanica, 1999.

La Mota y Escobar, Alonso de. *Descripción geográfica de los reinos de Nueva Galicia, Nueva Vizcaya y Nuevo León, colección histórica de obras facsimilares*. Jalisco: Gobierno del Estado de Jalisco, 1993 [1602–1605].

Mundy, Barbara. *The Mapping of New Spain: Indigenous Cartography and the Maps of the Relaciones Geográficas*. Chicago: University of Chicago, 1996.

Muñoz Camargo, Diego. *Histora de Tlaxcala*. Mexico City: Publicaciones del Ateneo Nacional de Ciencias y Artes de Mexico, 1947 [16th century].

Nash, Gary B. "The Hidden History of Mestizo America," *Journal of American History* 82, no. 3 (1995): 941–64.

Navarro García, Luis. *Las provincias internas en el siglo xix*. Seville: Escuela de Estudios Hispano-Americanos, 1965.

La política americana de José de Gálvez según su "Discurso y reflexiones de un vasallo." Málaga, Spain: Algazara, 1998.

Nevárez Pequeño, Napoleón. *Villa San Cristóbal Hualahuises.* Monterrey, Mexico: Editorial I.F.C.C., 1987.

Nikel, Herbert J. *El peonaje en las haciendas mexicanas: interpretaciones, fuentes, hallazgos.* Mexico City: Universidad Iberoamericana, 1991.

Nutini, Hugo. "Clan Organization in a Nahuatl-Speaking Village of the State of Tlaxcala, Mexico," *American Anthropologist* 63, no. 1 (1961): 62–78.

Ocaranza, Fernando. *Crónica de las Provincias Internas de la Nueva Espana.* Mexico: Editorial Polis, 1939.

Ochoa, Lorenzo. "Huastec." In *Oxford Encyclopedia of Mesoamerican Cultures*, ed. Davíd Carrasco. New York: Oxford, 2001.

Offutt, Leslie Scott. "Levels of Acculturation in Northeastern New Spain: San Esteban Testaments of the Seventeenth and Eighteenth Centuries," *Estudios de Cultura Náhuatl* 22 (1992): 409–43.

    Saltillo, 1770–1810: Town and Region in the Mexican North. Tucson: University of Arizona, 2001.

    "Defending Corporate Identity on Spain's Northeastern Frontier: San Esteban de Nueva Tlaxcala, 1780–1810," *Americas* 64, no. 3 (2007): 351–75.

O'Hara, Matthew. *A Flock Divided: Race, Religion and Politics in Mexico, 1749–1857.* Durham, NC: Duke, 2009.

O'Phelan Godoy, Scarlet. *Kuracas sin sucesiones: del cacique al alcalde de indios, Perú y Bolivia, 1750–1835.* Cuzco: Centro de Estudios Regionales Andinos Bartolomé de las Casas, 1997.

Orozco, Victor. "El conflicto entre Apaches, Raramuris, y mestizos en Chihuahua durante el siglo xix." In *Nómadas y sedentarios*, ed. Marie-Areti Hers. Mexico City: UNAM, 2000.

Osante, Patricia. *Orígenes de Nuevo Santander (1748–1772).* Ciudad Victoria, Mexico: Universidad Autónoma de Tamaulipas, 1997.

Ouweneel, Arij. "From Tlahtocayotl to Gobernadoryotl: A Critical Examination of Indigenous Rule in 18th-Century Central Mexico," *American Ethnologist* 22, no. 4 (1995): 756–85.

Owensby, Brian P. *Empire of Law and Indian Justice in Colonial Mexico.* Stanford, CA: Stanford University Press, 2008.

Pagden, Anthony. *The Fall of Natural Man: The American Indian and the Origins of Comparative Ethnology.* New York: Cambridge University Press, 1982.

    "Identity Formation in Spanish America." In *Colonial Identity in the Atlantic World, 1500–1800*, eds. Nicholas Canny and Anthony Pagden. Princeton, NJ: Princeton University, 1987.

    Spanish Imperialism and the Political Imagination: Studies in European and Spanish-American Social and Political Theory, 1513–1830. New Haven, CT: Yale, 1990.

    Lords of All the World: Ideologies of Empire in Spain, Britain, and France, c. 1500–1800. New Haven, CT: Yale, 1995.

    The Idea of Europe: From Antiquity to the European Union. Cambridge: Cambridge University, 2002.

Perkins, Stephen M. "Macehuales and the Corporate Solution: Colonial Secessions in Nahua Central Mexico," *Mexican Studies/Estudios Mexicanos* 21, no. 2 (2005): 277–306.

Phelan, John Leddy. *The Millennial Kingdom the Franciscans in the New World.* 2d rev. ed. Berkeley: U.C. Berkeley, 1970.

Phillips, William D. *Slavery from Roman Times to the Early Transatlantic Trade.*
Minneapolis: University of Minnesota, 1985.

Phillips, William D. and Carla Rahn Phillips. *The Worlds of Christopher Columbus.*
Cambridge: Cambridge University, 1992.

Pierce, Donna, Rogelio Ruiz Gomar and Clara Bargellini. *Painting a New World:
Mexican Art and Life, 1521–1821.* Denver, CO: Denver Art Museum, 2004.

Polzer, Charles, ed., *The Jesuit Missions of Northern Mexico.* New York: Garland, 1992.

Pope Pius VI. *Breve apostólico y estatutos generales para la erección y govierno de las
custodias de misiones Franciscanos Observantes de Propaganda Fide en las
Provincias Internas.* Madrid: Joachin Ibara, 1781.

Portillo Valdez and Pedro Gómez Danés. *La evangelización del noreste.* Monterrey,
Mexico: Arquidiócesis de Monterrey, 2001.

Powell, Phillip Wayne. *Capitán Mestizo: Miguel Caldera y la frontera norteña: la
pacificación de los chichimecas (1548–1597).* Trans. Juan José Utrilla. Mexico:
Fondo de Cultura Economica, 1980.

Soldiers, Indians, and Silver: The Northward Advance of New Spain, 1550–1600.
Berkeley: University of California, 1952.

Mexico's Miguel Caldera: The Taming of America's First Frontier, 1548–1597.
Tucson: University of Arizona, 1977.

"Franciscans of the Old Silver Frontier of Old Mexico." In *The Franciscan Missions of
Northern Mexico,* ed. Thomas E. Sheridan. New York: Garland, 1991.

Purnell, Jennie. *Popular Movements and State Formation in Revolutionary Mexico: The
Agraristas, and Cristeros of Michoacán.* Durham, NC: Duke, 1999.

Quiñones Keber, Eloise, Susan Schroeder and Frederic Hicks, eds. *Chipping Away on Earth:
Studies in Prehispanic and Colonial Mexico in Honor of Arthur J. O. Anderson
and Charles E. Dibble.* Lancaster, CA: Labyrinthos, 1994.

Radding, Cynthia. *Wandering Peoples: Colonialism, Ethnic Spaces, and Ecological
Frontiers, 1700–1850.* Durham, NC: Duke, 1997.

Ramos, Raul Alberto. "From Norteño to Tejano: The Roots of Borderlands Ethnicity,
Nationalism, and Political Identity in Béxar, 1811–1861." Ph.D Dissertation,
University of Texas, Austin, 1981.

Reff, Daniel T. *Plagues, Priests, and Demons: Sacred Narratives and the Rise of
Christianity in the Old World and the New.* New York: Cambridge, 2005.

Reinhartz, Dennis, ed. *The Mapping of the Entradas into the Greater Southwest.*
Norman: University of Oklahoma, 1988.

Rendón Garcini, Ricardo. *Breve historia de Tlaxcala.* Mexico City: Colegio de Mexico,
1996.

Reséndez, Andrés. *Changing National Identities at the Frontier: Texas and New Mexico,
1800–1850.* New York: Cambridge, 2005.

Restall, Matthew, *Maya Conquistador.* Boston: Beacon Press, 1998.

Seven Myths of the Spanish Conquest. New York: Oxford University Press, 2003.

The Black Middle: Slavery, Society, and African-Maya Relations in Colonial Yucatan.
Stanford, CA: Stanford University Press, 2009.

Restall, Matthew and Florine Asselbergs. *Spanish, Maya, and Nahuatl Accounts of the
Conquest Wars.* University Park, PA: Penn State University, 2007.

Ricard, Robert. *The Spiritual Conquest of Mexico: An Essay on the Apostolate and
Evangelizing Methods of the Mendicant Orders, 1523–1572.* Trans. Lesley Byrd
Simpson. Berkeley: University of California, 1966.

Rieu-Millan, Marie Laure. *Los Diputados Americanos en las Cortes de Cádiz.* Madrid: Consejo Superior de Investigaciones Científicas, 1990.

Ríos, Eduardo Enrique. *Fray Margil de Jesús: Apóstol de América,* 2d ed. Mexico City: Editorial Jus, 1955.

Robinson, David James. *Research Inventory of the Mexican Collection of Colonial Parish Registers.* Salt Lake City: University of Utah Press, 1980.

Rodríguez, Luis Gonzalez. "Los tobosos, bandoleros y nómadas: experiencias y testimonios historicos." In *Nómadas y sedentarios,* ed. Marie-Areti Hers. Mexico City: UNAM, 2000.

Rodríguez, Mario. *The Cádiz Experiment in Central America, 1808–1826.* Berkeley: U.C. Berkeley, 1978.

Rodríguez García, Martha. *Historias de resistencia y exterminio: los indios de Coahuila durante el siglo xix.* Mexico City: CIESAS, 1995.

La guerra entre bárbaros y civilizados: el exterminio del nómada en Coahuila, 1840–1880. Saltillo, Mexico: CIESAS, 1998.

Rodríguez O., Jaime, ed. *Mexico in the Age of Democratic Revolutions, 1750–1850.* Boulder: University of Colorado, 1994.

The Independence of Spanish America. New York: Cambridge, 1998.

Roel, Santiago. *Nuevo León: apuntes históricos.* Monterrey, Mexico: Estado de Nuevo León, 1938.

Roldan, Gerardo Adam, Maricela Hernandez Reyes and Luisa Ortiz Castro. *La esclavitud en la Nueva España siglo xvi.* Mexico: Instituto de Estudios y Documentos Históricos, 1982.

Rothschild, Nan A. *Colonial Encounters in a Native American Landscape: The Spanish and Dutch in North America.* Washington, DC: Smithsonian, 2003.

Russell, Lynette, ed. *Colonial Frontiers: Indigenous-European Encounters in Settler Societies.* Manchester, U.K.: Manchester University, 2001.

Sahlins, Peter. *Boundaries: The Making of France and Spain in the Pyrenees.* Berkeley: U.C. Berkeley, 1989.

Unnaturally French: Foreign Citizens in the Old Regime and After. Ithaca, NY: Cornell, 2004.

Salmon, Roberto Mario. *Indian Revolts in Northern New Spain (1680–1786).* Lanham, MD: University Press of America, 1991.

Sánchez Zamora, Fernando. "Descubrimiento del Río Blanco y su población." In *Historia de Nuevo León, con noticias sobre Coahuila, Tamaulipas, Texas y Nuevo Mexico, siglo xvii, notas de Israel Cavazos Garza.* eds. Alonso de León, Juan Bautista Chapa, and Fernando Sánchez de Zamora, Monterrey, Mexico: Ayuntamiento de Monterrey, 1980 [17th century].

Sarmiento Donate, Alberto, ed. *De las leyes de indias: antología de la recopilación de 1681.* Mexico City: Consejo Nacional de Fomento Educativo, 1985 [1681].

Schattschneider, E. E. *The Semisoverign People.* New York: Holt, Rinehart, Winston, 1960.

Schroeder, Susan. "Looking Back at the Conquest: Nahua Perceptions of Early Encounters from the Annals of Chimalpahin." In *Chipping Away on Earth: Studies in Prehispanic and Colonial Mexico in Honor of Arthur J. O. Anderson and Charles E. Dibble.* eds. Eloise Quiñones Keber, Susan Schroeder, and Frederic Hicks. Lancaster, CA: Labyrinthos, 1994.

Schwartz, Stuart B., ed. *Victors and Vanquished: Spanish and Nahua Views of the Conquest of Mexico.* Boston: Bedford/St. Martin's, 2000.

Tropical Babylons: Sugar and the Making of the Atlantic World, 1450–1680. Chapel Hill: University of North Carolina, 2003.

Seed, Patricia. "Social Dimensions of Race: Mexico City, 1753," *Hispanic American Historical Review* 62 (1982): 559–606.

Ceremonies of Possession in Europe's Conquest of the New World, 1492–1640. Cambridge: Cambridge University, 1995.

American Pentimento: The Invention of Indians and the Pursuit of Riches. Minneapolis: University of Minnesota, 2001.

Sego, Eugene B. "Six Tlaxcalan Colonies on New Spain's Northern Frontier; A Comparison of Success and Failure." Ph.D Dissertation, Indiana University, 1990.

Aliados y adversarios: los colonos tlaxcaltecas en la frontera septentrional de Nueva España. Colegio de San Luis Potosí, 1998.

Serulnikov, Sergio. *Subverting Colonial Authority: Challenges to Spanish Rule in Eighteenth-Century Southern Andes.* Durham, NC: Duke, 2003.

Sheridan, Thomas E., Charles Polzer, Thomas E. Naylor, and Diana W. Hadley, eds. *The Franciscan Missions of Northern Mexico.* New York: Garland, 1991.

Sheridan Prieto, Cecilia. "'Indios madrineros': colonizadores tlaxcaltecas en el noreste novohispano," *Estudios de Historia Novohispana* 24, no. enero-febrero (2001): 15– 51.

Sherwin-White, Adrian Nicholas. *The Roman Citizenship.* Oxford, U.K.: Oxford University, 1939.

Sims, Harold Dana. *The Expulsion of Mexico's Spaniards.* Pittsburgh, PA: University of Pittsburgh, 1990.

Spengler, Oswald. *The Decline of the West.* Trans. Charles Francis Atkinson. New York: Knopf, 1957 [1926].

Spicer, Edward Holland. *Cycles of Conquest: The Impact of Spain, Mexico, and the United States on the Indians of the Southwest, 1553–1960.* Tucson: University of Arizona Press, 1962.

Stavig, Ward. *The World of Túpac Amaru: Conflict, Community, and Identity in Colonial Peru.* Lincoln: University of Nebraska, 1999.

Stern, Steve. *Resistance, Rebellion, and Consciousness in the Andean Peasant World, 18th to 20th Centuries.* Madison: University of Wisconsin, 1987.

Tapia Mendez, Aureliano. "Fray Rafael José Verger y su técnico de misiones," *Humanitas* [Mexico] 16 (1975): 449–96.

La creacion del primitivo obispado de Linares, 1777. Mexico: Ediciones Al Voleo, 1979.

Taylor, William B. *Landlord and Peasant in Colonial Oaxaca.* Stanford, CA: Stanford University Press, 1972.

Drinking, Homicide, and Rebellion. Stanford, CA: Stanford University Press, 1979.

Magistrates of the Sacred: Priests and Parishioners in Eighteenth-Century Mexico. Stanford, CA: Stanford University Press, 1996.

Taylor, William B., and Franklin Pease, eds. *Violence, Resistance, and Survival in the Americas: Native Americans and the Legacy of Conquest.* Washington, DC: Smithsonian, 1994.

Tavárez, David. "La idolatría letrada: Un análisis comparativo de textos clandestinos rituals y devocionales en comunidades Nahuas y zapotecas, 1613–1654," *Historia Mexicana* 49, no. 2 (1999): 197–252.

Terraciano, Kevin. *The Mixtecs of Colonial Oaxaca: Ñudzahi History, Sixteenth through Eighteenth Centuries.* Stanford, CA: Stanford University Press, 1996.

"The 'Original Conquest' of Oaxaca: Late Colonial Nahuatl and Mixtec Accounts of the Spanish Conquest," *Ethnohistory* 50, no. 2 (2003): 349–96.

Thomas, Hugh. *Conquest: Montezuma, Cortés and the Fall of Old Mexico*. London: Hutchinson, 1993.

Thompson, Sinclair. *We Alone Rule: Native Andean Politics in the Age of Insurgency*. Madison: University of Wisconsin, 2002.

Todorov, Tzvetan. *The Conquest of America: The Question of the Other*. New York: Harper and Row, 1984.

Toro, Alfonso. *La Familia Carvajal*. El Paso: Texas Western Press, 2002.

Torre Curiel, Jose Refugio de la. *Vicarios en entredicho: crisis y destructuracion de la Provinica Franciscana de Santiago de Jalisco, 1749–1860*. Zamora, Michoacán: Colegio de Michoacán, 2001.

"*Conquering the Frontier. Contests for Religion, Survival, and Profits in Northwestern Mexico, 1765–1855*." Ph.D Dissertation, U.C. Berkeley, 2005.

Townsend, Camilla. *Malintzin's Choices: An Indian Woman in the Conquest of Mexico*. Albuquerque: University of New Mexico Press, 2006.

Here in This Year: Seventeenth-Century Nahuatl Annals of the Tlaxcala-Puebla Valley. Stanford, CA: Stanford University Press, 2010.

Toynbee, Arnold. *A Study of History*. Oxford: Oxford University, 1972 [1934].

Treviño Villarreal, Hector Jaime. *El señor de Tlaxcala en la historia de San Miguel de Bustamante*, series, Cuadernos del Archivo. Monterrey, Mexico: Achivo del Estado de Nuevo León, 1998.

Tutino, John. "Spanish Elites, Haciendas, and Indian Towns, 1750–1810." Ph.D Dissertation, U.T. Austin, 1976.

From Insurrection to Revolution in Mexico: Social Bases of Agrarian Violence, 1750–1940. Princeton, NJ: Princeton University, 1998.

Tyler, Lyman. *Two Worlds: The Indian Encounter with the European, 1492–1509*. Salt Lake City: University of Utah, 1988.

Usner, Daniel H. *Indians, Settlers, and Slaves in a Frontier Exchange Economy: The Lower Mississippi Valley before 1783*. Chapel Hill: University of North Carolina, 1990.

Valdes Dávila, Carlos Manuel and Ildefonso Dávila del Bosque, eds. *San Esteban de Nueva Tlaxcala: documentos para conocer su historia*. Saltillo, Mexico: Consejo Editorial del Estado, 1991.

eds. *Los Tlaxcaltecas en Coahuila, fuentes documentales*, 2d ed. San Luis Potosí: Colegio San Luis Potosí, 1999.

Van Young, Eric. *The Other Rebellion: Popular Violence, Ideology, and the Mexican Struggle for Independence, 1810–1821*. Stanford, CA: Stanford University Press, 2001.

Velasco Murillo, Dana. "The Creation of Indigenous Leadership in a Spanish Town: Zacatecas, Mexico, 1609–1752," *Ethnohistory* 56, no. 4 (Fall 2009): 669–97.

Viera Powers, Karen. *Andean Journeys: Migration, Ethnogenesis and the State in Colonial Quito*. Albuquerque: University of New Mexico Press, 1995.

Vignes, David M., trans. and ed. "Nuevo Santander in 1795: A Provincial Inspection by Félix María Calleja," *Southwestern Historical Quarterly* 75, no. 4 (1972): 461–506.

Villareal Arrabide, Carlos. *Obras Relativas a Cadereyta Jiménez*. Monterrey, Mexico, 2001.

Vinson, Ben. *Bearing Arms for His Majesty: The Free-Colored Militia in Colonial Mexico*. Stanford, CA: Stanford University Press, 2001.

Vizcaya Canales, Isidro. *Invasión de los indios bárbaros en el norte*. Monterrey, Mexico: ITESM, 1968 [1840–1841].

    "Montemorelos en la primera mitad del siglo xix," *Humanitas* [Mexico] 12 (1971): 325–30.

    "Don Andrés Ambrosio de Llanos y Valdez (1725–1805)," *Humanitas* [Mexico] 14 (1973): 457–67.

    En los albores de la independencia: las Provincias Internas de Oriente durante la insurgencia de Don Miguel Hidalgo. Monterrey, Mexico: ITESM, 1976.

Voekel, Pamela. *Alone before God*. Durham, NC: Duke, 2002.

Von Germeten, Nicole. *Black Blood Brothers: Confraternities and Social Mobility for Afro-Mexicans*. Gainesville: University Press of Florida, 2006.

Voss, Stuart. *On the Periphery of Nineteenth-Century Mexico: Sonora and Sinaloa, 1810–1877*. Tucson: University of Arizona, 1982.

Weber, David J. *The Spanish Frontier in North America*. New Haven, CT: Yale, 1992.

    On the Edge of Empire: The Taos Hacienda of los Martínez. Santa Fe: Museum of New Mexico, 1996.

    How Did Spaniards Convert Indians? Waco, TX: Baylor University Press, 2004.

    Bárbaros: Spaniards and Their Savages in the Age of Enlightenment. New Haven, CT: Yale, 2005.

    "The Spanish Borderlands, Historiography Redux," *History Teacher* 39, no. 1 (Nov. 2005): 43–56.

White, Richard. *The Middle Ground: Indians, Empires, and Republics in the Great Lakes Region, 1650–1815*. New York, Cambridge University Press, 1991.

Wightman, Ann. *Indigenous Migration and Social Change: The Forasteros of Cuzco*. Durham, NC: Duke, 1990.

Wood, Stephanie. *Transcending Conquest: Nahua Views of Spanish Colonial Mexico*. Norman: University of Oklahoma, 2003.

Yannakakis, Yanna. *The Art of Being In-Between: Native Intermediaries, Indian Identity, and Local Rule in Colonial Oaxaca*. Durham, NC: Duke, 2009.

Zapata Aguilar, Gerardo. *Bibliotecas antiguas de Nuevo León*. Monterrey, Mexico: UANL, 1996.

Zavala, Silvio. *La "Utopia" de Tomas Moro En La Nueva España y otros estudios*. Mexico: Antiguo Libreria Robredo, 1937.

    La filosofia politica en la conquista de América. Mexico City: Fondo de Cultura Economica, 1972.

    Ensayos sobre la colonización español en America. Mexico: Editorial Porrua, 1978.

    La defensa de los derechos del hombre en América Latina (siglos xvi-xviii). Mexico: UNAM/UNESCO, 1982.

    America en el espíritu francés del siglo XVIII. Mexico City: Colegio Nacional, 1983.

    El mundo americano en la época colonial, suplemento bibliográfico, 1967–1991. Mexico: Instituto Panamericano de Geografia e Historia, 1992.

    Entradas, congregas y encomiendas en el Nuevo Reino de León. Seville: Universidad de Seville, 1992.

    La encomienda indiana. Mexico City: Editorial Porrua, 1992.

    Suplemento documental y bibliográfico a la encomienda indiana. Mexico City: UNAM, 1994.

Zavala, Silvio, Udo Oberem, Jan Bazant, and Hermes Tovar. *Peones, conciertos, y arrendamientos en América Latina*. Bogotá: Universidad Nacional de Colombia, 1987.

Index

CPSIA information can be obtained at www.ICGtesting.com
Printed in the USA
LVOW12s2328140414

381678LV00004B/272/P